Strategic Marketing Management

The Framework

ALEXANDER CHERNEV

Kellogg School of Management

Northwestern University

Strategic Marketing Management | The Framework

ISBN: 978-1-936572-59-5

January 2019

Author website: Chernev.com

Supplemental materials: MarketingToolbox.com

Published by Cerebellum Press | Chicago, IL | USA

TABLE OF CONTENTS

ABOUT THE AUTHOR

Alexander Chernev is a professor of marketing at the Kellogg School of Management, Northwestern University. He holds a PhD in psychology from Sofia University and a PhD in business administration from Duke University.

Dr. Chernev has written numerous articles focused on business strategy, brand management, consumer behavior, and market planning. His research has been published in the leading marketing journals and has been frequently quoted in the business and popular press, including *The Wall Street Journal, Financial Times, The New York Times, The Washington Post, Harvard Business Review, Scientific American, Associated Press, Forbes,* and *Business Week.* He was ranked among the top ten most prolific scholars in the leading marketing journals by the *Journal of Marketing* and among the top five marketing faculty in the area of consumer behavior by a global survey of marketing faculty published by the *Journal of Marketing Education.*

Dr. Chernev's books—*Strategic Marketing Management, Strategic Brand Management, The Marketing Plan Handbook,* and *The Business Model: How to Develop New Products, Create Market Value, and Make the Competition Irrelevant*—have been translated into multiple languages and are used in top business schools around the world. He has served as an area editor for the *Journal of Marketing* and on the editorial boards of leading research journals, including the *Journal of Marketing Research, Journal of Consumer Research, Journal of Consumer Psychology, Journal of the Academy of Marketing Science, International Journal of Research in Marketing,* and *Journal of Marketing Behavior.*

Dr. Chernev teaches marketing strategy, brand management, and behavioral decision theory in MBA, PhD, and executive education programs at the Kellogg School of Management. He has also taught in executive programs at INSEAD in France and Singapore, at IMD in Switzerland, and at Hong Kong University of Science and Technology. He has received numerous teaching awards, including the Core Course Teaching Award, Faculty Impact Award, and the Top Professor Award from the Kellogg Executive MBA Program, which he has received eleven times.

In addition to research and teaching, Dr. Chernev is an Academic Trustee of the *Marketing Science Institute* and advises companies around the world on issues of marketing strategy, brand management, consumer behavior, pricing, strategic planning, and new product development. He has worked with Fortune 500 companies on ways to reinvent their business models, develop new products, and gain competitive advantage. He has helped multiple startups uncover market opportunities, discover new business models, and craft market strategies.

ACKNOWLEDGMENTS

This book has benefited from the wisdom of many of my current and former colleagues at the Kellogg School of Management at Northwestern University. I owe a considerable debt of gratitude to the "father" of modern marketing Philip Kotler, who sparked my interest in marketing management. I would also like to thank Andrea Bonezzi (New York University), Aaron Brough (Utah State University), Pierre Chandon (INSEAD), Akif Irfan (Goldman Sachs), Mathew Isaac (Seattle University), Ryan Hamilton (Emory University), Kevin Keller (Dartmouth University), Alexander Moore (University of Chicago), Ajay Kohli (Georgia Institute of Technology), and Jaya Sah (Goldman Sachs) for their valuable comments. I am also grateful to Joanne Freeman for editing this book with a very keen and helpful eye.

PREFACE

Marketing is both an art and a science. It is an art because intuition and creativity can play a major role in the development of a successful marketing campaign. Many brilliant marketers such as McDonald's founder Ray Kroc, Starbucks founder Howard Shultz, Microsoft founder Bill Gates, and Apple founder Steve Jobs did not have formal marketing training. Rather, they used their creativity and gut feel to build successful billion-dollar enterprises.

Marketing is also a science because it captures the generalized knowledge that reflects the experiences of multiple companies across a diverse set of industries. This knowledge complements managers' intuition and enhances their ability to design successful offerings that create market value. The scientific aspect of marketing that reflects the logic underlying the processes of creating and managing value is captured in the principles, theories, and frameworks outlined in this book.

This book delineates the fundamentals of marketing strategy, offers a systematic approach to marketing management, and presents a value-based framework for developing viable market offerings. The theory presented stems from the view of marketing as a value-creation process that is central to any business enterprise. In addition to theory, this book offers a set of practical tools that enable managers to apply the knowledge contained in the generalized frameworks to specific business problems and market opportunities.

The information contained in this volume is organized into five major parts. The first part defines the essence of marketing as a business discipline and outlines an overarching framework for marketing management that serves as the organizing principle for the information presented in the rest of the book. Specifically, we discuss the role of marketing management as a value-creation process, the essentials of marketing strategy and tactics as the key components of a company's business model, and the process of developing an actionable marketing plan.

Part Two covers issues pertaining to the development of a marketing strategy that will guide the company's tactical activities. Here we focus on three fundamental aspects of a company's marketing strategy: the identification of target customers, the development of a customer value proposition, and the development of a value proposition for the company and its collaborators.

Part Three focuses on the marketing tactics, viewed as a process of designing, communicating, and delivering value. We discuss how companies design their offerings and, specifically, how they develop key aspects of their products, services, brands, prices, and incentives. We further address the ways in which companies manage their marketing communication and explore the role of distribution channels in delivering the company's offerings to target customers.

The fourth part of the book focuses on managing growth. Specifically, we discuss strategies used by companies to gain and defend market position and, in this context, address the issues of pioneering advantage and managing sales growth. We further address the process of developing new market offerings and the ways in which companies manage product lines to create market value. We also discuss the key principles of managing product lines and ways in which companies can use product lines to gain and defend market position.

The final part of this book provides a set of tools that illustrate the practical application of marketing theory. Specifically, this part presents two workbooks: a workbook for segmenting the market and identifying target customers and a workbook for developing the strategic and tactical components of a company's business model.

The marketing framework outlined in this book applies to a wide range of companies—startups and established enterprises, consumer packaged goods companies and business-to-business enterprises, high-tech and low-tech ventures, online and brick-and-mortar entities, product manufacturers and value-added service providers, nonprofit organizations and profit-driven companies. This book combines theoretical rigor with practical relevance to strengthen the marketing skills of a wide array of business professionals—from those creating novel market offerings to those improving on existing ones, from entrepreneurs launching a new business to managers working in established corporations, and from product managers to senior executives.

This book is an abbreviated version of a more comprehensive volume, *Strategic Marketing Management: Theory and Practice*, which is intended for readers seeking broader and more in-depth discussion, detailed analysis, and additional perspectives on the topics presented in the current book.

PART ONE

The Framework for
Marketing Management

INTRODUCTION

It is possible to fail in many ways,
while to succeed is possible only in one way.
— Aristotle, Greek philosopher

The rapid growth of technological innovation, ever-increasing globalization, and the emergence of new business models have made today's markets more dynamic, unpredictable, and interdependent than ever. This increasingly complex environment in which companies operate underscores the importance of taking a systematic approach to marketing management. Such a systematic approach can be achieved by using frameworks.

The following chapters present an overarching framework that incorporates both strategic and tactical aspects of marketing management. By offering an integrative view of the key marketing concepts and frameworks, these chapters present a systematic and streamlined approach to marketing analysis, planning, and management. Specifically, the chapters included in this section address the following topics: *marketing as a business discipline, marketing strategy and tactics*, and *the marketing plan*.

- Understanding the role of **marketing as a business discipline** is the stepping stone for the development of a sound marketing program. Marketing is not just a set of tactical activities such as sales, advertising, and promotion; it also involves strategic analysis and planning, which are the foundation of the company's market success. The essence of marketing as a business discipline and its role as the growth engine of an organization are discussed in Chapter 1.

- **Marketing strategy and tactics** are the two building blocks of a company's business model. Strategy identifies the market in which the company operates and outlines the ways in which an offering will create value for the relevant market participants. Tactics, on the other hand, define the activities employed to execute a given strategy by designing, communicating, and delivering specific market offerings. The key aspects of developing an offering's strategy and its tactics are delineated in Chapter 2.

- **The marketing plan** delineates a course of action to translate an offering's strategy and tactics into a market reality. The development of an actionable marketing plan is guided by the G-STIC framework, which articulates the company's goal and delineates a course of action to reach this goal. The process of market planning and developing a viable marketing plan is discussed in Chapter 3.

The concepts, principles, and frameworks outlined in these three chapters serve as the foundation for the discussion of strategic marketing management presented in this book. They are the foundation on which a company's marketing programs and activities are built. To achieve market success, a company must have a solid understanding of the marketing function and its role within an organization, create a viable business model that defines the company's strategy and tactics, and develop an actionable marketing plan that translates its business model into a market reality.

Chapter One

Marketing as a Business Discipline

> *Good companies fulfill needs;*
> *great companies create new markets.*
>
> — Philip Kotler, founder of modern marketing theory

M arketing is both art and science. It is an intuitive skill and a set of principles soundly grounded in logic and academic scholarship. It reflects the individual experiences of companies across different industries, as well as a set of common principles that stem from these individual experiences and span companies and industries. Building on this view of marketing, this chapter addresses the essence of marketing as a business discipline, focusing on its role as a value-creator and the growth engine of an organization.

The Essence of Marketing

There are many ways to define marketing, each reflecting a different understanding of the role of marketing as a business discipline. Marketing has been defined as a functional area — similar to finance, accounting, and operations — that captures a unique aspect of a company's business activities. Some view marketing as a customer-centric business philosophy. Others see it as a process of moving products and services from concept to customers. Still others view marketing as a specific set of activities that typically involve a particular marketing function such as product development, pricing, promotion, and distribution. And for some, marketing is yet another department in the company's organizational grid.

These diverse views of marketing stem from marketing's numerous functions. Marketing is indeed everything that the above definitions imply: a business discipline, a functional area, a philosophy of thinking, a business process that encompasses a set of specific activities, and a distinct unit of an organization. Diverse as these views of marketing are, they are related conceptually. As a business discipline, marketing embraces a philosophy that gives rise to a set of processes and activities coordinated by the marketing department. Therefore, the key to defining marketing is delineating its core business function, which informs the specific processes and activities involved in marketing management.

Companies vary in the way they view the core function of marketing and its role within the organization. In particular, there are several commonly held, albeit erroneous, views of marketing that stem from the more general misunderstanding of marketing as a business discipline. One popular view is that marketing is a tactical activity tantamount to facilitating sales. This view is particularly common in organizations whose primary activity is selling large inventories of warehoused products and who see the goal of marketing as "selling more things to more people for more money, more efficiently." This view appeals to many managers because it is intuitive, clear, and succinct. The problem with this view is that it does not describe marketing. Rather, it describes sales, an activity related to—but distinct from—marketing. Given the popularity of the view of marketing as primarily sales, it is important to define the boundaries between the two activities.

Marketing is *not* equivalent to selling; it is much broader. Unlike selling, which usually begins once the company has a product to sell, marketing starts long before the product becomes a reality. Moreover, marketing does not stop with the sale of the product; it continues after the customer has made a purchase and involves managing the customer's entire experience with the product—including using, servicing, disposing of, and repurchasing the product. Marketing incorporates all aspects involved in developing the offering that is to be sold. As such, the product is the outcome of a company's marketing activities, not vice versa. The goal of marketing is to create a product that sells, not to sell a product.

The view of marketing as an overarching business discipline that guides a number of specific functions, including sales, is well articulated by the founder of modern management science, Peter Drucker, who writes:

> Marketing is not only much broader than selling, it is not a specialized activity at all. It encompasses the entire business. The aim of marketing is to make selling superfluous. The aim of marketing is to know and understand the customer so well that the product or service fits him and sells itself. Ideally, marketing should result in a customer who is ready to buy.[1]

The idea that marketing can replace sales may sound extreme, but what Drucker points out is that marketing and sales work in concert. A product that is poorly designed because of a lack of marketing insight will require tremendous selling effort, whereas a product that is designed to address an important unmet customer need is likely to generate much greater customer demand and, hence, will require relatively little sales effort. A company can have the best salesforce in the world and still fail in the marketplace if its offerings do not create customer value. On the other hand, a well-designed product requires much less sales effort and can almost sell itself. When Tesla offered its Model 3 electric car, the orders poured in—nearly 200,000 orders within the first 24 hours—because it had crafted a viable product that created customer value by addressing an unmet need.

Another common misconception is viewing marketing as a set of communication activities—advertising, public relations, and social networking—designed to promote the company's offering. The popularity of this view springs from the fact that communication, and especially advertising, is the most visible aspect of the company's marketing activities. Companies that subscribe to this view consider marketing as a means to inform their target customers about the offerings developed by the company's engineers and product designers and to persuade them to buy these products. The problem with this view is that communication, although important, is only one aspect of marketing. Marketing takes place long before the communication campaign is conceived: It guides the development of the offering that will later be communicated to target customers.

Marketing is also misconstrued when it is equated with sales promotions—including price discounts, coupons, rebates, and bonus offerings. The popularity of this view of marketing lies in the fact that sales promotions are a tool that a company can readily use to enhance the value of its offerings by temporarily decreasing their monetary cost. Because they can help the company bring attention to the product in a given market and facilitate adoption by target customers, sales promotions are often equated with marketing. Yet, nudging customers to purchase a company's products reflects only one facet of marketing. This view of marketing as an activity that helps bring products to market and entices customers to buy these products is oblivious to marketing's role in creating the very products that are being promoted.

Equating marketing with sales, advertising, and sales promotions, and thus, viewing it as a tactical activity is a common misperception. This myopic view limits the role of marketing to creating awareness, incentivizing customers to make a purchase, and facilitating sales and precludes a company from mobilizing marketing's full potential to develop a viable business strategy. The view of marketing only as a tactical activity fails to offer a clear understanding of how sales, advertising, and promotions align with and relate to the other tactical aspects of the marketing process, including product development, pricing, and distribution. Furthermore, viewing marketing as a tactical tool fails to take into account the need for an overarching logic that guides and melds the individual marketing activities in a way that creates value for customers, the company, and its collaborators.

Marketing is far more than tactics. It also involves the development of a strategic vision that determines the success of the tactical elements. Marketing encompasses all activities— tactical and strategic—that enable the company to create value in a given market. Marketing as a business discipline is about creating new markets and managing existing ones. Market success, in turn, is defined by the value exchanged by the different market participants: the company, its customers, and its collaborators. Consequently, the primary purpose of marketing is strategic rather than tactical: It is the creation of market value.

As a business discipline, marketing is first and foremost about creating value

Because the ability to create value defines a company's market success, marketing is strategic in nature. Marketing defines the market in which the company operates and the customer needs the company aims to fulfill with its offerings. The various tactical activities— such as sales, advertising, and promotion—are the means used to turn the company's strategy into reality, driven by the ultimate goal of creating market value. Focusing on value recognizes marketing as a pivotal function that pervades all areas of an enterprise. This view of marketing as an integral business discipline forms the basis of the marketing theory outlined in this book.

Marketing as a Value-Creation Process

The focus of marketing is the exchange of goods, services, and ideas that takes place in consumer and business markets. Because the driving force behind an exchange is the creation of value for participants, the concept of value is central to marketing. Accordingly, the discipline of marketing can be defined as follows:

Marketing is the art and science of creating value
by designing and managing viable market offerings

Marketing is an *art* that frequently relies on a manager's creativity and imagination. Brilliant marketers such as King Gillette, Ray Kroc, and Henri Nestlé relied not on formal schooling but on an innate ability to identify unmet customer needs and develop products to meet those needs.

Marketing is also a *science* that has produced a body of generalized knowledge about the process of creating market value. Based on investigation of the successes and failures of numerous companies over the years, this knowledge has allowed marketing science to articulate a set of general principles that distill the experiences of individual companies to capture the essence of the marketing processes. The scientific aspect of marketing that reflects the logic underlying the processes of creating and managing value underlies the principles, theories, and frameworks outlined in this book.

Because the main function of the market exchange is to create *value*, the concept of value is central to marketing. Value is a strategic concept that defines the benefits and costs that participants receive from the market exchange. Therefore, optimizing value for target customers, collaborators, and the company is the key principle that steers managerial decision making and is the foundation for all marketing activities.

The purpose of marketing is not limited to maximizing monetary outcomes such as net income and return on investment. Instead, marketing must be defined using the broader term *success*, which extends beyond monetary outcomes to include all forms of value created in the market. Thus, success is not always expressed in monetary terms such as net income, return on investment, and market share. Many organizations define success in nonmonetary terms that include technological vision, customer satisfaction, and social welfare. Therefore, the goal of marketing is to create value exchanges—whether or not their success is defined in monetary terms—that enable exchange participants to reach their goals.

Marketing aims to create superior value for target customers in a way
that enables the company and its collaborators to achieve their goals

As a value-creation process, marketing can be viewed as comprising four key aspects: (1) *identifying value*, which involves uncovering an unmet customer need that the company can fulfill better than the competition while creating value for itself and for its collaborators; (2) *designing value*, which involves developing the actual product or service, defining the brand, setting the price, and deciding on the sales promotions; (3) *communicating value*, which involves informing the relevant marketing entities—target customers, collaborators, and the company employees and stakeholders—about the offering; and (4) *delivering value*, which involves bringing the offering to target customers through a set of distribution channels. These four aspects of creating market value form the backbone of this book.

The Scope of Marketing

Marketing is not limited to products and services: It can also involve events, places, people, real estate, organizations, and even ideas. Anything that can be exchanged can be marketed. In this context, the scope of marketing as a business discipline is very broad, covering the value relationships among different business entities operating across diverse markets.

The market in which a company aims to create value is a central marketing concept. Companies often define their markets through the products they manufacture or the industry in which they operate. Despite its popularity, this is a myopic view of a company's market. Products, as well as entire industries, inevitably become obsolete. After enjoying periods of rapid growth, mainframe computers, VCR tapes, and DVDs faded into oblivion because they were replaced with alternative means—often coming from a different industry—that offered a superior solution for satisfying the same underlying customer need. A product-based definition of the market can also prevent a company from taking advantage of emerging market trends, making it fall behind the competition. Coca-Cola's rather narrow focus on its product—carbonated sodas—rather than on the underlying customer need for hydration and self-expression, made it overlook beverage trends toward fruit-flavored drinks such as Snapple, energy drinks such as Gatorade, and designer water brands such as Vitaminwater.

Customers and the needs that they aim to fulfill, rather than a company's products or the industry in which it operates, are the true defining aspects of a market. Products and industries are a consequence of customer needs; they provide the means of fulfilling customer needs using currently available technologies. Even as the demand for a specific product begins to decline in the face of a superior offering featuring a new technology, the underlying customer need addressed by these offerings persists. As a result, companies that define their markets in terms of products rather than customer needs are destined to decline along with the industries they represent.

Depending on the entities participating in the value exchange, there are three main types of markets: *business-to-consumer*, *business-to-business*, and *consumer-to-consumer*.

- **Business-to-Consumer (B2C)** markets involve offerings aimed at individuals who are typically the end users of these offerings. B2C markets are common for consumer packaged goods companies such as Procter & Gamble, Unilever, and Nestlé, as well as for consumer-focused service companies such as retail banks, hotels, and airlines.

- **Business-to-Business (B2B)** markets are similar to B2C markets, with the key difference that customers are business entities rather than consumers. For example, GE and Rolls-Royce supply engines to aircraft manufacturers Boeing and Airbus; Intel and Qualcomm supply computer chips to computer and smartphone manufacturers; and Robert Bosch, Johnson Controls, and Continental supply parts for companies in the automotive industry, including Ford, General Motors, and Mercedes-Benz.

- **Consumer-to-Consumer (C2C)** markets are those in which a company facilitates interactions between individual customers. These interactions can involve communications (Facebook, Instagram, Twitter), monetary transactions (eBay, PayPal, Square), and services (Uber, Airbnb, Freelancer). The C2C market can also involve a B2C market in which the company and its collaborators create value for their customers by providing a platform that enables customer-to-customer interactions.

Despite their differences, these three types of markets share the same ultimate goal—to create value for all relevant market participants. Accordingly, the core marketing concepts, principles, and frameworks outlined in this book apply to all three types of markets. Thus, while most of the examples used focus on consumer markets, the overarching principle of creating superior market value and the strategies and tactics that companies can employ to ensure market success are equally relevant in business markets.

Marketing as the Central Function of an Organization

Because growth is at the heart of every business, a primary function of an organization is successfully managing growth. Without a growth strategy, a company is in danger of losing market position and being outmaneuvered by the competition. To ensure its long-term market success, an enterprise must grow its current markets and develop new markets. The guiding discipline behind an organization's growth strategy is marketing.

Marketing fosters growth by exploring new opportunities, identifying new markets, and uncovering new customer needs. The role of marketing as a central business discipline defining the other business functions is captured in the words of Peter Drucker:

> Because the purpose of business is to create a customer, the business enterprise has two—and only two—basic functions: marketing and innovation. Marketing and innovation produce results; all the rest are costs. Marketing is the distinguishing, unique function of the business.[2]

Marketing and innovation foster growth through their symbiotic relationship. Innovation enables marketing by identifying novel means to address customer needs in a way that creates market value. Marketing empowers innovation by shaping new technologies and inventions and aligning them with market needs. Together, marketing and innovation spark growth.

In addition to empowering innovation, marketing facilitates the development of strategies that enable a company to take full advantage of emerging opportunities, capture uncontested markets, and discover the best means to fulfill unmet customer needs. Thus, marketing helps sustain and enhance a company's business position by focusing on new ways in which the company can create value for its customers, collaborators, and stakeholders.

The view of marketing as a central business function has important implications for the role of marketing in the organization. With its primary purpose of creating and sustaining value for customers, the company, and its collaborators, marketing should play a central role in any organization. Business success is only possible when all departments work together to create market value: Engineering designs the right products, finance furnishes the right amount of funding, purchasing buys the right materials, production makes the right products in the right time horizon, and accounting measures profitability in a meaningful way. This type of harmony can only coalesce around a unified interdepartmental focus on creating value—an outcome possible only in organizations where marketing plays a central rather than peripheral role.

The central role of marketing in business management implies that it is not just an activity managed by a single department; it spans all departments. To build a strong organization, managers across all departments must understand the fundamental marketing principles and align their activities in order to develop offerings that create market value. David Packard, cofounder of Hewlett-Packard, observed:

> Marketing is far too important to leave to the marketing department. In a truly great marketing organization, you can't tell who's in the marketing department. Everyone in the organization has to make decisions based on the impact on the customer.

The broad role marketing plays in an organization does not make marketing departments superfluous. On the contrary, marketing departments are the organizational units that guide the development and implementation of the marketing strategy and tactics. At the same time, because the scope of value creation encompasses broad aspects of a company's operations, the marketing department should work with other organizational units within a company to provide strategic direction for carrying out the marketing function.

Delegating the marketing function solely to the marketing department is counterproductive and reflects a short-sighted view of the role of marketing in an organization. To succeed, a company must ensure that the marketing focus permeates all of its organizational units, such that all departments think in terms of creating market value.

SUMMARY

As a business discipline, marketing is the art and science of creating value by designing and managing viable market offerings.

Marketing is often equated with tactical activities such as sales, advertising, and sales promotions. Yet, marketing is much broader than sales: It incorporates all aspects involved in developing the offering that is to be sold. The goal of marketing is to create a product that sells, not to sell a product. Marketing is also broader than the company's communication—advertising, public relations, and social networking—designed to promote the company's offering. Marketing takes place long before the communication campaign is conceived: It guides the development of the offering that will later be communicated to target customers.

Marketing is far more than tactics. It also involves the development of a strategic vision that is foundational to the success of the tactical elements. It encompasses all activities—both tactical and strategic—that enable the company to create value in a given market.

Marketing is not limited to products and services; it can also involve events, places, people, real estate, organizations, and even ideas. Depending on the entities participating in the value exchange, there are three main types of markets: business-to-consumer, business-to-business, and consumer-to-consumer.

As the growth engine of the organization, marketing empowers innovation by aligning new technologies and inventions with the current market needs. Marketing helps sustain and enhance a company's business position by focusing on new ways in which the company can create value for its customers, collaborators, and stakeholders.

MARKETING INSIGHT: THE ROLE OF FRAMEWORKS IN MARKETING MANAGEMENT

Frameworks facilitate decisions in several ways. They help identify alternative approaches to thinking about the decision task, thus providing managers with a better understanding of the problem they are trying to solve. In addition to helping formulate the problem, frameworks provide a generalized approach to identifying alternative solutions. Frameworks further enhance decision making by providing a shared vocabulary with which to discuss the issues, thus streamlining communication among the entities involved in the marketing process.

Because of their level of generality, frameworks are not intended to answer specific marketing questions. Instead, they provide a general approach that enables managers to identify the optimal solution to a particular problem. Using a framework calls for abstracting the problem at hand to a more general scenario for which the framework offers a predefined solution and then applying this solution to solve the specific problem. By relying on the abstract knowledge captured in frameworks, a manager can effectively sidestep the trial-and-error-based learning process (Figure 1).

The role of marketing frameworks in business management can be illustrated with the following example. Imagine a consultant who has been asked by a cereal manufacturer for advice on how to price a new cereal. After analyzing the industry dynamics, the consultant identifies five key factors that need to be considered when deciding on the price of the cereal: customer willingness to pay for the cereal; the availability and pricing of competitive offerings; the cost structure and profit goals of the company; the margins that suppliers and distributors charge; as well as more general context factors such as the current economic environment, consumption (health and diet) trends, and legal regulations concerning pricing strategies and tactics.

Figure 1. Making Decisions Using a Framework

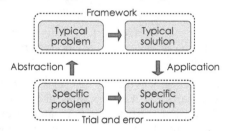

A month later the consultant receives an assignment from a different client, a gas pipeline manufacturer, asking for help with setting the price for a new pressure valve. The consultant diligently analyzes the industry and ends up suggesting the same five factors: customer willingness to pay, competitive pricing, company costs and goals, collaborator (supplier and distributor) margins, and the current context.

The following month the consultant receives another assignment from a telecommunications company, asking for advice on pricing its new mobile phone. By this time the consultant has realized that the three recent price-setting requests are conceptually similar. Moreover, the consultant realizes that the three tasks entail analyzing the same five factors: customer willingness to pay, competitor prices, company goals and cost structure, collaborator prices and margins, and the overall economic/regulatory/technological context in which the company operates. (These five factors comprise the 5-C framework, which is discussed in the following chapter.)

As the above example illustrates, the effective use of marketing frameworks as a managerial problem-solving tool involves three key steps. First, a manager needs to generalize the specific problem at hand (e.g., how to price a new mobile phone) to a more abstract problem that can be addressed by a particular framework (e.g., how to price a new product). Second, the manager needs to identify a framework that will help answer the specific problem (e.g., the 5-C framework) and use it to derive a general solution. Third, the manager needs to apply the generalized solution prescribed by the framework to the specific problem. The reliance on generalized knowledge captured in frameworks can help managers circumvent the trial-and-error approach to solving business problems.

Marketing frameworks build on already existing generalized knowledge to facilitate future company-specific decisions. In fact, many of the business problems companies face on a daily basis can be generalized into a framework that can be applied to solving future problems. The role of frameworks as a problem-solving tool is captured in the words of French philosopher René Descartes: *Each problem that I solved became a rule which served afterwards to solve other problems.*

CHAPTER TWO

MARKETING STRATEGY AND TACTICS

Strategy without tactics is the slowest route to victory.
Tactics without strategy is the noise before defeat.

—Sun Tzu, Chinese military strategist

The success of an offering is defined by the company's ability to design, communicate, and deliver market value. The particular way in which an offering creates value is determined by the company's business model and its two building blocks: strategy and tactics. The key aspects of developing an offering's strategy, designing its tactics, and crafting a market value map are the focus of this chapter.

Marketing Strategy and Tactics

A company's success is determined by the ability of its business model to create value in its chosen market. To create value, a company must clearly identify the target market in which it will compete; develop a meaningful set of benefits for its target customers, collaborators, and the company stakeholders; and design an offering that will deliver these benefits to the target market. These activities define the two key components of a company's business model: *strategy* and *tactics*.

- The term **strategy** comes from the Greek *stratēgía*—meaning "generalship"—used in reference to maneuvering troops into position before a battle. In marketing, strategy outlines a company's choice of the market in which it will compete and the value it intends to create in this market. Consequently, marketing strategy involves two key components: the *target market* in which it will compete and the *value proposition* for the relevant market entities—the company, its target customers, and its collaborators. The choice of the target market and the value proposition is the foundation of the company's business model and serves as the guiding principle for making the tactical decisions that define the company's offering.

- The term **tactics** comes from the Greek *τακτική*—meaning "arrangement"—used in reference to the deployment of troops during battle from their initial strategic position. In marketing, tactics refer to a set of specific activities, also known as the marketing mix, employed to execute a given strategy. The market tactics define the key aspects of the offering that the company introduces and manages in a given market, from the benefits this offering creates and how much it costs to how customers will hear about and buy it. The tactics logically follow from the company's strategy and

11

reflect the way the company will make this strategy a market reality. The tactics define the attributes of the market offering, namely, the product, service, brand, price, incentives, communication, and distribution.

A company's strategy and tactics are intricately related. Whereas the strategy defines the target market and the value the company aims to create in this market, the tactics define the attributes of the actual offering that creates value in the chosen market. Because the strategy defines the value that the company aims to create with its offering, deciding on the specific aspects of the offering—be it product features, brand image, pricing, sales promotions, communication activities, or distribution channels—is impossible without knowing whose needs the offering aims to fulfill, what those needs are, and what the competing options are for fulfilling these needs.

Marketing Strategy: The Target Market

The target market is the market in which a company aims to create and capture value. The choice of the target market is a crucial decision that can determine the viability of the company's market strategy. Indeed, because one of the main goals of a company is to create customer value, the choice of target customers for whom to create value is a key driver of the company's market success.

The target market is defined by five factors: *customers* whose needs the company aims to fulfill, *competitors* that aim to fulfill the same needs of the same target customers, *collaborators* that work with the company to fulfill customers' needs, the *company* managing the offering, and the *context* in which the company operates.

The five market factors are often referred to as the *Five Cs*, and the resulting framework is referred to as the *5-C framework*. This framework offers a simple yet very powerful tool for market analysis to guide the company's decisions and actions. The 5-C framework can be visually represented by a set of concentric ellipses, with target customers in the center; collaborators, competitors, and the company in the middle; and the context on the outside (Figure 1). The central placement of target customers reflects their defining role in the market; the other three entities—the company, its collaborators, and its competitors—aim to create value for these customers. The context is the outer layer because it defines the environment in which customers, the company, its collaborators, and its competitors operate.

Figure 1. Identifying the Target Market: The 5-C Framework

The Five Cs and the relationships among them are discussed in more detail in the following sections.

Target Customers

Target customers are the entities (individuals or organizations) whose needs the company aims to fulfill. Because a key goal of a company's offerings is to create customer value, identifying the right customers is essential for market success. In business-to-consumer markets, target customers are the individuals who are typically the end users of the company's offerings. In business-to-business markets, target customers are other businesses that use the company's offerings. Target customers are defined by two factors: *needs* and *profile*.

- **Customer needs** reflect the specific problem(s) faced by customers that the company aims to address. They determine the benefits that customers expect to receive from the company's offering. Although of critical importance to the company's ability to create customer value, customer needs are not readily observable and are often inferred from customers' demographics and behavior.

- **Customer profile** reflects customers' observable characteristics: *demographics* such as age, gender, income, occupation, education, religion, ethnicity, nationality, employment, social class, household size, and family life cycle; *geolocation* such as customers' permanent residence and their current location at a particular point in time; *psychographics* such as customers' personality, including moral values, attitudes, interests, and lifestyles; and *behavior* such as shopping habits, purchase frequency, purchase quantity, price sensitivity, sensitivity to promotional activities, loyalty, and social and leisure activities.

Both factors—needs and profile—are important in defining target customers. Customer needs determine the value the company must create for these customers, and the customer profile identifies effective and cost-efficient ways in which the company can reach customers with these needs to communicate and deliver its offering. To illustrate, consider the following examples:

iPhone fulfills customers' need for an all-in-one, always-on device that enables them to work, have fun, socialize, and even show off. Customers with this need have diverse profiles: Their ages range from teenagers to adults; they span social classes, income groups, and geographic locations; and they vary in occupation, hobbies, and lifestyles.

Starbucks fulfills customers' need for a place between home and work where they can relax, socialize, and enjoy indulgent coffee drinks handcrafted to their personal taste. Customers with these needs have different profiles: Most are adult urbanites aged 25 to 40 with relatively high incomes, professional careers, and a sense of social responsibility; the second-largest customer segment is young adults aged 16 to 24, many of whom are college students or young professionals.

The choice of target customers is determined by two key principles: The target customers should be able to create value for the company and its collaborators; and, vice versa, the company and its collaborators must be able to create superior value for these target customers relative to the competition. The selection of target customers determines all other aspects of the market: the scope of the competition, potential collaborators, company resources necessary to fulfill customer needs, and the context in which the company will create market value. A change in target customers typically leads to a change in competitors and collaborators, requires different company resources, and is influenced by different context factors. Because of its strategic importance, choosing the right target customers is the key to building a successful business model. The process of identifying target customers is discussed in more detail in Chapter 4.

Competitors

Competitors are entities that aim to fulfill the same need of the same customers as the company. Because the success of a company's offering hinges on its ability to create *superior* customer value, identifying the competitive offerings that customers will also consider when making a choice is essential to a company's ability to gain and defend its market position. Without knowing who the competitors are and what benefits they offer to target customers, it is difficult for a company to design an offering that will successfully provide superior value.

When defining their rivals, companies often fall prey to the myopic view of competition by defining it in traditional category and industry terms. For example, Blockbuster—the once ubiquitous chain of video rental stores—focused on competing with other movie rental businesses and missed the emerging competition from video streaming services such as Netflix and Hulu. In the same vein, Barnes & Noble and Borders booksellers focused exclusively on competing with other brick-and-mortar bookstores and overlooked the emerging online competition from Amazon.

Many companies do not realize that competitors are defined relative to customer needs, rather than the industry within which they operate. For example, digital camera manufacturers do not only compete with one another; they also compete with the manufacturers of smartphones because both digital cameras and smartphones can fulfill the same customer need of capturing a moment in time. By defining competitors based on the customer needs they aim to satisfy rather than a particular category, a company can gain a better understanding of who their current and future competitors are likely to be. To illustrate, consider some of the key iPhone and Starbucks competitors:

iPhone competes with smartphones from other manufacturers, including Samsung, HTC, Huawei, LG, and Xiaomi. It also competes with cameras from Canon, Fuji, Nikon, and Sony; portable music players from Sony, Pioneer, SanDisk, and Apple (iPod); and navigation services and devices from Garmin, Google, Magellan, and TomTom. It even competes with portable game consoles by enabling consumers to play games on their phones.

Starbucks competes with other chain stores offering drip and espresso-based coffee drinks, including Dunkin' Donuts, McDonald's, Costa Coffee, and Peet's Coffee. It also competes with boutique coffee shops offering handcrafted coffee drinks. In addition, Starbucks competes with offerings from the likes of Nespresso and Keurig, whose capsule-based technology enables consumers to easily make drip and espresso coffee drinks at home. Finally, Starbucks competes with traditional coffee producers including Folgers, Maxwell House, and Eight O'Clock Coffee.

Because competition is customer specific, companies that compete in one market can collaborate in another. For example, Apple competes with Microsoft in the market for personal computers and tablets while also collaborating with Microsoft to develop productivity software, including word processing and spreadsheet programs. Likewise, Samsung manufactures many iPhone components even though its Galaxy phones compete directly with the iPhone. Furthermore, because the competition is defined based on the ability of an offering to fulfill a particular customer need, different offerings in a company's product line can compete with one another. For example, different offerings in a company's product line can compete with one another. For example, different generations of Gillette's razors such as Sensor Excel, Mach3, and Fusion compete with one another to be the preferred shaving device for men.

Collaborators

Collaborators are entities that work with the company to create value for target customers. Because few, if any, companies possess all the resources necessary to create customer value, selecting the right collaborators is paramount for the company to compete in the chosen market. Value creation through collaboration represents a fundamental shift away from the conventional business paradigm in which value is created by the company and then delivered to the customer to a new paradigm in which the value is created jointly by the company and its collaborators. This value co-creation approach calls for involving collaborators in the very process of designing, communicating, and delivering value to target customers.

The choice of collaborators is driven by the complementarity of the resources needed to fulfill customer needs. Collaboration involves outsourcing the resources that the company lacks and that are required to fulfill the needs of target customers. Thus, instead of going through the risky and time-consuming task of building or acquiring resources that are lacking, a company can "borrow" them by partnering with entities that have these resources and can benefit from sharing them. Consider the collaborator networks of Apple and Starbucks:

iPhone benefits from Apple's collaboration with wireless service providers such as AT&T, Verizon, T-Mobile, and Sprint that ensure compatibility of the iPhone across different wireless networks. Apple also collaborates with numerous suppliers such as 3M, Corning, Intel, Foxconn, LG, Samsung, and Qualcomm. In addition, Apple collaborates with various retailers such as Walmart, Target, and Best Buy that make the iPhone available to the public.

Starbucks collaborates with numerous coffee growers around the globe to provide high-quality coffee beans. Starbucks also partners with suppliers that provide various non-coffee items such as water, pastries, snacks, and branded merchandise. In addition, Starbucks collaborates with a variety of retail outlets including grocery chains; mass-merchandisers; warehouse clubs; and convenience stores that sell coffee beans, instant coffee, and snacks.

Common types of collaborators include suppliers, manufacturers, distributors (dealers, wholesalers, and retailers), research-and-development entities, service providers, external salesforce, advertising agencies, and marketing research companies. For example, Procter & Gamble collaborates with the design firm IDEO to develop some of its products, with Diamond Packaging to provide packaging, and with retail giant Walmart for distribution. Walmart collaborates with Procter & Gamble to procure many of its products, with software solutions provider Oracle to streamline its logistics, and with shipping conglomerate Moller-Maersk to transport its goods.

Company

The company is the entity that develops and manages a given market offering. Understanding the goals the company aims to achieve and the resources it has to achieve these goals is important for determining the company's ability to successfully compete in the chosen market.

The company can be a manufacturer that produces the actual goods being sold (Procter & Gamble), a service provider (American Express), an entity engaged in brand building (Lacoste), a media company (Facebook), or a retailer (Walmart). The company is not limited to a single role; it can perform multiple functions. For example, a retailer might have its own production facility, engage in building its own brand, and offer a variety of value-added services.

In the case of enterprises with diverse strategic competencies and market offerings, the term *company* refers to the particular business unit (also called the *strategic business unit*) of the organization managing the specific offering. To illustrate, Apple comprises multiple strategic business units, including iPhone, iPod, iPad, Apple Watch, iTunes, and Apple TV, among others. In the same vein, GE, Alphabet (Google's parent company), and Facebook have multiple business units, each of which can be viewed as a separate company requiring its own business model.

A company's motivation and ability to create market value can be defined by two main factors: *goals* and *resources*.

- **Goals** reflect the end result that the company aims to achieve with a particular offering. Company goals can be monetary, such as maximizing profits, and strategic, such as establishing synergies with other company offerings and creating value for society at large.

- **Resources** reflect the company's characteristics, including the resources that determine its ability to create market value and a sustainable competitive advantage. A company's resources include its assets and competencies such as business facilities; suppliers; employees; know-how; existing products, services, and brands; communication and distribution channels; and access to capital.

To illustrate, consider the goals and resources of Apple and Starbucks.

Apple's (iPhone) resources are characterized by its production facilities; its relationships with suppliers, manufacturers, and distributors; its technology-savvy employees; its intellectual property including know-how, patents, and trademarks; its strong brand; its existing product and service ecosystem; its loyal customer base; and its vast cash reserves. Apple's goals are for the iPhone to be its key revenue and profit driver (monetary goal) and a cornerstone of the company's ecosystem of products and services (strategic goal).

Starbucks' resources are defined by its numerous retail locations, its relationships with coffee growers and distributors, its professionally trained employees, its intellectual property, its strong brand, its loyal customer base, and its access to capital markets. Starbucks' monetary goal—to generate revenues and profits for its shareholders—is complemented by its strategic goal to benefit society and promote social responsibility.

Context

Context describes the environment in which the company operates. Understanding the context is important because even small changes in the market environment can have major implications for the company's business model. The context is defined by five factors:

- **Sociocultural context** includes social and demographic trends, value systems, religion, language, lifestyles, attitudes, and beliefs.

- **Technological context** includes new techniques, skills, methods, and processes for designing, manufacturing, communicating, and delivering market offerings.

- **Regulatory context** includes taxes; import tariffs; embargoes; product specification, pricing, and communication regulations; and intellectual property laws.

- **Economic context** includes factors such as the overall economic activity, money supply, inflation, and interest rates.

- **Physical context** includes natural resources, climate, geographic location, topography, and health trends.

To illustrate, the context in which iPhone and Starbucks operate can be described as follows:

iPhone's context is characterized by people's mounting desire for mobile connectivity that enables them to search, share, and shop on the go; by rapid technological developments, including the availability and speed of wireless connectivity, improved battery life and processing speed, and enhanced image processing; by intellectual property laws enabling the company to protect its patents and trademarks; and by the overall economic conditions that determine customers' disposable income.

Starbucks' context is characterized by the growing popularity of crafted coffee drinks and the desire to socialize in person, as well as by the growing popularity of online communications; by the technological developments that enable the company to better understand its customers, track their buying behavior, and communicate with them on a one-on-one basis; by the favorable trade agreements that influence import tariffs on coffee; by various economic factors, including the state of the local economy and the global commodity prices for coffee; and by the climate and weather patterns across different geographic locations.

Unlike the other four Cs—customers, competitors, collaborators, and company—which describe the different market players in the value-exchange process, the context depicts the environment in which the value exchange takes place. Consequently, changes in the context can influence all the market participants and the ways in which they create and capture market value. In fact, changes in the context, whether they are new technological developments or changes in the regulatory environment, are often the impetus behind disruptive innovations that give birth to new markets and industries. Without thoroughly understanding the intricacies of the context in which a company operates, it is impossible to create a viable business model that will endure the test of time.

Marketing Strategy: The Value Proposition

The value proposition defines the value that an offering aims to create in a given market. A meaningful value proposition allows a company to craft an offering that creates value for all relevant parties in the market exchange—target customers, collaborators, and the company. The primary aspects of developing a value proposition are discussed below.

Defining the Value Exchange

The value proposition defines the value that an offering aims to create for market participants. Designing a meaningful value proposition calls for understanding the *value exchange* among the relevant market entities—customers, the company, its collaborators, and its competitors—that operate in a given context (Figure 2). Accordingly, the value exchange defines how different entities create and capture value in a given market.

Each of the relationships defining the value exchange is a process of giving (creating) and receiving (capturing) value. Thus, the relationship between the company and its customers is defined by the value the company creates for its customers as well as by the value created by these customers that is captured by the company. In the same vein, the relationship between the company and its collaborators is defined by the value the company creates for these collaborators as well as by the value generated by these collaborators that is captured by the company. The relationship between the company's customers and its collaborators is defined by the value these collaborators create for target customers as well as by the value generated by the target customers that is captured by collaborators.

Figure 2. Defining the Value Exchange

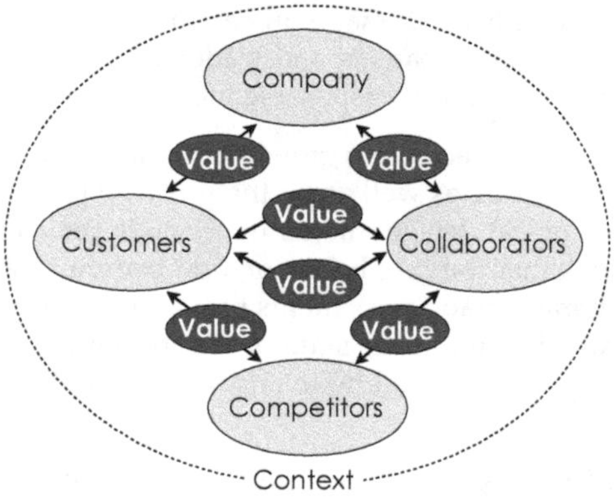

To illustrate, consider the relationship between a manufacturer, a retailer, and their customers. The manufacturer (the company) partners with a retailer (the collaborator) to deliver an offering to target customers. *Customers* receive value from the product (created by the manufacturer) they purchase as well as from the service (delivered by the retailer) involved in the buying process, for which they offer monetary compensation that is shared by both the manufacturer and the retailer. The *retailer* receives value from customers in the form of margins (the differential between the buying and selling price) as well as value from the manufacturer in the form of various trade promotions. The *manufacturer* receives value from customers in the form of the price they pay for its products (excluding the retailer markup) as well as from the retailer in the form of various services the retailer performs on the manufacturer's behalf.

The three value relationships between the company, its customers, and its collaborators reflect only the company side of the value exchange. No market exists without competitors that aim to create value for the same target customers. The competitive aspect of the value exchange mirrors the company side of the value exchange. Specifically, it consists of three types of value relationships: those between the company's target customers and its competitors, those between the company's target customers and competitors' collaborators (some or all of whom could also be the company's collaborators), and those between the competitors and their collaborators.

To succeed in a competitive environment, a company's offerings must beat the competition and create superior value for all three entities—customers, collaborators, and the company. This is the essence of the market value principle discussed in the following section.

The Market Value Principle

Creating value for all relevant entities involved in the market exchange—target customers, collaborators, and the company—is the overarching principle that guides all company actions. This is the market value principle that encapsulates the company's value proposition:

> *The offering must create superior value for its target customers and collaborators in a way that enables the company to achieve its goals*

The market value principle implies that when developing market offerings, a company needs to consider all three types of value: *customer value, collaborator value*, and *company value*.

- **Customer value** is the worth of an offering to its customers; it is customers' assessment of the degree to which an offering fulfills their needs. The value an offering creates for its customers is determined by three main factors: (1) the *needs* of these customers, (2) the benefits and costs of the company's offering, and (3) the benefits and costs of the alternative means (competitive offerings) target customers can use to fulfill their needs. Simply put, the customer value proposition answers the question: *Why would target customers choose the company's offering instead of the available alternatives?*

- **Collaborator value** is the worth of an offering to the company's collaborators; it is the sum of all benefits and costs that an offering creates for collaborators. The collaborator value reflects an offering's ability to help collaborators achieve their goals better than the alternative offerings. Simply put, the collaborator value proposition answers the question: *Why would collaborators choose the company's offering instead of the competitive offerings?*

- **Company value** is the worth of the offering to the company; it is the sum of all benefits and costs associated with an offering. The value of an offering is defined relative to the company's goal and the value of other opportunities that are available to the company, such as the value of other offerings that could be launched by the company. The company value proposition answers the question: *Why would the company choose this offering instead of the alternative options?*

Because the market value principle underscores the importance of creating value for the three key entities—target customers, the company, and collaborators—it is also referred to as the *3-V principle*. The market value principle implies that the viability of a business model is defined by the answers to three sets of questions related to the value of an offering for customers, collaborators, and the company:

- *What value does the offering create for its target customers? Why would target customers choose this offering? What makes this offering better than the alternative options?*

- *What value does the offering create for the company's collaborators? Why would the entities identified as collaborators (suppliers, distributors, and co-developers) partner with the company?*

- *What value does the offering create for the company? Why should the company invest resources in this offering rather than in an alternative offering?*

The need to manage value for three different entities raises the question of whose value to prioritize. Surprisingly, many companies find it difficult to reach a consensus because of the divergent priorities of the different stakeholders, often represented by different departments within the company. Marketing departments focus on creating customer value; finance departments and senior management focus on creating company (shareholder) value; and the salesforce focuses on creating value for collaborators, such as dealers, wholesalers, and retailers.

The "right" answer is that the company needs to balance the value among its stakeholders, customers, and collaborators to create an optimal value proposition. Here, the term *optimal value* means that the value of the offering is balanced across the three entities, such that it creates value for target customers and collaborators in a way that enables the company to achieve its strategic goals. Optimizing customer, company, and collaborator value is inherent in the market value principle, which is the cornerstone of market success (Figure 3).

Figure 3. The 3-V Market Value Principle

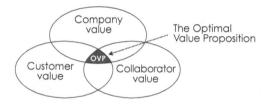

An offering that satisfies the market value principle is said to have an *optimal value proposition* (OVP). Failure to create superior value for any of the three market entities inevitably leads to an unsustainable business model and failure of the business venture. The root cause of virtually all business failures can be traced to the inability of the company's offering to deliver superior value to target customers, collaborators, and/or the company. Therefore, developing a value proposition that can fulfill the needs of all relevant participants in the value exchange is the overarching principle of any marketing activity.

The market value principle and the concept of the optimal value proposition can be illustrated with the following examples:

iPhone. Customers receive value through the functionality and prestige of the iPhone, for which they offer Apple and its collaborators monetary compensation. Collaborators (wireless service providers) receive the strategic benefit of associating their service with a product that is in high demand and likely to promote greater usage of their services. In return, these collaborators invest resources in making their services compatible with iPhone's functionality. Another set of collaborators (retailers) receives monetary benefit (profits) from selling the iPhone as well as the strategic benefit of carrying a traffic-generating product. Retailers, in turn, invest monetary and strategic resources (shelf space, inventory management, and salesforce) to deliver the iPhone to its customers. In return for developing, advertising, and distributing the iPhone, the company (Apple) receives monetary compensation from consumers purchasing the iPhone as well as the strategic benefit of strengthening its brand and its ecosystem of compatible Apple products.

Starbucks. Customers receive value through the functional benefit of a variety of coffee beverages as well as the psychological benefit of expressing certain aspects of their personality through the choice of a customized beverage, for which they deliver monetary compensation. Starbucks collaborators (coffee growers) receive monetary payments for the coffee beans they provide and the strategic benefit of having a consistent demand for their product, in return for which they invest resources in growing coffee beans that conform to

Starbucks' standards. By investing resources in developing and offering its products and services to consumers, the company (Starbucks) derives monetary benefit (revenues and profits) and the strategic benefits of building a brand and enhancing its market footprint.

The value proposition reflects the company's expectation of the value that the offering will create for the three key market entities. The value proposition is not a tangible offering in and of itself. Rather, value is created by specific offering(s) the company and its collaborators design, communicate, and deliver to target customers. The key aspects of developing offering(s) that create market value are discussed in the following section.

Marketing Tactics: The Market Offering

Marketing tactics define the company's offering by delineating the specific attributes describing the actual good that the company deploys to fulfill a particular customer need. Whereas a company's strategy determines its target market and the value it seeks to provide to relevant market participants, tactics determine the specific offering that will deliver the value outlined in the strategy. The key attributes defining a company's offering and the way they come together as a process of designing, communicating, and delivering value are outlined in the following sections.

The Seven Attributes Defining the Market Offering

A company's offering is defined by seven attributes: product, service, brand, price, incentives, communication, and distribution. These seven attributes are also referred to as the *marketing mix*—the combination of specific activities employed to execute the offering's strategy. These seven tactics defining the offering are the tools that managers have at their disposal to create market value (Figure 4).

Figure 4. Marketing Tactics: The Seven Attributes Defining the Market Offering

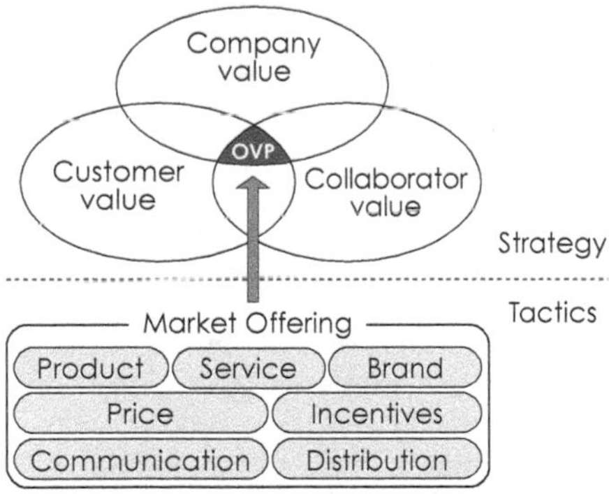

The seven attributes that delineate the market offering are defined as follows:

- The **product** aspect of an offering reflects the benefits of the good with which the company aims to create market value. Products can be both tangible (e.g., food, apparel, and automobiles) and intangible (e.g., software, music, and video). Products typically entitle customers to permanent rights to the acquired good. For example, a customer purchasing a car or a software program takes ownership of the acquired product.

- The **service** aspect of an offering reflects the benefits of the good with which the company aims to create value for its customers without entitling them to permanent ownership of this good (e.g., movie rental, appliance repairs, medical procedures, and tax preparation). The service aspect of the offering is closely related to its product aspect such that some offerings might be positioned as either a product or a service. For example, a software can be offered as a product, with customers purchasing the rights to a copy of the program, or as a service, with customers renting the program to temporarily receive its benefits. Many offerings involve both product and service components. For example, a mobile phone offering includes a product component—the physical device that customers acquire—as well as a service component that includes wireless connectivity and device repairs.

- The **brand** is a marketing tool that aims to inform customers about the source of the products and services associated with the brand. The brand helps identify the company's products and services, differentiate them from those of the competition, and create unique value beyond the product and service aspects of the offering. For example, the Harley-Davidson brand identifies its motorcycles; differentiates these motorcycles from those made by Honda, Suzuki, Kawasaki, and Yamaha; and elicits a distinct emotional reaction from its customers, who use Harley-Davidson's brand to express their individuality.

- The **price** is the amount of money the company charges its customers and collaborators for the benefits provided by the offering.

- **Incentives** are tools that enhance the value of the offering by reducing its costs and/or by increasing its benefits. Common incentives include volume discounts, price reductions, coupons, rebates, premiums, bonus offerings, contests, and rewards. Incentives can be offered to individual customers, the company's collaborators (e.g., incentives given to channel partners), and the company's employees.

- **Communication** informs the relevant market entities—target customers, collaborators, and the company's employees and stakeholders—about the specifics of the offering.

- **Distribution** defines the channel(s) used to deliver the offering to target customers and the company's collaborators.

The seven attributes defining the offering are illustrated by the following examples:

iPhone. The *product* is the actual phone, defined by its physical characteristics and functionality. The *service* is the wireless connectivity provided by the telecommunications companies as well as the assistance offered by Apple in using and repairing the phone. The *brand* is the iPhone identity marks (e.g., its name and logo) and the associations that it evokes in people's minds. The *price* is the amount of money Apple charges for the iPhone. *Incentives* are the promotional tools such as temporary price reductions that provide additional value for iPhone customers. *Communication* is the information conveyed by press conferences, media coverage, and advertisements that inform the public about the iPhone. *Distribution* encompasses the channels—Apple's own stores and authorized resellers—that make the iPhone available to the public.

Starbucks. The *product* is the variety of coffee and other beverages, as well as food items available. The *service* is the assistance offered to customers prior to, during, and after purchase. The *brand* is Starbucks' name, logo, and the associations it evokes in customers' minds. The *price* is the monetary amount that Starbucks charges customers for its offerings. *Incentives* are the promotional tools—loyalty programs, coupons, and temporary price reductions—that provide additional benefits for customers. *Communication* is the information disseminated via different media channels—advertising, social media, and public relations—informing the public about Starbucks' offerings. *Distribution* includes the Starbucks-owned stores and Starbucks-licensed retail outlets, through which Starbucks' offerings are delivered to its customers.

Marketing Tactics as a Process of Designing, Communicating, and Delivering Value

The seven marketing tactics—product, service, brand, price, incentives, communication, and distribution—can be viewed as a *process of designing, communicating, and delivering* customer value. The product, service, brand, price, and incentives are the aspects of the offering that define its value; communication is the process of communicating the offering's value; and distribution is the value-delivery aspect of the offering (Figure 5). Customer value is created across all three dimensions, with different attributes playing distinct roles in the value-creation process.

Figure 5. Marketing Tactics as a Process of Designing, Communicating, and Delivering Customer Value

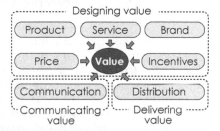

Because they define the key benefits and costs, the product, service, brand, price, and incentives are the *key value drivers* of the offering. Communication and distribution are the *channels* through which the benefits created by the first five attributes are communicated and delivered to target customers. Thus, communication informs customers about the functionality of a product or service, builds the image of its brand, publicizes its price, apprises buyers of sales promotions, and advises them about the availability of the offering. Likewise, distribution delivers a company's products and services, delivers customer payments to the company, and delivers the offering's promotional incentives to customers and collaborators.

The value-creation process can be examined from both the company and customer perspectives. From a company's perspective, value creation is a process of *designing, communicating,* and *delivering* value. From a customer's perspective, however, these three components of the value-creation process correspond to the *attractiveness, awareness,* and *availability* of the offering.[3] Thus, an offering's ability to create customer value is determined by the answers to the following three questions:

- *What makes the offering attractive to target customers?*
- *How will target customers become aware of the offering?*
- *How will target customers acquire the offering?*

The answer to the first question outlines the customer benefits and costs associated with the product, service, brand, price, and incentives aspects of the offering. The answer to the second question outlines the way in which the company will communicate the specifics of the offering to its target customers. The answer to the third question outlines the way in which the company will make the offering available to its target customers. In this context, the customer-centric approach to managing the *attractiveness*, *awareness*, and *availability* of an offering complements the company-centric approach to managing the process of *designing*, *communicating*, and *delivering* value to target customers (Figure 6).

Figure 6. Marketing Tactics: Company Actions and Customer Impact

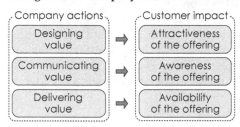

The process of designing, communicating, and delivering value can be illustrated with the following examples:

iPhone. The *value-design* component of this Apple offering involves development of the actual product (the iPhone) and service (Apple's own service and that of the wireless carriers), the creation of the iPhone brand (crafting the image that Apple wants to be associated with the iPhone in people's minds), setting the price, and deciding on the type of incentives to use to promote customer demand. The *value-communication* component of the iPhone involves communicating the features and benefits of the phone and the related services, communicating the elements of the iPhone brand, as well as informing customers about the iPhone price and incentives. Finally, the *value-delivery* aspect of the iPhone involves physically delivering the phone to buyers, servicing the phone, delivering the brand-related information, collecting payments, and delivering the incentives.

Starbucks. The *value-design* aspect of Starbucks' offerings involves the creation of its portfolio of products, ranging from espresso drinks to various food items and even wine; defining the service experience; designing its brand (defining what the Starbucks brand should mean to its customers); setting prices for all possible combinations of its various drinks and sizes; and deciding what, when, and how many sales promotions to offer (such as 2-for-1 promotions). The *value-communication* aspect of Starbucks involves informing and educating customers about different drinks and food items available, communicating Starbucks' service policies, promoting the meaning of the Starbucks' brand, communicating its prices, and informing customers about relevant incentives. Finally, the *value-delivery* aspect of Starbucks involves delivering its products and services to customers, delivering the brand-related information, collecting consumer payments, and delivering incentives to target customers using appropriate channels (e.g., newspaper inserts, online banner advertisements, and proximity-based mobile promotions).

The Market Value Map

For practical purposes, the strategy and tactics delineating a company's business model can be represented as a value map that outlines the ways in which an offering creates value for its target customers, collaborators, and the company. The market value map is a schematic presentation of the business model, enabling managers to clearly articulate the key aspects of the company's strategy and tactics. Thus, the primary purpose of the value map is to visually outline the key aspects of the business model and serve as a guide that lays out the company's strategy and tactics.

The market value map follows the structure of the business model and comprises the three key components—*the target market, the value proposition,* and *the market offering*—that define the offering's strategy and tactics. Accordingly, the market value map is visually represented as a matrix: The left side outlines the key elements of the company's strategy—the target market (customers, collaborators, company, competitors, and context) and the value proposition (customer value, collaborator value, and company value)—and the right side outlines the market offering defined by its seven key attributes (product, service, brand, price, incentives, communication, and distribution). The components of the market value map and the key questions defining each component are shown in Figure 7.

Figure 7. The Market Value Map

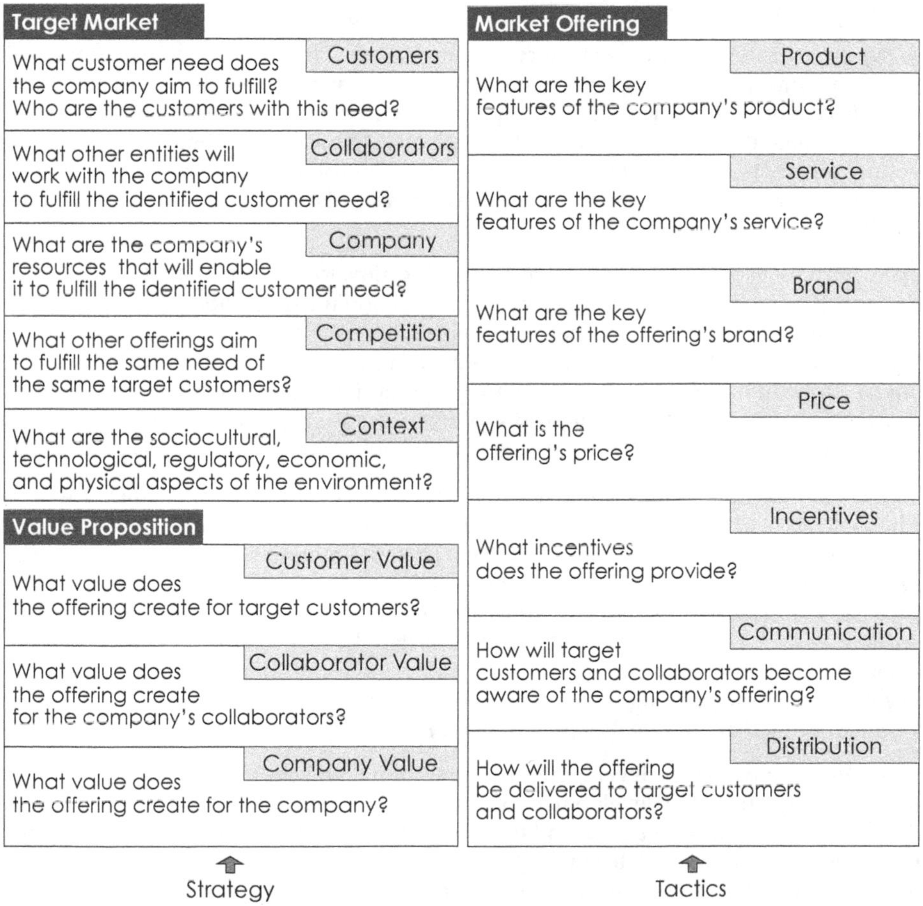

Target Market	Market Offering
Customers What customer need does the company aim to fulfill? Who are the customers with this need?	**Product** What are the key features of the company's product?
Collaborators What other entities will work with the company to fulfill the identified customer need?	**Service** What are the key features of the company's service?
Company What are the company's resources that will enable it to fulfill the identified customer need?	**Brand** What are the key features of the offering's brand?
Competition What other offerings aim to fulfill the same need of the same target customers?	**Price** What is the offering's price?
Context What are the sociocultural, technological, regulatory, economic, and physical aspects of the environment?	**Incentives** What incentives does the offering provide?
Value Proposition	**Communication** How will target customers and collaborators become aware of the company's offering?
Customer Value What value does the offering create for target customers?	**Distribution** How will the offering be delivered to target customers and collaborators?
Collaborator Value What value does the offering create for the company's collaborators?	
Company Value What value does the offering create for the company?	

⬆ Strategy   ⬆ Tactics

The market value map outlines the ways in which an offering creates value for the three relevant market entities—customers, collaborators, and the company. Because each of these entities requires its own value proposition and employs different tools to create value, the market value map can be divided into three, more detailed maps: a customer value map that reflects the way an offering creates value for target customers, a collaborator value map that reflects the way an offering creates value for the company's collaborators, and a company value map that reflects the way an offering creates value for the company. Examples of these three types of value maps are shown in Appendix B at the end of this book.

SUMMARY

A company's success is defined by its ability to create value in the chosen market. To create value, a company must clearly identify the target market in which it will compete, develop a meaningful value proposition that enables it to create and capture value in this market, and design a viable market offering. These key activities form the two building blocks of a company's business model: *strategy* and *tactics*.

Strategy identifies the market in which the company competes and the value the company intends to create in this market. Marketing strategy involves two components: the target market and the value proposition.

The *target market* is defined by five factors that form the 5-C framework: *customers* whose needs the company aims to fulfill, *competitors* that aim to fulfill the same needs of the same target customers, *collaborators* that work with the company to fulfill customers' needs, the *company* managing the offering, and the *context* in which the company operates. The choice of target customers determines all other aspects of the target market: the scope of the competition, potential collaborators, company resources necessary to fulfill customer needs, and the context in which the company will create market value.

The *value proposition* defines the value that an offering aims to create for target customers, collaborators, and the company. An offering's value proposition must provide a clear answer to three questions: Why would target customers choose the company's offering instead of the available alternatives? Why would collaborators choose the company's offering instead of the alternative options? Why would the company choose this offering instead of the alternative options? The *market value principle* states that to succeed in a given market the company must create superior value for its target customers and collaborators in a way that enables it to achieve its goals.

Tactics are the specific activities employed to execute the offering's strategy; they are the means that managers have at their disposal to create market value. Tactics outline the seven key attributes of the offering (also referred to as the *marketing mix*) that the company deploys in the target market: product, service, brand, price, incentives, communication, and distribution. Tactics can be viewed as a process of *designing, communicating,* and *delivering* value, where product, service, brand, price, and incentives compose the value-design aspect of the offering that defines its *attractiveness* for target customers; communication captures the value-communication aspect that aims to create *awareness* of the offering among target customers; and distribution reflects the value-delivery aspect of the offering that ensures the *availability* of the offering to target customers.

The value-based approach to developing a business model and crafting the strategy and tactics of a market offering guides the development of a *market value map* that outlines the specific ways in which an offering creates value for its target customers, collaborators, and the company. The market value map follows the structure of the business model and comprises three key components—the target market, the value proposition, and the market offering—that outline the offering's strategy and tactics.

Marketing Insight: 4-P and 5-Forces Frameworks

The Market Value framework outlined in this chapter is not the only business model framework in existence. There are a number of frameworks that address different aspects of business models. Two of these frameworks — the *4-P framework* and *5-Forces framework* — are outlined below.

The 4-P Framework

The 4-P framework, introduced by Jerome McCarthy in the 1960s, offers a tool for planning and analyzing the implementation of a given marketing strategy.[4] This framework identifies four key decisions that managers must make with respect to a given offering: (1) what features to include in the *product*, (2) how to *price* the product, (3) how to *promote* the product, and (4) in which retail outlets to *place* the product. These four decisions, often referred to as the marketing mix, are captured by the four Ps: product, price, promotion, and place (Figure 8).

Figure 8. The 4-P Framework

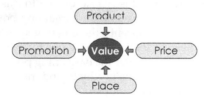

The 4-P framework is simple, intuitive, and easy to remember — factors that have contributed to its popularity. Despite its simplicity, the 4-P framework has a number of limitations that significantly limit its relevance in the contemporary business environment. One such limitation is that it does not distinguish between the product and service aspects of the offering. The fact that the 4-P framework does not explicitly account for the *service* element of the offering is a key drawback in today's service-oriented business environment, in which a growing number of companies are switching from a product-based to a service-based business model.

Another important limitation of the 4-P framework is that the *brand* is not defined as a separate factor and instead is viewed as part of the product. The product and brand are different aspects of the offering and can exist independently of each other. An increasing number of companies such as Lacoste, Prada, and Disney outsource their product manufacturing in order to focus their efforts on building and managing their brands.

The 4-P framework also comes up short in defining the term *promotion*. Promotion is a broad concept that includes two distinct types of activities: *incentives*, such as price promotions, coupons, and trade promotions; and *communication*, such as advertising, public relations, social media, and personal selling. Each of these two activities has a distinct role in the value-creation process. Incentives enhance the offering's value, whereas communication informs customers about the offering without necessarily enhancing its value. Using a single term to refer to these distinct activities muddles the unique role that they play in creating market value.

The limitations of the 4-P framework can be overcome by defining the market offering in terms of seven, rather than four, factors — product, service, brand, price, incentives, communication, and distribution — as outlined by the marketing tactics framework discussed earlier in this chapter. The four Ps can be easily mapped onto the seven attributes defining the market offering, whereby the first P comprises product, service, and brand; price is the second P; incentives and communication are the third P; and distribution is the fourth P (Figure 9). Thus, the marketing mix framework outlined earlier in this chapter presents a more refined version of the 4-P framework that offers a more accurate and actionable approach to designing a company's offering.

Figure 9. The Four Ps and the Marketing Mix

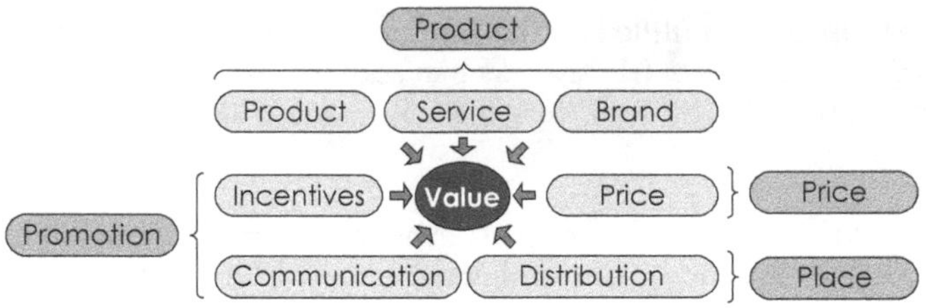

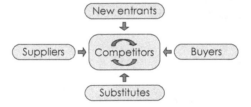

The Five Forces Framework

The Five Forces framework, advanced by Michael Porter, offers an industry-based analysis of the competition and is often used for strategic industry-level decisions such as evaluating the viability of entering (or exiting) a particular industry.[5] According to this framework, competitiveness within an industry is determined by five factors: the bargaining power of suppliers, the bargaining power of buyers, the threat of new entrants, the threat of substitutes, and rivalry among extant competitors (Figure 10). The joint impact of these five factors defines the competitive environment in which a firm operates. The greater the bargaining power of suppliers and buyers, the threat of new market entrants and substitute products, and the rivalry among existing competitors, the greater the competition within the industry.

Figure 10. The Five Forces of Competition

The Five Forces framework shares a number of similarities with the 5-C framework, as both frameworks aim to facilitate analysis of the market in which a company operates. At the same time, these frameworks differ in the way they define the market. The Five Forces framework takes an industry perspective to analyze the competition in the market. In contrast, the 5-C framework is customer centric rather than industry focused, meaning that it defines the market based on customer needs rather than the industry in which the company competes. As a result of its customer centricity, the 5-C framework defines competitors based on their ability to fulfill customer needs and create market value, and is not concerned with whether the company and its competitors operate within the bounds of the same industry. Accordingly, the concept of substitutes is superfluous in the context of the 5-C framework because from a customer's point of view, substitutes are merely cross-category competitors that aim to fulfill a particular customer need.

The industry focus of the Five Forces framework makes it particularly relevant to analyzing the competitive structure within a given industry. At the same time, when it comes to analyzing an offering's ability to create market value, the Five Forces approach has much lower explanatory power. In such scenarios, the 5-C framework is typically a better fit because of its customer focus and its view of the market as defined by customer needs rather than in terms of a particular industry.

CHAPTER THREE

MARKETING PLANNING AND MANAGEMENT

A man who does not think and plan long ahead
will find trouble right at his door.

— Confucius, Chinese philosopher

To achieve market success, a company needs to develop a sound marketing plan and create an organizational structure and a set of processes to manage its activities. The key aspects of the process of marketing planning and management are the focus of this chapter.

The G-STIC Framework for Marketing Management

A company's future hinges on its ability to develop successful market offerings that create superior value for target customers, the company, and its collaborators. Market success is rarely an accident; it is typically a result of diligent market analysis, planning, and management. To succeed in the market, a company must have a viable business model and an action plan to make this model a reality. The process of developing such an action plan is captured in the G-STIC framework discussed in the following sections.

The G-STIC Approach to Action Planning

The backbone of market planning is the action plan, which articulates the company's goal and delineates a course of action to reach this goal. The development of an action plan is guided by five key activities: setting a *goal*, developing a *strategy*, designing the *tactics*, defining an *implementation* plan, and identifying a set of *control* metrics to measure the success of the proposed action. These five activities comprise the G-STIC (Goal-Strategy-Tactics-Implementation-Control) framework, which is the cornerstone of marketing planning and analysis (Figure 1). The core of the action plan is the business model comprising the offering's strategy and tactics.

Figure 1. The G-STIC Framework for Marketing Management

The individual components of the G-STIC framework are outlined in more detail below.

- The **goal** identifies the ultimate criterion for success; it is the end result that the company aims to achieve. The goal has two components: the *focus*, which defines the metric reflecting the desired outcome of the company's actions (e.g., net income), and the performance *benchmarks* quantifying the goal and defining the time frame for it to be accomplished.

- The **strategy** defines the company's *target market* and its *value proposition* in this market. The strategy is the backbone of the company's business model.

- **Tactics** define the key attributes of the company's offering: *product, service, brand, price, incentives, communication,* and *distribution*. These seven tactics are the tools that the company uses to create value in the chosen market.

- **Implementation** defines the processes involved in creating the market offering. Implementation includes *developing* the company resources and the market offering and *deploying* the offering in the target market.

- **Control** evaluates the success of the company's activities over time by evaluating the company's *performance* and monitoring the changes in the market *environment* in which the company operates.

The key components of the marketing plan and the key factors describing each component are outlined in Figure 2.

Figure 2. The G-STIC Action-Planning Flowchart

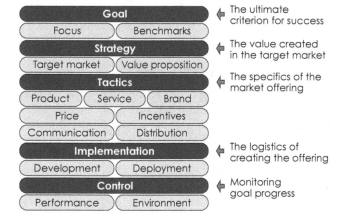

The G-STIC framework offers an intuitive approach to streamlining a company's activities into a logical sequence that aims to produce the desired market outcome. Note that even though the G-STIC framework implies a particular sequence, starting with the definition of the company's goal and concluding with identifying controls for measuring performance, marketing planning is an iterative process. Thus, even though the development of a marketing plan often starts with the identification of an unmet customer need that the company can fulfill better than the competition, it can also start with a technological invention that enables the company to create market value. In this context, the G-STIC framework describes the key elements of the iterative process of marketing planning (Goal, Strategy, Tactics, Implementation, and Control) and outlines a logical sequence of organizing these elements without prescribing the order in which these elements are developed.

The key aspects of the action plan are examined in more detail in the following sections. Because the offering's strategy and tactics were discussed in depth in the previous chapter, the focus here is on the remaining three aspects: goal, implementation, and control.

Setting a Goal

The marketing plan starts with defining the goal that the company aims to achieve. This goal then becomes the beacon that guides all company activities. Without a well-defined goal, a company cannot design a meaningful course of action and evaluate its success. The importance of having a clear goal is captured in the words of the English mathematician and author of *Alice's Adventures in Wonderland*, Lewis Carroll: *If you don't know where you're going, any road will get you there.* This insight applies to business as well: Without a set goal, a company is like a ship without a rudder.

Setting a goal involves two decisions: identifying the *focus* of the company's actions and defining the performance *benchmarks* to be achieved.

Defining the Goal Focus

The focus identifies the key criterion for a company's success; it is the metric defining the desired outcome of the company's activities. Based on their focus, goals can be monetary or strategic:

- **Monetary goals** involve monetary outcomes such as net income, profit margins, earnings per share, and return on investment. Monetary goals are the primary performance metric for for-profit enterprises.

- **Strategic goals** involve nonmonetary outcomes that are of strategic importance to the company. Common strategic goals include growing sales volume, creating brand awareness, increasing social welfare, enhancing the corporate culture, and facilitating employee recruitment and retention. Strategic goals are the main performance metric for nonprofit enterprises as well as for offerings of for-profit companies that have the primary function of supporting other, profit-generating offerings. For example, Amazon might break even (or even operate at a loss) in making, promoting, and distributing some of its Kindle devices and yet view them as a strategically important platform for its retail business.

Monetary goals and strategic goals are not mutually exclusive: A company might aim to achieve certain strategic goals with an otherwise profitable offering, and a strategically important offering might contribute to the company's bottom line. In fact, long-term financial planning must always include a strategic component in addition to setting monetary goals. In the same vein, long-term strategic planning must always include a financial component that articulates how achieving a particular strategic goal will translate into financial benefits.

Companies are increasingly looking beyond sales revenue and profit to consider the legal, ethical, social, and environmental effects of marketing activities and programs. For example, when Ben Cohen and Jerry Greenfield founded Ben & Jerry's, they divided the traditional financial bottom line into a "double bottom line" that also measured the environmental impact of their products and processes. That later expanded into a "triple bottom line"—people, planet, and profits—to reflect the societal impact of the firm's entire range of business activities.

Defining Performance Benchmarks

Performance benchmarks outline the quantitative and temporal criteria for reaching the goal. Consequently, there are two types of performance benchmarks that work in concert to define the company goal:

- **Quantitative benchmarks** define the specific milestones to be achieved by the company with respect to its focal goal. For example, goals such as "increase market share by 2%," "increase retention rates by 12%," and "improve the effectiveness of marketing expenditures by 15%" articulate benchmarks that quantify the set goal. Quantitative benchmarks can be expressed in either relative terms (e.g., increase market share by 20%) or absolute terms (e.g., achieve annual sales of one million units).

- **Temporal benchmarks** identify the time frame for achieving a particular milestone. Setting a timeline for achieving a goal is a key decision because the strategy adopted to implement these goals is often contingent on the time horizon. The goal of maximizing next quarter's profits will likely require a different strategy and tactics than the goal of maximizing long-term profitability.

Overall, the company goal must address three main questions: *what* is to be achieved (goal focus), *how much* should be achieved (quantitative benchmark), and *when* should it be achieved (temporal benchmark). To illustrate, a company might set the goal of generating net income (goal focus) of $50 million (quantitative benchmark) in one year (temporal benchmark). Answers to these questions capture the essence of the company's goal and serve as a beacon that guides the company's strategy and tactics.

Setting Market Objectives

Based on their focus, goals vary in their level of generality. Some goals reflect outcomes that are more fundamental than others. Therefore, a company's goals can be represented as a hierarchy headed by a company's ultimate goal, which is implemented through a set of more specific goals referred to as market objectives.

Unlike the ultimate goal, which is typically defined in terms of a company-focused outcome, *market objectives* delineate specific changes involving the relevant market factors—customers, the company, collaborators, competitors, and context—that will enable the company to achieve its ultimate goal. The different types of market objectives are illustrated in Figure 3 and outlined below.

Figure 3. Market Goals and Objectives

- **Customer objectives** aim to change the behavior of target customers (e.g., increasing purchase frequency, switching from a competitive product, or making a first-time purchase in a product category) in a way that will enable the company to achieve its ultimate goal. To illustrate, the company goal of increasing net revenues can be associated with the more specific customer objective of increasing the frequency with which customers repurchase the offering. Because the customers are the principal source of a company's revenues and profits, a company's ultimate goal typically involves a customer-focused objective.

- **Collaborator objectives** aim to elicit changes in the behavior of the company's collaborators, such as providing greater promotional support, better pricing terms, greater systems integration, and extended distribution coverage. To illustrate, the company goal of increasing net revenues can be associated with the more specific collaborator objective of increasing the shelf space available for the offering in distribution channels.

- **Company (internal) objectives** aim to elicit changes in the company's own actions, such as improving product and service quality, reducing the cost of goods sold, improving the effectiveness of the company's marketing actions, and streamlining research-and-development costs. For example, the company goal of increasing net revenues can be associated with the more specific internal objective of increasing the effectiveness and cost efficiency of its communication.

- **Competitive objectives** aim to change the behavior of the company's competitors. Such actions might involve creating barriers to entry, securing proprietary access to scarce resources, and circumventing a price war. For example, the company goal of increasing net revenues can be associated with limiting competitors' access to target customers by creating exclusive distribution agreements with retailers serving these markets.

- **Context objectives** are less common and usually implemented by larger companies that have the resources to influence the economic, business, technological, sociocultural, regulatory, and/or physical context in which the company operates. For example, a company might lobby the government to adopt regulations that will favorably affect the company by offering tax benefits and subsidies, and impose import duties on competitors' products.

Defining market objectives is important because without a change in the behavior of the relevant market entities, the company's ultimate goal is unlikely to be achieved. Indeed, if there is no change in any of the five market factors (the Five Cs), the company is unlikely to make progress toward its goals. To illustrate, a company's ultimate goal of increasing net income by $100 million by the end of the fourth quarter can involve different objectives. A customer-specific objective might be to increase market share by 10% by the end of the fourth quarter. A collaborator-related objective might involve securing 45% of the distribution outlets by the end of the fourth quarter. And a company's internal objective might call for lowering the cost of goods sold by 25% by the end of the fourth quarter.

Defining marketing objectives involves prioritizing different alternatives in order to determine the activities most likely to help the company achieve its ultimate goal. Prioritizing objectives is important because it enables the company to better manage resources by bringing into focus the activities that are most likely to accelerate the company's progress toward its ultimate goal. Prioritizing objectives also helps align potentially conflicting activities associated with these objectives. Indeed, while some objectives tend to complement one another (e.g., increasing market share and increasing the number of distribution channels), others might involve activities with conflicting outcomes. For example, increasing market share while decreasing marketing expenses could be challenging because increasing market share typically involves greater investment in various promotional activities.[6] In this context, prioritizing alternative objectives and honing in on the most important ones can help the company articulate the best course of action to achieve its ultimate goal.

Developing the Strategy and Tactics

The strategy and the tactics define the business model of an offering. The processes of developing the market strategy and designing the tactics were discussed in detail in Chapter 2. Consequently, this section offers only a brief outline of these two concepts.

Developing the Strategy

The strategy delineates the value created by the company in a particular market. It is defined by the company's *target market* and its *value proposition* for this market.

- The **target market** defines the market in which the company aims to create value. It is defined by five factors: *customers* whose needs the company aims to fulfill, *competitors* that aim to fulfill the same needs of the same target customers, *collaborators* that work with the company to fulfill the needs of customers, the *company* managing the offering, and the *context* in which the company operates.

- The **value proposition** reflects the benefits and costs of the company's offering that define the value the company aims to create in the target market. The value proposition has three components — *customer value*, *collaborator value*, and *company value* — which reflect the value created by the company for these market entities. The development of a value proposition is often complemented with the development of a *positioning* that defines the key benefit(s) of the company's offering in a competitive context.

Designing the Tactics

Tactics — also referred to as the *marketing mix* — define the actual offering that the company introduces in the target market. The tactics logically follow from the company's strategy and reflect the way the company will make this strategy a market reality. The tactics delineate the seven attributes that define the company's offering: *product, service, brand, price, incentives, communication,* and *distribution*. Working in concert, these attributes define the value that the company's offering creates in the target market.

Defining the Implementation

Marketing implementation is the process that turns a company's strategy and tactics into actions and ensures they accomplish the plan's stated goals and objectives. A brilliant marketing plan counts for little if not implemented properly. As the French writer Antoine de Saint-Exupéry succinctly put it: *A goal without a plan is just a wish.*

Implementation directly follows from the company's strategy and tactics, such that each strategic decision is translated into a set of tactics, which are then translated into an implementation plan. In this context, implementation defines the activities that aim to make the business model a reality. Implementation involves three key components: *developing the company resources*, *developing the offering*, and *commercial deployment of the offering*.

Developing the Company Resources

Resource development aims to secure the competencies and assets necessary to implement the company's offering. Resource development can involve developing *business facilities* such as manufacturing, service, and technology infrastructure; ensuring the availability of reliable *suppliers*; recruiting, training, and retaining *skilled employees*; developing relevant *products*, *services*, and *brands* that can serve as a platform for the new offering; acquiring the *know-how* needed to develop, produce, and manage the offering; developing *communication* and *distribution* channels to inform target customers about the company's offering and deliver the offering to them; and securing the *capital* necessary to develop these resources. The resources necessary to succeed in the chosen market are discussed in more detail in Chapter 4.

Developing the Market Offering

Offering development involves the processes that transform the company's strategy and tactics into an actual good that is communicated and delivered to the company's target customers. Offering development involves managing the flow of information, materials, labor, and money in order to create the offering that the company will deploy in the market. Thus, offering development involves designing the *product* (procurement, inbound logistics, and production) and *service* (installation, support, and repair activities); building the *brand*; setting retail and wholesale *prices* and *incentives* (coupons, rebates, and price discounts); designing the means of *communication* (message, media, and creative execution); and setting the channels of *distribution* (warehousing, order fulfillment, and transportation).

Commercial Deployment

Commercial deployment includes activities such as setting the timing of the offering's market launch, defining the resources involved in the launch, and determining the scale of the launch. It logically follows the process of developing an offering by delineating the process of bringing the offering to market. Commercial deployment can be selective, initially focusing on specific markets in order to assess the market reaction to the offering, or it can involve a large-scale rollout across all target markets. In cases of selective commercial deployment, the marketing plan defines the primary market in which the offering will first be introduced and outlines the key activities associated with the launch of the offering. The marketing plan further identifies the timing and the processes involved in expanding the offering beyond the primary market so that it can reach all target customers and achieve its full market potential.

Identifying Controls

The constantly changing business environment requires companies to be agile and continuously realign their actions with market realities. Most companies strive to make their marketing operations more effective and cost efficient and to better assess the return on their marketing investment in order to ensure that they are on the right track to achieve their goals. Controls help a company ensure that its actions are aligned with its strategy and tactics in a way that will enable the company to achieve its ultimate goal.

The primary function of controls is to inform the company whether to proceed with its current course of action, reevaluate its actions and realign the underlying strategy and tactics, or abandon its current course of action and develop a different offering that better reflects the current market realities. Controls involve two key components: *evaluating the company's performance* and *monitoring the market environment*.

Evaluating Performance

Evaluating performance involves tracking the company's progress toward its goal, as defined by its focus and benchmarks. Evaluating a company's monetary performance can involve assessing the top line by comparing the desired and actual sales revenue outcomes, as well as assessing the bottom line and identifying inefficiencies in its operations.

Performance evaluation can reveal one of two outcomes: adequate goal progress or a discrepancy (performance gap) between the desired and the actual performance. When the progress is adequate, the company can stay the course with its current action plan. In contrast, when performance evaluation reveals a gap whereby a company's performance lags behind the benchmarks set, the company's action plan must be modified to put the company back on track toward achieving its goal.

Monitoring the Environment

Monitoring the environment aims to identify market opportunities and threats. It enables the company to take advantage of new opportunities such as favorable government regulations, a decrease in competition, or an increase in consumer demand. It also alerts a company of impending threats such as unfavorable government regulations, an increase in competition, or a decline in customer demand.

Once the key opportunities and threats have been identified, the current action plan can be modified to take advantage of the opportunities and counteract the impact of threats. Because it aims to align a company's actions with the changes in the market in which it operates, monitoring the environment in which the company operates is a prerequisite for business agility and a necessary condition for sustainability of the company's value-creation model.

The Marketing Plan

The marketing plan is the central instrument for directing and coordinating a company's marketing efforts. It is a tangible outcome of a company's strategic planning process, outlining the company's ultimate goal and the ways in which it aims to achieve this goal. The function of the marketing plan, its key principles, structure, and updating process are outlined in the following sections.

The Purpose of the Marketing Plan

The ultimate purpose of the marketing plan is to guide a company's actions. To this end, the marketing plan must effectively communicate the company goal and proposed course of action to relevant stakeholders: company employees, collaborators, shareholders, and investors.

Because marketing covers only one aspect of a company's business activities, the marketing plan is narrower in scope than the business plan. In addition to focusing on the marketing aspect of the company's activities, the business plan addresses financial, operations, human resources, and technological aspects of the company's offerings. The marketing plan may include a brief overview of other aspects of the business plan, but only to the extent they are related to the marketing strategy and tactics.

The marketing plan serves three main functions: (1) delineate the company's goal and proposed course of action, (2) inform the relevant stakeholders about this goal and course of action, and (3) persuade the relevant decision makers of the viability of the goal and the proposed course of action. These functions are covered in more detail below.

- **Delineate the company goal and proposed course of action.** Because marketing plans are written documents, they often force managers to be specific in their analysis and articulate in greater detail different aspects of the proposed action. This greater level of detail enables the marketing plan to serve as a guide for tactical decisions such as product development, service management, branding, pricing, sales promotions, communication, and distribution. In addition to articulating the proposed course of action, the marketing plan can identify the composition of the team managing the offering and the allocation of responsibilities among individual team members.

- **Inform relevant stakeholders of the goal and proposed course of action.** By providing uniform information to all stakeholders, the marketing plan helps ensure that all relevant parties have an accurate understanding of the specifics of the offering. Because most offerings are developed, promoted, and distributed in collaboration with external entities, having a common understanding of the primary goal and the proposed course of action to achieve that goal is essential for an offering's success.

- **"Sell" the proposed goal and course of action.** An important and often overlooked function of the marketing plan is to persuade the relevant stakeholders of the viability of the set goal and the identified course of action. The marketing plan can be the key factor in senior management's decision to proceed with the proposed course of action and the primary driver of collaborators' decision to support the company's offering.

The overarching goal of the marketing plan is to inform relevant stakeholders about the company's action plan and ensure that their actions are consistent with the company's ultimate goal.

The Key Principles of Developing a Marketing Plan

Most marketing plans suffer from a common problem. Rather than fulfilling their vital mission of steering a company's actions to attain a stated goal, they are frequently written merely to fulfill the requirement of having a document filed in the company archives. As a result, instead of outlining a meaningful course of action, marketing plans often comprise exhaustive analyses of marginally relevant issues and laundry lists of activities without delineating whether and how these activities will benefit the company. This lack of internal logic and cohesiveness often leads to haphazard actions that fall far short of helping the company achieve its ultimate goal.

To be effective, the marketing plan must outline a sound goal, propose a viable action plan to achieve this goal, and communicate this goal and action plan to the target audience. To this end, the marketing plan must be *actionable*, *relevant*, *clear*, and *succinct*.

- **Actionable.** The marketing plan should be specific enough to guide the company's activities. It must delineate the proposed changes in the product, service, brand, price, incentives, communication, and distribution aspects of the company's offering. In addition, it also must present the specific time frame for implementing these changes and specify the entities responsible for implementing them.

- **Relevant.** The marketing plan should clearly articulate the company goal and specific objectives and delineate a course of action aimed at achieving the stated goal and objectives. To this end, the marketing plan must link each proposed activity with an objective and clearly articulate how this activity will benefit the company. Without relating the company actions to its goal and objectives, a marketing plan can become a list of unrelated activities that add little or no value to the company's ability to achieve its goal and can even end up being counterproductive by diverting resources from more meaningful activities.

- **Clear.** The marketing plan aims to inform the relevant stakeholders about a company's action plan and convince them of the viability of the proposed action. Therefore, the marketing plan should clearly articulate the goal the company aims to achieve and delineate the essence of the proposed action. Because the marketing plan contains information concerning different aspects of the proposed action — its goal, strategy, tactics, implementation, and metrics for evaluating its performance — this information must be presented in a systematic manner that underscores the logic of the proposed course of action. The clarity of a manager's thought process is reflected in the organization of the marketing plan: Streamlined marketing plans indicate streamlined business thinking.

- **Succinct.** Most marketing plans suffer from a common problem: They are unnecessarily long and filled with marginally relevant information. Managers developing such plans are often driven by the misguided notion that the length of the plan reflects the depth of thinking about the proposed course of action and, hence, that longer marketing plans are inherently more viable than shorter ones. While it is true that the length of the marketing plan is sometimes used as an indicator of broader analysis and deeper thinking, shorter plans are often more useful than longer ones. Indeed, in an environment where managers are overwhelmed with a plethora of company-specific and market-related information, streamlined marketing plans help focus managers' attention on what really matters by underscoring the key aspects of the proposed course of action. When it comes to writing marketing plans, it is often the case that *less is more*.

Following the above four principles — actionability, relevance, clarity, and conciseness — can help the company ensure that its marketing plan will effectively guide its market actions and enable the company to reach its strategic goals.

The Structure of the Marketing Plan

Most marketing plans share a common structure: They start with an executive summary, followed by a situation overview; they then set a goal, formulate a value-creation strategy, delineate the tactical aspects of the offering, articulate a plan to implement the offering's tactics, define a set of control measures to monitor the offering's progress toward its goals, and conclude with a set of relevant exhibits. The key components of the marketing plan and the main decisions underlying each individual component are illustrated in Figure 4 and summarized below.

Figure 4. The Marketing Plan

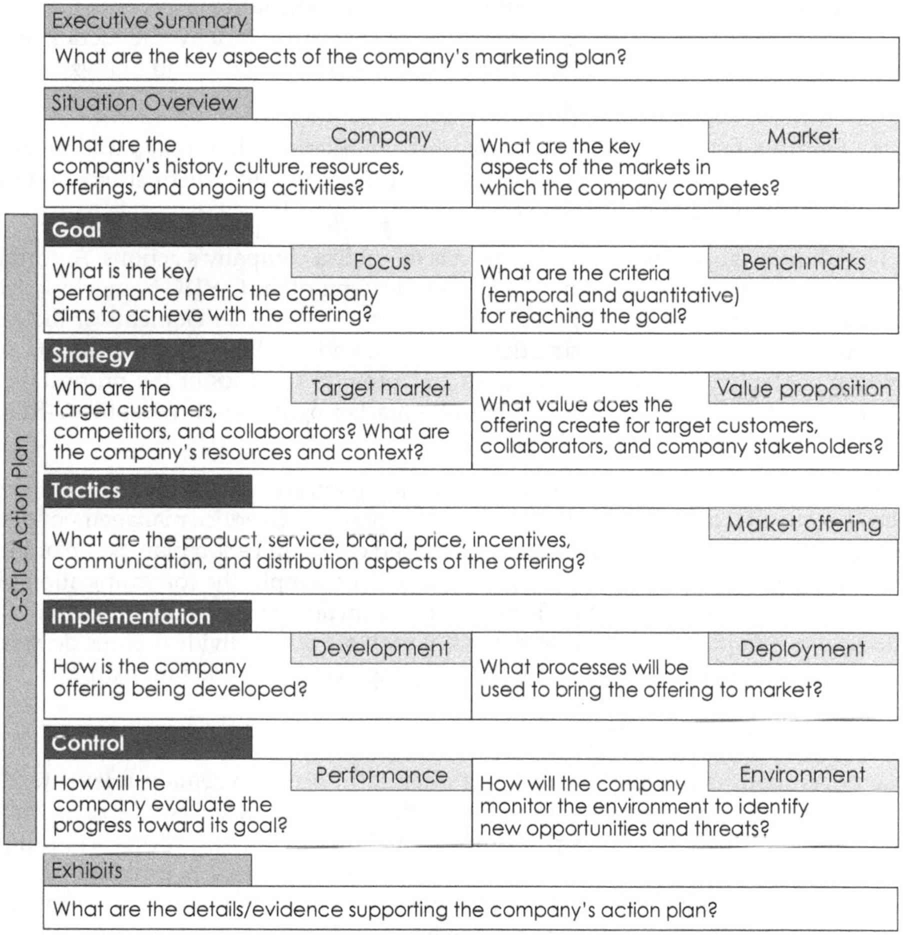

Executive Summary		
What are the key aspects of the company's marketing plan?		

Situation Overview		
Company What are the company's history, culture, resources, offerings, and ongoing activities?		**Market** What are the key aspects of the markets in which the company competes?

G-STIC Action Plan

Goal		
Focus What is the key performance metric the company aims to achieve with the offering?		**Benchmarks** What are the criteria (temporal and quantitative) for reaching the goal?

Strategy		
Target market Who are the target customers, competitors, and collaborators? What are the company's resources and context?		**Value proposition** What value does the offering create for target customers, collaborators, and company stakeholders?

Tactics		
Market offering What are the product, service, brand, price, incentives, communication, and distribution aspects of the offering?		

Implementation		
Development How is the company offering being developed?		**Deployment** What processes will be used to bring the offering to market?

Control		
Performance How will the company evaluate the progress toward its goal?		**Environment** How will the company monitor the environment to identify new opportunities and threats?

Exhibits		
What are the details/evidence supporting the company's action plan?		

- The **executive summary** is the "elevator pitch" for the marketing plan—a streamlined and succinct overview of the company's goal and the proposed course of action. The typical executive summary is one or two pages long, outlining the key issue faced by the company (an opportunity, a threat, or a performance gap) and the proposed action plan.

- The **situation overview** section of the marketing plan provides an overall evaluation of the company and the environment in which it operates, and identifies the markets in which it competes and/or will compete. Accordingly, the situation overview involves two sections: (1) the *company overview*, which outlines the company's history, culture, resources (competencies and assets), and its portfolio of offerings, and (2) the *market overview*, which outlines the markets in which the company operates and/or could potentially target.

- The **G-STIC** section is the core of the marketing plan. It identifies (1) the *goal* the company aims to achieve; (2) the offering's *strategy*, which defines its target market and value proposition; (3) the offering's *tactics*, which define the product, service, brand, price, incentives, communication, and distribution aspects of the offering; (4) the *implementation* aspects of executing an offering's strategy and tactics; and (5) *control* procedures that evaluate the company's performance and analyze the environment in which it operates.

- **Exhibits** help streamline the logic of the marketing plan by separating the less important and/or more technical aspects of the plan into a distinct section in the form of tables, charts, and appendices.

The ultimate goal of the marketing plan is to guide a company's actions. Accordingly, the core of the marketing plan is defined by the key elements of the G-STIC framework delineating the company's goal and the proposed course of action. The other elements of the marketing plan—the executive summary, situation overview, and exhibits—aim to facilitate an understanding of the logic underlying the plan and provide specifics of the proposed course of action. An outline of the key components of a marketing plan following the G-STIC framework is given at the end of this chapter.

In addition to developing an overall marketing plan, companies often develop more specialized plans that can include a product development plan, service management plan, brand management plan, sales plan, promotion plan, and communication plan. Some of these plans can, in turn, encompass even more specific plans. For example, the communication plan often comprises a series of activity-specific plans such as an advertising plan, public relations plan, and social media plan. The ultimate success of each of these individual plans depends on the degree to which they are aligned with the company's overall marketing plan.

Updating the Marketing Plan

Once developed, marketing plans need updating in order to remain relevant. Marketing management is an iterative process in which the company executes its strategy and tactics while simultaneously monitoring the outcome and modifying the process accordingly. Continual monitoring and adjustment enable the company to assess its progress toward the set goals as well as take into account the changes in the market in which it operates. The dynamic nature of marketing management is ingrained in the G-STIC framework, where the control aspect of planning (the "C" in the G-STIC framework) is explicitly designed to provide the company with feedback on the effectiveness of its actions and the relevant changes in the target market.

Updating a marketing plan involves modifying the company's current course of action and can include the need to reevaluate the current goal, redesign the existing strategy (identify new target markets, and modify the overall value proposition of the offering for customers, collaborators, and the company), change the tactics (improve the product, enhance the service, reposition the brand, modify the price, introduce new incentives, streamline communication, and introduce new channels of distribution), streamline the implementation, and develop alternative controls.

There are two main reasons for updating the marketing plan: to *close performance gaps* and to *respond to changes in the target market*. These two reasons are discussed in more detail below.

Closing Performance Gaps

Performance gaps involve a discrepancy between a company's desired and actual performance on a key metric defined by the company's goal, such as net income, profit margins, and sales revenues. Performance gaps typically stem from three main sources: *incomplete information* about the target market, *logic flaws* in the marketing plan, and *implementation errors* that involve poor execution of a viable marketing plan.

- **Incomplete information.** When developing the marketing plan, managers rarely have all the necessary information at their fingertips. It is often the case that, despite the voluminous amount of information accumulated by the company, certain strategically important pieces of information—competitive intelligence, technological developments, and future government regulations—are not readily available. As a result, managers must fill in the information gaps by making assumptions. Updating the plan to reduce the uncertainty contained in such assumptions and increasing the accuracy of the information that serves as the basis for the company's marketing plan can bolster the plan's effectiveness.

- **Logic flaws.** Another common source of performance gaps is the presence of logic flaws in the design of the marketing plan. For example, the proposed strategy might be inconsistent with the set goal, which means an otherwise viable strategy might not produce desired results. In the same vein, the offering's tactics might be inconsistent with the desired strategy, whereby product attributes might not create value for target customers, the price might be too high, and/or communication and distribution channels might be inadequate. The presence of logic flaws in the marketing plan necessitates revising the plan to eliminate any inconsistencies in the ways the company aims to create market value.

- **Implementation errors.** Performance gaps can also stem from implementation errors involving poor execution of an otherwise viable marketing plan. This type of error occurs because managers do not adhere to the actions prescribed by the marketing plan (e.g., because they are unfamiliar with the plan), because their (erroneous) intuition based on prior experience contradicts the proposed course of action, or because of lack of discipline (often imbued in a company's culture) to systematically implement the agreed-on marketing plan. The presence of implementation errors calls for revising the process of managing the offering and reevaluating the relevant personnel.

Responding to Market Changes

Market changes involve changes in one or more of the Five Cs: (1) changes in target customers' demographics, buying power, needs, and preferences; (2) changes in the competitive environment, such as a new competitive entry, price cuts, launch of an aggressive advertising campaign, and expanded distribution; (3) changes in the collaborator environment, such as a threat of backward integration from the distribution channel, increased trade margins, and consolidation among retailers; (4) changes in the company, such as the loss of strategic assets and competencies; and (5) changes in the market context, such as an economic recession, the development of a new technology, and the introduction of new regulations.

To illustrate, in response to the change in the needs and preferences of its *customers*, many fast-food restaurants, including McDonald's, redefined their offerings to include healthier options. To respond to the new type of *competition* from online retailers, many traditional brick-and-mortar retailers—such as Walmart, Macy's, Barnes & Noble, and Best Buy—redefined their business models and became multichannel retailers. In the same vein, many manufacturers redefined their product lines to include lower tier offerings in response to their *collaborators'* (retailers) widespread adoption of private labels. The development or acquisition of *company* assets, such as patents and proprietary technologies, can call for redefining the underlying business models in virtually any industry. Finally, changes in *context*, such as the ubiquity of mobile communication, e-commerce, and social media, have disrupted extant value-creation processes, forcing companies to redefine their business models.

To succeed, the ways in which a company creates market value must evolve with the changes in the market in which it operates. A number of formerly successful business models have been made obsolete by the changing environment. Companies that fail to adapt their business models and market plans to reflect the new market reality tend to fade away, their businesses engulfed by companies with superior business models better equipped to create market value. The key to market success is not only generating a viable market plan but also honing the ability to adapt this plan to changes in the market.

SUMMARY

Marketing planning is a process defined by five main steps: setting a *goal*, developing the *strategy*, designing the *tactics*, defining the *implementation* plan, and identifying the *control* metrics to measure progress toward the set goal. These five steps comprise the G-STIC framework, which is the backbone of market planning.

The *goal* identifies the ultimate criterion for success that guides all company marketing activities. Setting a goal involves identifying the *focus* of the company's actions and defining the specific quantitative and temporal performance *benchmarks* to be achieved. A company's ultimate goal is translated into a series of specific market objectives that stipulate the market changes that must occur in order for the company to achieve its ultimate goal.

The *strategy* delineates the value created by the company in a particular market, and is defined by the company's target market and its value proposition for this market. The *target market* defines the offering's target customers, collaborators, company, competitors, and context (the Five Cs). The *value proposition* specifies the value that an offering aims to create for the relevant market entities—target customers, the company, and its collaborators.

The *tactics* outline a set of specific activities employed to execute a given strategy. The tactics define the key attributes of the company's offering: product, service, brand, price, incentives, communication, and distribution. These seven tactics are the means that managers have at their disposal to execute a company's strategy.

The *implementation* outlines the logistics of executing the company's strategy and tactics, and involves developing the resources necessary to implement the company's offering, developing the actual offering that will be introduced in the market, and deploying the offering in the target market.

The *control* delineates the criteria for evaluating the company's goal progress and articulates a process for analyzing the changes in the environment in which the company operates in order to align the action plan with market realities.

The *marketing plan* can be formalized as a written document that communicates the proposed course of action to relevant entities: company employees, stakeholders, and collaborators. The core of a company's marketing plan is the G-STIC framework, which is complemented by an executive summary, a situation overview, and a set of relevant exhibits. To be effective, the marketing plan must be actionable, relevant, clear, and succinct. Once developed, marketing plans must be updated to remain relevant. To ensure that its plan is adequately implemented, a company must periodically conduct marketing audits to identify overlooked opportunities and problem areas and recommend a plan of action to improve the company's marketing performance.

MARKETING INSIGHT: THE SWOT FRAMEWORK

The SWOT framework offers a straightforward approach for evaluating a company's overall business condition. As implied by its name, the SWOT framework entails four factors: the company's *strengths* and *weaknesses*, and the *opportunities* and *threats* presented to the company by the environment in which it operates. The four factors are organized in a 2×2 matrix based on whether they are internal or external to the company, and whether they are favorable or unfavorable from the company's standpoint (Figure 5).

Figure 5. The SWOT Framework for Assessing a Company's Market Position

To illustrate, factors such as loyal customers, strong brand name(s), patents and trademarks, know-how, skilled employees, and access to scarce resources are typically classified as strengths, whereas factors such as disloyal customers, weak brand name(s), and lack of technological expertise are viewed as weaknesses. Similarly, factors such as the emergence of a new, underserved customer segment and a favorable economic environment are considered opportunities, whereas a new competitive entry, increased product commoditization, and increased buyer and supplier power are considered threats.

When evaluating the company strengths, one must consider the importance of each factor deemed a strength, the extent to which the company possesses this factor, and the degree to which the company can sustain this strength over time. Likewise, the assessment of company weaknesses must take into account the importance of each factor identified as a weakness, the extent to which it is relevant for the company, and the degree to which it is likely to persist over time.

In the same vein, when evaluating a potential opportunity, a company must consider two factors: the desirability of the outcome that ideally can be achieved by taking advantage of the opportunity and the likelihood that the company will succeed in achieving this outcome. Likewise, when evaluating a potential threat, a company must consider the potential impact of the threat should it become a reality as well as the likelihood that this threat will actually materialize.

The SWOT framework can also be thought of as a reorganization of the 5-C framework, in which the Five Cs are partitioned into favorable or unfavorable factors. Thus, the analysis of strengths and weaknesses focuses on the company, and the analysis of opportunities and threats focuses on the other four Cs describing the market in which the company operates, defined by customers, collaborators, competitors, and context.

MARKETING INSIGHT: DEVELOPING A MARKETING PLAN

There are two types of marketing plans: plans for launching a new offering and plans for managing an existing offering. Because these two types of plans share a similar structure, the template shown here applies to both cases. The main text reflects an outline of a marketing plan for launching a new offering, and the text in square brackets indicates the additional information that needs to be included when developing a plan for managing an existing offering.

Executive Summary

Provide a brief overview of the situation, the company's goal, and the proposed course of action.

Situation Overview

Provide an overview of the situation—current/potential customers, collaborators, competitors, and context—in which the company operates and identify relevant opportunities and threats. [Provide an overview of the company's progress toward its current goals. Highlight the recent changes in the market, such as changes in buyer preferences, a new competitive entry, and a change in the regulatory environment.]

Goal

Identify the company's primary goal and market-specific objectives.

- *Primary Goal*. Identify the company's ultimate goal by defining its focus and key performance benchmarks. [State the company's current progress toward this goal.]
- *Market Objectives*. Identify the relevant customer, collaborator, company, competitive, and context objectives that will facilitate achieving the primary goal. Define the focus and key benchmarks for each objective. [State the company's current progress toward each objective.]

Strategy: Target Market

Identify the target market in which the company will launch its new offering. [Underscore the key changes in the target market.]

- *Customers*. Define the need(s) to be fulfilled by the offering and identify the profile of customers with such needs. [Identify any recent changes in customer needs/profile.]
- *Collaborators*. Identify the key collaborators (suppliers, channel members, and communication partners) and their strategic goals. [Identify any recent changes in collaborators.]
- *Company*. Define the business unit responsible for the offering, the relevant personnel, and key stakeholders. Outline the company's core competencies and strategic assets, its current product line, and market position. [Identify any recent changes in the company's core competencies and strategic assets, its current product line, and market position.]
- *Competitors*. Identify the competitive offerings that provide similar benefits to target customers and collaborators. [Underscore any recent changes in the competitive environment.]
- *Context*. Evaluate the relevant economic, technological, sociocultural, regulatory, and physical context. [Identify any recent changes in the context.]

Strategy: Value Proposition

Define the offering's value proposition for target customers, collaborators, and the company.

- *Customer value proposition.* Define the offering's value proposition, positioning strategy, and positioning statement for target customers. [Highlight the proposed changes in the customer value proposition.]

- *Collaborator value proposition.* Define the offering's value proposition, positioning strategy, and positioning statement for collaborators. [Highlight the proposed changes in the collaborator value proposition.]

- *Company value proposition.* Outline the offering's value proposition, positioning strategy, and positioning statement for company stakeholders and personnel. [Highlight the proposed changes in the company value proposition.]

Tactics

Outline the key attributes of the market offering. [Highlight the proposed changes in tactics.]

- *Product.* Define relevant product attributes. [Highlight the proposed product changes.]

- *Service.* Identify relevant service attributes. [Highlight the proposed service changes.]

- *Brand.* Determine the key brand attributes. [Highlight the proposed changes to the brand.]

- *Price.* Identify the price(s) at which the offering is provided to customers and collaborators. [Highlight the proposed price changes.]

- *Incentives.* Define the incentives offered to customers, collaborators, and company employees. [Highlight the proposed changes to incentives.]

- *Communication.* Identify the manner in which the key aspects of the offering are communicated to target customers, collaborators, and company employees and stakeholders. [Highlight the proposed changes to communication.]

- *Distribution.* Describe the manner in which the offering is delivered to target customers and collaborators. [Highlight the proposed changes to the distribution.]

Implementation

Define the specifics of implementing the company's offering. [Highlight the proposed implementation changes.]

- *Resource development.* Identify the key resources needed to implement the marketing plan and outline a process for developing/acquiring deficient resources. [Highlight the proposed changes in the current resource-development approach.]

- *Offering development.* Outline the processes for developing the market offering. [Highlight the proposed changes to the current process of developing the offering.]

- *Commercial deployment.* Delineate the process for bringing the offering to target customers. [Highlight the proposed changes in the current market-deployment approach.]

Control

Identify the metrics used to measure the offering's performance and monitor the environment in which the company operates. [Highlight the proposed changes in the controls.]

- *Performance evaluation.* Define the criteria for evaluating the offering's performance and progress toward the set goals. [Highlight the proposed changes in the metrics used to evaluate performance.]

- *Analysis of the environment.* Identify metrics for evaluating the environment in which the company operates and outline the processes for modifying the plan to accommodate changes in the environment. [Highlight the proposed changes in the metrics used to evaluate the environment and modify the action plan.]

Exhibits

Provide additional information to support specific aspects of the marketing plan. This information may include target market data (e.g., industry overview, company overview, and customer trend analyses); financial calculations (e.g., break-even analysis, best/worst case scenario analysis, and customer value analysis); details pertaining to the marketing mix (e.g., product specifications, communication plan, and distribution structure); implementation (e.g., an overview of the processes of developing and deploying the offering); and control (e.g., performance metrics and analysis of the environment).

PART TWO

DEVELOPING A MARKETING STRATEGY

INTRODUCTION

All men can see the tactics whereby I conquer,
but what none can see is the strategy out of which victory is evolved.
—Sun Tzu, Chinese military strategist

M arketing strategy articulates the logic of the value-creation process. Specifically, strategy identifies the market in which the company operates and outlines the ways in which it creates market value. The following chapters outline the key aspects of developing an offering's strategy: identifying target customers whose needs the company aims to fulfill with its offering, developing a value proposition for these customers that can fulfill their needs better than competitive options, and creating value for the company that can enable it to achieve its strategic goals. Specifically, the chapters included in this section address the following topics:

- **Identifying target customers** is the stepping stone for developing an effective marketing strategy. The identification of target customers involves selecting which segments to target and determining actionable strategies to reach the selected customers. Because the ultimate goal of identifying target customers is to create market value for customers, collaborators, and the company, the basic principles of segmentation and targeting hold for both consumer and business markets. The key aspects of identifying target customers are discussed in Chapter 4.

- **Developing a customer value proposition** articulates the value of the company's offering for target customers. Specifically, the value proposition delineates all relevant benefits and costs that reflect the value customers are likely to receive from the company's offering. The value proposition is augmented by formulating a positioning that underscores the offering's most important benefit(s). The process of developing a value proposition and positioning is discussed in Chapter 5.

- **Creating company value** delineates the ways in which an offering will benefit the company and enable it to achieve its goals. To build a successful offering, a manager must understand not only how to develop an offering desired by target customers but also how to design it in a way that enables the company to capture value for its stakeholders. The ways in which a company creates value for its stakeholders are discussed in Chapter 6.

These three aspects of a company's strategy—identifying the target market, developing a customer value proposition, and creating company value—stem from the key marketing principle: The success of an offering is determined by its ability to create superior value for its target customers in a way that benefits the company and its collaborators. Hence, the following chapters delineate the processes by which the company identifies customers whose needs it can fulfill better than the competition and develops an optimal value proposition to meet these needs and create company value.

CHAPTER FOUR

IDENTIFYING TARGET CUSTOMERS

Where your talents and the needs of
the world cross, there lies your calling.
— Aristotle, Greek philosopher

The cornerstone of developing a viable marketing strategy is deciding which customers to target and how to reach these customers in an effective and cost-efficient manner. Failure to identify the right target customers is one of the most common and at the same time most dangerous marketing mistakes. Indeed, it is virtually impossible to develop a meaningful value proposition without clearly identifying customers whose needs the company aims to fulfill with its offering. The concept of targeting and the process of identifying the right target customers are the focus of this chapter.

Targeting as a Marketing Concept

Targeting is the process of identifying customers for whom the company will optimize its offering. Simply put, targeting reflects the company's choice of which customers it will prioritize and which customers it will ignore when designing, communicating, and delivering its offering. The logic of identifying target customers and the strategic and tactical aspects of this process are discussed in more detail below.

The Logic of Targeting

Imagine a company operating in a market in which there are two customers with different needs. Which of these customers should the company serve? The intuitive answer is—both. Indeed, all else being equal, the greater the customer base, the greater the company's profit potential. Should the company choose to target both customers, it has two options for developing an offering. One approach is to develop the same offering for both customers (one-for-all strategy), and the other is to develop different offerings based on the needs of each customer (one-for-each strategy).

The *one-for-all strategy* of developing a single offering for the entire market is not very effective for satisfying customers with different needs because the offering will not create value for at least one of the customers (and perhaps even both). For example, if the customers vary in terms of their price sensitivity, developing either a high-quality, high-priced offering or a low-priced, low-quality offering will inevitably fail to fulfill the needs of one of these customers because one will find the offering too expensive and the other will deem it of insufficient quality. Furthermore, developing a mid-priced, mid-quality offering will likely fail to fulfill the needs of both because the offering will still be too expensive for one of the customers and of insufficient quality for the other.

The *one-for-each* strategy of developing a separate offering for each customer might not be effective because the company might not have the resources to develop offerings that meet the needs of both customers. For example, the company might not have the scale of operations to develop a low-priced offering for the price-sensitive customer and lack the technological know-how to develop a high-performance offering for the quality-focused customer. Furthermore, even if the company has the resources to develop separate offerings, both customers might not be able to create value for the company. For example, the customer for the high-quality product might not have the financial resources to afford the company's offering or might have needs that the company cannot fulfill without incurring costs that exceed the benefits received from serving this customer.

The discussion so far has focused on a scenario in which a company operates in a market comprised of two customers. While such markets do exist, especially in a business-to-business context, they are the exception rather than the rule: Most markets comprise thousands and often millions of buyers. This scenario is different not only in the number of customers but also in that some customers are likely to have fairly similar needs that could be fulfilled by the same offering. In such cases, rather than developing individual offerings for each customer, a company might consider developing offerings for groups of customers—commonly referred to as *customer segments*—that share similar characteristics.

The concept of segment-based targeting is illustrated in Figure 1. Here, individual customers are represented by varying shapes based on the differences in their underlying needs. For example, circles might represent quality-focused customers, triangles might represent price-sensitive customers, and squares might represent customers who are looking for a compromise between price and quality. In this context, Figure 1 depicts a scenario in which a company targets quality-oriented customers for whom it will develop high-end offerings, while ignoring the other two customer segments.

Figure 1. Segment-Based Targeting

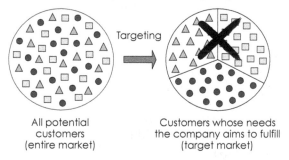

All potential customers (entire market)   Customers whose needs the company aims to fulfill (target market)

Grouping customers into segments enables a company to improve the cost efficiency of its marketing activities by not having to customize the offering for individual customers, usually with minimal sacrifice to the effectiveness of the offering. From a conceptual standpoint, the process of identifying target customers is virtually the same whether it involves individual customers or customer segments. The key difference is that in addition to identifying the needs of the target customers, segment-based targeting involves grouping customers with similar needs into segments—a process commonly referred to as segmentation.

The logic of the segmentation process and the key segmentation principles are outlined in more detail later in this chapter.

Strategic and Tactical Targeting

Based on the criteria used to identify customers, targeting can be strategic or tactical. *Strategic targeting* identifies customers whose needs the company aims to fulfill by tailoring its offerings to fit these needs. In contrast, *tactical targeting* aims to identify the ways in which the company will reach strategically important customers. These two types of targeting are inseparable components of the process of identifying target customers.

Strategic and tactical targeting vary in their goals. Strategic targeting involves trading off market size for a better fit between the offering's benefits and customers' needs. Instead of trying to reach the entire market with an offering that attempts to appeal to a wide variety of customers with diverse needs, strategic targeting calls for a conscious decision to ignore some potential customers in order to better serve others by tailoring the offering to their specific needs. Tactical targeting, on the other hand, does not aim to exclude any potential customers. Instead, it aims to reach *all* strategically important customers in a way that is both effective and cost efficient for the company.

Because they have different goals, strategic and tactical targeting prioritize different factors. Strategic targeting focuses on the *value* that the company can create for and capture from target customers. In contrast, tactical targeting focuses on the *means* by which the company can reach these customers. Working in concert, strategic and tactical targeting aim to answer two questions: *Who* are the customers with whom the company can establish a mutually beneficial relationship? *How* can these customers be reached in the most effective and cost-efficient manner? Here, the first question focuses on the offering's strategy, and the second question addresses the offering's tactics.

Given its focus on creating and capturing value, strategic targeting is concerned with customer needs and preferences (which define the value the company needs to create for these customers) and their resources (which define the value these customers can create for the company). Tactical targeting, on the other hand, is concerned with the customer profile, which reflects customers' readily observable characteristics such as age, gender, income, social status, geographic location, and buying behavior.

Focusing on value is the starting point of the targeting process because value creation is the ultimate goal of any business activity. The drawback of focusing on value is that value is unobservable, which makes it difficult for the company to reach its target customers in order to communicate and deliver the company's offering to them. Focusing on the customer profile, on the other hand, can be beneficial because it is observable, which enables the company to make customers aware of the offering and deliver the offering to them in an effective and cost-efficient manner. The downside of focusing on the profile is that it provides little or no insight into customer needs and preferences, thus making it difficult for the company to create value for its customers. Because neither of the two customer descriptors — value and profile — is sufficient on its own to ensure an offering's market success, targeting must incorporate both factors, with strategic targeting focusing on customer value and tactical targeting focusing on the customer profile.

The two aspects of targeting, strategic and tactical, are discussed in more detail in the following sections.

Strategic Targeting

The process of identifying target customers is guided by the company's ability to develop an offering that will fulfill the needs of these customers better than the competition, and do so in a way that creates value for the company. In this context, strategic targeting starts with identifying the specific customer need(s) that the company aims to fulfill with its offering.

Strategic targeting involves making tradeoffs: It ignores some customers in order to better serve others. Deciding to deliberately forgo some potential customers is one of the most important and at the same time most difficult decisions a company must make. Many companies have failed because they were unwilling to sacrifice market breadth in order to focus only on those customers for whom their offering could create superior value. The key to meaningful targeting is identifying not only customers that the company aims to serve but also those it chooses deliberately *not* to serve. A viable market strategy is not possible without choosing to ignore some customers in order to offer better service to others.

A key consideration when selecting target customers is determining how large the target segment should be. The tradeoff here is between the breadth of the target market and the strength of the company's competitive positioning in that market. Choosing a relatively narrow target market can help the company establish a strong competitive position but at the same time limits the market potential of the offering. Choosing a very broad market segment, on the other hand, presents greater market potential but limits the company's ability to establish a strong competitive advantage.

> *When identifying target customers, a company must strive to select the largest*
> *market segment for which it can establish a meaningful point of difference*

As a general rule, developing a separate offering for each customer segment is beneficial when the incremental value created by customizing the offering outweighs the costs of developing the offering. To illustrate, when the cost of customization is relatively high (as with durable goods such as cars, household appliances, and electronic equipment), companies tend to develop offerings that serve relatively large groups of customers, whereas in industries where the cost of customization is relatively low (as in the case of delivering online information), offerings can be tailored for smaller groups of customers.

Strategic targeting is guided by the company's ability to develop an offering that will fulfill the needs of its customers better than the competition, while benefiting the company and its collaborators. Accordingly, when evaluating the viability of a particular customer segment, a manager must address two key questions:

- *Can the company create superior value for these customers?*
- *Can these customers create superior value for the company?*

The answer to the first question is determined by the degree to which the company's resources are compatible with the needs of target customers, that is, the extent to which the company has the assets and competencies necessary to create customer value. The answer to the second question is determined by the degree to which target customers are attractive to the company in terms of their ability to create company value. These two principles of strategic targeting — *target compatibility* and *target attractiveness* — are illustrated in Figure 2 and discussed in more detail below.

Figure 2. Strategic Targeting: Key Principles

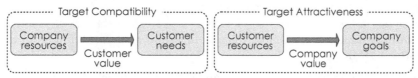

Target Compatibility

Target compatibility reflects the company's ability to fulfill the needs of its customers better than the competition. Simply put, target compatibility is a company's ability to create superior customer value. Target compatibility is a function of the company's resources and the degree to which these resources enable it to create value for target customers. Having relevant resources is important because it enables the company to fulfill customer needs in an effective and cost-efficient manner and create an offering that delivers superior value relative to the competition.

The key resources that are essential for the success of a company's targeting strategy include: *business infrastructure, access to scarce resources, skilled employees, collaborator networks, know-how, strong brands, an established ecosystem,* and *access to capital.*

- **Business infrastructure** involves several types of assets: manufacturing infrastructure that comprises the company's production facilities and equipment; service infrastructure, such as call-center and customer relationship management solutions; supply-chain infrastructure, including procurement infrastructure and processes; and management infrastructure, defined by the company's business management culture.

- **Access to scarce resources** provides the company with a distinct competitive advantage by restricting the strategic options of its competitors. For example, a company can benefit from access to unique natural resources, from securing prime manufacturing and retail locations, as well as from acquiring a memorable web domain.

- **Skilled employees** are the company's human resources with technological, operational, and business expertise. For many companies—such as those involved in research and development, education, and consulting—human capital is a key strategic asset.

- **Collaborator networks** include two types of interactions: vertical networks in which collaborators are located along the company's supply chain (suppliers and distributors) and horizontal networks that collaborate with the company in developing and promoting the offering (research and development, manufacturing, and promotion collaborators).

- **Know-how** is the relevant expertise needed to address a particular customer need, including a company's proprietary processes, technologies, and intellectual property such as patents and trade secrets.

- **Strong brands** create value by identifying the offering and generating meaningful associations that create value above and beyond the value created by the product and service aspects of the offering. Brands are particularly important in commoditized industries where the differences between the competing products and services are relatively minor or nonexistent.

- **Established ecosystem** includes relevant products, services, and brands that can facilitate the adoption of the offering by its target customers. For example, the Windows operating system can be viewed as a strategic asset for Microsoft because it ensures product compatibility, thus facilitating customer adoption of related software offerings.

- **Access to capital** provides the company with access to the financing needed to design, produce, communicate, and deliver offerings to target customers.

A company's resources are target-specific: Resources that enable the company to create value for one segment might not create value for another segment. For example, a brand associated with a casual image is likely to be an asset when targeting customers seeking to convey a casual image and a liability for customers seeking to project a more upscale, exclusive image. In the same vein, a company specialized in manufacturing special-order precision medical equipment might not have the resources necessary to produce low-priced mass-market medical devices. Therefore, when choosing a target market a company needs to evaluate its assets from the viewpoint of the particular target segment to ensure the compatibility of customer needs with its own resources.

A company's ability to create value for target customers is a necessary but not sufficient condition for successful targeting. The second important criterion for identifying target customers is the ability of these customers to create value for the company. Thus, in addition to being compatible with the company's resources, the target must be attractive for the company. The key factors in evaluating target attractiveness are discussed in the following section.

Target Attractiveness

Target attractiveness reflects the ability of a given market segment to create superior value for the company. Thus, when selecting customers for whom to tailor its offering, a company must assess the degree to which different market segments can create value for the company and select the segment(s) that best fit the company's goals. A target customer can create two types of value for a company: *monetary* and *strategic*.

Monetary Value

Monetary value refers to customers' ability to generate profits for the company. Monetary value is a function of the *revenues* generated by a particular customer segment and the *costs* associated with serving this segment.

- **Customer revenues** involve money received from customers for the right to own and/or use a company's offering. Customer revenues are influenced by a number of factors, including the size of the market and its growth rate; customers' buying power, brand loyalty, and price sensitivity; the company's pricing power; competitive intensity; as well as various context factors such as the state of the economy, government regulations, and the physical environment.

- **Costs of serving target customers** involve expenses necessary to tailor the offering's benefits to fit target customers' needs as well as to communicate and deliver the offering to these customers. The cost of serving target customers can also include the expenses incurred in acquiring and retaining these customers such as customer incentives, post-purchase support, and loyalty programs.

When assessing the monetary value of a target audience, the revenues received from providing an offering to these customers must be weighed against the costs involved in providing it. Thus, a segment that brings in less revenue but demands a less costly offering might prove to be of greater monetary value to a company than a segment that generates more revenue but demands an offering that is costly to produce, communicate, and distribute. In general, the greater the revenues derived from a particular customer segment and the lower the costs of serving that segment, the more attractive it is to the company.

Because customer revenues and costs are relatively easy to quantify, many companies tend to focus almost exclusively on the monetary aspect of the value created by a given customer segment, while overlooking the strategic value it can create. This is a rather narrow view because the strategic value can be a significant component of the overall value created by target customers.

Strategic Value

Strategic value refers to customers' ability to create nonmonetary benefits for the company. Based on the nature of the value created by customers, there are three main types of strategic value: *social value*, *scale value*, and *information value*.

- **Social value** reflects customers' ability to impact other potential buyers. Indeed, customers might be attractive not only because of the sales revenues they can generate for the company but also because of their social networks and ability to influence other buyers. For example, a company might target opinion leaders, trendsetters, and mavens because of their ability to promote and endorse the company's offering.

- **Scale value** refers to the benefits received from the scale of the company's operations. For example, a company might target low-margin or even unprofitable customers because of the economics of its business model. This is especially true in the case of companies such as airlines, hotels, and cruise lines, which have large fixed costs and relatively small variable costs. Furthermore, a company in its early stages of growth might target low-margin customers in order to build a product and user ecosystem that will serve as a platform for future growth. The success of Uber, Airbnb, Microsoft, eBay, and Facebook networks illustrates the benefits of building large-scale user networks.

- **Information value** reflects the worth of the information provided by customers. A company might target customers because they furnish the company with data about their needs and profile that can help design, communicate, and deliver value to other customers with similar needs. A company might also target customers whose needs precede those of the mass market and who are likely to be early adopters of the company's offering—commonly referred to as lead users—to benefit from their feedback on how to modify and enhance the offering.

A key challenge in assessing the strategic value of different customer segments is that, unlike monetary value, strategic value is often not readily observable and is difficult to quantify. For example, a customer's ability to influence others often cannot be directly observed by the company, and even when it can be observed (for example, by assessing the number of followers on social media), the impact of such influence on other customers' preference for the company's offerings is difficult to assess. In the same vein, the likelihood that a prospective customer might provide the company with relevant information, as well as the value of this information, is often difficult to assess in advance. Despite the difficulty in assessing strategic value, it can play a significant role in choosing target customers, either as a complement to the monetary value of these customers or as the main driver of company value. For example, a company might target highly influential customers who might never generate money for the company directly but may influence broader and more profitable segments of the market to take up the company's offering.

Identifying unmet customer needs that a company can fulfill in a meaningful way is a challenging task. Companies with different strategic goals are likely to vary in the way they evaluate the attractiveness of different segments, such that the same customers might be viewed as desirable by some companies and undesirable by others. For example, executives of large companies are often focused exclusively on segments that are likely to generate revenues and profits that are significant enough to have a material impact on the company's bottom line. As a result, these managers tend to ignore smaller, albeit inherently profitable, segments because they are not aligned with the company's appetite for profits. Yet, many of the customer segments that large companies end up competing for in the future are, in fact, the same segments these companies overlooked in the past when they lacked the scale to match the profit goals of these companies. Therefore, when assessing the attractiveness of a given segment, a company must consider not only this segment's current size but also its growth potential and long-term strategic impact.

Targeting as a Means of Creating a Competitive Advantage

Creating and capturing customer value almost always occurs in a competitive context. As a result, to create market value, a company must assess the compatibility and the attractiveness of a given customer segment vis-à-vis the competitors' ability to effectively and profitably serve this segment. Therefore, a key principle of strategic targeting is that the choice of customers should be driven by the company's ability to create an offering that delivers *superior value* to these customers relative to the competition. A company's ability to create a superior offering stems from its resources and the degree to which its resources are superior to those of the competition. This is the resource advantage principle: *To create superior market value, a company must have superior resources relative to the competition.*

Because serving different customer segments often calls for distinct core competencies and strategic assets, the choice of target customers is crucial in defining a company's resource advantage over the competition. The uniqueness of customer needs determines the degree to which a company requires specialized resources to fulfill these needs, as well as the degree of competition for this customer segment. In general, the more unique the customer needs, the more the company requires specialized resources to serve those customers, and the fewer viable competitors likely to exist in the market. Thus, many niche markets tend to require higher levels of specialization from the companies serving them and typically attract fewer competitors compared to mass markets.

From a competitive perspective, the process of identifying a company's target customers is a function of three key factors: customer needs, company resources, and competitor resources. The relationship among these three factors is illustrated in Figure 3. A company's "ideal" target customers are those whose needs the company can fulfill in a way its competitors cannot. Because of their attractiveness and lack of competition, such markets are often referred to as "blue oceans." In contrast, markets in which the company and its competitors have matching resources are characterized by intense competition and are often referred to as "red oceans."

Figure 3. The Resource Advantage Principle

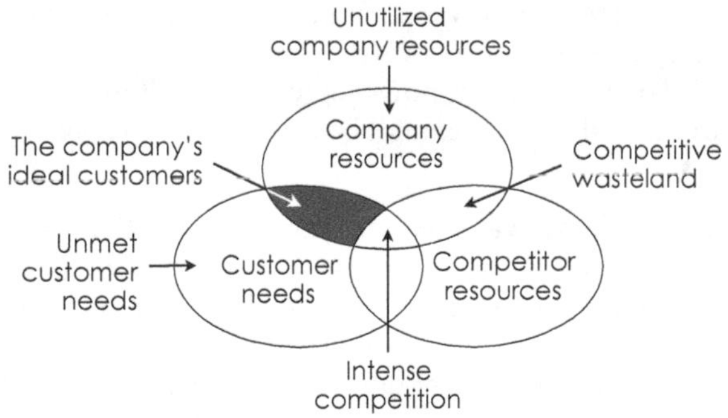

The development of market offerings should always be driven by customer needs. Yet, obsession with the competition often leads companies astray, encouraging them to develop offerings that match those of competitors even in the absence of an underlying customer need. Such a competitor-driven, rather than customer-driven, approach creates a competitive wasteland, squandering company resources by replicating competitors' mistakes while missing real market opportunities. For example, following PepsiCo's launch of Crystal Pepsi, a caffeine-free soda promoted as a "clear alternative" to normal colas, Coca-Cola launched its own clear soda, Tab Clear. Sales were dismal due to lack of customer demand for a clear soda, and both offerings were pulled off the market less than a year after being introduced.

Because a company's resources do not perfectly overlap with customer needs, some of these resources will remain unutilized when serving a particular segment, and some of the customer needs will remain unmet by the company's offering. These unutilized needs and resources can provide the company with directions for future development. Thus, unmet customer needs present the company with an opportunity to develop the necessary resources to create offerings that will fulfill these needs. In the same vein, unutilized company resources call for identifying unmet customer needs and developing offerings to fulfill those needs.

Tactical Targeting

Tactical targeting is similar to strategic targeting in that it involves identifying target customers. However, unlike strategic targeting, which aims to determine which customers to target and which to ignore, tactical targeting aims to identify an effective and cost-efficient approach to communicating and delivering the offering to already selected target customers. The key aspects of tactical targeting are discussed in more detail below.

Defining the Customer Profile

Following the identification of a strategically viable target market, a company must identify the profile of these customers in order to communicate and deliver its offering to them. The challenges in identifying target customers, the essence of profile-based targeting, and its pros and cons are outlined in the following sections.

The Customer Identification Problem

Because strategic targeting reflects a company's ability to create and capture customer value, identifying strategically viable customers is the key to the success of an offering. Identifying target customers based on their needs, however, can be challenging because these needs are not readily observable and therefore cannot be acted upon to communicate and deliver the company's offering.

The challenge of identifying ways to reach customers with a particular need is referred to as the *identification problem*. The issue here is that without being able to identify ways to reach the strategically viable customers whose needs it aims to fulfill with its offering, the company would have to communicate the offering and make it available to *all* customers — an approach that in most cases is neither effective nor cost efficient.

Despite the challenges in identifying target customers, value-based segmentation is almost always the starting point of targeting analysis. This is because the ultimate goal of targeting is to identify customers for whom the company can create superior value relative to the competition, not merely customers whose characteristics the company can readily observe. Only after target customers have been selected based on their potential value to the company would a company seek to find these customers in the broader population. To reach the high-value customer segments in an effective and cost-efficient manner, companies need to identify a set of readily observable characteristics that describe these segments and use these observable characteristics to communicate and deliver its offerings. The process of linking value-based segments to corresponding observable and actionable profiles is the essence of tactical targeting.

Profile-Based Targeting

Tactical targeting identifies effective and cost-efficient ways to communicate and deliver an offering to strategically viable customers by linking the need the company aims to fulfill to observable customer characteristics. These observable factors — referred to as the customer profile — involve four types of factors: *demographic, geographic, behavioral,* and *psychographic.*

- **Demographic factors** include customers' descriptive characteristics such as age, gender, income, occupation, level of education, religion, ethnicity, nationality, employment status, population density (urban or rural), social class, household size, and stage in the life cycle. For example, one of the commonly used demographic factors is that of generation, such as Baby Boomers (1946–1964); Generation X (1965–1981); Generation Y, also referred to as Millennials (1982–2000); and Generation Z (2001–present). When target customers are companies rather than individuals, they are identified by factors referred to as firmographics: size, organizational structure, industry, growth, revenues, and profitability.

- **Geographic (geolocation) factors** reflect customers' physical location. Unlike demographic data, which describe *who* the target customer is, geographic data describe *where* this customer is. Some of the geographic indicators — such as a customer's permanent residence, including country, state, city, and neighborhood where the customer lives — are more enduring, whereas others — such as a customer's current location at a particular point in time — are dynamic and frequently change over time. The proliferation of mobile devices that are uniquely tied to individual customers and have the ability to pinpoint their location has dramatically increased the importance of geographic factors in targeting.

- **Behavioral factors** reflect customers' actions. Common behavioral factors include customers' prior experience with the company's offering (e.g., customers new to the category, competitors' customers, current customers, or loyal customers), the frequency with which they purchase the offering, the quantity typically purchased, price sensitivity, sensitivity to the company's promotional activities, loyalty, mode of purchase (online or offline), frequently used retail outlets, role in the decision process (e.g., initiator, influencer, decider, buyer, or user), and the stage in their customer decision journey. Behavioral factors can also include the ways in which customers learn about new products, socialize, and spend their free time.

- **Psychographic factors** reflect facets of an individual's personality, including moral values, attitudes, interests, and lifestyles. Psychographics differ from demographic, geographic, and behavioral factors in that they link observable and unobservable characteristics of target customers. Although values, attitudes, interests, and lifestyles can be ascertained by directly asking individuals about them, psychographics are often not readily observable and instead are inferred from a customer's observable characteristics and actions. For example, a customer's interest in sports (psychographic factor) can be inferred from observing this customer's behaviors, such as subscriptions to sports magazines, viewing sports programming, gym membership, and purchases of sports equipment. Psychographics can be viewed as a bridge between readily observable factors describing target customers (demographics, geolocation, and behavior) and the specific unobservable customer need that the company's offering aims to fulfill.

The proliferation of online communication and e-commerce has heightened the importance of psychographics by making customer moral values, attitudes, interests, and lifestyles readily accessible to companies. Using their customers' demographic, geographic, and behavioral data, social media companies such as Facebook, Google, and Twitter are able to construct actionable psychographic customer profiles. The same is true for traditional media companies, credit card providers, and online retailers that have data linking individuals' demographic, geographic, and behavioral profiles with their moral values, attitudes, interests, and lifestyle.

The Pros and Cons of Profile-Based Targeting

Because certain demographic, geographic, behavioral, and psychographic characteristics are readily observable, managers often define target customers in terms of their profiles without necessarily focusing on their underlying needs. This approach is based on the notion that customers with similar profiles often share similar needs. For example, customers in the 50+ age group are more likely to use hair replacement and hair coloring aids, skin-tightening creams, and nutritional supplements.

Although intuitively viable, focusing primarily on customer profiles rather than customer needs can lead to misidentifying the target market. The problem with focusing exclusively on customer profiles is that customers with the same demographic, geographic, and behavioral profiles might have different needs, while customers with different profiles might share the same needs. For example, millennials vary in their preferences for soft drinks, with some favoring Pepsi, others preferring Coke, and some opting for non-cola beverages like 7UP and Mountain Dew. At the same time, the profile of loyal Pepsi drinkers extends beyond millennials to include consumers from all generations.

Profile-only targeting can lead not only to misunderstanding customer needs but can also result in misidentifying the company's true competitors. For example, if Pepsi defines its target market as everyone who drinks carbonated soft drinks (behavior-based target), its competitors would be other carbonated soft drink companies. However, if Pepsi targets all individuals who seeks to quench their thirst (need-based target), its competition would include noncarbonated soft drinks, bottled water, fruit juices, tea, and coffee.

Rather than focusing only on the readily observable characteristics of target customers reflected in their profiles, managers should think of profile-based and need-based descriptions of the target market as overlapping sets of identifiers, where the degree of overlap reflects the extent to which a company can use the customer profile as a proxy for the underlying customer need (Figure 4).

Figure 4. Customer Profile and Customer Needs

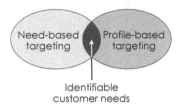

In cases when the degree of overlap is high, meaning that customers with the same profile are likely to have similar needs, profile-based targeting can be used as a proxy for need-based targeting. For example, age is a good indicator of when men begin shaving, which enables companies like Gillette, Schick, and Harry's to successfully use demographics to target boys in their late teens. In contrast, when the degree of overlap is low, meaning that customers with similar profiles are likely to have different needs, then customer needs, rather than profile, should guide the company's targeting activities. For example, using age as a proxy for the type of car consumers purchase—a sedan, a sports car, or an SUV—is often inappropriate because customers in the same age group might have different needs and, hence, seek different types of cars.

In general, even though profile-based targeting could yield similar results to need-based targeting, such cases are the exception rather than the rule. In most cases, focusing only on customer profile without considering the underlying customer needs can dramatically reduce the accuracy of the company's targeting efforts. The customer need, rather than customer profile, should be the main criterion underlying the company's targeting decision.

Aligning Customer Value and Customer Profile

An important aspect of tactical targeting involves identifying the profile characteristics of strategically important value-based customer segments. The process of linking value-based and profile-based aspects of target customers and the key factors determining the effectiveness and cost efficiency of the company's targeting activities are discussed in more detail in the following sections.

Identifying Target Customers by Linking Their Value and Profile Characteristics

The relationship between strategic and tactical targeting is illustrated in Figure 5. Strategic targeting is value focused and is a function of the company's ability to create customer value (target compatibility) and customers' ability to create company value (target attractiveness).

The focus on value, although crucial for the success of the company's offering, has the important shortcoming that value is unobservable and, hence, cannot readily be acted on to reach target customers. This shortcoming is addressed by tactical targeting, which involves identifying the demographic, geographic, psychographic, and behavioral profile of the strategically selected target customers. Thus, strategic and tactical targeting are two inseparable and complementary aspects of the process of identifying target customers.

Figure 5. Linking Customer Value and Profile

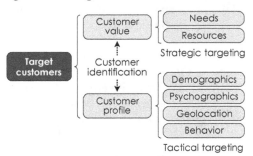

To illustrate, consider a company launching a new credit card featuring a loyalty program that rewards customers with travel benefits, including airline tickets and hotel stays. The strategically important customers include those who need a credit card and would enjoy the travel benefits offered by the card (customer value), use the card frequently, and do not default on the payments (company value). The problem faced by this company is that customer needs are unobservable, meaning that, a priori, it is difficult to know which consumers might enjoy the travel benefits offered by the card. In addition, customers' future use of the credit card and the likelihood of their not defaulting on payments are likewise unobservable. The unobservable nature of the characteristics defining segment attractiveness to the company and segment compatibility with the company's resources makes it difficult for the company to effectively communicate with and deliver the card to target customers.

To solve this problem, the company must link the value-based customer segment with the observable characteristics of customers in this segment. Thus, to identify customers with high card usage and a low likelihood of default, the company might consider customers' credit scores, demographics, geolocation, and purchase behavior, including their buying patterns, items purchased, and credit card usage frequency. Furthermore, to identify customers for whom the company can create value (e.g., those looking for travel rewards), the company might seek out customers who are likely to travel more frequently, read travel magazines and/or watch travel shows, and tend to seek travel-related information. Consequently, to reach these customers, the company might utilize travel-related communication channels to promote its offerings. Thus, by focusing on customers whose profiles are aligned with the value-based target segment, a company can maximize the effectiveness and cost efficiency of its targeting activities.

Reaching target customers in an effective and cost-efficient manner is crucial in order to avoid wasting resources on customers who are either unlikely to benefit from the company's offering or unlikely to create value for the company. Targeting that is too narrow is ineffective because it might overlook strategically important customers. Overly broad targeting, on the other hand, is not cost efficient because it wastes resources on reaching customers that are unlikely to respond favorably to the company's offering. Therefore, when evaluating different tactical targeting options, a manager needs to answer two key questions:

- *Does the company reach **all** of its target customers to communicate and deliver the offering?*
- *Does the company reach **only** its target customers to communicate and deliver the offering?*

The above two questions reflect the two main principles of tactical targeting: *effectiveness* (whether the company can reach all target customers) and *cost efficiency* (whether the company's resources are deployed in a way that reaches only its target customers). These two principles are discussed in more detail below.

Targeting Effectiveness

The effectiveness of a company's targeting efforts reflects the degree to which its actions are able to reach *all* of its target customers. Effective targeting must ensure that all strategically viable customers—those whose needs can be fulfilled by the offering in a way that benefits the company and its collaborators—are aware of the company's offering and have access to it.

In an ideal scenario, often referred to as *sniper* targeting, the company communicates and makes its offering available to all strategically viable customers and only to those customers. Such precise targeting, however, rarely happens, especially in markets comprising a large number of individual customers. The two common errors that result in ineffective targeting are choosing profile-based segments that overlap too narrowly with a selected value-based segment or do not overlap with the value-based segment at all (Figure 6). Narrow, or *slice-of-the-pie*, targeting reaches only a subset of target customers that represent a value-based segment, thus missing the opportunity to capture a larger share of the market. Off-base, or *shot-in-the-dark*, targeting occurs when the company tries to communicate and deliver its offering to customers who are not strategically viable and are unlikely to respond favorably to the company's offering.

Figure 6. Tactical Targeting: Effectiveness

"Sniper" targeting (optimal) "Slice-of-the-pie" targeting (too narrow) "Shot-in-the-dark" targeting (off base)

● Value-based segment
☐ Profile-based segment

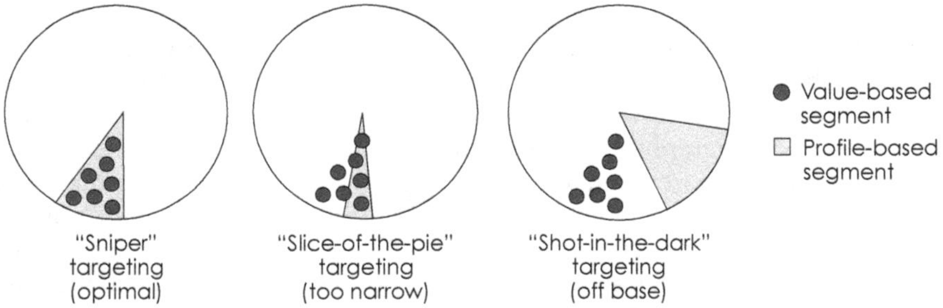

To illustrate, a credit card company targeting a customer demographic that falls in the 18–24 age group might have an overly narrow definition of its target market and could be overlooking buyers who are interested in the company's offering but fall outside of the company-defined age group. Likewise, a company promoting a credit card featuring travel benefits to customers who are not frequent travelers and are not interested in travel benefits exemplifies an off-base targeting approach with little, if any, overlap between customer needs and the offering's benefits.

Targeting Cost Efficiency

The cost-efficiency principle requires that the company's communication and distribution reach *only* its target customers. This principle is focused on managing resources to minimize (and ideally eliminate) expending resources on customers whose needs cannot be effectively addressed by the company's offering or who cannot create value for the company.

The most common error that leads to inefficient targeting involves casting a communication and distribution net that is broader than the desired target customer segment (Figure 7). The problem with this approach, often referred to as *shotgun targeting*, is that it wastes company resources such as time, effort, and money by promoting and distributing offerings to customers who are not interested in the company's offering and/or are unlikely to be able to create value for the company.

Figure 7. Tactical Targeting: Cost Efficiency

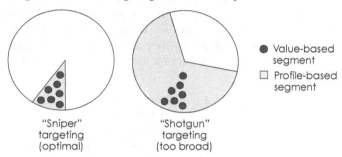

To illustrate, a company promoting a credit card featuring travel benefits using a variety of mass-media channels targeting diverse customer audiences is likely to cast a very broad net trying to reach customers who will appreciate its unique benefits. Such an approach is effective in the sense that it is likely to reach customers who are the ultimate targets of the company's marketing efforts. Yet, it is cost inefficient because, in addition to target customers, the company bears the cost of reaching customers who are unlikely to be interested in the company's offering.

Segmenting the Market

The process of identifying target customers, which thus far has been the focus of discussion, assumes that customers have already been assigned to distinct segments. In this section, the discussion centers on the key principles that drive the process of dividing potential buyers into market segments.

Segmentation as a Marketing Concept

Segmentation lays the foundation for selecting which customers to target and which to ignore. Dividing customers into distinct groups enables the company to streamline its targeting decisions by combining customers with similar needs and resources into larger segments and consequently dealing with these segments as if they were a single customer.

Segmentation is a categorization process that groups customers by focusing on those differences that are relevant for targeting and ignoring those differences that are irrelevant.

The process of segmentation is based on the notion that the efficiency of a company's marketing activities can be improved by ignoring the nonessential differences among customers and treating customers with similar needs and resources as if they were a single entity. Consequently, segmentation focuses marketing analysis on the important aspects of customer needs, enabling managers to group customers into distinct segments and develop offerings for each segment rather than for each individual customer.

Segmentation involves two opposing processes—differentiation and agglomeration. On one hand, segmentation is a differentiation process that aims to *divide* all buyers in the market into groups by focusing on the differences in their needs and resources with respect to the company's offering. On the other hand, segmentation is an agglomeration process that aims to *group* individual buyers into segments by focusing on the similarities in their needs and resources with respect to the company's offering. Both differentiation and agglomeration aim to produce segments comprising customers with homogeneous preferences, such that customers in each segment are similar to one another and at the same time different from customers in the other segments. Thus, even though differentiation and agglomeration are opposite processes, they aim to achieve the same goal—the creation of distinct segments comprising customers that are likely to respond in the same way to the company's offering.

A common misperception is that the process of identifying target customers starts with dividing customers into segments, and that the decision of which segments to target and which to ignore is made only after market segments have been identified. This is a myopic view of segmentation. There are countless ways to divide potential customers into distinct segments. As a result, without knowing the criteria that are relevant for the purposes of targeting, a company might develop a segmentation that is unrelated to the company's targeting strategy. In this context, segmenting the market without a particular targeting decision in mind is likely to end up an exercise in futility.

Note that although for presentation purposes segmentation typically precedes targeting, from a conceptual standpoint segmentation and targeting are an iterative process of identifying target customers. To be relevant, customer segments must be defined in a way that facilitates targeting. To ensure such relevance, prior to segmenting the market, a manager should have a general idea of who the company's target customers might be and what value the company might be able to create for these customers. Segmentation is targeting-specific, meaning that markets are segmented in a way that facilitates targeting. By the same token, targeting is segment-driven, meaning that a segment must already be defined in order to be selected as a target.

Strategic and Tactical Segmentation

Because segmentation aims to facilitate targeting, it shares many of the same core principles. Based on the choice of criterion used to divide customers into segments, segmentation involves two types of processes: *strategic* and *tactical*.

- **Strategic segmentation** groups customers based on the *value* that the company can create and capture from these customers. Strategic segmentation lays the groundwork for strategic targeting, which involves selecting one (or more) of the identified segments that the company will serve by tailoring its offering to the needs of targeted customers.

- **Tactical segmentation** groups customers into segments based on their *profile* characteristics: demographics and behavior. Tactical segmentation lays the groundwork for tactical targeting, which identifies the specific channels to be used to reach strategically viable customers in order to communicate and deliver the company's offering.

The two types of segmentation and the corresponding targeting decisions are illustrated in Figure 8. The process of identifying target customers is driven by two key decisions: (1) identifying customer needs that the company can fulfill better than the competition can in a way that benefits the company and its collaborators (strategic targeting) and (2) identifying effective and cost-efficient ways to reach these customers to communicate and deliver the company's offering (tactical targeting). Each of these targeting decisions is facilitated by a corresponding segmentation: (1) strategic (value-based) segmentation groups customers based on their needs and the value they can create for the company and (2) tactical (profile-based) segmentation identifies ways (the specific communication and distribution channels) in which the company can reach these customers to communicate and deliver its offering.

Figure 8. Strategic and Tactical Segmentation Facilitates the Process of Identifying Target Customers

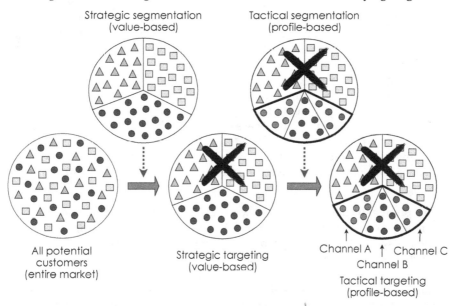

The strategic and tactical aspects of the process of identifying target customers can be described as follows. The first step in identifying target customers involves strategic targeting, which aims to identify a customer need that the company can meet better than the competition in a way that creates value for the company and its collaborators. This strategic targeting is enabled by tactical targeting, which groups customers based on the value they expect to receive and can create for the company. Therefore, once the strategically viable customer segment has been selected, the next step involves tactical targeting, which aims to identify effective and cost-efficient channels to reach this segment. The process of tactical targeting is enabled by a tactical segmentation that aims to identify the demographic, geographic, psychographic, and behavioral profile of customers for whom the company has decided to tailor its offering in order to communicate and deliver the offering to these customers in the most effective manner.

Key Segmentation Principles

To be effective, segmentation should conform to three main principles. It should be *relevant* with respect to the targeting goals; involve segments that are *similar* (homogeneous) with respect to underlying needs; and be *comprehensive*, whereby the segmentation comprises all potential buyers in the market.

- **Relevance.** Because segmentation aims to facilitate targeting, it should group customers based on their likely response to the company's offering. There are countless criteria that could be used to divide customers into segments. Most of these criteria, however, are unrelated to factors that underlie the company's targeting strategy and, as a result, produce market segments that do not facilitate the development of a meaningful strategy and tactics. Accordingly, segmenting markets without a particular targeting purpose in mind is most often a waste of company resources that ends up distracting rather than facilitating managerial decision making.

- **Similarity.** Segmentation aims to group customers so that those within each segment are similar to one another (have homogeneous preferences) in the way they are likely to respond to the company's offering. In general, a larger number of segments leads to greater similarity among the customers within each segment, with the resulting segments more likely to comprise customers with uniform preferences. At the same time, a more granular segmentation calls for the development of a greater number of customized offerings—an approach justified only in cases when the underlying differences between these segments are essential to the company's ability to create customer value. Therefore, to be effective, a segmentation must balance the advantage of creating more homogeneous segments with the disadvantage of creating segments that are not significantly different from one another with respect to the company offering.

- **Comprehensiveness.** Segments should be comprehensive: They should include all potential customers in a given market, with each customer assigned to a segment. Thus, segmentation should produce segments that are collectively exhaustive, meaning that no potential customers are left unassigned to a segment. Not including a particular subset of the market in the segmentation is particularly problematic because it effectively excludes these potential customers from even being considered when identifying potentially viable target customers. In this context, having an exhaustive segmentation that involves all potential customers in a given market is of crucial importance for a meaningful targeting strategy.

Figure 9 illustrates segmentations that violate these three principles. The first scenario (Figure 9A) illustrates a segmentation that uses an irrelevant criterion, such that the resulting segmentation does not capture important differences in customer needs. The second scenario (Figure 9B) illustrates a segmentation that violates the similarity principle, whereby customers in one of the segments have heterogeneous preferences. Finally, the third scenario (Figure 9C) illustrates a non-exhaustive segmentation that fails to include all potential customers.

Figure 9. Common Segmentation Errors

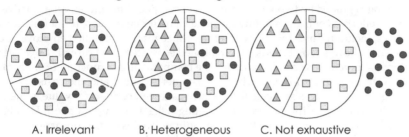

  A. Irrelevant   B. Heterogeneous   C. Not exhaustive

To illustrate, consider a credit card company that offers travel-related benefits such as airline miles and hotel points. If this company groups its potential customers based on their affinity to different types of cuisine, in most cases this is likely to produce a segmentation that is irrelevant (it is more likely to be relevant for a restaurant than for a credit card). If this company groups customers based on their income but does not group them based on their affinity for travel, the resulting segments are likely to be heterogeneous (because it includes both people who are interested in travel and those who are not). Finally, if this company focuses solely on certain demographics, such as only those who fall in the 18–55 age group, the resulting segmentation would be non-exhaustive.

A simplified version of the key segmentation principles is the MECE rule, which states that segmentation should yield segments that are both *mutually exclusive* and *collectively exhaustive*. This rule combines two of the three segmentation principles—similarity and comprehensiveness. The requirement that segments be mutually exclusive means that these segments must be sufficiently different from one another and should not overlap. This requirement can be related to the principle of similarity in segmentation. Indeed, if customers within each segment are similar to one another in the way they are likely to respond to the company's offering, they are also likely to be different from customers in other segments. Likewise, the requirement that segments be collectively exhaustive means that the segmentation is comprehensive and the identified segments include *all* customers in a given market.

Note that the comprehensiveness principle applies to the majority of situations, although not all. Thus, it is possible that a company might deliberately focus on a particular subsegment in order to segment the market even further based on additional criteria. In such cases, focusing on a particular sub-segment without explicitly considering the other subsegments is not an issue as long as the company is cognizant of and has considered all subsegments when selecting target customers.

The development of a sound segmentation is crucial for selecting a viable target market. Segmentation and targeting are two complementary aspects of the process of identifying target customers, such that errors in segmenting the market are likely to lead to a suboptimal choice of target customers. Following the key segmentation principles—relevance, similarity, and comprehensiveness—can help ensure the soundness of the resulting segmentation and its feasibility as a basis for identifying viable target customers.

SUMMARY

Targeting is the process of identifying customers for whom the company will optimize its offering. Targeting involves two decisions: strategic and tactical.

Strategic targeting involves identifying which customers (segments) to serve and which to ignore. Strategic targeting is guided by two key factors: target compatibility and target attractiveness. *Target compatibility* reflects a company's ability to create value for customers; it is a function of a company's resources, including: business infrastructure, scarce resources, skilled employees, collaborator networks, know-how, strong brands, an established ecosystem, and capital. *Target attractiveness* reflects customers' potential to create value for the company; it is a function of monetary factors such as the revenues generated by a particular customer segment and the costs associated with serving this segment, as well as strategic factors such as a segment's social value, scale value, and information value. A key principle of strategic targeting is that the company should be able to create superior value for its customers relative to the competition. To this end, a company must follow the *resource advantage principle* and identify markets in which it has superior resources relative to the competition.

Tactical targeting involves identifying effective and cost-efficient ways to reach strategically viable customers. Tactical targeting links the (typically unobservable) value-based segments to specific observable and actionable characteristics. Such observable characteristics, also referred to as the *customer profile*, include demographic (e.g., age, gender, and income), geographic (e.g., permanent residence and current location), psychographic (e.g., moral values, attitudes, interests, and lifestyle), and behavioral (e.g., purchase frequency, purchase quantity, and price sensitivity) factors. Tactical targeting is guided by two key factors: effectiveness (a company's ability to reach all target customers) and cost efficiency (a company's ability to deploy its resources in a way that reaches only its target customers).

Segmentation is a categorization process that groups customers by focusing on those differences that are relevant for targeting and ignoring those differences that are irrelevant. Segmentation enables managers to group customers into larger segments and develop offerings for the entire segment rather than for each individual customer.

Segmentation involves two types of processes: *strategic* and *tactical*. Strategic segmentation lays the groundwork for strategic targeting by grouping customers based on the *value* that the company can create and capture from these customers. Tactical segmentation lays the groundwork for tactical targeting by grouping customers into segments based on their *profile* characteristics: demographics, geolocation, psychographics, and behavior.

Segmentation must follow three *principles*: relevance (customers must be grouped on characteristics that are relevant to their likely response to the offering), similarity (segments must comprise customers with similar characteristics), and comprehensiveness (segmentation must include all potential customers).

CHAPTER FIVE

DEVELOPING A CUSTOMER VALUE PROPOSITION

*We would take something old and tired and common — coffee
— and weave a sense of romance and community around it.*

— Howard Schultz, founder of Starbucks

The customer value proposition articulates the specific benefits and costs that a company's offering aims to create for its target customers. The customer value proposition guides all tactical decisions involved in designing, communicating, and delivering the company's offering to its customers. The key aspects of developing a customer value proposition are the focus of this chapter.

Developing a Value Proposition

The development of a meaningful value proposition is a central element of a viable marketing strategy. The key issues involved in the development of a value proposition— *understanding the way customers form value judgments, identifying the key competitors, defining the offering's points of difference and points of parity,* and *creating a sustainable competitive advantage* — are discussed in more detail in the following sections.

The Customer Value Proposition as a Marketing Concept

The customer value proposition articulates the value—benefits and costs—a company aims to create for its target customers. The essence of the value proposition and its relation to the process of identifying target customers, the concept of customer value as a reflection of customer needs and offering attributes, the three dimensions of customer value, and a general framework for creating customer value in a competitive context are detailed in the following sections.

Identifying Target Customers and Developing a Value Proposition

Creating customer value is a central component of a company's market strategy, which is built on identifying target markets and developing a value proposition. Crafting a customer value proposition follows the identification of customers that the company will serve with its offering (discussed in more detail in Chapter 4). In this context, an offering's value proposition delineates the value—defined by the specific benefits and costs—that target customers will receive from the offering.

The development of a customer value proposition is intricately related to the identification of target customers. In fact, the processes of identifying target customers and creating a value proposition for these customers are often thought of as a progression. The development of these processes, however, is iterative, such that crafting the value proposition both determines and follows from the choice of target customers. The development of a value proposition determines the identification of target customers because the company's ability to create superior customer value is a key targeting criterion. At the same time, the development of a value proposition follows from the selection of target customers because a meaningful value proposition necessitates focusing on specific customer needs.

For example, a credit card company might identify target customers who like to vacation in different locations and offer these customers reward points redeemable for airline tickets and hotel stays. At the same time, the company's choice of target customers is also driven by its ability to procure travel rewards that are attractive to customers at a cost that will make offering these rewards feasible for the company.

Recognizing the iterative nature of the processes of identifying target customers and the development of a value proposition, the following discussion bases the key aspects of developing a value proposition on the assumption that target customers have already been identified. In this context, the sections below address the concept of the customer value proposition and the role of the competitive context in defining the offering's benefits and costs.

Customer Value as a Function of Customer Needs and Offering Attributes

Customer value reflects the worth of an offering; it is a customer's assessment of the ability of the company's offering to fulfill this customer's needs. The value of an offering is determined by the fit between this offering's attributes and the needs of the target customers: The better the offering's attributes fit the needs of its target customers, the greater the customer value created by this offering (Figure 1).

Figure 1. Value as a Function of Customer Needs and Offering Attributes

Two aspects of value merit attention: Value is intangible and idiosyncratic. Because it is a customer's subjective evaluation of the worth of the company's offering, value is *intangible*; it does not physically exist in the market. Value is not an attribute of a company's offering; it is created when a customer interacts with the company's offering. Only when an offering's attributes are considered by a customer whose needs could be fulfilled by these attributes does the value created by the offering emerge.

Furthermore, because value reflects a customer's assessment of the offering, it is *idiosyncratic*, whereby the same offering can create different value for different customers. Thus, an offering that is appealing to one customer might be of little or no value to another customer. For example, a credit card offering travel benefits can be attractive to a frequent traveler but hold little value for a person who rarely travels or one whose travel expenses are covered by a third party. In the same vein, a lower priced, lower quality offering is likely to be attractive to price-conscious customers and unattractive to those customers seeking high performance and exclusivity.

Dimensions of Customer Value

Depending on the underlying customer needs, an offering can create value across three domains: *functional*, *psychological*, and *monetary*. These three domains of customer value are depicted in Figure 2 and briefly outlined below.

Figure 2. Dimensions of Customer Value

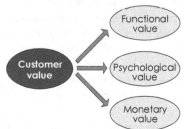

- **Functional value** is defined by the benefits and costs directly related to an offering's performance. Attributes that create functional value include performance, reliability, durability, compatibility, ease of use, customization, form, style, and packaging. For offerings that serve primarily utilitarian functions, such as office and industrial equipment, functionality is often the paramount consideration. The functional value of an offering is gauged by the answer to the question: *What is the functional value of the offering for target customers?*

- **Psychological value** is defined by the psychological benefits and costs associated with the offering. Psychological value goes beyond the functional benefits of the offering to create psychological benefits for target customers. For example, customers might value the emotional benefits provided by a car, such as the joy of driving a high-performance vehicle as well as the social status and lifestyle conveyed by the car. In categories such as luxury and fashion, where customers seek emotional and self-expressive benefits, the psychological value conveyed by the offering is of primary importance. The psychological value of an offering is gauged by the answer to the question: *How do target customers feel about the offering?*

- **Monetary value** is defined by the monetary benefits and costs associated with the offering. Attributes that create monetary value include the offering's price, fees, discounts, and rebates, as well as the various monetary costs associated with using and disposing of the offering. Even though monetary value is typically associated with costs, an offering can also carry monetary benefits such as cash-back offers, monetary bonuses, cash prizes, financial rewards, and low-interest financing. In commoditized categories with undifferentiated offerings, the monetary aspect of the offering is often the dominant criterion for choice. The monetary value of an offering is gauged by the answer to the question: *What are the monetary benefits and costs of the offering for target customers?*

Even though they represent different dimensions of customer value, these domains are not mutually exclusive. For example, the customer value of Apple's iPhone is defined by its performance across all three dimensions. The *functional value* of the iPhone is defined by factors such as its mobile connectivity; its ability to make phone calls, send text messages, and take pictures; and the benefits offered by millions of productivity and entertainment apps. Its *psychological value* stems from factors such as the satisfaction of using an aesthetically pleasing, user-friendly device; from peace of mind that the iPhone will function as described; and from the iPhone's ability to convey one's personality and social status. Finally, the iPhone's *monetary value* is defined by factors such as its price, any available promotional incentives, and its resale value.

In the same vein, Starbucks serves fresh-brewed coffee to millions of customers around the world every week, in the process delivering value across all three domains. Starbucks creates *functional value* for its customers by providing them with energy (caffeine); promoting productivity; and offering them a physical space in which to relax, work, and socialize. Starbucks delivers *psychological value* by becoming part of customers' daily routine, giving them a sense of belonging and a means to express their identity by creating their "own" beverages, in addition to fostering the feeling of moral satisfaction derived from supporting a socially responsible company. Finally, Starbucks' *monetary value* is reflected in its prices and various monetary incentives, including loyalty points, buy-one/get-one offers, and promotional discounts.

The dimensions of consumer value are not universally positive. Because value stems from both benefits and costs, costs might outweigh the benefits on a particular dimension. In most cases, the functional value and psychological value, which reflect the core benefits of the offering, are positive, whereas the monetary value, which involves the price paid by customers for the offering, is negative. For example, a consumer might appreciate the functional benefits of the iPhone and find the Apple brand highly relevant but derive negative value from iPhone's price. Because value is a function of benefits and costs, to create value the benefits across all three dimensions should outweigh the corresponding costs.

Creating Customer Value in a Competitive Context

To create superior market value, it is vital that managers understand the way in which a company's offering creates customer value and how this value compares to the value created by competitors' offerings. The value an offering creates for its customers is determined by three main factors: (1) the needs of these customers, (2) the value created for these customers by the company's offering, and (3) the value created by the alternative means (e.g., competitive offerings) these customers can use to fulfill their needs (Figure 3). Accordingly, the customer value proposition must answer the question: *Why would target customers choose the company's offering instead of the available alternatives?*

Figure 3. The Customer Value Proposition

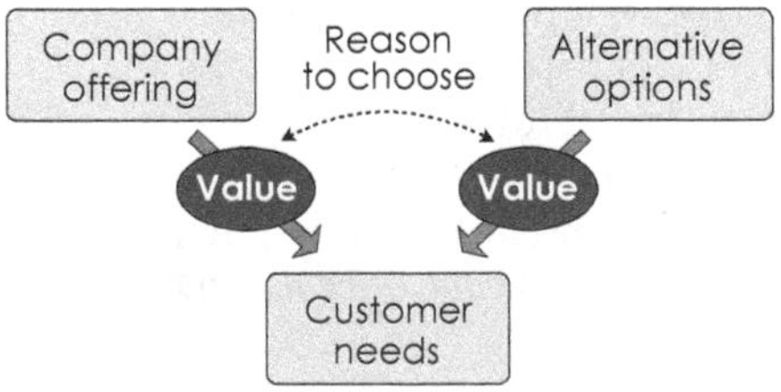

The alternative options are not limited to competitive offerings; they might include a company's own products and services (as is the case when a market leader introduces a new version of its offering that aims to replace the old one) or even makeshift solutions created by customers themselves. Because in most cases the key alternative to a company's offering is an offering developed by another company, the rest of this chapter uses the term competitive offerings in reference to offerings developed by other companies.

To create a meaningful value proposition for its target customers, a company must design an offering that delivers superior benefits relative to the competition. Yet companies often launch products and services without a clear understanding of who their competitors are and why their target customers would choose their offering over competitive offerings. Unfortunately, these companies realize the importance of understanding the competition only after their offering is engulfed by it. Overlooking the competition prevents the company from delivering on one of the key marketing principles: *The success of an offering is defined by its ability to create greater value for target customers than the competition.* Identifying the key competitors and creating a sustainable competitive advantage are key to market success.

Identifying the Key Competitors

Identifying an offering's key competitors is essential to the development of a customer value proposition. Without knowing what other options are available, it is virtually impossible to design an offering that can create superior customer value for target customers. A company's competitors include not only the similar offerings that exist within the same industry but all means that can fulfill the same customer need as the company's offering seeks to do.

Depending on whether or not competitive offerings belong to the same industry and product category, competition can be either direct or indirect. *Direct competitors* are offerings that come from the same industry (or product category) and aim to fulfill the same customer need as the company's offering. For example, Coca-Cola competes directly with Pepsi, Canon cameras compete with Nikon, and Marriott competes with Hilton. *Indirect competitors* are those with offerings that compete across different industries (product categories) to fulfill the same customer need. For example, Coca-Cola competes with a variety of non-cola beverages, including juices and water. Canon competes with smartphones like iPhone, Pixel, and Samsung Galaxy. Marriott competes with peer-to-peer online apartment rental platforms such as Airbnb. Thus, indirect competitors include all alternative means outside of the offering's industry that aim to address a particular need.

Because competition is defined relative to the customer need being fulfilled, not industry or product category affiliation, the distinction between direct and indirect competitors is inconsequential. Indeed, customers typically consider offerings that promise to address their needs without regard for industry or category affiliation. Therefore, to ensure market success, a company must look beyond the boundaries of the industry in which it operates and the product category in which it competes and design an offering that creates greater customer value than all alternative means of fulfilling the identified customer need.

A practical approach to identifying a company's key competitors is to evaluate the market through the eyes of target customers, examine the ways in which the company's offering fits into their lives, and pinpoint the alternative means that these customers can use to fulfill the identified need. In particular, there are three key questions that a manager should ask to identify the competition:

- *What means are target customers currently using to fulfill the need addressed by the company's offering?*

- *If the company does not introduce its offering, what would these customers do?*
- *What product, service, or behavior does the company's offering aim to replace?*

The first question aims to identify the competition by examining the *current behavior* of target customers. Specifically, this question aims to uncover the default option against which the company's offering will be evaluated. Identifying customers' current behavior is important because the value of an offering is defined relative to the option(s) that this offering aims to replace.

The second question seeks to identify the competition by examining the *counterfactual behavior* of target customers—their behavior in the absence of the company's offering. The option likely to be chosen if the company's offering were not available is the offering that will end up competing with the company's offering when it is introduced.

The third question aims to identify the competition by examining the *substitution behavior* of the target customers. Because customers often face resource constraints on factors such as time, money, and space, the introduction of a new offering will not necessarily result in an additional purchase; instead the new offering might replace an offering that customers have purchased in the past. Simply put, the introduction of a new offering does not mean that customers will end up buying *more* items but rather that they will buy *different* items. The item(s) customers might forgo by purchasing the company's offering are this offering's competitors.

To illustrate, consider a company launching a new protein snack that offers a nutritious meal on the go for health-conscious consumers. To identify its competitors, a manager can start by examining the *current behavior* of its target customers—what snacks they currently consume. A manager can further examine the *counterfactual behavior* of its target customers and identify the means these customers can use to fulfill their need for on-the-go healthy snacks should the company not introduce its new snack. A manager can also examine the *substitution behavior* that is likely to be displayed by customers: How would their behavior change when the new snack is introduced? What would they take out of (or not put in) their shopping basket if they were to choose the new snack?

The above questions examining customers' current, counterfactual, and substitution behavior represent different ways to identify the competitive offerings. Because these questions examine the same pattern of behavior by target customers, the answers to all three questions should converge on the same set of competitors.

Defining the Offering's Points of Difference and the Points of Parity

In an ideal world, a company's offering would surpass the competitive offerings on all attributes. In reality, however, this is rarely the case. Most offerings have both strengths and weaknesses relative to the competition. Because companies vary in their resources, their offerings differ in the benefits they deliver to target customers. Based on whether an offering's benefits are similar to or different from those of its competitors, the value proposition can be defined on three dimensions: *points of dominance*, *points of parity*, and *points of compromise*.

- **Points of dominance** (PoD) are the dimensions on which a company's offering is superior to the competition. The points of dominance define a company's *competitive advantage*. For example, an offering might have higher reliability, greater comfort, and better performance than the competition.

- **Points of parity** (PoP) are the dimensions on which a company's offering is equal to the competition; these are the attributes on which the company's offering is at *competitive parity* with the competition. For example, an offering's durability might be identical to that of its competitors. Note that the competitive offerings need not be literally identical in their performance to be at parity; the key is that the customers perceive them to offer benefits that are not meaningfully different.

- **Points of compromise** (PoC) are the dimensions on which a company's offering is inferior to the competition. The points of compromise define a company's *competitive disadvantage*. These are the attributes on which customers must compromise in order to receive the unique benefits afforded by the offering. For example, customers might compromise on price in order to gain the higher levels of reliability, comfort, and performance provided by the company's offering.

Each of the above dimensions — points of dominance, points of parity, and points of compromise — reflects the way customers *perceive* the market offerings rather than the actual performance of these offerings. As such, minor differences in market offerings that are not noticed by customers or deemed to be irrelevant do not constitute a competitive advantage.

Creating a competitive advantage is not just about differentiation: It is about differentiation that is meaningful to customers. Because competitive advantage is determined by an offering's ability to create superior customer value, only attributes that are relevant to customer needs can create a competitive advantage. Differentiating on attributes that do not add value for customers does not lead to a competitive advantage. Moreover, differentiation on irrelevant attributes might even decrease the perceived value of the offering if customers believe that the irrelevant attributes come at the expense of other, more important benefits.

The advantages and disadvantages of an offering relative to the competition can be illustrated using a *competitive value map*, which identifies the key attributes that are important to target customers and highlights the competitive advantage, parity, and disadvantage of the company's offering on these attributes (Figure 4). The horizontal axis of the competitive value map identifies the key offering attributes, ordered in terms of their importance to target customers. The vertical axis indicates customers' valuation of the benefits of the available offerings on these attributes. Attributes on which the company's offering can create superior customer value relative to competitive offerings define its competitive advantage, attributes on which it is inferior define its competitive disadvantage, and attributes on which offerings are equivalent define the points of competitive parity.

Figure 4. Competitive Value Map

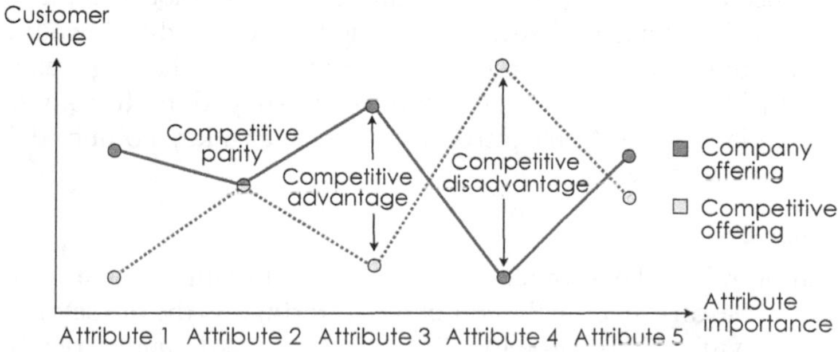

Creating a Sustainable Competitive Advantage

The competitive advantage of an offering reflects its ability to fulfill a particular customer need better than the alternative means of satisfying the same need. An offering's competitive advantage gives customers a reason to choose this offering instead of the other available options. In this context, there are three core strategies to design a value proposition that stand out from the competition: *differentiate on an existing attribute*, *introduce a new attribute*, and *build a strong brand*.

Differentiate on an Existing Attribute

This is the quintessential strategy for creating a competitive advantage. For example, Gillette sets itself apart from its competitors on the quality of its shave. Dollar Shave Club—an online shaving supplies retailer—has established price as its competitive advantage over premium brands such as Gillette. Online shoe retailer Zappos has differentiated itself from its competitors based on the level of customer service it provides. BMW differentiates itself from the competition by the driving experience its vehicles deliver, Volvo differentiates itself by focusing on safety, and Rolls-Royce sets itself apart by emphasizing luxury.

Although differentiating on an important attribute is the most intuitive way to create a competitive advantage, it is often difficult to achieve because as the overall performance of all offerings improves they become more similar. For example, with advancements in the overall quality of television sets, the differences among the available options have become less pronounced, making them more similar to one another in customers' eyes.

Introduce a New Attribute

Instead of enhancing an offering's performance on one of the existing attributes, a company might create a competitive advantage by introducing a new attribute that differentiates its offering. For example, PepsiCo has differentiated its lemon-lime soft drink Sierra Mist by using only all-natural ingredients. Dollar Shave Club introduced subscription-based, direct-to-consumer shipping of shaving supplies. TOMS introduced a "buy one, give one" social responsibility program as an important dimension that differentiates it from traditional shoe manufacturers. Uber introduced cash-free ride payment to streamline the monetary transaction between customers and drivers. The Nest thermostat introduced machine learning as an alternative approach to controlling the temperature in one's home.

Note that differentiating through the introduction of a new attribute does not necessarily mean inventing a completely new attribute. It can also involve focusing on an existing attribute that has been neglected by all competitors and making it a point of difference. For example, household cleaning products manufacturer Method Products has differentiated its offerings by designing aesthetically pleasing packaging, thus introducing a new dimension of competitive differentiation in a category where packaging was viewed as a purely functional attribute. In the same vein, with its egg-shaped, multi-colored iMac enclosed in a translucent plastic case, Apple introduced design as a key point of difference in the personal computer category.

Build a Strong Brand

A powerful brand can be a source of sustainable competitive advantage and provide customers with a reason to choose the company's offering. As the old saying goes, nobody ever got fired for buying IBM because the IBM brand signified quality, reliability, and compatibility. Likewise, Harley-Davidson owes its success not only to the design of its motorcycles but to a large degree to the strength of its brand. What separates Coca-Cola from the other cola drinks is not just its taste but its image, which has transcended national borders and cultural barriers to reach almost everyone on the planet.

The power of a brand as a source of differentiation is particularly prominent in commoditized product categories such as cereal, soft drinks, and alcoholic beverages. To illustrate, Grey Goose has successfully positioned its product as the World's Best Tasting Vodka, allowing the company to charge significantly higher prices compared to many of its competitors. Grey Goose's example is particularly telling because the underlying product (vodka) is effectively a commodity, defined as "neutral spirits so distilled as to be without distinctive character, aroma, taste, or color."[7] Thus, for most customers who cannot tell the difference in the taste of different premium vodkas, the Grey Goose brand is the main purchase driver.

Managing Competitive Differentiation

The above three strategies enable a company to create and enhance its competitive advantage. Despite their common goal, these strategies vary in the ways they elicit competitive differentiation. The first two strategies—*differentiating on an important attribute* and *introducing a new attribute*—involve modifying the actual product or service that the company deploys in a given market. In contrast, the third strategy—*building a strong brand*—changes the ways customers think about the company's products and services without necessarily changing the actual offering.

The three strategies are not mutually exclusive. They can be employed simultaneously to solidify an offering's competitive advantage. When deciding which strategies to pursue and how to prioritize them, a manager must choose the strategy that creates the greatest value for target customers, the company, and its collaborators. To create a meaningful advantage and make the competition irrelevant, a manager must develop an offering that creates market value in a way that cannot be readily copied by the competition.

Positioning the Offering

Positioning builds on the offering's value proposition to define the key reason(s) for customers to choose the offering. Unlike the value proposition, which identifies all of the benefits and costs of an offering, positioning focuses only on its primary benefit(s). The essence of positioning and the process of developing a positioning strategy are outlined in the following sections.

Positioning as a Strategic Decision

Positioning is a process of designing a company's offering so that it occupies a distinct place in the minds of its target customers; it is the process of creating a meaningful and distinct image of the company's offering in customers' minds.[8] For example, BMW positions its cars as delivering the ultimate driving experience, Volvo emphasizes safety, Toyota focuses on reliability, Ferrari prioritizes speed, and Rolls-Royce underscores luxury. In this context, positioning is akin to the process of developing a value proposition with the key difference that the value proposition reflects *all* benefits and costs of the offering while positioning focuses on the *most important* benefit(s) that tend to drive consumer choice.

The concept of positioning can be better understood when related to the concept of the value proposition. Unlike the value proposition, which reflects *all* aspects of an offering, positioning focuses customers' attention only on the *most important* aspect(s) of the offering. Furthermore, unlike the value proposition, which captures both the benefits and the costs of the offering, positioning focuses only on the benefits in order to accentuate the advantages of the company's offering in a way that provides customers with a compelling reason to choose this offering (Figure 5).

Figure 5. Customer Value Proposition and Positioning

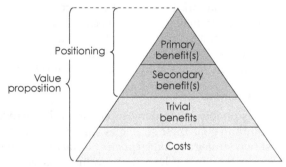

The need to "position" a company's offering in the minds of its customers stems from the fact that most individuals cannot process and remember all the benefits of a company's offering. Rather than presenting its customers with information about all aspects of its offering, a company can make a conscious decision not to promote some of the offering's benefits in order to focus only on the most important ones. Thus, a company might hone in on one or more primary benefits that are of utmost importance to its target customers, while placing relatively less emphasis on benefits that are of secondary importance.

Positioning is a strategic concept that steers the company's tactical decisions, including product and service design, brand building, pricing, development of incentives, and communication and delivery of the offering to target customers. A key component of an offering's strategy, positioning is not directly shared with the company's customers. Rather, positioning is reflected through the choice of the offering's tactics and, most prominently, in its communication. For example, Domino's' focus on speed led to the tagline *Fresh, hot pizza delivered in 30 minutes or less, guaranteed.* Papa John's Pizza's focus on quality resulted in the tagline *Better Ingredients. Better Pizza.* Tide's focus on cleaning power generated the tagline *If it's got to be clean...it's got to be Tide.* Avis's focus on service resulted in the tagline *We try harder.* Visa's focus on worldwide acceptance spawned the tagline *It's everywhere you want to be.*

The development of a positioning strategy involves three key decisions: *how many benefits to promote*, *which benefits to promote*, and *how to frame these benefits*.

Deciding How Many Benefits to Promote

Positioning is a process of prioritizing the benefits of an offering and selecting the one(s) that a company desires to be most prominently engraved in a customer's mind. Because customers often make decisions relying only on the key benefits of the offering, positioning involves tradeoffs—deciding not to promote certain benefits in order to bring others into focus. Specifically, positioning involves two types of decisions: (1) identifying all benefits that target customers view as important (rather than trivial) and (2) identifying the benefit(s) that target customers view as having primary importance. The process of establishing the hierarchy of benefits based on their impact on target customers is often referred to as *benefit laddering*.

Based on the number of benefits promoted and the nature of these benefits, there are three common positioning strategies: *single-benefit positioning, multi-benefit positioning,* and *holistic positioning.*

- **Single-benefit positioning** emphasizes an attribute the company believes will most likely provide customers with a compelling reason to choose its offering. Single-attribute positioning does not imply that the offering is inferior on its secondary attributes; it simply highlights the importance of a single attribute in order to establish a distinct message in the minds of customers. Typically, the primary benefit reflects the most important point of dominance, with the other points of dominance and points of parity the secondary benefits. For example, despite offering multiple benefits that include performance, prestige, luxury, comfort, and safety, the BMW brand underscores a single benefit: performance. In the same vein, GEICO emphasizes the low price of its insurance products, Swatch emphasizes the self-expressive fashion of its watches, and Visa emphasizes the worldwide acceptance of its credit cards.

- **Multi-benefit positioning** emphasizes two (or more) attributes of the offering. For example, even though Bayer's Aleve offers multiple benefits—including fast, longer lasting, effective, and safe pain relief—its positioning focuses on its strength and long-lasting effect, captured in the motto *Aleve. All day strong. All day long.* In the same vein, Apple promoted the iPad as a *Magical and Revolutionary Device at an Unbelievable Price,* and Walmart's motto *Save Money. Live Better* highlights the quality and low price of its offerings.

- **Holistic positioning** emphasizes an offering's overall performance without highlighting individual benefits, thus enticing customers to choose the offering based on its performance as a whole rather than on particular benefits. For example, Gillette's positioning as *The best a man can get* aims to create a perception of superior overall performance. Colgate Total, as implied by its name, claims to offer the best overall package of category benefits. Similarly, Amoco's positioning as *America's number one premium gasoline,* Tylenol's positioning as *The brand most hospitals trust,* and Hertz's positioning as the *#1 car rental company in the world* emphasize market leadership to signal superior overall performance.

Single-benefit positioning is perhaps the most common strategy. The logic behind single-benefit positioning is threefold. First, focusing on a single benefit can help the company's message break through the media clutter and create a meaningful impression in customers' minds. This is because people tend to form simplified judgments to deal with information overload and focus only on the distinctive aspects of the offering. Another reason favoring single-benefit positioning is that choosing the offering that excels on an important attribute is often considered a valid reason for choice, helping buyers justify their choices to others as well as to themselves. Finally, people tend to believe that a specialized offering that does only one thing must do it very well, whereas an offering that does many things is unlikely to excel in any of them.[9]

Deciding Which Benefits to Promote

In addition to choosing how many benefits to promote, a company must also decide which benefits to feature in its positioning. As a general principle, the choice of the benefits to promote is driven by two key considerations: (1) relevance to customer needs, meaning that these benefits should have primary importance for customers, and (2) compatibility with the company's resources, meaning that the company's offering should be able to deliver superior performance on these attributes.

To decide which benefits to promote, a company must first identify the extent to which it can create value for its target customers in each of the three domains — functional, psychological, and monetary — and then assess the degree to which positioning in these domains is sustainable over time. These two aspects of developing a positioning strategy are outlined in more detail below.

Positioning on Functional, Psychological, and Monetary Benefits

Based on the domain of the focal benefits — functional, psychological, or monetary — a company can follow three distinct positioning strategies:

- **Positioning on functional benefits** aims to create customer value by emphasizing the functionality of the company's offering. For example, Energizer emphasizes the longevity of its batteries, Tide emphasizes the cleaning power of its detergents, and BMW emphasizes the driving experience. Functional benefits vary in their scope, such that certain benefits are more specific than other, higher level benefits. For example, in its campaign *Go Tagless*, Hanes underscores the fact that its T-shirts feature a tag that is imprinted directly on the shirt rather than sewn on. Likewise, Arm & Hammer underscores the fact that its toothpaste contains baking soda, and Coca-Cola promotes the natural sweetener stevia as a key ingredient in some of its low-calorie sodas. These specific benefits, in turn, can be related to higher level functional benefits: an imprinted rather than sewn-on tag (specific benefit) implies comfort (general benefit), the presence of baking soda (specific benefit) implies cleaning power (general benefit), and stevia (specific benefit) is associated with managing weight gain (general benefit).

- **Positioning on psychological benefits** emphasizes the psychological value associated with the offering. For instance, offerings such as Montblanc, Rolls-Royce, and Dom Pérignon are positioned to instill feelings of luxury, exclusivity, and prestige. An offering's positioning may also be influenced by the company's positioning as a leader in product innovation, as in the case of Apple, Google, and Samsung, or by its image as a socially responsible organization, as in the case of Ben & Jerry's, Newman's Own, and Ecolab. An offering may also be positioned by emphasizing its risk-minimizing benefits, such as reducing uncertainty and providing peace of mind — a strategy exemplified by Allstate Insurance's tagline, *You're in good hands with Allstate*.

- **Positioning on monetary benefits** emphasizes the monetary value associated with the offering. To illustrate, Aldi, Walmart, and Priceline.com emphasize low cost as a key aspect of their value proposition, and Discover credit card emphasizes its monetary value as *America's number one cash rewards program*. Positioning on monetary benefits is sustainable only when the company has the low-cost structure to ensure the competitiveness of its offering on price.

The above three positioning strategies are not always mutually exclusive. In some cases, it is possible to develop a positioning that bridges different strategies. For example, Volkswagen has positioned its cars as being both reliable (functional benefit) and economical (monetary benefit). In the same vein, Starbucks is positioned as a purveyor of high-quality coffee (functional benefit) as well as a place where customers can feel at home (psychological benefit). Likewise, Walmart's motto *Save Money. Live Better* reflects its strategy of offering low prices (monetary benefit) and making shoppers feel good about savings they can use to enhance other aspects of their lives (psychological benefit).

Developing a Sustainable Positioning Strategy

An important aspect of deciding how to position an offering is ensuring that it is unique and cannot easily be copied by competitors. In this context, positioning strategies can be ordered in terms of their ability to create a sustainable competitive advantage, with price-based positioning often the easiest to replicate and positioning based on psychological benefits the most difficult to imitate (Figure 6).

**Figure 6. Positioning Strategies Based on their Ability
to Create a Sustainable Competitive Advantage**

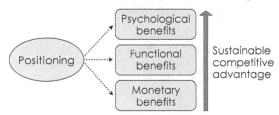

Because customers typically buy products and services based on their functional value, positioning on functional benefits is perhaps the most common type of positioning. The degree to which positioning on functional benefits offers a sustainable competitive advantage depends on the type of featured benefit. In general, positioning on specific features tends to offer a competitive advantage that is more difficult to sustain than the advantage stemming from positioning on higher level benefits. For example, a competitor can readily replace sewn-on tags with imprinted ones, add baking soda to toothpaste, and use stevia as a low-calorie sweetener. As a result, many companies choose to position their offerings on more general benefits in order to make it more difficult for competitors to imitate them. For example, rather than focusing on specific features such as engine performance, anticorrosion technology, and extended warranty, Toyota's positioning is focused on the more general benefit of reliability. In the same vein, rather than focusing on specific features such as crash resistance, automatic emergency braking, and number of airbags, Volvo's positioning reflects the more general benefit of safety.

Functional-benefit positioning has an important limitation with respect to its ability to differentiate a company's offerings from the competition. As an increasing number of products and services reach relatively high performance levels, customers are becoming more indifferent to the variations among competitive offerings because all of them deliver benefits that are satisfactory to most customers. For example, Toyota's long-standing positioning on reliability and Volvo's positioning on safety have been weakened by the fact that at present most cars have satisfactory performance on these two dimensions.

Unable to create a sustainable competitive advantage on monetary and functional benefits, many companies are turning to differentiating on psychological benefits, such as enabling customers to self-express through their brands (e.g., Harley-Davidson, Abercrombie

& Fitch, and Porsche), appealing to their sense of social responsibility (Starbucks, Product Red, and Google), or building an emotional connection (Disney, Hallmark, and Dove). Rather than relying on monetary and functional benefits to convince customers to *buy the company's offering*, positioning on psychological benefits aims to convince customers to *buy into the company's brand*. Because it reflects customers' personality and self-identity, and is therefore the most difficult to imitate, positioning on psychological benefits is a key factor in creating a sustainable competitive advantage. The role of brands as a means of differentiation is discussed in more detail in Chapter 9.

Deciding How to Frame Relevant Benefits

Value judgments do not occur in a vacuum: Value is defined relative to a reference point used to assess the benefits and costs of an offering. The same offering can be viewed as attractive when compared to an inferior offering and as unattractive when compared to a superior offering. Therefore, along with highlighting the benefits of an offering, positioning also includes a frame of reference—the benchmark against which customers will evaluate the benefits of the offering.

The choice of a reference point is of utmost importance when developing an offering's positioning. Because the reference point helps define the benefits of the offering, the same offering can be framed in different ways depending on the specific benefit that the company aims to highlight. Consider Glacéau Vitaminwater—nutrient-enhanced water marketed by the Coca-Cola Company. Vitaminwater has several potential benefits, each requiring a different frame of reference. Thus, as a source of hydration, Vitaminwater can be compared to regular water; as a source of nutrients, it can be compared to vitamins; as a source of energy, it can be compared to energy drinks such as Red Bull and Monster Energy; and to promote its thirst-quenching benefits, it can be compared to other thirst-quenching drinks such as Gatorade and Powerade.

Based on the choice of reference point, five frames of reference can be distinguished: *need-based, category-based, user-based, competitive*, and *product-line framing*.

- **Need-based framing** directly links the benefits of the offering to a particular customer need. For example, Coca-Cola's (1929) positioning as *The pause that refreshes* appealed directly to customers' need for a refreshment. In the same vein, Disneyland's (1955) positioning as *The Happiest Place on Earth*, Miller Lite's *Great Taste . . . Less Filling!* positioning, and Walmart's *Save Money. Live Better* positioning relate the benefits of the offerings to particular customer needs.

- **Category-based framing** defines the offering by relating it to an already established product category. For example, Coca-Cola's (1906) positioning as *The great national temperance beverage* defined Coke through its category membership and BMW's positioning as *The ultimate driving machine* defines its offerings relative to the automobile category. In addition to directly relating an offering to a product category, a company might seek to convey category membership by associating its offering to other offerings that are prototypical for the product category. For example, Chevrolet might relate its hybrid car Volt to Toyota's Prius, which pioneered the hybrid car category, Mercedes might associate its super luxury Maybach with Rolls-Royce, and Tesla might associate its cars with Ferrari to convey membership in the race car category. Note that the association in this case is not driven by the desire to compete for the same customers (as in the case of competitive framing) but rather to use an exemplar to establish category membership.

- **User-based framing** defines the offering by linking it to a particular type of user. For example, Pepsi's classic campaign *Choice of a New Generation* featuring mega-stars like Michael Jackson and Tina Turner aimed at positioning Pepsi as the soft drink for people who saw the "young view of things." In the same vein, Harley-Davidson positions itself as the motorcycle manufacturer for "macho guys (and 'macho wannabes'), mostly in the United States, who want to join a gang of cowboys, in an era of decreasing personal freedom."[10] Luxury brands like Rolls-Royce, Louis Vuitton, and Patek Philippe are often associated with the upper social class and are often used to convey the image of high status and exclusivity.

- **Competitive framing** defines the offering's value proposition by explicitly contrasting it to competitors' offerings and highlighting those aspects of the offering that differentiate it from the competition. For example, Dollar Shave Club positioned itself directly against Gillette, Apple defined the benefits of its Mac computers relative to Microsoft, and Microsoft positioned its search engine Bing against Google. In the same vein, Truvía positioned itself as a natural sweetener against Splenda, Equal, and Sweet'N Low; and Monster Energy positioned itself against Red Bull by introducing an innovative 16-ounce can and a wide variety of energy drinks. Rather than a particular competitor, the frame of reference can also be a competitive category, as in the case of DiGiorno's *It's not delivery. It's DiGiorno positioning*, 7UP's positioning as the *Un-cola, and* T-Mobile's positioning as the *Un-carrier*.

- **Product-line framing** defines the offering by comparing it to other offerings in the company's product line. Product-line framing highlights the differences between generations of the same offering and typically involves contrasting the benefits of the newly released product with those of the product it aims to replace. For example, Procter & Gamble used the tagline *Five Is Better than Three* to differentiate its five-blade Gillette Fusion razor from its three-blade predecessor, Mach3. Product-line framing is particularly common among market leaders operating in rapidly evolving product categories where technology innovations force companies to constantly upgrade their offerings.

The above five frames of reference can be grouped into the more general categories of noncomparative and comparative frames. *Noncomparative framing* directly relates the value of the offering to the reference point without explicitly contrasting it to other offerings. Need-based, category-based, and user-based frames of reference tend to be noncomparative. In contrast, *comparative framing* defines the offering by contrasting it to other offerings instead of (or in addition to) relating it to particular needs. Competitive framing and product-line framing typically involve comparative frames of reference.

As a general rule, comparative positioning is employed by lesser known offerings trying to gain share from the market leader. Comparative positioning is rarely used by the market leader because by comparing its offering with a lesser known offering with a smaller share, the market leader often ends up implicitly promoting the referent offering. For example, Google's positioning does not involve a comparison with other search engines because it stands to gain relatively little from such comparisons. In contrast, Microsoft introduced its

Bing search engine by (favorably) comparing itself to the market leader, Google, aiming to attract some of Google's customers.

Crafting a Positioning Statement

The desired positioning of a company's offering is typically captured in an internal document commonly referred to as a positioning statement. The primary purpose of this document is to share the key aspects of an offering's strategy with the relevant stakeholders involved in the development and management of the offering. The key principles of developing a positioning statement are outlined in the following sections.

The Positioning Statement as a Means of Communication

The positioning statement is a succinct document—usually consisting of a single sentence—that delineates the key components of an offering's strategy. The positioning statement is broader than the offering's positioning in that, along with delineating the offering's positioning, it also identifies its target customers. The primary purpose of the positioning statement is to guide tactical decisions related to the product, service, brand, price, incentives, communication, and distribution aspects of the offering. As such, the positioning statement seeks to communicate the essence of the offering's strategy to all stakeholders in order to ensure that their activities are aligned with the company's goals.

The positioning statement plays an important role because different managers within the company might not have an accurate understanding of the offering's strategy: who the offering's target customers are, why they would choose this offering over a competitor's, and how this offering benefits the company. Accordingly, the positioning statement aims to foster a shared view of the offering's strategy to all relevant entities in the company.

In addition to informing different company entities about the offering's strategy, the positioning statement has an important role in ensuring that the company's external collaborators—including research and development and product design partners, advertising and public relations agencies, channel partners, and external salesforce—correctly understand this strategy. Communicating the offering's strategy to the company's collaborators is particularly important because these entities are typically less familiar with the company's goals and strategic initiatives.

The positioning statement is often confused with an offering's positioning. Although directly related, these concepts reflect different aspects of an offering's strategy. Positioning is narrower in scope, focusing on the key aspect of the offering's value proposition. In contrast, the positioning statement has a broader scope and includes not only the offering's positioning but also a description of how the offering creates value for target customers, the company, and its collaborators.

The positioning statement is also confused with the brand motto and communication tagline. This is because all three capture certain aspects of the offering's strategy. Despite their similarities, however, the positioning statement, the brand motto, and the communication tagline have different functions and are written for different audiences. The positioning statement is an internal company document aimed at company employees and collaborators, and is not intended to be seen by customers. In contrast, the brand motto and the communication tagline are explicitly written for the company's customers. Consequently, the brand motto and communication tagline use catchy, memorable phrases designed to capture customers' attention, whereas the positioning statement is written in a straightforward manner with a focus on the logic rather than on the form of expression.

To illustrate, Gillette's positioning promises the best shaving performance. Its positioning statement can be written as: *For all men who shave, Gillette provides the best shaving experience because it uses the most innovative shaving technology.* Gillette's brand motto is much more succinct and memorable: *Gillette. The Best a Man Can Get.* Finally, one of Gillette's communication taglines for its Fusion ProGlide razor highlights a particular aspect of its razor: *Less Tug and Pull.* In the same vein, BMW's positioning promises a superior driving experience. Its positioning statement can be articulated as: *BMW is the best vehicle for drivers who care about performance because it is designed to be the ultimate driving machine.* BMW's brand motto is: *The Ultimate Driving Machine.* A recent advertising tagline is: *BMW. We Make Only One Thing: The Ultimate Driving Machine.*[11]

Structuring the Positioning Statement

A typical positioning statement involves three components: *target customers, frame of reference,* and *primary benefit(s).* These three aspects of the positioning statement are outlined below.

- **Target customers** are buyers for whom the company will tailor its offerings. These customers are defined by their needs, the key benefit(s) they seek to receive from the offering, as well as by their demographic and/or behavioral profile. The selection of target customers is discussed in more detail in Chapter 4.

- The **frame of reference** identifies the reference point used to define the offering. The frame of reference can be either noncomparative or comparative. *Noncomparative* framing relates the value of the offering to the customer need it aims to fulfill without explicitly comparing it to other offerings; in contrast, *comparative* framing defines the offering by contrasting it to other offerings.

- The **primary benefit** identifies the primary reason why customers will consider, buy, and use the offering. The primary benefit typically highlights the key value driver(s) defining the worth of the offering for target customers. The primary benefit could also involve a *justification* (reason to believe) for why the offering can claim this benefit. Common benefit justifications involve the presence of desirable ingredients (e.g., the presence of hyaluronic acid as a moisturizing ingredient in beauty care products), exceptional performance on a key attribute (e.g., the fastest speed and best coverage among wireless service providers), and brand reputation (e.g., having the best consumer rankings in a given product category).

The customer-focused positioning statement is a blueprint of the way(s) in which the company will create customer value. Accordingly, the core question that the customer-focused positioning statement must answer is: *Who are the offering's target customers and why would they buy and use the company's offering?* The organization and the key components of a customer-focused positioning statement can be illustrated with the following examples.

Example A (Noncomparative Positioning): For [target customers][offering] offers [frame of reference] that is [primary benefit] because [justification of the benefit].

> For the tradesman who uses power tools to make a living, DeWalt offers dependable professional tools that are engineered to be tough and are backed by a guarantee of repair or replacement within 48 hours.

Example A (Comparative Positioning): For [target customers][offering] offers [frame of reference] that is more [primary benefit] than [competition] because [justification of the benefit].

> For the tradesman who uses power tools to make a living, DeWalt offers professional tools that are more dependable than any other brand because they are engineered to be tough and are backed by a guarantee of repair or replacement within 48 hours.

Example B (Noncomparative Positioning): For [target customers][offering] is the [frame of reference] that provides the best [primary benefit] because [justification of the benefit].

> For all men who shave, Gillette Fusion is the razor that provides the best shaving experience because it uses the most innovative shaving technology.

Example B (Comparative Positioning): For [target customers][offering] is the [frame of reference] that provides a better [primary benefit] than [competition] because [justification of the benefit].

> For all men who shave, Gillette Fusion is the razor that provides a better shaving experience than Mach 3 because it has the latest shaving technology.

SUMMARY

The value proposition reflects all benefits and costs associated with an offering. Because value is a function of customers' needs, an offering's ability to create value is customer-specific: An offering that creates value for some customers might fail to do so for others.

An offering's *value proposition* is determined relative to the competitive offerings. The value proposition can be defined on three dimensions: points of dominance (dimensions on which a company's offering is superior to the competition), points of parity (dimensions on which a company's offering is equal to the competition), and points of compromise (dimensions on which a company's offering is inferior to the competition). There are three core strategies for designing an offering that dominates the competition: differentiate on an existing attribute, introduce a new attribute, and build a strong brand.

Positioning is the process of creating a meaningful and distinct image of the company's offering in target customers' minds. The development of a positioning strategy involves three key decisions: how many benefits to promote, which benefits to promote, and how to frame these benefits. Based on the *number of benefits*, there are three common positioning strategies: single-benefit positioning, multi-benefit positioning, and holistic positioning. Based on the domain of the *primary benefit*, positioning can highlight functional benefits, psychological benefits, and monetary benefits. Based on the choice of a reference point, positioning can involve need-based framing, which directly links the benefits of the offering to a particular customer need; category-based framing, which defines the offering by relating it to an already established product category; user-based framing, which associates the offering with a particular type of customer; competitive framing, which defines the offering by explicitly contrasting it with competitors' offerings; and product-line framing, which defines the offering by comparing it with other company offerings.

The *positioning statement* is an internal company document that outlines an offering's strategy to guide tactical decisions. A typical positioning statement involves three components: target customers, frame of reference, and primary benefit(s).

CHAPTER SIX

CREATING COMPANY VALUE

You can't have a healthy society unless you have healthy companies that
are making a profit, that are employing people, and that are growing.
— Michael Porter, professor at the Harvard Business School

Markets comprise companies and customers that interact with one another to create a mutually beneficial value exchange. To build a successful market strategy, a manager must understand not only how to design an offering that is desired by target customers but also that enables the company to create value for its stakeholders. The ways in which a manager can develop offerings that create company value are the focus of this chapter.

Dimensions of Company Value

Companies are entities established for the purpose of creating value for their stakeholders. To this end, companies develop market offerings that create value for their target customers and at the same time capture value from these customers to create value for their stakeholders and collaborators. Because creating and capturing value is the central function of the company, understanding the ways in which a company can create value for its stakeholders is paramount for the development of a sound business strategy.

A company creates market value by designing, communicating, and delivering offerings in the markets it decides to serve. The value that these offerings generate for the company can be divided into two categories: *monetary* and *strategic*. These two types of value are illustrated in Figure 1 and outlined in more detail below.

Figure 1. Dimensions of Company Value

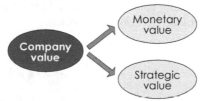

- **Monetary value** involves the monetary benefits of the offering. It is directly linked to a company's desired financial performance and typically includes factors such as net income, profit margins, sales revenue, and return on investment. For example, an offering can generate revenues that, in turn, can increase a company's bottom line. Monetary value is the most common type of value sought by for-profit companies.

- **Strategic value** involves nonmonetary benefits that are strategically important to the company. An offering can create strategic value by facilitating the demand for other offerings in the company's portfolio, by strengthening the company's reputation, and by providing the company with information about its target customers. For example, a free software can create value for the company by providing it with a technological platform for developing high-margin offerings, by promoting the company's brand, and by gaining information about customers' preferences and behavior. Offerings that demonstrate market leadership can create value for the company by helping to attract valuable employees and promote brand loyalty. Socially responsible actions that preserve the environment and support important social causes can create company value by strengthening the corporate brand and culture.

Consider the ways in which the iPhone generates value for Apple. The company receives monetary benefits from selling the iPhone. The iPhone also delivers the strategic benefit of creating a strong consumer brand, strengthening Apple's other brands, and expanding Apple's ecosystem of compatible products and services. In the same vein, Starbucks derives monetary benefit from selling its products and services to its customers. Starbucks also receives the strategic benefit of creating a strong consumer brand, enhancing its market footprint, and broadening its portfolio of offerings.

The two dimensions of company value correspond to the two types of company goals—monetary and strategic—whereby the monetary value is reflected in an offering's ability to meet the company's financial goals and strategic value reflects an offering's ability to fulfill a company's strategic goals. The two dimensions of company value are discussed in more detail in the following sections.

Managing Monetary Value

Because creating monetary value is the primary goal for the vast majority of companies, most offerings must either directly or indirectly be linked to profitability. The key profit drivers and strategies to grow profits are discussed in more detail below.

The Key Profit Drivers

To maximize profits, a manager must understand the key drivers of a company's bottom line, prioritize their impact, and focus on changes that will have the greatest impact on profits. The key profit drivers can be presented in the form of a tree-like diagram that delineates the individual factors contributing to the company's bottom line. These profit drivers are outlined in Figure 2 and discussed in more detail below.

Figure 2. The Key Profit Drivers

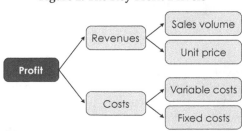

On the most general level, a company's profit is defined as the difference in revenues and costs. Revenues are a function of the sales volume and the unit price. Costs involve *fixed costs*, which are expenses that do not fluctuate with the number of units produced (e.g., the cost of research and development, equipment, advertising, rent, and salaries), and *variable costs*, which are expenses that fluctuate in direct proportion to the number of units produced and sold (e.g., the cost of raw materials, incentives, and sales commissions). Because some of the fixed costs (e.g., research and development and equipment) are amortized over a long period of time, they are prorated based on the proportion of relevant resources used during the time frame in which profit is being assessed. Accordingly, a company's profit formula can be summarized by the following equation:

$$\text{Profit} = \text{Sales volume} \cdot \text{Unit price} - \text{Variable costs} - \text{Prorated fixed costs}$$

Even though both increasing sales revenues and decreasing costs can have a significant impact on profits, growing revenues rather than cutting costs is more likely to produce sustainable profit growth. Indeed, for most offerings, there are fewer limits on continuously increasing revenues than on continuously reducing costs. Similarly, even though price optimization can have a significant impact on profits, increasing sales volume rather than modifying price is usually the key source of sustainable profitability. This is because in most cases there are greater limits to a company's ability to increase or lower prices compared to its ability to increase its customer base. In this context, growing sales volume is often viewed as the main source of profit growth, subject to optimizing the offering's price and the costs.

The most effective strategy to grow profits depends on a company's goals, resources, and the specific market conditions. In some cases, profitability can best be achieved by increasing sales volume—by attracting new customers or generating incremental volume from current customers. In other scenarios, profit growth might also involve lowering costs—for example, by streamlining operations or reducing marketing expenses. Finally, in some cases profit growth can also be achieved by optimizing (raising or lowering) prices in order to increase profit margins or grow customer demand. Different strategies for achieving profit growth are outlined in more detail in the following sections.

Managing Profits by Increasing Sales Revenues

Increasing sales revenues is the prevalent approach to achieving long-term profitability. Sales growth can be achieved using internal resources—an approach referred to as "organic" growth—or by acquiring or merging with another company. The focus of this section is on organic growth, which is arguably the most common sales growth strategy. In this context, there are two main approaches for increasing sales revenues: *growing sales volume* and *optimizing price*. These two strategies are discussed in more detail in the following sections.

Increasing Sales Revenues by Growing Sales Volume

There are two general strategies to grow sales volume: A company can focus on its current customers by increasing the quantity and frequency of their purchases, or it can focus on acquiring customers that it does not currently serve. Both strategies can play an important role in growing sales volume. Increasing sales to current customers is often considered the path of least resistance to maximize revenues from company customers. Customer acquisition, on the other hand, is essential for driving long-term profitability because of the inevitable attrition that erodes the company's current customer base.

Growing sales volume through customer acquisition can follow two paths: growing the size of the entire market by attracting customers who are new to the product category (market-growth strategy) and attracting customers who already buy similar offerings from competitors (steal-share strategy). Growing sales volume from current customers (market-penetration strategy), on the other hand, aims to increase usage of the company's offerings. These three basic strategies for increasing sales volume—market growth, steal share, and market penetration—are illustrated in Figure 3 and discussed in more detail below.

Figure 3. Strategies for Growing Sales Volume

- The **market-growth strategy** (also referred to as primary-demand strategy) involves increasing sales volume by attracting new-to-the-category customers who currently are not using either the company's or competitors' offerings. Growing the entire market is particularly beneficial for companies that are most likely to gain from the influx of new customers to the market—typically companies with a dominant market share and those who have offerings with a distinct benefit that is highly valued by target customers. The market-growth strategy also tends to be more effective in the early stages of a given category when sales growth is fueled by new customers entering the category, the competition is less intense, and the need to attract competitors' customers is less pronounced. For example, when Red Bull was first introduced to the United States in 1997, much of its strategy involved growing the relatively undeveloped energy drink market.

- The **steal-share strategy** involves growing sales volume by attracting customers who are already category users that buy competitors' offerings. The steal-share strategy is often employed by direct competitors aiming to gain share at the expense of their counterparts. The steal-share strategy is common in mature categories where few new customers are entering the market and the competition for existing customers is relatively intense. The decades-long competition between Pepsi and Coca-Cola is an example of competitors in a mature market engaging in a steal-share strategy.

- The **market-penetration strategy** involves increasing sales volume by increasing the quantity purchased by the company's own customers rather than explicitly trying to "steal" competitors' customers or attract new buyers to the product category. Market penetration can be achieved by increasing the frequency with which customers use and repurchase the company's offering, as well as by encouraging (upselling) customers to purchase the company's other offerings. Because the market-penetration strategy implies that a company already has solidified its market position, this strategy is more appropriate for established enterprises with a loyal customer base than for companies that do not have a strong market presence. For example, Campbell's attempt to increase the consumption of its soups during the summer is an attempt at increasing sales volume from existing customers.

The effectiveness of the market-growth, steal-share, and market-penetration strategies depends on the strategic goals and resources of the company and the specifics of the market in which it competes. In general, the market-growth strategy tends to be more effective in the early stages of the product life cycle, whereas the steal-share and market-penetration strategies are more common in mature markets when market growth has slowed down and companies are seeking alternative strategies to grow their market position. These three strategies are discussed in more detail in Chapter 14.

Increasing Sales Revenues by Optimizing Price

Setting prices is a vital component of managing sales revenues. The impact of pricing on sales revenues depends on the way customers react to changes in price. On the one hand, raising prices increases profit margins, which has a positive impact on sales revenues. On the other hand, raising prices tends to decrease sales volume because of the lower customer value associated with a higher price. Thus, sales revenues can be increased by raising prices in cases when the positive impact of increasing prices is greater than the negative impact of the corresponding decrease in sales volume. Alternatively, sales revenues can be increased by lowering prices in cases when the positive impact of the increase in sales volume is greater than the negative impact of the decrease in price.

The impact of price on sales volume is a function of customers' price elasticity, which reflects the degree to which a change in price leads to a change in quantity sold. The lower the price elasticity, the less sensitive consumers are to price increases, and the more likely it is that raising the price can increase sales revenues (see Chapter 10 for more details). Consequently, in cases where price elasticity is low and the decrease in sales volume caused by a higher price can be offset by an increase in revenues attributed to the higher price, raising prices can lead to greater sales revenues. Alternatively, when price elasticity is high and lost revenues from a price cut can be offset by an increase in sales volume, lowering price can lead to higher sales revenues.

Two issues in managing price merit attention. First, the term *price* is used fairly broadly to reflect not only the list price of an offering but also various monetary incentives that typically accompany the list price. These incentives include price reductions, coupons, rebates, and trade discounts such as volume discounts and trade allowances. Consequently, managing sales revenues requires optimizing not only an offering's price but also the price incentives associated with it. A more detailed discussion of managing price and incentives is offered in Chapters 10 and 11.

Second, because a manufacturer's offerings are in most cases sold by a third party (wholesalers, retailers, distributors, and dealers), its sales revenues are determined not so much by the retail price that customers pay as by the (wholesale) price the company charges its channel partners. Therefore, managing price involves managing not just the final customer price but also managing the prices throughout the retail channel. A more detailed discussion of the company's relationship with its channel partners and the different distribution strategies available is offered in Chapter 13.

Managing Profits by Lowering Costs

An alternative strategy to growing profits involves lowering costs rather than increasing sales revenues. Based on the type of expense, costs can be grouped into four categories: cost of goods sold, research-and-development costs, marketing costs, and other costs such as general and administrative expenses and the cost of capital. The four types of costs are illustrated in Figure 4, and the corresponding strategies for lowering costs are discussed in more detail below.

Figure 4. Managing Profits by Lowering Costs

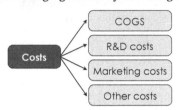

- **Lowering the cost of goods sold.** The term *cost of goods sold* (COGS) describes expenses directly related to creating the goods or services being sold and can have both a variable component (e.g., the cost of raw materials and the cost of turning raw materials into goods) and a fixed component (e.g., the depreciation of equipment). There are two basic ways to lower the cost of goods sold. The first is to *lower the costs of inputs* — such as raw materials, labor, and inbound logistics — used to develop the company's offering. Lowering the costs of inputs can be achieved by outsourcing, switching suppliers, and adopting alternative technologies that use more cost-effective inputs. For example, reducing the costs of ball bearings used as an input by an automaker helps create monetary value. The second approach to managing the cost of goods sold is to *lower the costs of the processes* that transform the inputs into the end product, such as optimizing operations and adopting alternative technologies that use more cost-effective processes. For example, an industrial robot manufacturer might create monetary value for an automaker through the introduction of a new machine that uses less electricity per operation.

- **Lowering research-and-development costs.** Research and development typically involves fixed costs necessary for designing the company's offering, and in many industries accounts for a significant portion of the overall costs. Strategies for decreasing research-and-development costs include adopting technologies that shorten the product development cycle, minimizing equipment costs, and reducing labor costs. For example, the adoption of a novel technology that can significantly abbreviate the time and lower the costs involved in testing the effectiveness of new drugs can be the source of monetary value for a pharmaceutical company.

- **Lowering marketing costs.** Depending on the company's business model, marketing costs can account for a significant portion of the overall costs associated with the offering. Marketing costs involve several types of expenses. The *cost of incentives* includes consumer-focused promotions such as price reductions, coupons, rebates, contests, sweepstakes, and premiums. *Communication costs* comprise advertising, public relations, and salesforce expenditures. *Distribution costs* reflect the margins received by distributors; cost of the salesforce;[12] and trade incentives such as trade allowances, volume discounts, and co-op advertising allowances. *Miscellaneous marketing costs* reflect the costs of factors such as marketing research and marketing overhead. Thus, a company might lower its marketing costs by improving the effectiveness and cost efficiency of its sales promotion, communication, distribution, and market research activities.

- **Lowering miscellaneous other costs.** In addition to decreasing the cost of goods sold, research and development expenditures, and marketing expenses, overall costs can be lowered by decreasing all other costs such as administrative costs, legal costs, and cost of capital. For example, a company might be able to reduce administrative costs by implementing enterprise resource planning software, consolidating its administrative offices, and streamlining its management structure.

The above four types of costs vary in their impact on a company's profit. Cost of goods sold typically is a variable cost, whereas research and development and many of the other costs tend to be fixed (meaning that they are not a direct function of the quantity produced and sold). Marketing costs fall into either the variable or fixed category depending on their type, with most advertising expenses being fixed costs and most incentives (discounts, rebates, and trade promotions) being variable costs.

Managing Strategic Value

Not all offerings are designed to generate profits: Some aim to create brand awareness, promote other offerings in the company's product line, enhance the corporate culture, and facilitate talent recruitment and retention. The ways in which offerings can create strategic value for the company and strategies for showcasing the financial benefits of strategic offerings are discussed in the following sections.

Designing Strategic Value

Although they do not directly generate profits, strategic offerings contribute to the overall profitability of the company through synergies with other profit-generating offerings. Thus, even though a particular offering does not yield profits, it still can be an important component in creating company value by increasing the desirability of the other offerings in the company's product line (Figure 5).

Figure 5. The Profit Impact of Strategic Offerings

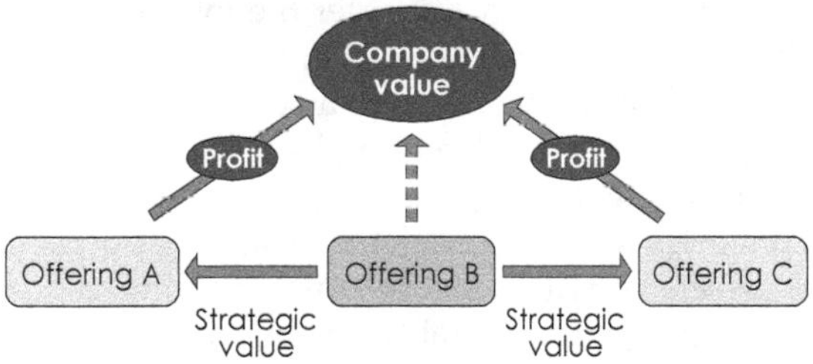

Consider, for example, an offering that is part of a two-tier product line in which the basic version of the product or service is offered for free while giving the customer an option to upgrade to a fully functional paid version. Here, the free version of the offering considered by itself generates a loss for the company, since it brings no revenues but incurs development, support, and sales costs. Yet, this offering creates strategic value for the company by promoting the paid version of the offering, which it enables consumers to experience at no cost. For example, Dropbox, Hulu, and Pandora make available both a free basic version of their offerings as well as a paid, fully functional (unrestricted) version.

Another type of strategic offering that delivers product line synergies is the loss-leader strategy employed by many retailers. This strategy entails setting a low price for an offering (often at or below cost) in an attempt to increase the sales of other products and services. For example, a retailer might set a low price for a popular item in an attempt to build store traffic, thus increasing the sales of other, more profitable items. In addition to generating traffic, the loss-leader strategy might have the secondary benefit of strengthening customers' perceptions of the retailer as having low prices.

Communicating Strategic Value

The issue of relating strategic value to monetary outcomes is particularly important for companies that offer functionally superior offerings at a higher price than their low-price, low-quality competitors. Because buying decisions are often made by purchasing managers whose primary focus is on monetary benefits, many of these managers tend to overlook some of the benefits that do not directly create monetary value.

To better communicate the value of its offerings to financially minded managers, a company might consider expressing the strategic benefits of the offering in monetary terms—a process commonly referred to as *economic value analysis*. The economic value analysis is predicated on the idea that the strategic benefits of an offering can be quantified and monetized based on the long-term financial impact of these benefits on the company (Figure 6).

Figure 6. Economic Value Analysis

Economic value analysis is frequently used by companies selling high-value, high-price offerings to justify their premium prices. Consider the following example: A manufacturer is selling a commercial grade 3-D printer priced at $180,000, which is $25,000 higher than similar offerings from its competitors. At first glance, the company's printer appears overpriced, and the company is considering lowering its price so that it can effectively compete with low-price rivals. Despite its intuitive appeal, this approach often results in foregone revenues and profits for the manufacturer. An alternative approach involves assessing all the benefits and costs associated with the company's offering, monetizing the value of the strategic benefits, and comparing the overall value of the company's offering to that of the competition.

In the above example, the value analysis reveals that four key attributes of strategic importance to buyers include durability, reliability, warranty, and the speed of service. Furthermore, competitive benchmarking shows that on all these attributes the company's offering is superior to the competition. Specifically, the company's offering has greater durability, which translates to two additional years of product usage; greater reliability, which translates to two fewer breakdowns per year; two additional years of warranty; and, on average, speedier repairs thanks to response times for service calls four hours faster than the competition.

Monetizing these benefits suggests that the value of two extra years of printer usage is $6,000; the value of the two fewer breakdowns over the 10-year life of the printer is $14,000; the value of the two years of extra warranty covering service calls and the replacement parts is $9,500; and the value of not having four hours of downtime while waiting for the printer to be serviced during its 10-year life is $11,500. This economic value analysis in this case can be illustrated as shown in Figure 7.

Figure 7. Analyzing the Value of a Company's Offering in a Competitive Context

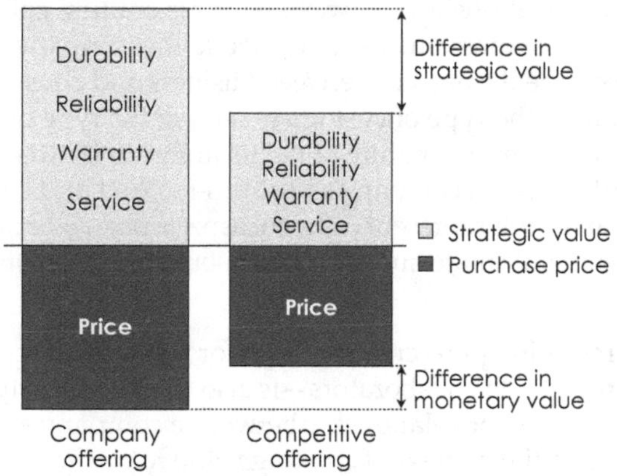

The above analysis indicates that the customer value of the functional benefits delivered by the company's offering is $41,000, which is significantly greater than the $25,000 price difference between the offerings. Specifically, this analysis shows that rather than being overpriced by $25,000, the company's offering is actually *underpriced* by $16,000 relative to the competition. Instead of lowering the price, the company might consider clearly documenting the value of the offering to its customers to shift their focus from factors readily expressed in monetary terms to the overall value of the offering, which includes the monetary (economic) value of the strategic benefits.

Because it estimates the long-term monetary impact of strategic benefits, economic value analysis is related to the notion of the total cost of ownership. Similar to economic value analysis, the total cost of ownership monetizes the nonmonetary aspects of the offering. Unlike economic value analysis, however, the total cost of ownership focuses mostly on the cost side of the value created by the offering. In this context, the concept of total cost of ownership is somewhat narrower in scope compared to the economic value analysis, which examines both the cost savings and revenue increases associated with the functional benefits of the offering.

Creating Market Value Through Collaboration

Collaboration involves entering into a relationship with another entity and delegating to it a subset of the company's activities for the purpose of creating superior market value. The key aspects of managing collaborator relationships are discussed in the following sections.

The Essence of Collaboration

Value creation through collaboration reflects a fundamental shift away from a business paradigm in which a company alone creates customer value to a new paradigm in which the value is jointly created by the company and its collaborators. The shift toward collaborative business enterprises stems from the belief that greater effectiveness and cost efficiency can be achieved from greater expertise and a broader scale of operations achieved through collaboration. Accordingly, collaboration brings together different entities—suppliers, manufacturers, distributors (dealers, wholesalers, and retailers), research-and-development companies, service providers, external salesforce, advertising agencies, and market research companies—to create an effective and cost-efficient value exchange.

Because it involves relationships between business entities, collaboration is often viewed strictly as a business-to-business process unrelated to the company's consumer-focused activities. This view reflects the differences between business and consumer markets on a number of dimensions, including the type of customers served, the type of products and services offered, the selling process, and the nature of the relationship between the buyer and the seller. Yet, despite their differences, a company's business-focused and consumer-focused activities are closely related. They both represent different aspects of an overarching value-creation process that determines the ultimate success of both business-to-business and business-to-consumer activities.

The key marketing principle—creating superior value for target customers in a way that benefits the company and its collaborators—is also the key principle that guides all aspects of collaboration. Therefore, the relationship between a company and its collaborators should always be considered in the context of creating value for target customers. In fact, there are few, if any, "pure" business-to-business relationships that can be considered independently from their ability to create customer value. Most business-focused relationships are business-to-business-to-consumer collaborations, meaning that the business-to-business component can meaningfully exist only as part of the broader customer-focused process of creating market value (Figure 8).

Figure 8. Creating Market Value Through Collaboration

To illustrate, consider the collaboration between a manufacturer and a retailer. The success of this collaboration is determined to a large degree by the ability of the manufacturer to create value not only for the retailer but also for the end customer. If the manufacturer's offerings fail to create value for the customer, the retailer, in turn, will find it difficult to sell the company's offerings to these customers, which ultimately will hinder its collaboration with the manufacturer.

To succeed as a business-to-business enterprise, the manufacturer must envision the entire value-creation chain and design its offering to create value for both its collaborators and end customers. As a result, the sustainability of collaboration depends on the degree to which actions of the companies involved create value for target customers. Failure to create customer value will threaten the viability of the entire collaboration.

Types of Collaboration

Because collaboration centers on creating value, it spans the processes of understanding, designing, communicating, and delivering value to target customers. Accordingly, collaboration can typically occur in four domains:

- **Market-insight collaboration** involves entities that work with the company to better understand the company's customers, collaborators, competitors, and the overall context in which the company operates. For example, consumer packaged goods manufacturers SC Johnson, Kellogg, and Kraft Heinz collaborate with marketing research companies such as Nielsen, Kantar, and IRI in areas involving the analysis of retail data and test marketing of new products.

- **Value-design collaboration** involves entities that partner on product and service development, brand building, price setting, and incentive design. For example, Nike, Samsung, and PepsiCo collaborate with the design company IDEO to develop innovative consumer products. AT&T, Verizon, and Sprint routinely outsource their customer support service to call centers in regions in which these services are more cost efficient. Citibank, MasterCard, and American Airlines combine their branding efforts to create a co-branded credit card. Hotels, airlines, and rental car companies often join in special pricing collaborations offering shared price discounts.

- **Value-communication collaboration** involves partnerships in areas such as advertising, public relations, and social media. For example, to promote their offerings and build strong brands, many Fortune 500 companies partner with media conglomerates WPP, Omnicom, Publicis, Interpublic, Dentsu, and Havas for assistance with promoting their offerings, building strong brands, and managing company reputation.

- **Value-delivery collaboration** involves partnerships with suppliers and distribution channels to provide materials to the company and facilitate the delivery of its offerings to target customers. For example, consumer packaged goods manufacturers such as Nestlé, Unilever, and Kraft Heinz make their offerings available to customers by relying on retail partners such as Walmart, Carrefour, and Tesco.

Note that even though they can serve different functions in the value-creation process, collaborating entities can be involved in all four aspects of understanding, designing, communicating, and delivering value. For example, in addition to delivering the company's offerings to target customers, distribution channels can play an important role in identifying customer needs and preferences, customizing the product, augmenting the service, setting the price, and managing incentives, as well as communicating the offering's benefits by means of in-store advertisements, displays, and direct mail. In the same vein, along with communicating the value of an offering, advertising agencies can gather market insights, facilitate its branding, optimize its pricing, and design and distribute targeted incentives.

The Pros and Cons of Collaboration

Despite a company's efforts to optimize the value of its offerings for collaborators, the goals of the company and collaborators often are not perfectly aligned. As a result, collaborator relationships can spawn tensions resulting from the different goal-optimization strategies pursued by the collaborating entities. Such tensions are often facilitated by the power imbalance of the collaborators and frequently lead to explicit conflicts.

Like most business relationships, collaboration has its advantages and drawbacks. Specifically, collaboration offers several important *benefits* for participating entities:

- **Effectiveness.** Collaboration enables companies to specialize in a particular aspect of the value-delivery process such as research and development, manufacturing, communication, and distribution. Because collaboration enables each party to take advantage of the other's expertise, it can provide both entities with a competitive advantage stemming from greater specialization.

- **Cost efficiency.** In addition to facilitating the effectiveness of the value-creation process, collaboration can also increase its cost efficiency because each collaborator can achieve greater economies of scale and experience by specializing in a given function. Specialization might also encourage a company to invest in new technologies that it would not invest in if it lacked a larger scale of operations.

- **Flexibility.** Relative to developing the necessary in-house expertise, collaboration requires a lesser commitment of resources, thus offering much greater flexibility in terms of switching technologies, entering new markets, and exiting existing ones. For example, the development of a new distribution channel requires substantial resources and calls for a long-term commitment, whereas partnering with an already existing distribution channel requires fewer resources and offers much greater flexibility.

- **Speed.** Collaboration enables a company to achieve the desired results much faster than building in-house expertise. For example, a manufacturer can gain access to target markets virtually overnight using an existing distribution chain, whereas launching its own distribution channel would take considerably longer.

Despite its numerous benefits, collaborating with other entities has several important *drawbacks*:

- **Loss of control.** Delegating certain aspects of a company's activities to an external entity often leads to loss of control over the value-creation process. For example, outsourcing manufacturing operations frequently hinders a company's ability to monitor production processes and product quality. Outsourcing also diminishes the company's ability to monitor the financial aspects of the value-creation process.

- **Loss of competencies.** Outsourcing key activities tends to weaken a company's core competencies. For example, outsourcing research-and-development activities over time tends to diminish a company's ability to drive innovation. In the same vein, outsourcing logistics and manufacturing activities can diminish a company's competency in supply-chain management.

- **Empowering the competition.** Outsourcing key activities also might enable collaborating entities to develop a set of strategic competencies, thus becoming a company's future competitor. For example, a collaborator assembling medical devices on behalf of the company might develop its own line of medical devices that will compete with the devices it assembles for the company.

As with most business decisions, entering into a collaborative relationship involves weighing the relevant benefits and costs. When the benefits from the collaboration outweigh the corresponding costs for both the company and its collaborators, the collaboration tends to be sustainable. In contrast, when the collaboration fails to create superior value for either party, the collaboration might be dissolved as the partners pursue alternative options such as finding new collaborators or insourcing.

Crafting Company and Collaborator Positioning Statements

To ensure market success, a company must develop a viable positioning for its collaborators and stakeholders. Thus, similar to the way in which managers develop a customer positioning statement, they must also develop a positioning statement geared toward the company's collaborators and its senior management and stakeholders. The key aspects of collaborator and company positioning statements are discussed in more detail in the following sections.

Developing a Collaborator Positioning Statement

To succeed, an offering has to create value not only for its target customers but also for the company's collaborators. Accordingly, in addition to developing a customer-focused positioning statement, managers need to develop a positioning statement outlining the offering's value for its collaborators.

The collaborator-focused positioning statement is similar to the customer-focused positioning statement (discussed in Chapter 5), with the main difference that instead of identifying target customers and the key aspects of the offering's value proposition for these customers, it identifies the company's key collaborators and delineates the key aspects of the offering's value proposition for these collaborators. The key question that the collaborator-focused positioning statement must answer is: *Who are the offering's key collaborators and why would they work with the company to support its offering?*

The typical collaborator-focused positioning statement consists of three key components: *collaborators, the frame of reference,* and *the primary benefit(s).* The overall structure of the collaborator-focused positioning statement is similar to the structure of the customer-focused statement. Examples of collaborator-focused positioning statements are shown below.

Example A (Noncomparative Positioning): [Offering][frame of reference] is an excellent choice for [collaborators] because [primary benefit].

DeWalt power tools are a great choice for retailers because they are profitable.

Example A (Comparative Positioning): [Offering][frame of reference] is a better choice for [collaborators] than [competition] because [primary benefit].

DeWalt power tools are a better choice for retailers than Makita because they offer price protection from discount retailers.

Example B (Noncomparative Positioning): For [collaborators] who seek [primary benefit], [offering] is an excellent [product category] because [justification of the benefit].

For mass-market retailers who seek to grow profits, Gillette Fusion offers a consumer staple that will generate high profit margins.

Example B (Comparative Positioning): For [collaborators] who seek [primary benefit], [offering] is a better [frame of reference] than [competition] because [justification of the benefit].

For mass-market retailers who seek to grow sales revenues and market share, Gillette Fusion offers a consumer staple that will generate higher profit margins than Gillette Mach3.

Developing a Company Positioning Statement

The company-focused positioning statement identifies the company's business unit managing the offering and outlines its key value proposition for the business unit and the company. The company-focused positioning statement aims to justify the viability of the offering to the senior management and key stakeholders (e.g., company directors) by articulating how the offering will help the company achieve its goals. The key question that this positioning statement must answer is: *Why should the business unit and the company invest in this offering?*

A typical company-focused positioning statement consists of three key components: *the company, the frame of reference,* and *the primary benefit(s).* The overall structure of the company-focused positioning statement is similar to the structure of the customer-focused statement. Examples of company-focused positioning statements are shown below.

Example A (Noncomparative Positioning): [Offering] is an excellent [frame of reference] for [company] because [the primary benefit derived from the offering].

> DeWalt power tools are an excellent choice for Black & Decker because they offer high profit margins.

Example A (Comparative Positioning): [Offering] is a better [frame of reference] for [company] than [alternative options] because [primary benefit].

> DeWalt power tools are a better strategic option for Black & Decker than Black & Decker Professional power tools because they have a larger margin and generate greater sales volume.

Example B (Noncomparative Positioning): [Offering] is an excellent choice for [company] because [the primary benefit derived from the offering].

> Fusion is an excellent option for Gillette because it will assert Gillette's position as the leader in the wet-shaving market and will ensure high profit margins.

Example B (Comparative Positioning): [Offering] is the [frame of reference] that gives [company] greater [primary benefit] than [alternative options] because [justification of the benefit].

> Fusion is the wet-shaving system that gives Gillette greater market share than Mach3 because it has higher profit margins.

SUMMARY

The company is an entity established for the purpose of creating value for its stakeholders. To this end, the company develops market offerings that fulfill the needs of target customers and collaborators while at the same time capturing value for its stakeholders. An offering can create two types of value for the company: *monetary* and *strategic.*.The monetary value corresponds to the company's financial goals, and the strategic value reflects the offering's ability to fulfill a company's strategic goals.

Achieving sustainable profit growth is the ultimate goal for most companies. Profit growth is achieved by increasing sales revenues and reducing costs. Increasing *sales revenues* is the prevalent approach to achieving long-term profitability. Increasing sales revenues can be achieved through two basic strategies: growing sales volume and optimizing price.

Strategies for growing *sales volume* include the market-growth strategy, which aims to attract customers who are new to the particular product category; the steal-share strategy, which aims to attract customers who are currently buying similar offerings from competitors; and the market-penetration strategy, which aims to increase consumption by the company's current customers.

The impact of *varying the price* on sales revenues depends on the way customers react to changes in price. Sales revenues can be increased by raising (lowering) prices in cases when the positive impact of increasing revenues (sales volume) is greater than the negative impact of the corresponding decrease in sales volume (revenues).

Profit growth can also be achieved by *lowering costs*, including the cost of goods sold, research-and-development costs, marketing costs, and miscellaneous other costs such as general and administrative costs and cost of capital.

The profit impact of *strategic offerings* is measured by assessing the monetary value they create through synergies with other profit-generating offerings. To better communicate the value of its offerings, companies often express the strategic benefits of the offering in monetary terms—a process referred to as economic value analysis.

To succeed in the market, most companies collaborate with other entities to understand, design, communicate, and deliver value to target customers. Accordingly, collaboration can typically occur in four domains: *market insight, value design, value communication,* and *value delivery*. The relationship between a company and its collaborators should always be considered in the context of creating value for their ultimate customers.

To ensure market success, a company must develop a viable positioning for its collaborators and stakeholders. Thus, managers must also develop a *collaborator-focused positioning statement*, which articulates the key aspects of the offering's value proposition for the company's collaborators and a *company-focused positioning statement*, which articulates the offering's value proposition for the company stakeholders.

MARKETING INSIGHT: QUANTIFYING MARKET PERFORMANCE

To effectively manage their companies, managers must identify the key performance dimensions and quantify their companies' performance on these dimensions. Quantifying market performance is relevant not only for for-profit companies but also for nonprofit organizations that seek to have an impact on individual consumers, the markets in which these consumers interact with one another and the company, and society as a whole. Specifically, quantifying market performance involves analyses in four areas: *assessing key performance metrics, developing an income statement, conducting a margin analysis,* and *break-even analysis*.

Key Performance Metrics

Market Share: An offering's share of the total sales of all offerings within the product category in which the company's offering competes. Market share is determined by dividing an offering's sales volume by the total category sales volume. Sales can be defined in terms of revenues or on a unit basis (e.g., number of items sold or number of customers served).

$$\text{Market share} = \frac{\text{An offering's sales in a given market}}{\text{Total sales in a given market}}$$

Net Income: Gross revenue minus all costs and expenses (cost of goods sold, operating expenses, depreciation, interest, and taxes) during a given period of time. Net income is also referred to as net earnings.

$$\text{Net income} = \text{Gross revenue} - \text{Total costs}$$

Return on Investment (ROI): Net income as a percentage of the investment required for generating this income.

$$\text{ROI} = \frac{\text{Gain from an investment} - \text{Cost of investment}}{\text{Cost of investment}}$$

Return on Marketing Investment (ROMI): A measure of the efficiency of a company's marketing expenditures, typically calculated in terms of incremental net income, sales revenues, market share, or contribution margin. ROMI can also be calculated with respect to the overall marketing expenditures or to a specific marketing mix variable (e.g., branding, incentives, or communication).

$$\text{ROMI} = \frac{\text{Incremental net income generated by the marketing investment}}{\text{Cost of the marketing investment}}$$

Return on Sales (ROS): Net income as a percentage of sales revenues.

$$\text{ROS} = \frac{\text{Net income}}{\text{Sales revenues}}$$

The Income (Profit and Loss) Statement

The income statement (also referred to as the *profit and loss statement*) is a financial document enumerating a company's income and expenses during a given period. It typically identifies revenues, costs, operating expenses, operating income, and earnings (Figure 9).

Figure 9. The Income (Profit and Loss) Statement

Gross Revenues	
Sales revenues	$ 18,000
Returns and allowances	(3,000)
Total (Gross) Revenues	15,000
Cost of Goods Sold	
Product costs	(4,500)
Services costs	(1,500)
Total Cost of Goods Sold	(6,000)
Gross Profit	9,000
Gross Margin	60%
Operating Expenses	
Sales and marketing	5,000
General and administrative	1,000
Research and development	1,500
Total Operating Expenses	7,500
Operating Income	1,500
Operating Margin	10%
Other Revenues (Expenses)	
Interest expense	(250)
Depreciation and amortization	(100)
Income tax expense	(400)
Total Other Revenues (Expenses)	(750)
Net Income (Earnings)	750
Net (Profit) Margin	5%

Gross (Profit) Margin: The ratio of gross (total) profit to gross (total) revenue. Gross margin analysis is a useful tool because it implicitly includes unit selling prices of products and services, unit costs, and unit volume. Gross margin is different than contribution margin (discussed later): Contribution margin includes all variable costs, whereas gross margin includes some—but often not all—variable costs, a number of which can be part of the operating margin.

$$\text{Gross margin} = \frac{\text{Gross profit}}{\text{Gross revenue}} = \frac{\text{Gross revenue} - \text{Cost of goods sold}}{\text{Gross revenue}}$$

Gross Profit: The difference between gross (total) revenue and total cost of goods sold. Gross profit can also be calculated on a per-unit basis as the difference between unit selling price and unit cost of goods sold. For example, if a company sells 100 units, each priced at \$1 and each costing the company \$.30 to manufacture, then the unit gross profit is \$.70, the total gross profit is \$70, and the unit and total gross margins are 70%.

$$\text{Gross profit}_{Total} = \text{Revenue}_{Total} - \text{Cost of goods sold}_{Total}$$

$$\text{Gross profit}_{Unit} = \text{Price}_{Unit} - \text{Cost of goods sold}_{Unit}$$

Gross Revenue: Total receipts from a company's business activities.

Net Margin: The ratio of net income to gross (total) revenue.

$$\text{Net margin} = \frac{\text{Net income}}{\text{Gross revenue}}$$

Operating Expenses: The costs, other than cost of goods sold, incurred to generate revenues (e.g., sales, marketing, research and development, and general and administrative expenses).

Operating Income: Gross profit minus operating expenses. Operating income reflects the firm's profitability from current operations without regard to the interest charges accruing from the firm's capital structure.

$$\text{Operating income} = \text{Gross profit} - \text{Operating expenses}$$

Operating Margin: The ratio of operating income to gross (total) revenue.

$$\text{Operating margin} = \frac{\text{Operating income}}{\text{Gross revenue}}$$

Margin Analysis

Contribution Margin (\$): When expressed in monetary terms (\$), contribution margin typically refers to the difference between total revenue and total variable costs. The contribution margin can also be calculated on a per-unit basis as the difference between the unit selling price and the unit variable cost. The per-unit margin, expressed in monetary terms (\$), is also referred to as the contribution (i.e., the dollar amount that each unit sold "contributes" to the payment of fixed costs).

$$\text{Contribution margin (\$)}_{Total} = \text{Revenue}_{Total} - \text{Variable costs}_{Total}$$

$$\text{Contribution margin (\$)}_{Unit} = \text{Price}_{Unit} - \text{Variable costs}_{Unit}$$

Contribution Margin (%): When expressed as a percentage (%), contribution margin typically refers to the ratio of the difference between total revenue and total variable costs to total revenue. The contribution margin can also be expressed as the ratio of unit contribution to unit selling price.

$$\text{Contribution margin (\%)} = \frac{\text{Revenue}_{\text{Total}} - \text{Variable costs}_{\text{Total}}}{\text{Revenue}_{\text{Total}}}$$

$$\text{Contribution margin (\%)} = \frac{\text{Price}_{\text{Unit}} - \text{Variable costs}_{\text{Unit}}}{\text{Price}_{\text{Unit}}}$$

Marginal Cost: The cost of producing one additional unit.

Trade Margin: The difference between unit selling price and unit cost at each level of a distribution channel. Trade margins can be expressed in monetary terms or as a percentage (Figure 10). Margins are typically calculated based on sales revenue (sales price) rather than based on cost (purchase price).

Figure 10. Calculating Trade Margins

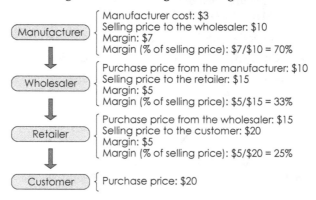

Marketing Insight: Break-Even Analysis

Break-even analysis aims to identify the point at which the benefits and costs associated with a particular action are equal, and beyond which profit occurs. The most common types of break-even analyses include break-even of a fixed-cost investment, break-even of a price cut, and break-even of a variable-cost increase.

Break-even analysis of a fixed-cost investment identifies the unit or dollar sales volume at which the company is able to recoup a particular investment, such as research-and-development expenses, product improvement costs, and the costs of an advertising campaign. The break-even volume (BEV) of a fixed-cost investment is the ratio of the size of the fixed-cost investment to the unit margin.

$$\text{BEV}_{\text{Fixed-cost investment}} = \frac{\text{Fixed-cost investment}}{\text{Unit margin}} = \frac{\text{Fixed-cost investment}}{\text{Unit selling price} - \text{Unit variable cost}}$$

The break-even analysis of a fixed-cost investment can be illustrated as shown in Figure 11. Here the break-even point indicates the sales volume beyond which the offering starts generating profits.

For example, consider an offering priced at $100 with variable costs of $50 and fixed costs of $50M. In this case, BEV = $50M/($100 – $50) = 1,000,000. Thus, for a $50M fixed-cost investment to break even, sales volume should reach 1,000,000 items.

Figure 11: Break-Even of a Fixed-Cost Investment

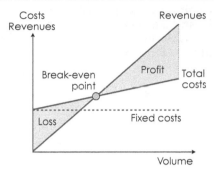

In addition to the break-even analysis of a fixed-cost investment associated with launching a new offering, a company may need to calculate the break-even volume of a change (most often an increase) in its current fixed-cost investment. Typical problems to which this type of analysis can be applied are estimating the incremental increase in sales necessary to cover the costs of a research-and-development project, the costs of an advertising campaign, and even the costs of an increase in the compensation package of senior executives.

To illustrate, consider the impact of an increase in fixed costs from $50M to $60M for a product priced at $100 with variable costs of $50. In this case, BEV = ($60M - $50M)/($100 – $50) = 200,000. Thus, for the $10M fixed-cost investment to break even, sales volume should increase by 200,000 items.

Break-even analysis of a price cut estimates the increase in sales volume needed for a price cut to have a neutral impact on company profits. To break even, lost profits resulting from a lower margin after a price cut must be equal to the additional profits generated by the incremental sales volume from the lower price. BEV Price cut is expressed

$$\text{BEV}_{\text{Price cut}} = \frac{\text{Margin}_{\text{Old price}}}{\text{Margin}_{\text{New price}}}$$

To illustrate, consider the impact of a price cut from $100 to $75 for a product with a variable cost of $50. In this case, Margin $_{\text{Old price}}$ = $100 – $50 = $50 and Margin $_{\text{New price}}$ = $75 – $50 = $25. Therefore, BEV $_{\text{Price cut}}$ = $50/$25 = 2. Thus, for the price cut to break even, sales volume should double at the lower price.

Break-even analysis of a variable-cost increase identifies the sales volume at which a company neither makes a profit nor incurs a loss after increasing variable costs. Typical problems to which this type of analysis can be applied are estimating the incremental increase in sales necessary to cover an increase in the cost of goods sold, estimating the costs associated with increasing an item-specific level of service, and estimating the costs associated with running item-specific incentives (e.g., premiums). The basic principle of calculating the break-even point of an increase in an offering's variable costs is similar to that of estimating the break-even point of a price cut. The difference is that a decrease in the margin generated by the new offering stems from an increase in the offering's costs rather than a decrease in revenues.

$$\text{BEV}_{\text{Variable cost increase}} = \frac{\text{Margin}_{\text{Old variable cost}}}{\text{Margin}_{\text{New variable cost}}}$$

To illustrate, consider the impact of an increase in variable costs from $50 to $60 for a product priced at $100. In this case, Margin $_{\text{Old variable cost}}$ = $100 – $50 = $50 and Margin $_{\text{New variable cost}}$ = $100 – $60 = $40. Therefore, the break-even volume of a variable cost increase can be calculated as BEV $_{\text{Variable cost increase}}$ = $50/$40 = 1.25. Thus, for the variable-cost increase to break even, the ratio of the new to old sales should be 1.25, meaning that sales volume should increase by a factor of .25, or by 25%.

PART THREE

DESIGNING THE MARKETING TACTICS

INTRODUCTION

*Everything should be made as simple
as possible, but not simpler.*
— Albert Einstein, theoretical physicist

Marketing tactics translate a company's strategy into a set of actionable decisions that define the offering the company will deploy in the target market. In this context, marketing tactics refer to a set of specific activities, also known as the marketing mix, employed to execute a given strategy. The marketing tactics reflect all attributes of a specific offering, from the benefits it creates and how much it costs to how customers will hear about it and buy it. The chapters included in this section address the following topics:

- **Managing products** involves crafting the product-related aspects of the company's offering. The key issues involved in managing a company's products are discussed in Chapter 7.

- **Managing services** involves crafting the service-related aspects of the company's offering. The key issues involved in managing a company's services are discussed in Chapter 8.

- **Managing brands** involves crafting and managing the brand image associated with the company's offering(s). The key branding decisions involved in managing a company's offering(s) are the focus of Chapter 9.

- **Managing price** involves setting and managing the monetary aspect of the offering; it defines the amount of money the company charges for the offering. The key pricing decisions are outlined in Chapter 10.

- **Managing incentives** involves a variety of tools, typically short term, aimed at enhancing the value of the offering by providing additional benefits or reducing costs. The key decisions involved in managing incentives are discussed in Chapter 11.

- **Managing communication** articulates the ways in which the company informs the relevant market entities about its offerings. The key decisions involved in managing communication are discussed in Chapter 12.

- **Managing distribution channels** involves defining the ways in which a company delivers its offerings to target customers. The key aspects of managing distribution are discussed in Chapter 13.

The key to designing a successful offering is to ensure that it can deliver superior value to the relevant market entities — target customers, the company, and its collaborators. To this end, the different aspects of the offering should be aligned in a way that optimizes the value delivered to these three entities. A systematic approach to developing and managing the value-design elements of a company's offering is outlined in the following chapters.

CHAPTER SEVEN

MANAGING PRODUCTS

A market is never saturated with a good product,
but it is very quickly saturated with a bad one.

— Henry Ford, founder of Ford Motor Company

A company's products—along with its services and brands—are a key source of customer value and one of the primary reasons why customers buy and use a company's offering. In this context, product management aims to optimize the value that a company's products deliver to target customers and do so in a way that benefits the company and its collaborators. The key product-management decisions are the focus of this chapter.

Product Management as a Value-Creation Process

A key consideration in product management is creating superior customer value. To this end, a manager must understand the role of products as a means of creating market value and the relationship between product attributes and customer benefits. These three aspects of product management are discussed in the following sections.

The Product as a Tool for Creating Market Value

The product is a good designed to create value in a particular market. It is one of the seven attributes defining the company's offerings. Working together with the other marketing tactics defining the offering—service, brand, price, incentives, communication, and distribution—the product aims to create value for the relevant market entities: the company, its customers, and its collaborators (Figure 1).

Figure 1. Product Management as a Value-Creation Process

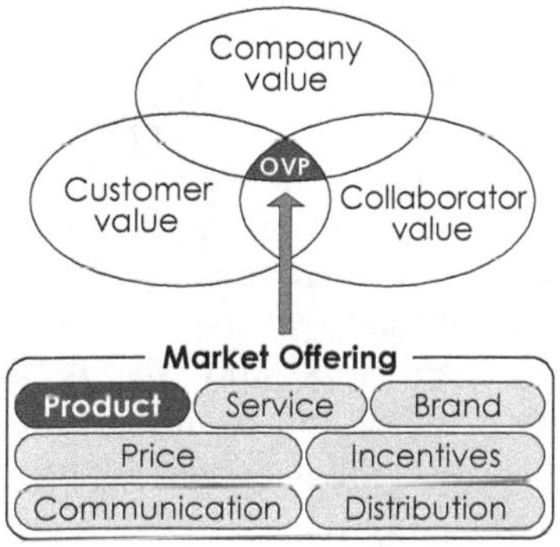

A manager's ultimate goal is to design products that create superior value for target customers in a way that benefits the company and its collaborators. To ensure a product's success, a manager must address three key questions:

- *Does the product create superior value for target customers relative to the competition?*
- *Does the product create superior value for the company's collaborators relative to the other options these collaborators might pursue?*
- *Does the product create superior value for the company relative to the other alternatives available to the company?*

An affirmative answer to these questions implies that the product has an optimal value proposition (OVP) that creates value for target customers, the company, and its collaborators. The development of a meaningful optimal value proposition is the overarching principle guiding all product decisions. To this end, a company must identify the benefits that customers seek to receive from the company's offering and then translate these benefits into specific product features and experiences in a way that enables the company and its collaborators to achieve their goals.

Product Attributes and Customer Benefits

Products are defined by a combination of attributes that deliver particular customer benefits. *Attributes* are objective characteristics of a product, such as certain levels of performance, reliability, and durability. In contrast, *benefits* reflect the subjective value customers derive from using the product. Product attributes can be related to specific benefits, although this relationship is not unidimensional: A particular attribute might be associated with one or more benefits, and a given benefit might stem from multiple attributes (Figure 2).

Figure 2. Product Attributes and Customer Benefits

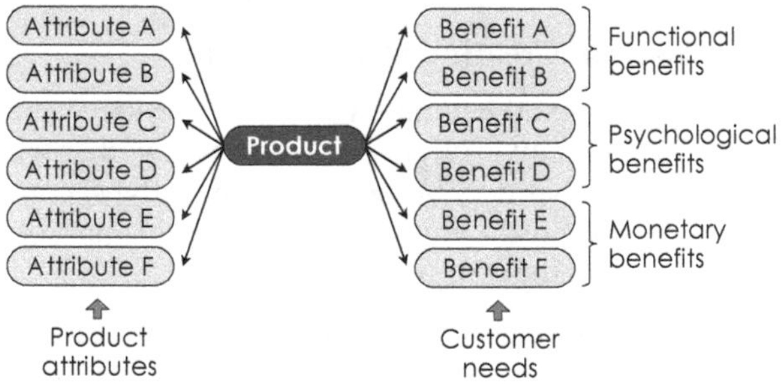

Depending on the underlying customer needs, product benefits can be classified into one of three types: functional benefits that are directly related to a product's performance, psychological benefits that reflect the emotional and self-expressive impact of the product, and monetary benefits that reflect the financial implications of using the product. Accordingly, when developing a new product or modifying an existing one, managers must ask three key questions: *How does the product's functional performance benefit customers? How do customers feel about different product attributes?* and *What is the monetary impact of the different aspects of the product on customers?* Providing meaningful answers to these questions and incorporating them into the product design can help ensure the product's market success.

The relationship between product attributes and customer benefits is better understood in the context of product design and consumption. Product attributes are defined by engineers who are in charge of designing and manufacturing the product. Once customers acquire the product, they experience the benefits stemming from the product's attributes. Thus, while engineers tend to think in terms of product attributes, customers tend to think in terms of the benefits delivered by the product. In this context, a manager's task is to ensure that the product designed by the engineers performs in a way that creates value for target customers — in other words, that product attributes are aligned with the benefits customers expect to receive from the offering.

Key Product Decisions

On the most general level, product development involves four key decisions: defining product functionality, designing the physical appearance of the product, delineating product guarantees and warranties, and creating the product packaging. The first three product decisions are outlined in more detail below and the decisions concerning product packaging are discussed in the following section.

Defining Product Functionality

Defining product functionality involves a series of decisions concerning attributes such as *performance, consistency, reliability, durability, compatibility, ease of use,* and *degree of customization.* These factors are discussed in more detail below.

- **Performance** reflects the key functional attributes of the offering. Products vary in their performance on different attributes. For example, cars vary in engine power, acceleration, comfort, safety, and fuel efficiency; computers vary in processing power, battery life, display size, and connectivity; and snacks vary in taste, nutritional value, and calorie content. In general, higher levels of performance are associated with greater customer benefits, although in some cases the performance on one attribute comes at the expense of the performance on another (e.g., taste and healthiness of a snack).

- **Consistency** reflects the degree to which in-kind products are identical and offer consistent performance. Simply put, consistency means that the same type of product (same SKU) manufactured at different points in time and in different facilities should deliver the same benefits. A popular approach to managing product consistency is the *Six Sigma* methodology of optimizing business processes, which builds on the idea that for an offering to be consistent with specifications, the difference between the actual and desired outcomes should not exceed six standard deviations (a level of consistency that implies that there should be fewer than 3.4 defective items per million outcomes).[13]

- **Reliability** refers to the extent to which a product fulfills its function each and every time it is used over a period of time. Specifically, reliability reflects the probability that the product will operate according to its specifications for the duration of its projected life cycle. Product reliability depends on a variety of factors that include its technical design, the quality of its materials and components, and the degree of care with which it is made and assembled. In general, higher levels of reliability are associated with greater customer benefits, although reliability typically involves greater costs from a company's perspective.

- **Durability** reflects the expected length of the offering's life cycle. Because durability is often an important consideration in a buyer's decision process, products that are more durable tend to be preferred by customers. At the same time, while durable products help companies attract new customers and build loyalty among existing customers, durability tends to have a negative impact on the frequency of repeat purchases because users are often reluctant to replace fully functioning products with new ones. As a result, when designing new offerings, manufacturers have to determine the optimal product durability that will create superior customer value and at the same time leave room for the company to offer meaningful upgrades in the future.

- **Compatibility** refers to the degree to which a product is consistent with certain already existing standards and complementary offerings. Compatibility can be used strategically by companies to create barriers to entry by ensuring that offerings are uniquely compatible with customers' existing systems and processes. Compatibility is also important in networked environments that force users to adhere to a certain standard. To illustrate, the popularity of Microsoft products is to a great degree a function of the need for compatibility when sharing information. Compatibility is also a key consideration in multipart products, where different components must be compatible with one another (e.g., razors and blades).

- E**ase of use** reflects the amount of effort—cognitive, emotional, and physical—involved in using the product. A common misconception is that greater functionality, such as a greater number of features, inevitably leads to greater satisfaction. In reality, however, this is not the case: Adding functionality, especially when customers lack the knowledge necessary to utilize it, can backfire. To illustrate, in an attempt to incorporate the latest technology in its redesigned 7-series sedan, BMW introduced iDrive, an over-engineered computer system used to control most secondary functions of a car, including the audio system, climate, and navigation. Designed to manage more than 700 functions with a single knob, the iDrive had a steep learning curve and quickly became the most controversial feature of the car.

- **Degree of customization** reflects the extent to which the company's products are personalized to fit the needs of individual customers. At one extreme, a company might decide to pursue a mass-production strategy, offering the same products to all customers. At the other extreme, the company might pursue a one-to-one customization in which the company's products are customized for each individual customer. A compromise between the mass-production approach and the one-to-one customization approach is segment-based customization. By developing offerings for groups of customers with similar needs, segment-based customization allows companies to develop fewer offerings while ensuring that these offerings fit well with customer needs. To illustrate, Porsche offers nearly 1,000 customization options for its flagship 911 Carrera, and Nike offers more than 10,000 different design and color sport-shoe customization options through its website nikeid.com. The Coca-Cola Freestyle soda machine can dispense over 100 sparkling and still beverages that customers can mix to match their own taste.

Designing the Product's Physical Attributes

Product design typically involves decisions concerning the physical appearance of the offering, such as its size, shape, and structure. Design plays an important role in manufacturing, transporting, storing, inventorying, and consuming the product. Because customers vary in their preferences and the amounts they consume, packaged goods are often available in a variety of sizes and shapes. For example, Johnson & Johnson's pain relief medicine Tylenol is available in more than fifty different SKU[14] forms—regular, extra strength, and children's dosages; normal and extended relief; tablets, caplets, gelcaps, geltabs, and liquid—all in a variety of sizes.

The look and feel of an offering are particularly important for products that have a primarily aesthetic and self-expressive function, such as luxury cars, designer furniture, and fashion apparel, but are relatively less pertinent for functional products such as manufacturing equipment. Because product styling can create value above and beyond the functional characteristics of the product, it is particularly important in commoditized product categories. For example, Apple revolutionized the personal computer industry by designing computers that were not only powerful and fast but also aesthetically pleasing. Method Products, a home and personal cleaning products company, has managed to successfully differentiate its products through the innovative, futuristic styling of its containers. Tesla managed to build a striking electric car that people *want* to drive, instead of a mediocre car that environmentally conscious consumers feel that they *have* to drive. By using innovative product design, Apple, Method, and Tesla have been able to develop products that stand out in a crowded marketplace in which multiple products are fighting for a share of buyers' attention and buyers' wallets.

In addition to delivering functional benefits, attracting buyers' attention, and creating an emotional connection, product design can also influence consumption. For example, while developing a packaging that would successfully challenge Coca-Cola's iconic 6.5-oz. "swirl" bottle, Pepsi discovered that the design of the bottle influences not only whether buyers will pick it up from the store shelf but also how much they'll drink once they bring it home. The larger the bottle, the greater the rate of consumption. The observation that larger bottles lead to a greater rate of consumption resulted in the development of the two-liter bottle, which has since become one of the most popular containers in the non-alcoholic carbonated beverage category.

Delineating Product Guarantees and Warranties

In addition to creating customer value via the benefits offered by the product, a company can also create value by offering customers reassurance that the product will perform as described and promising some form of reparation should the product fail to meet expectations. Such reassurance can be conveyed by product guarantees and warranties.

A *guarantee* is an assurance that if a product does not function as promised by the company and/or expected by customers, some form of compensation will be provided by the company. Guarantees create value for customers by reducing the functional and monetary risk associated with using the product, by adding credibility to the company's claims, and by delineating the process of addressing eventual product failures. In addition to minimizing customer risk, guarantees can convey product quality by signaling the company's willingness to stand by its products. Guarantees can also benefit the company by sharpening its focus on the customer experience, establishing accountability, facilitating the development of performance standards, and offering guidelines for recovering from failures.

Guarantees can be *overall satisfaction* guarantees that apply to any aspect of the overall product experience regardless of whether it stems from the actual quality of the product or customers' assessment of the product quality, and *specific attribute* guarantees that apply to a particular aspect of the product such as performance, reliability, and durability. In addition, guarantees can be valid for a specific period of time, such as one year, or they can be stipulated for a variable time frame such as for the duration of product ownership by the original buyer.

Warranties are similar to guarantees in terms of the benefits they provide to customers and the company. At the same time, they differ on at least two dimensions. First, warranties are usually associated with a repair or a replacement of the purchased item, whereas guarantees can also involve returning the product for a refund. In addition, guarantees are always free and do not require an added payment. In contrast, warranties that extend the product's existing free warranty can be purchased either when the product is bought or at a later date.

While enhancing customer value, guarantees and warranties come at a cost to the company. In general, the more generous the guarantees and warranties, the higher the company cost of offering these benefits to customers. Therefore, when designing product guarantees and warranties, a company must carefully consider their pros and cons and their overall impact on the offering's ability to create market value.

Product Packaging as a Tool for Creating Market Value

Packaging refers to the process of enclosing products for distribution, storage, sale, and use. The importance of the packaging stems from the fact that it is a buyer's first encounter with the product, which can determine this buyer's interest in the product and shape the subsequent product evaluation and purchase decision. Because of its ability to influence customer choice, many companies strategically use packaging to create distinct customer value and differentiate their products from the competition.

The Role of Packaging in Product Design

Packaging serves several key functions: *protecting* the product during transportation and storage; physically *containing* liquid, powder, and granular goods; *agglomerating* small items into larger packages; *preventing* tampering, counterfeiting, and theft; providing *convenience* during transportation, handling, storage, display, sale, and consumption; offering *information* on how to transport, store, use, and dispose of the product; *differentiating* the company's product from the competition; and *promoting* the product to potential buyers by providing them with reasons to choose it.

In addition to facilitating the distribution, storage, sale, and use of products, packaging can also be used to create value above and beyond the value created by the product itself. To illustrate, Tiffany's signature blue box highlights the exclusivity of the offering, strengthens the company's brand image, and helps differentiate it from the competition. The role of packaging as an aspect of the offering's brand is further discussed in Chapter 9.

An important aspect of packaging is the *label*, which refers to any written, electronic, or graphic communication placed directly on the package or otherwise associated with the product (e.g., an information tag attached to the product). The primary functions of the label are to communicate information to buyers, channel members, and the company to facilitate identification of the offering; delineate the key attributes of the product; highlight product benefits; provide information about the use, storage, and disposal of the product; increase the product's aesthetic appeal; as well as build and leverage the brand associated with the product.

Packaging involves two key decisions: designing the packaging for a new offering and deciding whether and how to modify the packaging of an existing offering. These two decisions are discussed in more detail below.

Designing the Packaging

The development of effective packaging follows a set of core principles that determine the product's ultimate success in the market. These principles are *visibility*, *differentiation*, *value transparency*, and *consumption impact*.

- **Visibility.** Shoppers are frequently overwhelmed with information from companies trying to promote their offerings. This information overload often forces customers to tune out and ignore much of the information they deem irrelevant and that does not help them with the decision process. Therefore, effective packaging must stand out in order to break through the clutter, grab shoppers' attention, and persuade them to favorably consider and ultimately purchase the offering.

- **Differentiation.** In addition to attracting shoppers' attention, packaging can help differentiate the company's offering from the competition. Thus, when confronted with multiple options, customers who are pressed for time often use packaging as a key source of information about the offering. Shoppers' reliance on packaging as a key input in their buying decision is further driven by the fact that many companies use packaging as a branding tool, which, in turn, makes it easy for shoppers to identify the brands they are looking for by merely looking at the packaging.

- **Value transparency.** Packaging's visibility and ability to differentiate the company's offering from the competition, although important, do not address another important function of packaging—namely, its ability to clearly communicate the value of the offering to its target customers. Because shoppers typically interact with the packaging at the time of purchase, effective packaging must make transparent the offering's value proposition to shoppers and give them a reason to buy the offering.

- **Consumption impact.** The role of packaging is not limited to influencing shoppers' buying decisions: Packaging can also influence the ways in which customers use the offering. In this context, packaging can have an impact on usage frequency—how often customers use the company's offerings—and usage quantity—how much they consume on each usage occasion. For example, Coca-Cola was able to increase consumption by introducing refrigerator-friendly fridge packs that stack 12 cans in a longer and narrower space and allow individual cans to be dispensed. Heinz boosted consumption of ketchup by introducing a series of packaging design innovations that made it easier to get ketchup out of its container. To this end, Heinz switched from glass bottles to squeezable plastic containers, put the mouth of the container at its base, and widened the opening used to dispense ketchup.

A number of the functions performed by packaging are similar to those performed by advertising. Indeed, both serve as means of communication, informing buyers about the company's offering. Despite their similarities, packaging and advertising vary in the ways in which they convey information as well as in the type of information they aim to convey. Advertising typically strives to create memorable impressions that buyers will act upon in the future. In contrast, because buyers often observe the packaging at the point of purchase, packaging can have almost an instant impact on customers, influencing their purchase decision. Furthermore, in the case of low-priced, familiar products, customers usually spend little time evaluating the available options and often rely on the visual properties of products and their packaging to make a choice. As a result, packaging is often designed to have a more direct, visual impact on the buyer.

Managing the Product Life Cycle

Once introduced in the market, products do not stay static; instead, products have a life cycle where they evolve along with the changes in customer demand, competition, and the overall market conditions. The key issues involved in managing products over their life span involve *understanding the dynamics of the product life cycle, extending the product life cycle,* and *managing product obsolescence.*

The Dynamics of the Product Life Cycle

The concept of a product life cycle is based on the idea that products and product categories have a finite life in which they go through four distinct stages: introduction, growth, maturity, and decline.[15] These stages vary on several dimensions, including the number of product offerings in the market, the nature of communication, the size of the market and its growth rate, the competitive intensity of the market, as well as the revenues and profits generated at each stage. The overall pattern of a product's financial performance across the four stages is illustrated in Figure 3 and outlined in more detail below.

Figure 3. Managing the Product Life Cycle[16]

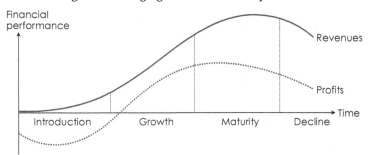

- **Introduction.** At the introduction (also referred to as market development) stage, companies typically offer a single product targeted to the most likely adopters. At this early stage, communication aims primarily to create awareness of the offering among early adopters. The overall size of the market is rather small and growing at a relatively slow pace. Because the market viability of the product is uncertain, there are relatively few competitors entering the market. Given the small but growing market, the revenues are relatively small, albeit showing an upward trend. Because new product development typically involves substantial costs, the profits at this stage are usually negative, meaning that the company is operating at a loss.

- **Growth.** As the product enters the growth stage, the number of customer adoptions increases, and so does the diversity of customers' needs. To address the diverse needs of its target customers, companies begin to introduce product variants designed to better meet the needs of different customer segments. As product sales take off during the growth stage, the number of competitors entering the market increases as more companies recognize the market potential. The size of the market continues to increase and its growth rate accelerates dramatically. Despite the growing number of competitors, the competitive intensity of the market is relatively tame, in part because the market growth leads companies to focus their efforts on attracting new customers to the market instead of trying to steal share from one another. The rapidly growing market and limited competition contribute to the largest rate of revenue and profit growth among all four life-cycle stages. At this stage profits tend to turn positive and the rate of profit growth reaches its peak—the inflection point at which the profit curve turns from convex to concave and the rate of profit growth starts to decline.

- **Maturity.** During the maturity stage, the number of product variants typically peaks as the company develops offerings that appeal to diverse market segments. Because the majority of customers are already aware of the product benefits and many have had a chance to experience the product, communication shifts from building primary demand to differentiating the company's offering by highlighting its benefits vis-à-vis the competition. The market size reaches its peak, but its growth rate starts to decelerate. As the inflow of new customers into the product category slows down, the competition intensifies and companies start competing directly with one another to steal customers and grow market share. Furthermore, as the number of products and competitors tends to peak, the market becomes saturated, and the intensified competition leads to a plateauing and decline in market revenues and profits.

- **Decline.** This stage is characterized by a shrinking market and falling demand for the product. The number of product variants starts decreasing as the product enters the decline stage, profit margins shrink, and companies focus on their best-selling products, phasing out product variants with insufficient volume to meet their profit goals. As the category enters its decline stage, communication continues to emphasize differentiation; however, at this point overall communication expenditures tend to diminish. Competition can become less intense due to fewer competitors because of consolidation and market exit. The overall market growth is negative, and both revenues and profits continue to decline.

Note that the above discussion examines the product life cycle from a product category standpoint rather than from the perspective of a particular company. This distinction is important because a company might not be the first entrant in a given product category and, instead, might enter the market at a later stage of the product life cycle. Regardless of the timing of market entry, the company's performance is likely to be influenced by the dynamics of the market defined by the particular life-cycle stage of the product category.

Extending the Product Life Cycle

As products reach the end of their life cycle, they are often replaced by a new generation of products that take advantage of changes in target markets, including changes in customer preferences, alterations in the competitive landscape, advances in technology, and changes in the regulatory environment. The finite nature of the product life cycle raises the question of whether and how a company can manage its products to prolong their market life. In this context, an important aspect of product management involves actively managing the evolution of the company's offerings over time. Rather than passively waiting for its products to follow their life course and ultimately decline and disappear, a company might choose to plan ahead and develop the next generation of products that will inevitably replace its current offerings.

There are two core approaches to extend the product life cycle: market expansion and product innovation. Market expansion can involve increasing the frequency of usage among the current users of the product, promoting new uses for the product among current users, and discovering new markets for the product. Even though market expansion can help the company extend the life of its products, it does not involve substantive changes in the actual product, leaving it vulnerable to obsolescence caused by the emergence of new technologies. In this context, product innovation, rather than market expansion, is often viewed as a more effective approach to ensure the longevity of a company's products.

The key to successful product innovation is to identify customer needs that are not being met by the current products and develop alternative products that can address these needs. This approach involves applying the product's core technology to new generations of the current product that are better, simpler, more convenient, and/or cheaper. Using such product innovations, a company can create a series of sequential generations of products that extend the product life cycle far beyond the decline stage of the original product (Figure 4). To illustrate, consider Gillette's product development strategy leading to the introduction of Fusion, its eighth-generation wet-shaving razor. Gillette's original razor, introduced in 1903, was replaced by the second-generation Trac II razor (1971), followed by the Sensor (1990), Sensor Excel (1995), Mach3 (1998), Mach3 Turbo (2002), M3Power (2004), Fusion (2006), Fusion ProGlide (2010), and Fusion FlexBall (2014).

Figure 4. Extending the Product Life Cycle Through Innovation[17]

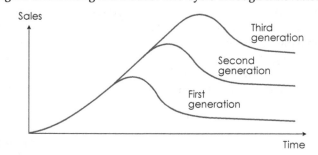

There is a common misconception that succeeding product generations should be more complex and offer more features than the ones they are replacing. This is not always correct. Even though enhancing already existing product attributes and adding new ones can increase the attractiveness of the product for customers, simplifying the product and removing some of its attributes to lower its price can also create customer value. The true criterion for the success of new products is their ability to create greater customer, collaborator, and company value than the current offerings.

Managing Product Obsolescence

Product obsolescence refers to a decrease in the availability of and/or the demand for the product, although its functionality has not decreased. Obsolescence often results in a company limiting or discontinuing the production, promotion, distribution, and support of the product. Based on how the product obsolescence came about, it can be either *involuntary* or *planned*.

Involuntary Obsolescence

Involuntary obsolescence happens when a product can no longer perform its core functions in a way that creates market value. Product obsolescence is often caused by entirely new technologies that replace old ones. For example, the traditional cameras using photographic film, which were the dominant form of photography until the early 21st century, have been made obsolete by the emergence of digital cameras and by the advancements in image-processing software. Other products that have been rendered obsolete by the emergence of new technologies include typewriters (replaced by computers), dedicated MP3 players (replaced by smartphones and wearable devices), pagers (replaced by smartphones), and printed phone directories (replaced by search engines and online phone directories).

Obsolescence can also occur when a product is no longer desirable because its design is outdated or its style is out of fashion. This type of obsolescence is particularly important in the fashion industry where tastes, styles, and designs can change virtually overnight, and fashion apparel and accessories often have a single-season life span. In this case, obsolescence is caused by consumers' desire to have a more current version of the product even though the new product is functionally equivalent to the older version. A particular feature of obsolescence in fashion is that it is rarely permanent; rather, it follows "fashion cycles" in which stylistically outdated products eventually regain popularity and cease to be obsolete. Examples of such in-and-out obsolete products include fedora hats, saggy and skinny jeans, cargo and harem pants, neon-colored accessories, and furs.

Planned Obsolescence

Planned obsolescence occurs when a company intentionally shortens the longevity of its products. Planned obsolescence is particularly common in industries where technological advances have made it possible to design reliable and durable products with a life span that does not necessitate frequent replacement. There are three common types of planned obsolescence: *generation obsolescence*, *product obsolescence*, and *component obsolescence*.

- **Generation obsolescence** aims to make the earlier generation of products obsolete by reducing their functionality in order to transition users to the new generation. Generation obsolescence often involves designing new products in a way that makes prior generations inferior on key dimensions such as functionality, compatibility, and style. For example, to facilitate user migration to later versions of their software, companies systematically terminate support for earlier versions.

- **Product obsolescence**, also referred to as built-in obsolescence, involves designing products so that they wear out or become obsolete at a particular point in time. Product obsolescence can also involve designs that artificially shorten the product's life span in order to force users to repurchase the product even when the new product has the same functional benefits. For example, an appliance manufacturer can design a refrigerator to last five years even when the cost of doubling its lifetime is relatively small. As a result, customers are likely to repurchase the prematurely obsolete products more frequently, thus increasing the manufacturer's revenues and profits.

- **Component obsolescence**, also referred to as value engineering, is another form of planned obsolescence that involves optimizing the performance of the individual components of the product for its expected lifetime. For example, from a cost perspective, it might not be feasible for a product to include a component that lasts much longer than the average life span of its other components. As a result, a company expecting its product to be obsolete within a given time frame might optimize costs by designing the durability of its components according to the expected product lifetime.

Companies use a variety of strategies to manage different types of obsolescence. *Generation obsolescence* is often driven by the emergence of new technologies that bring greater customer benefits and/or are more cost efficient and strategically important for the company. *Product obsolescence*, on the other hand, reflects a company's efforts to design products that reflect customers' willingness to pay for durability and at the same time allow the company to achieve its monetary and strategic goals. Finally, *component obsolescence* is particularly relevant for products comprising multiple components, as it helps reduce costs by not overspending on components that would significantly outlast the life of the entire product.

SUMMARY

Product management aims to optimize the value that a company's products deliver to target customers and do so in a way that benefits the company and its collaborators. To this end, a company must identify the benefits that customers seek to receive from the company's offering and then translate these benefits into specific features and experiences that define the company's products.

Product development involves four key decisions: defining product functionality, designing the physical appearance of the product, delineating product guarantees and warranties, and creating the product packaging.

Defining *product functionality* involves a series of decisions concerning attributes such as performance, consistency, reliability, durability, compatibility, ease of use, and degree of customization. *Product design* typically involves decisions concerning the physical appearance of the offering, such as its size, shape, and structure. *Product guarantees and warranties* offer customers reassurance that the product will perform as described and promise some form of reparation should the product fail to meet expectations.

Packaging serves multiple functions that range from protecting the product during transportation and storage and offering product information to differentiating the company's product from the competition and promoting the product to potential buyers. The development of effective packaging follows four principles: visibility, differentiation, value transparency, and consumption impact.

Managing the *product life cycle* involves optimizing the products as they progress through different stages in the marketplace: introduction, growth, maturity, and decline. Because the stages in the product life cycle are characterized by different market conditions, different stages require different marketing strategies. The two core approaches to extend the product life cycle are market expansion and product innovation.

Product obsolescence refers to a purposeful decrease in the availability of and the demand for the product. Based on how the product obsolescence came about, it can be either involuntary obsolescence, which occurs when a particular product can no longer perform its core functions in a way that creates market value, or planned obsolescence, which occurs when a company intentionally shortens the longevity of its products.

CHAPTER EIGHT

MANAGING SERVICES

There is no such thing as service industries. There are only industries whose service components are greater or less than those of other industries. Everybody is in service.

—Theodore Levitt, marketing educator

Service management aims to optimize the value that a company's services deliver to target customers and do so in a way that enables the company and its collaborators to achieve their goals. Managing services—in concert with managing products and brands—aims to define the benefits that the company's offering will create for target customers. The key service decisions are the focus of this chapter.

Service Management as a Value-Creation Process

The role of services as a key source of customer value has increased in recent years as many companies including Adobe, Apple, and Microsoft have transitioned from predominantly product-based to more service-oriented offerings. This shift toward services is, in part, driven by companies' desire to enhance the value customers derive from their offerings as well as to ensure a superior user experience, greater satisfaction, and deeper loyalty.

Service as a Tool for Creating Market Value

Service is one of the seven attributes defining the company's offerings. Working together with the other marketing tactics defining the offering—product, brand, price, incentives, communication, and distribution—the service aims to create value for the relevant market entities: the company, its customers, and its collaborators (Figure 1).

Figure 1. Service Management as a Value-Creation Process

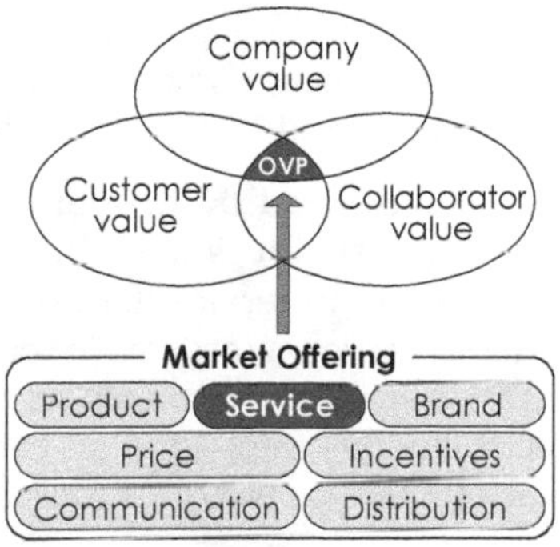

A manager's ultimate goal is to design services that create superior value for target customers in a way that benefits the company and its collaborators. To ensure that the service aspect of the offering creates market value, a manager must address three key questions:

- *Does the service create superior value for target customers relative to the competition?*
- *Does the service create superior value for the company's collaborators relative to the other options these collaborators might pursue?*
- *Does the service create superior value for the company relative to the other alternatives available to the company?*

An affirmative answer to these questions implies that the service has an optimal value proposition (OVP) that creates value for target customers, the company, and its collaborators. The development of a meaningful optimal value proposition is the overarching principle guiding all service decisions. To this end, a company must identify the benefits that customers seek to receive from the company's offering and then translate these benefits into specific service features and experiences in a way that enables the company and its collaborators to achieve their goals.

The Service Aspects of an Offering

Products and services are closely related and share a number of commonalities, which sometimes makes it difficult to draw a clear distinction between them. At the same time, there are several distinctive characteristics that separate services from products. The three main differences are: *ownership*, *separability*, and *variability*.

- **Ownership.** Unlike products, which typically change ownership (from the seller to the buyer) during purchase, services do not usually involve a change in ownership; instead, the customer acquires the right to use the offering and receive its benefits within a given time frame. For example, travel, hospitality, and professional services deliver their benefits to target customers without providing permanent legal entitlement to the underlying goods.

- **Separability.** Unlike products, which can be physically separated from the manufacturer and distributed by a third party, services are usually delivered and consumed at the same time. Inseparability makes services difficult to inventory—an important consideration in industries such as airlines, hotels, and call centers, where companies with a fixed service capacity face fluctuating customer demand. In such industries, yield management—optimizing the balance of supply and demand—is of utmost importance to ensure customer satisfaction and enable service providers to achieve their goals. For example, an airline can raise prices at times of peak demand and offer sales promotions to stimulate demand in off-peak times.

- **Variability.** Services are characterized by greater variability in performance than products, meaning that service delivery is more likely to vary across different occasions. Indeed, the human element in service delivery makes it difficult to standardize. As a result, service quality varies across service occasions depending on the type of customer, the particular service provider, and the interaction between the service provider and the customer. To illustrate, different customers might receive varying levels of service from the same service provider, and the same service provider might have different interactions with different customers depending on their specific needs and behavior.

Many offerings comprise a combination of products and services. For example, even mundane products such as toothpaste, soap, and milk are accompanied by a service provided by retailers carrying these products, including sales support and returns. More complex products such as cars, consumer electronics, and household appliances are augmented with technical support, delivery, and repair services. At the same time, many services include product components. For example, airlines offer meals, snacks, and drinks; hotels offer toiletries; and car rental companies provide customers with temporary use of automobiles.

Key Service Decisions

Designing the service component of a company's offerings involves three types of decisions: Defining the functional aspects of the service, delineating service guarantees and warranties, and defining the physical context of service delivery. These three aspects of service design are outlined in the following sections.

Defining Service Functionality

The attributes defining service functionality are similar to those defining the functional aspects of the company's products. Thus, creating and managing services involves a series of decisions concerning factors such as *performance, consistency, reliability, compatibility, ease of use,* and *degree of customization.*

- **Performance** reflects the key functional aspects of the service. Key performance dimensions include service quality—that is, the degree to which the service can fulfill the core needs of its target customers—and service speed, which reflects the temporal dimension of the service delivery. For example, in the case of professional services, performance can be defined in terms of the quality of the service (legal advice, tax preparation, medical treatment) and the expediency with which the service was delivered.

- **Consistency** reflects the degree to which a company can deliver the same quality of service over time. Because variability is a key characteristic of service, consistency is of vital importance in service delivery and one of the main contributors to the success of companies such as McDonald's, Starbucks, and Ritz-Carlton. Because consistent performance makes future service outcomes more predictable, consistency is a key prerequisite for building a strong service brand.

- **Reliability** refers to the degree to which a service is likely to be delivered according to its specifications. Reliability is often used as a differentiating point to create a unique positioning for a company's services. For example, FedEx promises "absolutely, positively overnight" delivery service, discount brokerage TD Ameritrade guarantees that certain trades will be executed within five seconds, and Verizon claims to be the most reliable wireless network in the United States, with a call-completion rate of more than 99.9%.

- **Compatibility** refers to the degree to which a service is consistent with already existing standards and complementary offerings. Compatibility is particularly important in networked environments incorporating multiple services from different providers that must interact with one another to deliver a seamless user experience. Compatibility is also important in the case of technology-enabled services that are associated with frequent service modifications and updates that require a smooth transition between the current and the new version of the service. For example, a video streaming service must be compatible with the hardware and software of the device on which it is displayed. In the same vein, different apps must be compatible with the software platform on which they will operate.

- **Ease of use** reflects the amount of cognitive, emotional, and physical effort involved in using a particular service. Easy-to-use services tend to enjoy faster adoption and a more loyal user base because customers might be unwilling to invest the extra effort to switch to competitors offering a more complex service. As in the case of products, a greater number of service options does not always lead to greater customer satisfaction, especially in cases when customers lack the knowledge necessary to utilize these options. For example, Quicken Loans, the largest retail lender in the United States, promotes its Rocket Mortgage services as the easiest and the fastest in the industry. In the same vein, GEICO, one of the largest U.S. auto insurers, emphasizes the ease of receiving an insurance quote.

- **Degree of customization** reflects the degree to which a company's services are personalized to address the needs of each individual customer. Service customization can be contrasted to a scenario in which customers are offered the same type and level of service regardless of their needs and preferences. Customization can be achieved by creating a service that perfectly fits a customer's needs as well as by providing a menu of options to enable customers to tailor the service to their own needs. For example, a news provider might use customers' behavior to infer their preferences and offer news programming that fits those preferences or, alternatively, it might let customers self-select the news they would like to receive. Overall, customization tends to increase perceived service quality, customer satisfaction, and ultimately customer loyalty to the service provider.

Delineating Service Guarantees and Warranties

Service guarantees reflect an assurance that a service will be delivered as promised by the company and expected by customers and that the company will offer some form of compensation in the event the service is found lacking. Guarantees create value for customers by reducing the functional and monetary risk associated with using the service. Guarantees further create customer value by adding credibility to the company's claims and delineating the process of addressing eventual service failures. In addition to creating customer value, guarantees can benefit the company by sharpening its focus on the customer experience, establishing accountability and facilitating the development of performance standards, and offering guidelines for recovering from service failures.

As in the case of products, service guarantees can involve customers' overall satisfaction or satisfaction with a specific attribute of the service. Overall satisfaction guarantees apply to any aspect of the service experience, regardless of whether it stems from the actual quality of the service or customer assessment of the service quality. For example, hotels such as Radisson Blu, Hampton Inn, and Fairfield Inn offer a 100% satisfaction guarantee that their guests will be pleased with their stay. In the same vein, many retailers such as Amazon,

Nordstrom, and Neiman Marcus guarantee customer satisfaction with the shopping experience and offer a "no questions asked" return policy on most of their items.

Service warranties differ from guarantees in two basic ways: They are usually associated with a correction or replacement of the purchased service (rather than a refund) and may involve additional payments (unlike guarantees, which are always free). Accordingly, service warranties are particularly relevant in cases when the delivered service can be rectified (rather than refunded). For example, services involving repair and maintenance of purchased items often offer warranties promising to address defects in materials and workmanship after the original manufacturer's warranty has expired. Service warranties may also cover loss or damage not covered under the original manufacturer's warranty.

Designing the Physical Context of Service Delivery

Unlike products, which in most cases have physical properties, services are largely intangible and do not have physical attributes. In this context, one might assume that packaging as a marketing concept does not apply to services. This is not the case. Although services are intangible, the process of service delivery involves tangible components. For example, FedEx uses airplanes and trucks to deliver packages, Marriott offers hospitality services through its hotels, and 7-Eleven retails convenience products in its vast network of franchisee-operated stores. In the same vein, theme parks are the physical environments in which Disney delivers its magic and creates memorable experiences.

The fact that services are largely intangible, variable, and experiential in nature (meaning that they are difficult to observe prior to being consumed) makes it more challenging for companies to describe and differentiate their services. Indeed, for many physical products, buyers can draw quality and performance inferences based on their readily observable attributes. In contrast, in the case of services, buyers are often faced with a much greater level of uncertainty because of the scarcity of physical cues from which to draw inferences. As a result, companies must seek ways to offer physical evidence that will inform buyers about the key aspects of their services. This physical evidence is often provided by the tangible elements of the service delivery.

The physical aspect of the service delivery can play a key role in creating market value. Augmenting the service with tangible attributes can benefit the company by enhancing buyers' confidence in the offering. For example, financial institutions aim to convey strength by embedding their services in a physical environment—including the exterior of the building, design of the lobby and reception area, the furnishings, and employee uniforms—that projects stability and permanence. In addition, some companies use symbols that aim to "tangibilize" the intangible aspects of their offerings. To illustrate, Prudential's logo features the Rock of Gibraltar to symbolize financial stability, ING's logo features a lion to signal strength, and Expedia's logo substantiates its services by featuring an airplane flying around the globe.

Delivering Superior Services

Delivering stellar service is at the heart of any customer-centric organization. Service quality is a powerful differentiator that can meaningfully distinguish the company's offerings from the competition and create superior value for customers and the company.

Because services are characterized by great variability stemming from their delivery by employees with varying levels of motivation and expertise, service outcomes are difficult to standardize in a way that ensures superior service quality across all customers and occasions. As a result, understanding and streamlining the processes by which a company can consistently deliver excellent customer service is crucial to a company's ability to generate value for its customers, collaborators, and stakeholders.

The ways in which a company can create market value through superior service, the core principles of managing employee performance, and the process of building and enhancing the company culture are discussed in the following sections.

Creating Market Value Through Superior Service

The key to designing a service-focused organization is understanding that delivering superior service creates value not only for the company's customers but that it is also a key driver of the company's own success. "A business absolutely devoted to service will have only one worry about profits," advocated Henry Ford. "They will be embarrassingly large." To succeed in today's competitive market, a company must harness the power of customer service as a source of creating market value and a tool for competitive differentiation. Customer focus and the ability to deliver superior customer service must become a core competency for any company that aims to achieve market success.

A well-designed service strategy can lead to a virtuous cycle that serves as an engine to create value. This cycle begins with selecting the right employees, providing these employees with adequate training, and motivating them to deliver excellent customer service. Trained, motivated employees are competent at doing their jobs and are content and satisfied with their work and being a part of the company. Competent employees that enjoy their work are, in turn, likely to deliver high-quality service that creates customer value by meeting and exceeding customer needs and expectations.

Customers who are satisfied and delighted with the company's service tend to stay loyal to the company and shift more of their business to the company. Greater customer loyalty means that the company receives greater revenues from its customers while having to spend much less than usual on customer retention, which translates into greater company profitability. As a result of this cycle, the company is able to reinvest some of the profits into hiring, training, and retaining skilled employees, enabling it to continue delivering superior customer value and sustain customer loyalty (Figure 2).

Figure 2. Creating Market Value Through Superior Customer Service

Managing employees—from selecting the right people to ensuring that they deliver superior service—is at the heart of creating customer value and company profits. "If you take care of your employees, your employees will take care of your customers, and your customers will take care of your shareholders," maintains the founder of Virgin Group, Richard

Branson. The key role that company employees play in creating market value underscores the importance of building a customer-focused employee culture and developing actionable strategies for managing employee performance. These issues are addressed in more detail in the following sections.

Managing Employee Performance

Superior customer service is the result of deliberate design of the service-delivery process and the painstaking implementation that translates this design into reality. A crucial component of this process is managing the performance of employees whose job is to ensure that the company delivers the service it has promised its customers.

Managing employee performance starts with *recruiting* the right employees, followed by a process of *training* these employees, providing them with the *information* they need to address customers' needs, offering a meaningful incentive structure to *motivate* employees to deliver quality service, *empowering* employees by delegating decision-making responsibilities to them, *monitoring* their performance to ensure consistent service quality, and ultimately developing a company *culture* that helps create and reinforce a customer-centric attitude as a norm of behavior among employees. The key components of managing employee performance are illustrated in Figure 3 and discussed in more detail below.

Figure 3. Managing Employee Performance

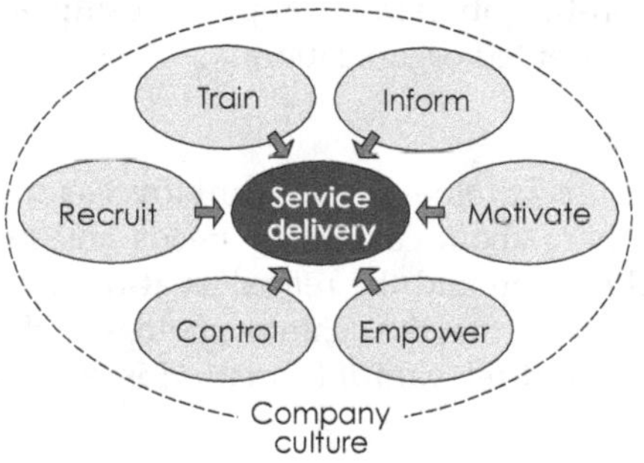

Recruiting Employees

Because services typically involve direct interaction between the company employees and customers, the process of delivering superior customer service begins with the selection of employees who are both capable and motivated to delight the company's customers. Given the importance of front-line employees in shaping a customer's experience, companies often use a systematic process to evaluate candidates and identify the best people for the job.

After it has found the right employees, a company must persuade them to join its ranks—a task that can be challenging in cases of experienced and highly skilled candidates. In general, a company's ability to recruit competent employees depends on three factors: *financial compensation*, including base salary and performance bonuses; *nonmonetary benefits* such as working conditions, availability of flexible work schedules, vacation time, and health insurance; and *self-fulfillment benefits* such as moral satisfaction from creating societal value and gaining a sense of achievement, personal growth, and professional development.

Company culture and reputation can play an important role in the hiring and retaining of skilled employees. Employees often place a premium on working for companies whose brands resonate with their own needs, preferences, and value system. As a result, companies with strong reputations find it easier to attract talented employees and keep these employees from leaving. In fact, employees are sometimes ready to accept a lower salary to work for a company with a culture consistent with their own value system.

Training Employees

Even though companies aim to recruit qualified personnel, in most cases new employees need to be informed about the specifics of their job requirements, familiarized with the workflow within their team and the company, and immersed in the company culture. In addition to introducing new employees to their responsibilities within the company, training programs can also promote personal growth by helping employees overcome deficiencies in their skill set and enhance their strengths. Thus, professional training programs might focus on improving specific skills such as technical, communication, teamwork, and management and leadership skills.

Professional training can be carried out using different formats. Formal training programs provide employees with relevant information organized in a structured format and presented in a way that makes it easy to understand and internalize. In addition to formal training programs, both formal and informal mentoring programs play an important role in employee training by providing guidance on how to behave in specific situations, some of which might not be covered in the training programs. In this context, providing an environment that is conducive to on-the-job training, apprenticeship, and mentoring is a key ingredient in building a service-oriented organization.

Informing Employees

To effectively deliver superior customer service, employees must have at their fingertips the data necessary to inform them about customers' needs and preferences, the nature of the problem they are currently facing and the remedies at the company's disposal to address this problem, as well as the value that the customer brings to the company. Providing front-line employees with timely and relevant information is essential to their ability to satisfy and delight customers.

Informing employees can involve three main types of information: (1) information about customers' needs and preferences to help employees deliver better service to these customers, (2) information about customers' touch points with the company to help ensure consistency of the delivered service, and (3) information about the lifetime value of individual customers to help prioritize customers based on their value to the company. To gather this information and furnish it in a timely manner to customer service representatives, companies use market research and data analytics to develop customer relationship management programs designed to provide up-to-date, customer-specific data that can facilitate the service-delivery process.

Empowering Employees

Empowering employees means shifting the decision-making power from management to front-line personnel. Depending on the nature of the company and the industry in which it operates, employee empowerment can be implemented in a variety of ways. For example, The Ritz-Carlton has instituted a policy that the first employee who encounters a customer's problem "owns" the problem until it is resolved. To this end, The Ritz-Carlton sees to it that everyone—not just the senior management—has $2,000 per day per guest to fix or improve a guest's experience.

Empowering employees can enhance service quality in multiple ways. First, it can lead to a faster resolution of customer problems since empowered employees can make a decision on the spot without involving a higher level of management. Empowerment can also lead to a more effective resolution of a customer's problem. Indeed, the problems faced by customers can often be addressed by a variety of possible solutions that customers might be unaware of or might be reluctant to use. In this context, being able to directly interact with customers enables empowered employees to identify the outcome that is likely to be optimal from customers' point of view.

Empowering employees can further increase the efficiency of the organization by cutting down on intra-office communication and shortening the approval-granting process. Another benefit of empowerment is that it delegates responsibility to employees, which can make them feel more engaged, motivate them to perform their jobs more effectively, and increase their overall satisfaction at working for the company. Finally, a company's ability to quickly identify and solve a customer's problem not only can lead to greater customer satisfaction and loyalty but can also become a reputation-builder for the company as customers share their experience with others.

Motivating Employees

Informing and empowering employees is a necessary but often insufficient condition for allowing a company to deliver superior customer service. Indeed, even though some employees might be intrinsically motivated to do their best, not all employees will feel the same way. To motivate all employees and ensure that they are fully engaged in trying to delight customers, companies often implement incentive systems designed to reward employees who take to heart the company's customer service policies.

A company can reward its employees using three basic types of incentives: financial payments such as pay raises and bonuses, nonmonetary benefits such as days off and paid vacations, and psychological rewards such as recognition of accomplishments and achievement awards. In addition to offering rewards, a company can motivate its employees by building a customer-centric culture that makes the drive to delight customers the norm rather than the exception. Employee motivation can also be enhanced by having resources—cash payments, vouchers, free services, and bonus products—at their disposal to address a customer's problem. The availability of such resources is another way in which a company can signal to front-line employees the importance of their role as touch points between the company and its customers.

Controlling Employees

Monitoring employee performance is important to ensure consistent delivery of superior customer service and identify and correct service breakdowns in a timely fashion. Service breakdowns can stem from a variety of factors such as the lack of employee engagement with the service, insufficient or inadequate training, as well as from misalignment of the employee and company incentives. Consider a customer service representative trying to appease an angry customer who calls to complain about the poor service she received from another employee. As soon as the service representative realizes that he is unlikely to be able to resolve the problem and might instead become the lightning rod for this customer's dissatisfaction, he might be tempted to hang up the phone and move on to the next call.

Monitoring employees' behavior can help a company achieve multiple goals such as assessing the service delivery, identifying skills gaps, providing training to overcome deficiencies, and rewarding outstanding performance. At the same time, enforcing accountability can help ensure that front-line employees follow the customer service guidelines prescribed by the company. In addition to ensuring a superior customer experience, employee monitoring also can help with loss prevention—an issue particularly relevant for employees dealing with money and high-value items.

To effectively monitor the service delivered by its employees, a company must develop internal service quality standards, policies, and guidelines that can be used as a benchmark for evaluating employee performance. To this end, a company can develop a service-quality dashboard that comprises the key performance indicators of successful service delivery and can serve as the basis for an internal service-quality audit.

Building a Service-Oriented Company Culture

A service-oriented culture results from a concerted effort of both company management and employees. Building a meaningful company culture is guided by several factors. It starts with the beliefs held by the management about the company values and the types of behavior endorsed by the company. These management beliefs are then reflected in the company's service policy and used to guide the process of recruiting the right employees, defining the norms of employee behavior, and promoting teamwork. The key components of building a service-oriented company culture are outlined in Figure 4 and discussed in more detail below.

Figure 4. Building a Service-Oriented Company Culture

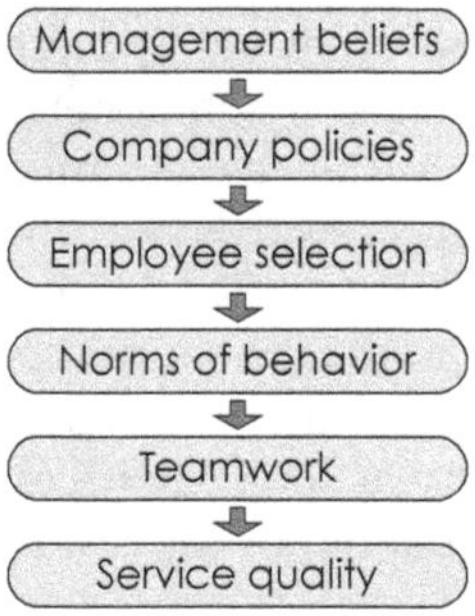

- **Management beliefs** define the set of values that guide the company; these values indicate the type of actions that are encouraged by the company and those that are discouraged. Management beliefs set the tone of the company culture and have a major impact on the way employees interact with customers. Managers that understand the importance of delivering superior service are likely to instill a customer-centric culture in their companies. For example, Amazon founder Jeff Bezos describes his view of the role of customer service in the company's business model as follows: "We see our customers as invited guests to a party, and we are the hosts. It's our job every day to make every important aspect of the customer experience a little bit better." This view has fostered a customer-focused culture that permeates all aspects of Amazon's business activities.

- **Company policies.** To be effective and have a lasting impact, management beliefs are formalized into a set of policies that outline the core values and principles that should guide the service-delivery process. In addition to outlining the overarching company beliefs, policies delineate how these beliefs apply in specific situations and how company employees are expected to behave when interacting with customers and with one another. Service policies address a variety of aspects of employee behavior, from the language used to refer to customers to the remedial actions needed in the case of service recovery.

- **Employee selection.** Because the culture resides with the company employees, employee selection can make or break the company culture. Accordingly, when making hiring decisions, service-oriented companies like Zappos, Southwest Airlines, and REI place utmost importance on the degree to which an employee's motivation, personality, and value system fit the company's culture. To this end, having a service-oriented culture—reflected in the company's value system, attitude toward customers and customer service, and its expectations of employee behavior—can greatly facilitate a company's ability to identify individuals that not only will fit the company's culture but will also help reinforce and elevate it.

- **Norms of behavior.** Even the best laid policies are useless unless they are internalized and followed by the company employees. Indeed, some companies have well-articulated policies designed to impart a service-oriented culture that exist only on paper and are largely ignored by employees. As new employees join the company, in addition to reading the company's written policies, they also observe the actual company culture as it is reflected in the norms of behavior that are deemed acceptable in the company's day-to-day activities. In this context, the unwritten norms of behavior that guide how employees act in situations not explicitly addressed by company policies are essential components in helping to shape the company culture.

- **Teamwork.** A company's culture is a shared experience that involves individual employees subscribing to a set of common values and norms of behavior. Because of its shared nature, a strong service culture almost by definition involves employee interaction and seamless teamwork. As an integral component of the company culture, teamwork benefits both customers and employees. Customers benefit from employees coming together to resolve customer problems and provide a better service experience. For employees, teamwork facilitates professional growth while offering an environment in which to enjoy social interactions, develop personal connections, and gain emotional support.

Consider Zappos, an online apparel retailer owned by Amazon and known for its outstanding customer service. Zappos prioritizes cultural fit when hiring new employees, and the cultural fit interview often carries half the weight in the hiring decision. Newly recruited employees spend their first month manning phones in the company's call center, learning how to interact with customers. Upon completion of their time in the call center, Zappos employees are offered $3,000 to leave the company—a strategy used to ensure that employees are committed to the company culture. To provide consistent customer service, Zappos does not hire temporary employees, so all employees are expected to sign up for shifts in the call center during the busy seasons. Call center employees are fully empowered to serve customers and do not have to ask for a manager's approval to address a customer's request. To build such a customer-centric culture, Zappos allocates a portion of its budget to team building. Managers at Zappos play a key role in fostering the company culture and are expected to spend up to 20 percent of their time on employee team-building activities.[18] Zappos' actions aim to ensure that every aspect of service delivery—from articulating management beliefs and setting service policies to recruiting employees, defining the norms of behavior, and fostering teamwork—are aligned with its strategic goal of delivering superior customer experience.

Summary

Service management aims to optimize the value that a company's services deliver to target customers and do so in a way that benefits the company and its collaborators.

Services are defined by three main characteristics: *ownership*, *separability*, and *variability*. Unlike products, which typically change ownership (from the seller to the buyer) during purchase, services do not usually involve a change in ownership; instead, the customer acquires the right to use the offering and receive its benefits within a given time frame. Furthermore, unlike products, which can be physically separated from the manufacturer and distributed by a third party, services are usually delivered and consumed at the same time. Finally, services are characterized by greater variability in performance than products, meaning that service delivery is more likely to vary across different occasions.

Designing services involves three types of decisions: defining the functional aspects of the service, delineating service guarantees and warranties, and defining the physical context of service delivery. *Service functionality* defines the core benefits delivered by the service provider on attributes such as performance, consistency, reliability, compatibility, ease of use, and degree of customization. *Service guarantees and warranties* reflect assurance that a service will be delivered as promised by the company and expected by customers and that the company will offer some form of compensation in the event the service is found lacking. The *physical aspect* of the service delivery involves augmenting the service with tangible attributes in order to optimize the service experience and strengthen the offering's brand.

A key aspect of service delivery is managing the performance of a company's employees. *Managing employee performance* starts with *recruiting* the right employees, followed by a process of *training* these employees, providing them with the *information* they need to address customer needs, offering meaningful incentives to *motivate* employees to deliver quality service, *empowering* employees by delegating decision-making responsibilities to them, *monitoring* employee performance to ensure consistent service quality, and ultimately developing a *company culture* that helps create and reinforce a customer-centric attitude as a norm of behavior among employees.

A company's culture is an integral component of the service-delivery process. The culture captures the personality of the company and serves as a moral compass guiding the discretionary behavior of its employees. A *service-oriented culture* results from a concerted effort of both company management and employees. Building a meaningful company culture is guided by several factors: It starts with the beliefs held by the management about the company values and the types of behavior endorsed by the company. These management beliefs are then reflected in the company's service policy and used to guide the process of recruiting the right employees, defining the norms of employee behavior, and fostering teamwork.

CHAPTER NINE

MANAGING BRANDS

If you are not a brand, you are a commodity.
— Philip Kotler, founder of modern marketing theory

Brands are one of the company's most valuable assets. Brands benefit customers by creating value that goes beyond the product and service aspects of the offering. By bolstering customer demand, brands enable the company to capture greater value from its customers while at the same time strengthening the impact of the other marketing tactics, ensuring greater collaborator support, and facilitating the hiring and retaining of skilled employees. The key aspects of creating and managing brands are the focus of this chapter.

Branding as a Value-Creation Process

Branding is the process of endowing a company's offerings with a unique identity in order to differentiate them from the competition and create value above and beyond the value delivered by the other aspects of the offering. The role of brands as a tool for creating market value and the ways in which companies create a distinct image in the minds of its target customers are discussed in more detail in the following sections.

Brands as a Tool for Creating Market Value

Brands have a long history as a means of distinguishing the goods of one producer from those of another. Some of the earliest known brands were used to mark the identity of a good's maker or owner. These simplest forms of branding were observed in the ancient civilizations of Egypt, Crete, Etruria, and Greece. During the Roman Empire, more distinctive forms of branding, including the use of word marks in addition to graphics, began to emerge.

The importance of brands dramatically increased by the end of the 19th century when the proliferation of mass-produced, standardized products—a direct consequence of the Industrial Revolution—created the need for unique marks to help consumers distinguish between these products. As manufacturers began producing on a larger scale and gained wider distribution, they started engraving their mark into the goods to distinguish themselves from their competition. Along with these changes, the nature of brands was transforming from simply marking the ownership of the product to identifying its maker and serving as a symbol of product quality.

Brands have become ubiquitous in modern society. They are not limited to physical goods such as food products, cars, cosmetics, and pharmaceuticals. Brands are used to identify services (American Express, Netflix, and Uber); companies (Procter & Gamble, Walmart, and Starbucks); nonprofit organizations (UNESCO, FIFA, and American Red Cross); events (Olympic Games, Wimbledon, and Super Bowl); individuals (Lady Gaga, Madonna, and Michael Jordan); groups (music groups, sport teams, and social clubs); administrative units (countries, states, and cities); geographic locations (Champagne, Cognac, and Camembert); and ideas and causes (education, social justice, and health).

Brands are one of the seven attributes defining the company's offerings. Together with the other attributes of the offering—product, service, price, incentives, communication, and distribution—brands aim to create an optimal value proposition (OVP) for the company, its customers, and its collaborators (Figure 1). Therefore, a manager's goal is to build brands that create superior value for target customers in a way that benefits the company and its collaborators.

Figure 1. Branding as a Value-Creation Process

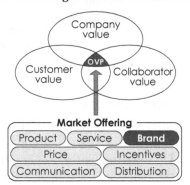

Creating value for target customers in a way that benefits the company and its collaborators is the overarching principle guiding all branding decisions. The means by which brands create customer, company, and collaborator value are outlined in more detail in the following sections.

Creating a Meaningful Brand Image

Building strong brands calls for creating a meaningful brand image in customers' minds. The brand image is the network of all brand-related associations that exist in a customer's mind. It reflects how customers see a particular brand through the lens of their own set of values, beliefs, and experiences.

Brand image can be visually represented as an association map delineating the key concepts linked to the brand name. Figure 2 illustrates streamlined brand association maps representing a customer's (hypothetical) image of the Apple and Starbucks brands. Here, the nodes represent the different concepts related to each of these brands in this customer's mind, and the lines connecting them represent the brand associations. The nodes closer to the brand indicate thoughts that are directly associated with the brand, and the nodes that are farther away indicate the secondary associations that are less prominent in a customer's mind.

Figure 2. Brand Association Maps of Apple and Starbucks

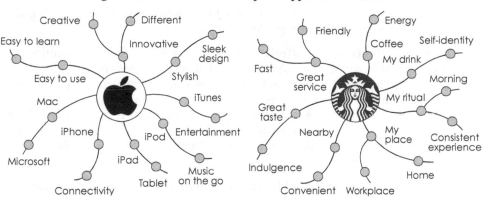

The type of associations brands evoke, as well as the breadth, strength, and attractiveness (positive vs. negative) of these associations, reflect the degree to which a given brand has successfully created a relevant, well-articulated, and positive image in a customer's mind. The stronger the brand, the greater the number of relevant benefits, usage occasions, experiences, concepts, products, and places associated with it—and the stronger and more positive these associations are. In this context, brand management aims to facilitate the formation of a variety of strong, meaningful, and positive brand associations in the minds of its target customers.

Ideally (from a company's standpoint), the brand image that exists in the mind of each of its customers should be consistent with the image the company aims to project. In reality, however, this is not always the case. Because the brand image exists in a customer's mind and stems from this customer's individual needs, values, and knowledge accumulated over time, the same brand might evoke different brand images across customers. For example, some customers might associate the Starbucks brand with handcrafted espresso coffee drinks while for different customers it might represent a part of their daily routine; others might think of Starbucks as a place to meet with friends. In the same vein, different customers might associate the Apple brand with user-friendly technology; with particular products such as the iPhone, iPad, or Apple Watch; with innovation, creativity, and being different; with other technology brands such as Microsoft, Google, and Samsung; and even with the company's own retail stores.

Brand Strategy

The process of building strong brands is guided by a clear understanding of the value they create for target customers, the company, and its collaborators. The different ways in which brands create market value are discussed in the following sections.

Brands as a Means of Creating Customer Value

One of the primary goals of brands is to create value for their target customers. To this end, brands create three types of customer value: *functional, psychological,* and *monetary.*

Functional Value

Brands can create functional value in two ways: by *identifying* a company offering and by *signaling* specific aspects of the offering's functionality.

- **Identifying the company offerings.** Brands enable customers to identify a company's products and services and distinguish them from those of its competitors. For example, if Tide laundry detergent was not associated with a unique brand, customers would have difficulty locating it and would have to examine the ingredients of many detergents to ensure that the product they purchase is indeed the Tide detergent produced by Procter & Gamble. The identification function of brands is particularly important in the case of commoditized products that are similar in their appearance and performance.

- **Signaling performance.** In addition to identifying the offering, brands can inform customers about the functional performance of the products and services associated with the brand. For example, the Tide brand signals cleaning power, the Crest brand signals effective cavity protection, and the DeWalt brand signals durability. Not only can brands inform customers about the performance of products and services, but in some cases they can also change the way customers experience these products and services. For example, the taste of beer, the scent of perfume, and even the effectiveness of a drug might be influenced by customers' knowledge of their brand names.

Psychological Value

Psychological value is often the key source of the market value created by brands. Indeed, because brands evoke specific associations in a customer's mind, they can convey a wider range of emotions and deeper meaning than the other attributes of the offering. Specifically, the psychological value created by brands stems from three types of benefits: *emotional, self-expressive*, and *societal*.

- **Emotional value.** Brands can create emotional value by evoking an affective response from customers that can involve a wide range of positive emotions. For example, Allstate Insurance Company (*You're in good hands with Allstate*) aims to convey peace of mind with its brand, and Hallmark (*When You Care Enough to Send the Very Best*) evokes the feeling of love and affection.

- **Self-expressive value.** In addition to creating emotional benefits, brands can create self-expressive value by enabling individuals to express their identity. For example, brands like Harley-Davidson, Oakley, and Abercrombie & Fitch stand for different lifestyles, enabling consumers to express their unique personality by displaying these brands. In addition to allowing consumers to express their individuality, brands like Rolls-Royce, Louis Vuitton, and Cartier create psychological value by enabling their customers to highlight their wealth and socioeconomic status.

- **Societal value.** Brands can also create societal value by conveying a sense of moral gratification from contributing to society. For example, brands like TOMS, Product Red, UNICEF, Doctors Without Borders, and Habitat for Humanity that represent humanitarian causes create customer value by taking a stand on relevant social issues and implementing a variety of socially responsible programs.

Monetary Value

In addition to creating functional and psychological value, brands can also create monetary value. Specifically, brands can create two types of monetary benefits: *signaling price* and generating *financial value*.

- **Signaling price.** Brands can signal the overall level of prices associated with the company's products and services. For example, the Walmart brand conveys the idea of low prices, fostering the belief that its offerings are priced lower than its competitors. The price image conveyed by a brand is particularly important when buyers are unaware of the competitiveness of the price of a given offering. In such cases, consumers often rely on the brand to infer the attractiveness of an offering's price.

- **Financial value.** In addition to signaling an offering's monetary value, brands can also carry inherent monetary benefits, which are reflected in the higher price of branded offerings on the secondary market. For example, a Louis Vuitton handbag commands a much higher resale price compared to a functionally equivalent unbranded handbag. In fact, the financial benefit of brands is one of the key factors in valuing alternative investments such as wine, watches, and automobiles.

Not every brand creates all three types of customer value. In fact, some of the positioning strategies implied by the different types of brand value might be mutually exclusive. For example, a brand signaling monetary benefits (e.g., low price) might not be credible in signaling product performance and conveying wealth and social status. In this context, the different types of customer value can serve as a guide to developing a brand's value proposition rather than as a requirement that a brand create value for customers on each of the three dimensions.

Brands as a Means of Creating Company Value

Brands can create company value on two main dimensions: *strategic* and *monetary*. The specific ways in which brands create strategic and monetary value for the company are outlined below.

Strategic Value

The strategic value created by brands reflects the nonmonetary benefits that a company derives from associating its products and services with a given brand. Specifically, brands can *bolster customer demand, amplify the impact of the other marketing tactics, ensure greater collaborator support*, and *facilitate the hiring and retaining of skilled employees*.

- **Bolstering customer demand.** Because brands create customer value, they generate incremental demand for a company's offerings. Thus, a customer who is not interested in an unbranded product might be interested in a branded version of the same product, provided that this customer finds the brand meaningful and relevant. In addition to increasing the attractiveness of the company's offerings, brands might facilitate product/service usage, which often leads to greater repurchase frequency. Offerings associated with an attractive brand are also more likely to encourage customer advocacy, which, in turn, is likely to further promote sales. For example, Zappos, Harley-Davidson, Apple, and Abercrombie & Fitch have a loyal consumer following that helps expand the demand for offerings associated with these brands.

- **Amplifying the impact of other marketing tactics.** In addition to directly bolstering customer demand, brands can increase the effectiveness of the other attributes defining the company's offering. Thus, brands can enhance customer perceptions of product performance by making branded products appear more powerful, reliable, durable, safe, attractive, tasty, or visually appealing than their unbranded counterparts. For example, consumers are likely to think that a drug is more effective if it is associated with a reputable pharmaceutical brand. Furthermore, because brands create incremental customer value, companies tend to charge higher prices for branded products than for unbranded products. For example, Advil-branded ibuprofen is priced significantly higher than the generic version, and Morton-branded salt commands a substantial price premium over the unbranded version. Not only do customers find branded products more attractive and pay extra for them, they are also more willing to search for the branded product across distribution channels and bypass more convenient retailers that do not carry their favorite brand even when a functionally equivalent substitute is readily available. Customers are also likely to react more favorably to incentives and communication from a brand they patronize and ignore those from unbranded products.

- **Ensuring greater collaborator support.** Strong brands can create value for the company by securing greater support from its collaborators. For example, strong brands give manufacturers power over retailers, enabling them to negotiate more advantageous agreements, resulting in a better distribution network and greater promotional support (on-hand inventory, product placement, and sales support). In the same vein, retailers with a strong brand can command greater support and better margins from manufacturers of products that are either unbranded or associated with weak brands.

- **Facilitating the recruiting and retaining of skilled employees.** Employees often place a premium on working for companies whose brands resonate with their own needs, preferences, and value systems. As a result, companies with strong brands find it easier to attract and retain talented employees. Moreover, employees are sometimes ready to sacrifice part of their compensation and accept a lower salary to work for a company with a favorable brand.[19] An additional benefit of brand power is a brand's ability to build, enhance, and sustain the company culture. This is because a brand can create a strong sense of identification among its employees, increase their morale, and bolster their teamwork.

Monetary Value

Along with their strategic benefits, brands can create monetary value for the company by *generating incremental revenues and profits*, *increasing company valuation*, and *creating a separable company asset*.

- **Generating incremental revenues and profits.** A brand's ability to generate incremental demand and command higher prices naturally leads to higher sales revenues and profits. In addition, customers' affinity for a particular brand can enable the company to negotiate better financial terms with its collaborators (e.g., suppliers and distributors), further increasing the company's profit margins.

- **Increasing the valuation of the company.** Brands' ability to generate incremental net income can, in turn, enhance the monetary value of the company, such that companies with strong brands receive higher market valuations. In this context, the monetary value of the brand (brand equity) is determined by the future value of the cash flow that is likely to be generated by the company's brand.

- **Creating a separable company asset.** In addition to contributing to a company's valuation, brands might generate additional value for the company if they are acquired by another entity. Thus, certain brands might have significantly higher value when acquired by another company with better opportunities to unlock the true value of the brand.

Brands as a Means of Creating Collaborator Value

Similar to the ways in which brands create company value, brands create two types of value for collaborators: *strategic* and *monetary*.

- **Strategic value.** The strategic value created by a given brand reflects the nonmonetary benefits that a company's collaborators derive from associating the brand with their offerings. Specifically, partnering with a strong brand can generate incremental demand for collaborators' products and services. For example, collaborating with established airline, hotel, and retail brands can bolster the demand for a bank's credit cards by attracting customers that are loyal to its branding partners. In addition to bolstering customer demand, partnering with a strong brand can strengthen collaborator brands. Thus, cobranding with a well-established and well-liked brand can have a "halo" (spillover) effect, adding credibility to a collaborator that is less known or less relevant.

- **Monetary value.** In addition to strategic value, brands can create monetary value for collaborators by generating incremental revenues and profits. Greater customer demand for company-branded offerings usually leads to higher sales revenues and profits for the company's collaborators. For example, cobranding with Intel (*Intel Inside* campaign) has enabled computer manufacturers to charge higher prices for their products, thus increasing their profit margins. In the same vein, partnering with fashion brands like Chanel, Prada, and Giorgio Armani enables Luxottica, the world's largest eyewear manufacturer, to sell its designer-designated offerings at a premium compared to products sold under its own brand name.

Brand Positioning

To create a meaningful value proposition and brand image, a company must identify the strategically important brand associations and make them primary in target customers' minds. Therefore, in addition to defining the functional, psychological, and monetary value that the brand creates for target customers, the company must develop a clear brand positioning strategy that reflects the company's view of how its target customers should think about the brand.

The term *positioning* is used in reference to both the *process* of creating a meaningful and distinct image in customers' minds, and the *outcome* of the positioning process—the mental image that the company aims to create in customers' minds. The latter meaning of brand positioning is akin to *brand image*, with the key difference that brand positioning is the set of brand associations that the company *aims to create* in its customers' minds, whereas the brand image consists of the brand associations that *actually exist* in a customer's mind. Furthermore, unlike brand image, which is an idiosyncratic representation of the brand in a customer's mind, brand positioning reflects a set of common benefits that the brand aims to create for all target customers. In this context, the brand image reflects the ways in which individual customers internalize the brand's positioning.

The general principles that apply to positioning an offering (discussed in Chapter 5) also apply to positioning the offering's brand. Because the brand is one of the attributes of the company's offering, the positioning of the offering's brand at least partially overlaps with the overall positioning of the offering. At the same time, brands that span product categories usually have a broader positioning than the actual products and services that carry the brand name. For example, the positioning of BMW as the ultimate driving machine is defined by a set of higher level, more general benefits compared to the positioning of the company's individual offerings—including its sedans, coupes, roadsters, sport activity vehicles, and sport wagons. Indeed, while consistent with the positioning of the BMW brand as the ultimate driving machine, the specific BMW vehicles offer different sets of benefits, target different customers, and have different competitors.

Brand Tactics

Brand tactics are the key characteristics defining the brand; they are the tools that the company uses to position the brand and create the desired brand image in customers' minds. Brand tactics are defined by two types of attributes: brand identifiers and brand referents.

Brand identifiers are brand attributes that are created, managed, and owned by the company for the primary purpose of identifying the brand and differentiating it from the competition. Common brand identifiers include brand name, logo, motto, character, soundmark, product design, and packaging. *Brand referents* are brand attributes whose value the company aims to leverage by associating them with its brand name. Unlike brand identifiers, brand referents typically exist independently of the company; they are not created, managed, and owned by the company. Brand referents help create meaningful associations in customers' minds by relating the brand to things that are meaningful to these customers.

The key brand identifiers and brand referents, and their use as brand design elements, are discussed in more detail in the following sections.

Brand Identifiers

Brand identifiers are the brand elements that are developed, managed, and owned by the company. The primary function of brand identifiers, as the name suggests, is to uniquely identify the company's offering and differentiate it from the competition. For example, the Coca-Cola name, logo, and swirling bottle design help differentiate the company's offerings by enabling its customers to easily locate the company's products, which, in turn, enables The Coca-Cola Company and its distributors to capture the revenues generated by these products. In a legal context, brand identifiers are similar to trademarks. The key brand identifiers are the *name, logo, motto, character, soundmark, product design*, and *packaging*.

- The **brand name** is the key brand element that links all other brand elements. The choice of a brand name involves a tradeoff between the ease of communicating the essence of the brand and the degree to which a brand is afforded legal protection.

Descriptive names such as Whole Foods, Wonderful Pistachios, Designer Shoe Warehouse readily communicate the type of offerings associated with the brand and, thus, require fewer resources (time, money, and effort) to establish a meaningful brand image in customers' minds. On the downside, however, from a legal standpoint, descriptive names are the most difficult to protect. Fabricated names such as Google, Kodak, Xerox, and Häagen-Dazs, that involve words that do not have any particular meaning and have been invented for the sole purpose of serving as a brand name, benefit from the greatest degree of legal protection. Because fabricated names are devoid of inherent meaning, however, creating a meaningful brand image in this case is associated with the need to expend significantly more resources.

- **Brand logo** is a sign comprising a unique combination of letters, fonts, shapes, colors, and/or symbols that aim to visually identify the brand. The choice of the logo elements is important because in addition to differentiating the brand they can also help convey a particular meaning. Thus, Coca-Cola's red color might be perceived to be more energetic compared to the more peaceful brown color featured by UPS. Similarly, fonts used by Disney in different movie franchises are more playful, whereas fonts used by FedEx, UPS, and DHL are more serious. In the same vein, the Rock of Gibraltar in Prudential's logo symbolizes financial stability, the lion in ING's logo conveys financial strength, and the crown in the Rolex logo symbolizes prestige and achievement.

- The **brand motto** is a phrase that identifies the brand by articulating the brand's positioning to its target customers. The choice of the brand motto is important because it directly relates the essence of the brand to its customers. To be effective, the motto must articulate the brand mantra for its target customers in a way that identifies the brand, differentiates it from the competition, and creates unique customer value. The choice of the specific motto is determined by the overall positioning of the brand and the image it aims to establish in customers' minds.

- The **brand character** is a fictional personality that embodies the essence of the brand. Popular brand characters include the Michelin Man, Johnnie Walker, and Mr. Peanut. Brand characters are especially important for commoditized products and services where the actual differences between the competitive market offerings are not well pronounced. A character's personality can add a deeper meaning to the brand and succinctly express more complex values, ideas, and emotions than can be communicated by words and graphics. In addition, customers (especially children) often find it easier to establish a meaningful connection with brand characters, especially when the brand characters are anthropomorphized and have a distinct personality. For example, brand characters such as Tony the Tiger, Betty Crocker, and the Nesquik Bunny create value by humanizing the company's offering and establishing an emotional connection between the brand and its target customers. Finally, because they are vivid, rich in imagery, and memorable, characters can help brands break through communication clutter and create a distinct image in customers' minds.

- The **brand soundmark** uses sound to identify a particular brand. Soundmarks help increase brand recognition, establish an emotional connection with a brand, enhance the brand meaning, and foster brand engagement. Common types of soundmarks include tune (e.g., Intel's chime), music (e.g., James Bond theme song), and jingle (e.g., McDonald's *I'm Lovin' It*). Soundmarks introduce another dimension on which a company can identify its offering(s), differentiate them from the competition, and create distinct market value. The importance of soundmarks in creating a relevant and memorable brand is heightened by the fact that different sensory modalities (e.g., sound and vision) tend to work together to strengthen the overall brand image.

- **Packaging** can serve as a brand identifier by associating an offering with a particular brand. Packaging elements that commonly play the role of brand identifiers include shape, color, graphics, and text. Individual packaging elements need not be unique to serve as brand identifiers; however, the combination of elements (the overall look and feel) must enable customers to identify the brand. Examples of product packaging that serves as a brand identifier include Coca-Cola's swirl bottle, the Heinz octagonal ketchup bottle, Grey Goose's frosted glass bottle with a silhouette of flying geese, Red Bull's packaging with the words "Red Bull" in a red font placed centrally between the blue and silver trapezoids, and Tiffany's robin's-egg blue box wrapped with a white bow.

- **Product design** can serve as a brand identifier when it indicates the source of the product and distinguishes it from products offered by others. Product design elements that commonly play the role of brand identifiers include shape, color, flavor, texture, scent, and sound. Examples of product design that serves as a brand identifier include the design of the Hermès Birkin bag, the pink color of Owens Corning fiberglass insulation, the shape of the Volkswagen Beetle, the shape and color of the bright-orange Goldfish crackers by Pepperidge Farm, the pale-blue color and diamond shape of Pfizer's drug Viagra, the taste and texture of Oreo cookies, the fragrance of Chanel N° 5 perfume, and the red soles of Christian Louboutin shoes.

Brand Referents

Brand referents are the brand elements whose value the company aims to leverage by linking them to its brand name. For example, BMW associates its brand with referents such as performance, driving experience, luxury, precision engineering, adventure, and Germany; Starbucks associates its brand with referents such as coffee, espresso, custom-crafted drinks, great taste, friendly service, and social impact; and Apple associates its brand with innovation, style, creativity, functionality, and ease of use.

Brand referents are similar to brand identifiers in that they aim to create a set of meaningful associations in people's minds. However, unlike brand identifiers, which are owned and managed by the company, brand referents exist independently of the company. Furthermore, unlike brand identifiers whose primary function is to identify the company's offering, brand referents typically do not uniquely identify the company's offerings. For example, although *coffee* is a brand referent for Starbucks, it also is used by other coffee chains such as Peet's Coffee, Seattle's Best Coffee, Tim Hortons, Costa Coffee, and Lavazza. Rather than uniquely identifying a company's products and services, the primary function of brand referents is to enhance the value of the brand by "borrowing" the meaning associated with the referents. Thus, using relevant brand referents enables the company to shape the image of the brand in customers' minds.

Brand referents can be thought of as nodes in the network of associations defining the image of a given brand in customers' minds. To illustrate, in the Starbucks map depicted in Figure 2 earlier in this chapter, *indulgence, energy, convenience,* and *self-identity* illustrate the needs the company seeks to fulfill and the benefits customers expect to receive from the brand; *great service, friendly, fast, consistent experience,* and *perfect taste* describe brand-specific experiences; *morning* and *my ritual* define the usage occasions typically associated with the brand; *nearby* reflects the place where the brand is usually consumed; and *coffee* defines the relevant product category. In the Apple map, *entertainment, music-on-the-go, connectivity, stylish,* and *sleek design* depict the need fulfillment and the benefits customers expect to receive from the brand; *different, innovative,* and *creative* are brand-related concepts representing abstract ideas and general notions; *easy-to-use* and *easy-to-learn* describe the brand-specific experience; *phone* and *tablet* define the product categories associated with the brand; and *Mac, iPhone, iPad, iPod, iTunes,* and *Microsoft* are the brands associated with the Apple brand.

The choice of brand referents is important because they help customers form brand associations by linking the brand name with important mental constructs—needs, benefits, experiences, occasions, activities, places, people, concepts, objects, products and services, and other brands—that are meaningful to target customers. To ingrain their brands in customers' minds and make these brands more relevant, companies use multiple referents, each designed to create a distinct and meaningful brand association. Because brand referents (together with brand identifiers) are the tools a company uses to create a favorable brand image, the individual brand elements must converge in a way that leads to a consistent and meaningful value proposition and positioning.

Managing Brand Portfolios

As companies grow, they expand their offerings to appeal to a broader range of customers. As a result, an important decision facing a company is whether its new offerings should be associated with the same brand or use different brands. There are three core approaches to building brand portfolios: *single-brand strategy*, *multi-brand strategy*, and *cobranding strategy*.

Single-Brand Strategy

Single-brand strategy (also referred to as *umbrella branding* or *branded house*) involves using the same brand across a variety of diverse offerings. For example, BMW, Mercedes, GE, Heinz, and FedEx use a single brand for nearly all their products and services. In this case, the individual offerings are differentiated by generic designators rather than brands. For example, Mercedes uses letters, BMW uses numbers, and GE combines the GE brand with common words such as aviation, healthcare, power, oil and gas, and transportation to reference the individual offerings in their company portfolios. In addition to using the same brand name, a more subtle form of the single-brand strategy involves using names with the same prefix to highlight the commonality across individual brands. For example, Nescafé, Nesquik, Nestea, and Nespresso are used by Nestlé to brand different beverages.

The single-brand strategy has a number of important advantages: It leverages the equity of an existing brand, benefiting from the instant recognition of this brand while avoiding the costs associated with building a new brand. Using a single brand can also strengthen the brand by increasing its visibility across product categories and purchase occasions.

Despite its advantages, the single-brand strategy has several drawbacks. One such drawback is that the single-brand strategy makes it difficult to establish a meaningful brand image across a broad set of product categories and purchase occasions. For example, Bic faced challenges when it tried to use its brand—primarily known for ballpoint pens, cigarette lighters, and disposable razors—in product categories such as perfume and underwear. Using a single brand also carries the risk of a spillover of negative information across brands, whereby poor performance by any product in the brand portfolio can hurt the reputation of the entire brand. Furthermore, using a single brand does not take advantage of the opportunity to build a new brand, thus creating a separable company asset that can increase the value of the company.

Multi-Brand Strategy

Multi-brand strategy (also referred to as a *house of brands*) involves using separate brands for different products and/or product lines. For example, Tide, Ariel, Cheer, Bold, and Era are individual brands of laundry detergent managed by Procter & Gamble, which also owns a variety of brands across different product categories, including Charmin, Bounty, Old Spice, Pampers, Luvs, Gillette, Crest, and Pantene. Diageo manages dozens of alcoholic beverage brands including Smirnoff, Tanqueray, Johnnie Walker, José Cuervo, Baileys, Hennessy, Guinness, Dom Pérignon, and Moët & Chandon. Yum! Brands owns KFC, Pizza Hut, and Taco Bell.

The multi-brand portfolio strategy has a number of important advantages. Using multiple brands enables a company to establish a unique brand identity for different product categories and purchase occasions—a strategy particularly relevant when targeting diverse customer segments across different product categories. Using multiple brands also limits the possibility of a spillover of negative information about a specific brand to other brands in a company's portfolio. A portfolio of unique brands also has greater market value because each brand represents a distinct company asset that has its own valuation and, if needed, can be divested.

Despite its advantages, the multi-brand strategy has several drawbacks. Because each brand has its own identity and is designed to create unique value for its target customers, creating a portfolio of distinct brands involves substantial financial and managerial resources. Furthermore, the multi-brand strategy does not capitalize on the breadth of the company's portfolio of offerings to enhance brand visibility and impact. Another downside is that for a brand to have a relevant and meaningful image in customers' minds, it must be internalized by customers and related to a particular set of needs, values, and purchase occasions—a process that can take years and even decades.

Cobranding Strategy

Cobranding involves using two (or more) of the company's brands, with one of the brands typically serving as an umbrella brand. Cobranding can involve one of two core strategies: *sub-branding* and *endorsement branding*.

- **Sub-branding** combines an umbrella brand with a lower tier brand in a way that underscores the umbrella brand. Sub-branding is very common among car manufacturers. For example, Jeep Cherokee, Jeep Renegade, and Jeep Wrangler are sub-brands of Jeep, which serves as the anchor brand. In the same vein, Dodge sub-brands—Dodge Charger, Dodge Durango, and Dodge Viper—underscore the parent brand.

- **Endorsement branding** combines an umbrella brand with a lower tier brand in a way that underscores the lower tier brand, with the umbrella brand playing a secondary role. For example, Courtyard by Marriott, Residence Inn by Marriott, and

SpringHill Suites by Marriott showcase the individual brands, with the Marriott umbrella brand used to support the focal brand. In the same vein, Kit Kat, Carnation, Toll House, and Coffee-mate are free-standing brands, all of which also feature the Nestlé brand that serves as an endorser.

Cobranding is often viewed as the middle ground between single-brand and multi-brand portfolio strategies. As such, it combines the benefits of these two strategies: single branding's cost efficiency and multi-branding's ability to create a unique brand identity tailored to different needs and purchase occasions.

Despite its advantages, cobranding has several important drawbacks. Compared to the single-brand strategy, cobranding involves building individual brands, which can involve significant financial and managerial resources. Furthermore, associating the same umbrella brand with different brands can make it more difficult for these brands to establish their own unique identity. Cobranding can also facilitate a spillover of negative information across brands, whereby negative information associated with one brand can spread to other brands (although spillover is less likely compared to the single-brand strategy).

Choosing a Brand-Portfolio Strategy

A company's options when designing its brand portfolio can be viewed as a continuum on which different strategies—single-brand, new sub-brand, new endorsed brand, and independent new brand—are arranged based on the degree to which offerings in the company's product portfolio share the same brand (Figure 3).

Figure 3. Single-Brand, Cobranding, and Multi-Brand Portfolio Strategies

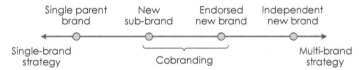

Because each brand-portfolio strategy has its pros and cons, the choice of a specific branding strategy is driven by the overarching goal the company aims to achieve with its products, services, and brands. Thus, the single-brand strategy is more common for companies that operate within a single industry and, hence, are less likely to benefit from having brands with distinct identities and meanings. In contrast, companies with product and service portfolios that span diverse categories are more likely to benefit from having multiple brands, with each brand tailored to specific customer needs.

The single-brand strategy is also more likely to be used by companies whose expertise is in domains other than brand building, such as technology development and product design. In contrast, the multi-brand strategy is more common for companies with brand-building expertise that understand the value created by brands and have the resources to build new brands in an effective and cost-efficient manner. The multi-brand strategy is also more common for consumer companies that cater to diverse customer segments and less common for industrial companies that often use a single brand to differentiate their offerings.

The cobranding strategy offers a compromise between having to invest time, money, and effort to build a new brand from scratch, and the limitation of being constrained by the meaning contained in a single brand. As a result many companies are using cobranding—

sub-branding or endorsement branding—as a way to build on the strength of their existing brands, while at the same time enabling these companies to develop unique identifiers and meanings to differentiate their products and services.

Brand Dynamics

Once created, brands don't stay still; they evolve over time as markets change. Thus, changes in customer needs, strategies adopted by competing brands, and goals that the company aims to achieve with its brand serve as the impetus for managers to modify their brands. There are two common ways in which managers can modify their brands: *extending the brand*, which involves broadening the set of offerings associated with the brand, and *repositioning the brand*, which involves changes to the identity and meaning of a company's brand.

Extending the Brand

Extending the brand involves using an existing brand in a different context, such as a different product category or a different price tier. For example, when launching an ice cream product line, Starbucks used its current brand, thus extending the meaning of the brand beyond coffee to include frozen packaged goods sold in traditional grocery stores. Depending on whether the newly added products are substantively different in functionality or price, there are two types of brand extensions: *vertical* and *horizontal*.

Vertical Brand Extensions

Vertical brand extensions stretch the brand to a product or service in a different price tier. Depending on the direction in which the brand is being extended, there are two types of brand extensions: upscale extensions in which the brand is associated with an offering in a higher price tier, and downscale extensions in which the brand is associated with an offering in a lower price tier (Figure 4).

Figure 4. Vertical Brand Extensions

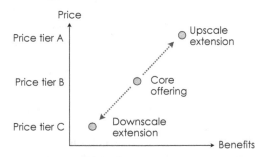

Upscale brand extensions associate an existing brand with offerings in a higher price tier with which the brand is not currently associated. For example, Apple extended its product line with the Apple Watch Edition series featuring 18-karat gold and priced between $10,000 and $17,000. Volkswagen introduced Volkswagen Phaeton, a luxury car with prices starting at around $70,000 and extending as high as $100,000. E. & J. Gallo Winery introduced its Gallo Signature Series collection of premium wines priced significantly higher than its mainstream wines.

Upscale brand extensions are appealing to companies for several reasons. The first and perhaps most obvious reason is that using an existing brand is much easier and more cost effective than building a new brand. Another factor adding to the appeal of upscale brand extensions is that they can help raise the image of the core brand. For example, adding the Watch Edition series underscores Apple's positioning as a self-expressive luxury brand—an important aspect of Apple's brand image in many developing countries. In the same vein, introducing Phaeton helped Volkswagen raise its brand image, and adding the Signature Series wines helped E. & J. Gallo Winery enhance the image of its core Gallo brand.

Despite their benefits, upscale brand extensions have important drawbacks. The key disadvantage of extending a brand upwards is that the existing brand associations tend to hurt rather than help the upscale extension. For example, adding the Gallo brand to a premium wine might make it less attractive to consumers who associate the Gallo brand with more affordable wine. In the same vein, one of the key reasons for Phaeton's commercial failure was that it was branded as a Volkswagen; consumers did not want to pay $80,000 for a car prominently featuring the VW logo and sold in Volkswagen dealerships. Because of these limitations, successful upscale brand extensions are rare.

Downscale brand extensions use an existing brand for offerings in a lower price tier with which the brand is not currently associated. For example, Mercedes-Benz introduced its Mercedes-branded A-Class, which was significantly more affordable than its core product line. In the same vein, BMW extended its product line downscale by introducing the BMW 1-Series, Porsche launched its entry-level Porsche Boxster, and Giorgio Armani introduced a more affordable version of its offerings with Armani Exchange.

Downscale brand extensions offer a number of important benefits. First, they enable a company to leverage an established brand name to new offerings without investing the time and resources needed to build a new brand. In addition, unlike upscale brand extensions, where the core brand often is a liability, for downscale extensions, the core brand is an asset that adds value to the new offering. Downscale extensions further benefit the company by introducing its brand to target customers who currently might not be able to afford the brand's higher end offerings but are likely to be able to do so in the future. For example, high-end retailer Neiman Marcus and upscale fashion designers including Carolina Herrera, Marc Jacobs, and Oscar de la Renta have partnered with Target to develop an entry-level luxury collection to attract younger, less affluent consumers who in the future might become customers of their pricier fashions.

On the downside, downscale brand extensions face several important challenges. Associating an upscale brand with an affordable product can hurt the brand image. For example, Jaguar's brand image was negatively influenced by the launch of its entry-level X-Type sedan, which was built on a Ford platform and used many components from Ford's mainstream vehicles. Another drawback of downscale brand extensions is that they can increase the likelihood of product line cannibalization, whereby the sales of the downscale offering come at the expense of the company's higher priced offerings. For example, instead of buying higher end Mercedes, BMW, or Audi models, customers might purchase their lower end models while still receiving the benefit of being associated with a premium brand. Because the lower end models also tend to have lower profit margins, product line cannibalization associated with downscale brand extensions is usually detrimental to company profitability.

Horizontal Brand Extensions

Horizontal brand extensions involve using a brand in a product category with which it is not currently associated (Figure 5). For example, Armani extended its brand from clothing to home furnishings, such as bedding and towels, and even to hotels; Timberland extended its brand from boots to outerwear and travel gear; Porsche extended its brand from sports cars to sedans and sport utility vehicles; and Yamaha extended its brand from musical instruments to multiple categories including audio equipment, golf products, and motorcycles.

Figure 5. Horizontal Brand Extensions

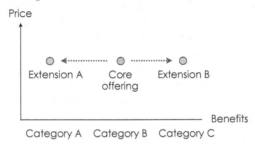

Horizontal brand extensions offer several important benefits to companies. Similar to vertical extensions, they use an existing brand to launch an offering—an approach that is much more cost efficient and involves less time and effort compared to building a new brand. For example, Crest leveraged its reputation in dental care to extend its brand to teeth whitening with the launch of Crest Whitestrips. Horizontal brand extensions also enable a company to leverage the power of its core brand by adding value to newly launched offerings. Unlike downscale extensions, which enable customers to purchase less expensive offerings carrying the same brand name, horizontal extensions offer different functionality that might complement rather than substitute for the brand's core offerings.

Horizontal brand extensions—such as different beverage flavors—also help fulfill the variety-seeking needs of customers without their having to leave the brand family. Presence in different product categories helps increase a brand's visibility across a variety of usage occasions and attain greater prominence in retail stores. For example, Montblanc, Ralph Lauren, Armani, and Oakley have benefited from cross-category availability because they offer more opportunities for customers to express their identity with their brands.

Despite their advantages, horizontal brand extensions have important drawbacks. A key concern with horizontal brand extensions is brand dilution, which can occur when a brand is extended to diverse product categories. For example, extending the Starbucks brand to non-coffee products that include ice cream, craft beer, wine, and small food plates might detract from its perceived coffee-related expertise. In addition to diluting the image of the core brand, brand extensions might detract from rather than add value to the new offering. For example, Colgate-Palmolive launched ready-to-eat meals branded as *Colgate Kitchen Entrees*, even though the Colgate brand was strongly associated with toothpaste rather than food.

Repositioning the Brand

Repositioning a brand involves changing the brand strategy—its target customers and/or its value proposition. For example, Philip Morris' flagship brand, Marlboro, originally introduced in 1924 as a women's cigarette tagged *Mild as May*, in 1954 was repositioned around the rugged cowboy image of the Marlboro Man, which was more relevant to male smokers. Target, which in the '90s was seen as just another discount retailer selling average-quality products at low prices, repositioned its brand to focus on value-priced designer apparel and merchandise, and, in the process, became the second-largest value retailer in the United States, after Walmart. Pabst Blue Ribbon, once considered a working-class beer, repositioned itself to appeal to a new customer segment and become the beer of choice for hipsters, college students, and millennials.

Brand repositioning is distinct from brand extension in that brand extension involves associating the brand with new products and/or services that previously were not associated with it. In contrast, brand repositioning involves a change in the meaning of the brand without necessarily changing its scope by adding new products and/or services. Whereas brand extension typically aims to preserve the meaning of the brand and expand it to a broader range of offerings, brand repositioning aims to change the meaning of the brand.[20]

A common reason for repositioning a brand is to ensure that it remains relevant to the changing needs of its target customers. For example, to increase its appeal to younger customers, Procter & Gamble repositioned its half-century-old beauty brand, Oil of Olay, by abbreviating the name to Olay (to avoid associations equating oil to "greasy"), streamlining the design of its logo, and replacing the woman's image (which resembled a nun) on the label with that of a younger woman. In the same vein, to reverse the decline in market share and attract new customers, Procter & Gamble repositioned Old Spice from a stale baby boomer brand to a contemporary male grooming brand for younger consumers.

Brand repositioning, although common, is not the only option to better align the meaning of the brand with the current market realities. Rather than reposition a brand—a process that involves a major change in its value proposition—a company might choose to make more subtle changes to the brand's value proposition. These changes, dubbed *brand revitalization*, typically involve relatively minor changes in the brand tactics, such as refreshing the brand logo, modifying the brand motto, and replacing the brand spokesperson. Unlike brand repositioning, however, brand revitalization involves changes that concern the peripheral aspects of the brand while leaving its core value proposition intact.

Brand Valuation

There are several reasons why a company can benefit from having an accurate estimate of the value of its brands. Knowing the monetary value of a brand is important in *mergers and acquisitions* to determine the premium over the book value of the company that a buyer should pay. Knowing the monetary value of its brand(s) is also important in order to determine the value of the entire company for *stock valuation* purposes. Brand valuation is also important in *licensing* to determine the price premium that brand owners should receive from licensees for the right to use their brand. Having an accurate estimate of the value of the brand also matters in *litigation* cases involving damages to the brand to determine the appropriate magnitude of monetary compensation. Assessing brand equity is also important for evaluating the *effectiveness* of a company's brand-building activities and for cost-benefit analysis when deciding on the allocation of resources across brands in a company's portfolio.

For a company to succeed in building strong brands, it must have a clear understanding of how the brand creates market value, as well as the metrics and processes for assessing the value of the brand. The two aspects of brand value—*brand equity* and *brand power*—are outlined in more detail in the following sections.

Brand Equity as a Marketing Concept

Brand equity is the monetary value of the brand. It is the premium that is placed on a company's valuation because of brand ownership. The monetary value of a brand is reflected in the financial returns that the brand will generate over its lifetime. Understanding the concept of brand equity, managing its antecedents and consequences, and developing methodologies to measure brand equity are of utmost importance for ensuring a company's financial well-being.

For years, companies spent millions of dollars on brand building without established accounting procedures to assess the value of the brands they created. The issue of brand valuation came into prominence in the 1980s when the wave of mergers and acquisitions, including the $25 billion buyout of RJR Nabisco, served as a natural catalyst for the increased interest in brand valuation and the development of more accurate brand valuation methodologies. Because the value of the brands owned by a company is not reflected in its books,[21] setting a fair price for brand assets that a firm has built over time is of utmost importance, especially given the fact that the value of a company's brands could exceed its tangible assets.

Brand equity is a part of goodwill, an accounting term referring to the monetary value of all intangible assets of a company. Goodwill is a way to document that—in addition to tangible assets such as property, plants, materials, and investments—a company's assets also include an intangible component comprising brands, patents, copyrights, know-how, licenses, distribution arrangements, company culture, and management practices. Thus, goodwill is much broader than brand equity and includes not only the value of the company's brand, but also the value of the company's other intangible assets.

Goodwill is recorded on a company's books when it acquires another entity and pays a premium over the listed book value of assets. For example, if a company pays $1 billion to acquire another company with book assets of $500 million, the other $500 million would be recorded in the books of the acquirer as goodwill. One of the reasons for the discrepancy between the book value and the market value of a brand is that acquired brands are recognized as assets for tax and accounting purposes, whereas internally generated brands are not.[22] Thus, a company that has built a brand from scratch cannot recognize it as an asset in its financial statements because it developed these brands internally and charged the related costs to expenses. In this context, goodwill is a way to recognize the market value of a brand when it is acquired.

Brand Power as a Marketing Concept

Unlike brand equity, which reflects the monetary value of the brand to the company, brand power reflects the brand's ability to influence the behavior of the relevant market entities—target customers, company collaborators, and company employees. Thus, brand power reflects the difference in the ways customers, collaborators, and company employees respond to the brand. For example, if knowledge that an offering is associated with a particular brand makes it more likely that customers will buy this offering, the brand has power. On the other hand, if brand knowledge has no impact on customers' response, the brand is lacking in power and the company's offering is effectively a commodity.

The relationship between brand power and brand equity is depicted in Figure 6. A company's branding activities facilitate the formation of a brand image in customers' minds. Based on the value it creates for target customers, this brand image influences customer behavior by increasing the likelihood that customers will buy, use, and endorse the branded offering, thus creating value for the company. In this context, brand power is a brand's ability to influence customers' behavior, and brand equity is the monetary value that this change in behavior creates for the company. Thus, the key driver of brand power is the brand image, which reflects all beliefs, values, emotions, and behaviors customers associate with the brand. To build a powerful brand, a company must focus its activities on creating a meaningful brand image in customers' minds that can influence their behavior in a way that creates value for the company.

Figure 6. Brand Power and Brand Equity

In addition to influencing customer behavior, brand power benefits the company by influencing the behavior of its collaborators and employees. Thus, brand power benefits the company by increasing the likelihood that target customers will purchase the branded offering, will use it frequently, and will be more likely to endorse this offering. Greater brand power also influences collaborators' behavior by increasing their willingness to work with the company. In addition, brand power helps the company attract a skilled workforce while enhancing employee loyalty and productivity.

Aligning Brand Power and Brand Equity

Greater brand power does not automatically lead to greater brand equity. For example, the brand equity of Nissan is estimated to be higher than the brand equity of Porsche even though Porsche is a stronger brand, as reflected in its greater price premium compared to Nissan. Likewise, even though Armani and Moët & Chandon have greater brand power than Gap and McDonald's, the brand equity of the latter is estimated to be higher.[23]

Because brand equity is a function of brand power as well as a company's ability to utilize this power in a given market, brand equity is not always a perfect indicator of brand power. Instead, brand equity reflects the degree to which the company is able to utilize the power of the brand. Brand power, in turn, is determined by the company's strategy and tactics as well as the impact of the various market forces: customer needs; competitor and collaborator actions; and the economic, technological, sociocultural, regulatory, and physical context in which the company operates.

Because brand power and brand equity are not perfectly correlated, it is possible to identify instances in which a brand's power exceeds its monetary value, as well as instances in which a brand's monetary valuation is overstated relative to the brand's power. A brand is undervalued when its brand equity does not take into account the full market potential of the power of this brand. In contrast, a brand is overvalued when its equity overstates the underlying brand power. From a marketing perspective, brands whose brand equity is undervalued, meaning that their brand power is not fully monetized by the company, present brand-building opportunities. From a financial perspective, undervalued brands present acquisition opportunities for companies that can unleash the hidden power of these brands.

SUMMARY

Brand management is a process of designing and sustaining a mental image in people's minds that enables the company to identify its products and services, differentiate them from the competition, and create distinct market value.

Brands create functional, psychological, and monetary *customer value*. Brands create functional value by enabling customers to identify a company's offering and by signaling the offerings' functionality. Brands create psychological value by offering emotional, self-expressive, and societal benefits to its customers. Brands create monetary value by signaling the offerings' monetary cost and enhancing the financial value of the offering.

Brands create strategic and monetary *company and collaborator value*. Brands create strategic value for the company by bolstering customer demand, amplifying the impact of the other marketing tactics, ensuring greater collaborator support, and facilitating the hiring and retaining of skilled employees. Brands create monetary value for the company by generating incremental revenues and profits, increasing the valuation of the company, and creating a separable company asset. In addition, brands create value for the company's collaborators by strengthening collaborators' own brands as well as by generating incremental demand, revenues, and profits.

To create market value, a brand must establish a meaningful and distinct image in target customers' minds—a process referred to as *brand positioning*.

Brand attributes are the tools that the company uses to position the brand and create the desired brand image in customers' minds. Brand building involves two types of attributes: *brand identifiers*, which are owned and managed by the company, and *brand referents*, which are not owned by the company but whose value the company aims to leverage by linking them to its brand name. The key brand identifiers are the name, logo, motto, character, soundmark, product design, and packaging. Common brand referents include needs, benefits, experiences, occasions, activities, places, people, concepts, objects, products and services, and other brands.

Building *brand portfolios* involves one of three core strategies. The *single-brand strategy* involves using the same brand across diverse offerings. The *multi-brand strategy* involves using separate brands for different products and product lines. *Cobranding* involves using two (or more) of the company's brands, with one of the brands typically serving as an umbrella brand. Cobranding can involve sub-branding, which underscores the umbrella brand, and endorsement branding, in which the umbrella brand plays a secondary role.

Brand extension involves using an existing brand name in a different context, such as a different product category or a different price tier. *Vertical brand extensions* stretch the brand to a product or service in a different price tier. Upscale extensions associate the brand with an offering in a higher price tier, whereas downscale extensions associate the brand with an offering in a lower price tier. *Horizontal brand extensions* stretch the brand to a category with which it is not currently associated.

Brand repositioning involves changing the meaning of the brand—without extending the brand to unrelated product categories.

Brand valuation involves assessing brand equity and brand power. *Brand equity* is the monetary value of the brand: It reflects the financial returns that the brand will generate over its lifetime. Brand equity stems from *brand power*, which is the brand's ability to influence the behavior of the relevant market entities—target customers, collaborators, and company employees. A brand is undervalued when its brand equity does not take into account its full market potential. In contrast, a brand is overvalued when its equity overstates the underlying brand power.

CHAPTER TEN

MANAGING PRICE

Price is what you pay. Value is what you get.
— Warren Buffett, American investor and philanthropist

Pricing directly influences the monetary value that the offering creates for target customers, the company, and its collaborators. Setting the right price enables the company to capture market value and achieve its monetary and strategic goals. Even though setting the perfect price cannot guarantee success, erroneous pricing can lead to a failure in the marketplace. The key aspects of price management are the focus of this chapter.

Pricing as a Value-Creation Process

Many companies do not think strategically about pricing. Instead, they consider pricing merely as a means to achieve a certain level of profits based on costs incurred in developing, manufacturing, and promoting their offerings, while taking into account the prices of competitive offerings. This approach lacks a clear understanding of pricing as an important attribute of their offering, which, in concert with the other offering attributes, can create superior value for target customers, the company, and its collaborators. The role of price as a tool for creating market value and the key factors that a company must consider when setting a price are discussed in the following sections.

Price as a Tool for Creating Market Value

The price is the amount of money the company charges its customers and collaborators for the benefits provided by the offering. Pricing is an important marketing decision that influences the value created by an offering for its customers, collaborators, and the company. From a customer's perspective, the price is a key factor in defining the offering. In fact, the price–quality tradeoff (giving up product benefits in order to pay less or vice versa) is one of the most important decisions that customers weigh when making a choice. Furthermore, because prices are readily observable, customers often rely on prices to infer the offering's performance on unobservable attributes such as durability, reliability, as well as overall quality.

In addition to playing a key role in influencing customer choice, pricing also plays an important role in creating value for the company. Price is the only attribute defining the company's offering that directly creates revenues for the company; all other offering attributes—product, service, brand, incentives, communication, and distribution—incur costs. Because of their direct impact on a company's bottom line, pricing decisions can make or break the company's financial performance. Finally, an offering's price defines the value of an offering to the company's collaborators by determining the monetary benefits and costs created by this offering.

Because of its direct impact on the monetary value it creates for customers, the company, and collaborators, setting the price is an integral aspect of defining the value of the offering. As one of the seven attributes defining the market offering, price works in tandem with the other marketing tactics to create an optimal value proposition (OVP). In this context, the optimal price complements the offering's product, service, brand, incentives, communication, and distribution aspects to create superior value for target customers in a way that benefits the company and its collaborators (Figure 1).

Figure 1. Pricing as a Value-Creation Process

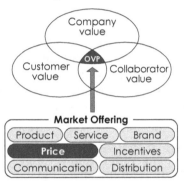

Despite the fundamental role price plays in designing and managing a company's offerings, there is little consensus on what constitutes the optimal pricing strategy. Although pricing approaches vary, successful pricing strategies share an understanding that the pricing decision should not be made in isolation but must be treated as an integral component of the offering's strategy and tactics. Accordingly, setting the optimal price is driven by a variety of considerations, including the company's strategic goals, customers' price elasticity, and the psychological aspects of customers' response to the offering's price. The role of these factors in setting the optimal price is discussed in more detail in the following sections.

Key Factors in Setting the Price

When setting the price, managers must consider two types of factors: *strategic factors* that address the market in which the company's offering aims to create value and *tactical factors* that address the ways in which price interacts with the other marketing tactics—product, service, brand, incentives, communication, and distribution—to create market value. These two types of factors are outlined in more detail below.

Strategic Factors Influencing the Price

The Five Cs—customers, company, collaborators, competitors, and context—are of strategic importance in setting and managing prices. Thus, price is a function of customers' willingness to pay for the offering's benefits, such that greater willingness to pay typically translates into higher prices. Pricing is also a function of the company's goals and cost structure, whereby aggressive sales goals and lower cost structure often result in lower prices. In addition, pricing is influenced by the company's collaborators (e.g., channel partners), such that more powerful channels (e.g., Walmart, Costco, and Carrefour) require lower prices. Because most purchase decisions involve choosing between competing offerings, an offering's price is also influenced by competitors' prices. Moreover, pricing is a function of various economic, technological, sociocultural, regulatory, and physical factors of the environment in which the company operates.

Optimal pricing policies take into account all five of the above factors. Yet, for a variety of reasons—simplicity, lack of relevant data, or mere ignorance of the market forces—some companies use simplified pricing approaches that rely on a single factor. For example, *demand pricing* sets prices based on customers' willingness to pay for the benefits afforded by the company's offering, *cost-plus pricing* and *markup pricing* add a premium to the cost of the product, and *competitive pricing* uses competitors' prices as benchmarks. While each of these methods has merit, taking into account only a subset of factors that could potentially influence the market value created by an offering provides a limited understanding of the market forces and often leads to suboptimal pricing policies.

Tactical Factors Influencing the Price

In addition to being a function of the Five Cs, price is also influenced by the other marketing tactics: product and service characteristics, brand, incentives, communication, and distribution. Thus, attractive and unique products and services command higher prices compared to less differentiated offerings. Price is also a function of the offering's brand, with strong brands commanding substantial price premiums over weaker brands and unbranded offerings, even when the actual quality of the offering is the same.

In addition to the product, service, and brand aspects of the offering, pricing depends on the available incentives (e.g., promotional allowances, price discounts, and coupons), which determine the final amount buyers pay for an offering. Price can also be influenced by a company's communication and set in a way that facilitates communication. For example, Subway's pricing was in part driven by its ability to create a memorable advertising campaign promoting $5 footlong sandwiches. An offering's price is also a function of its distribution, such that channels with a lower cost structure are able to offer lower prices.

Setting the Price to Create Customer Value

A key criterion when setting the price is to ensure that the company's offering can create value for its target customers, meaning that the benefits customers receive from the offering correspond to its price. To this end, a manager must know how to assess customers' price elasticity, understand how to use price as a segmentation and targeting tool, and recognize the importance of the psychological aspects of pricing.

Understanding Price Elasticity

To set the optimal price, a manager must understand the relationship between the offering's price and customer demand for that offering. Typically, sales volume is inversely related to price: Lowering the price results in an increase in the sales volume, and vice versa. The degree to which changing the price influences sales volume is referred to as *price elasticity*. Lowering the price in order to increase volume is most effective in cases where demand is elastic, meaning that a small change in price leads to a large change in sales volume. In contrast, in cases where demand is inelastic, profits might often be increased by raising the price because the decrease in sales volume resulting from the change in price is likely to be relatively small.

To illustrate, consider the price–quantity relationship illustrated in Figure 2, which depicts the impact of a price drop on purchase quantity for two products associated with different price elasticity. Even though for both products the change in price is identical — a price drop from $15 to $10 — the impact of this price drop on consumer demand is not the same. For the product with inelastic demand, the quantity sold increased from 20 to 25 units, whereas for the product with elastic demand, the quantity sold increased from 20 to 50 units. In this way, elasticity determines the impact that a change in price will have on sales of a product.

Figure 2. The Price Elasticity of Demand

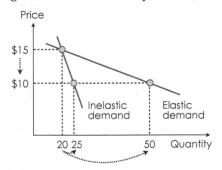

Price elasticity is quantified as the percentage change in quantity sold ($\Delta Q\%$) relative to the percentage change in price ($\Delta P\%$) for a given product or service. Because in most cases the quantity demanded decreases when the price increases, this ratio is negative; however, for practical purposes, the absolute value of the ratio is used, and price elasticity is often reported as a positive number.

$$E_p = \frac{\Delta Q\%}{\Delta P\%} = \frac{\Delta Q \cdot P}{\Delta P \cdot Q}$$

To illustrate, a price elasticity of 2 means that a 5% price increase will result in a 10% decrease in the quantity sold. In cases where (the absolute value of) price elasticity is greater than 1, demand is said to be elastic, meaning that a percentage change in price causes a larger percentage change in quantity demanded. In contrast, when (the absolute value of) price elasticity is less than 1, demand is said to be inelastic, meaning that a percentage change in price results in a smaller percentage change in quantity demanded. When (the absolute value of) price elasticity is equal to 1, demand is said to be unitary, meaning that a change in price results in an equal change in quantity demanded. In general, the higher the elasticity, the greater the volume increase resulting from a price reduction.

Because price elasticity reflects proportional changes, it does not depend on the units in which the price and quantity are expressed. Furthermore, because price elasticity is a function of the initial values, the same absolute changes in price can lead to different price elasticity values at different price points. For example, the volume decline resulting from lowering the price by five cents might be 5% when the initial price is $1.00 but is only 1% when the initial price is $5.00.

In general, buyers tend to be more price sensitive when an offering is perceived to be a commodity and there are many alternative options available. In contrast, buyers tend to be less price sensitive when they pay only a fraction of the total cost (as in the case of medical products and services largely covered by insurance) and when the purchase price is a relatively small component of the total cost of the offering over its lifetime (as in the case of printers, where the cost of cartridges vastly exceeds the price of the device).

Price elasticity has important implications for setting the offering's price. Thus, if demand is elastic, lowering the price (or running sales promotions) might have a positive impact on the company's net income because the decline in profit margins stemming from the price drop might be offset by a corresponding increase in the sales volume. In contrast, when demand is inelastic (meaning that the buyers are relatively insensitive to changes in price), raising the price might be a viable option to increase the company's net income because in this case the loss of volume due to the increase in price might be offset by the corresponding increase in profit margins.

Price as a Targeting Tool

Companies typically do not set a single price for an offering but rather implement a pricing structure that involves different price points based on the specifics of the markets in which they intend to compete. Because buyers' willingness to pay is one of the key market characteristics, companies use pricing as a tool to segment and target different customer segments.

The practice of charging a different price for the same good or service is referred to as price segmentation (in economics literature, price segmentation is commonly referred to as price discrimination). Price segmentation benefits companies by enabling them to customize the value they capture from individual customers. The ability to offer different price levels for their products and services and, specifically, the ability to offer lower prices to certain customers also allows companies to serve different market segments that they might not be able to serve using a universal price policy. In addition, charging different prices at different points in time helps companies better manage the customer flow—an approach commonly referred to as yield pricing. For example, many restaurants offer "happy hour" pricing during off-peak periods to smooth demand as well as to attract more price-sensitive customers that otherwise might not end up patronizing the establishment.

In the ideal scenario, a company would segment customers based on their willingness to pay for the company's offering. In reality, however, customers' willingness to pay is not readily observable and must be inferred from the visible customer characteristics and the purchase occasion. Commonly used characteristics that can serve as a proxy for customers' willingness to pay include customer demographics, geolocation, and behavior.

Customer demographics typically used to segment customers based on price include age, income, occupation, employment status, population density of their location (urban or rural), social class, household size, and stage in the product's life cycle. For example, a company might offer lower prices to children and seniors, large families, and low-income consumers. Customer geolocation can be used to segment customers based on the availability of competitive options. For example, a company might set lower prices to match the competitive offerings available in physical proximity to the customer.

Instead of (or in addition to) setting prices based on customer demographics, a company might also set prices based on customers' buying behavior. In this context, commonly used segmentation criteria involve purchase quantity (e.g., offering lower prices to customers purchasing larger quantities), time of purchase and use (e.g., yield-management pricing including peak-load pricing and early-/late-purchase discounts), and distribution channel (e.g., offering different prices in different retail channels).

A meaningful price-based targeting requires that a company be able to identify different segments that vary in their willingness to pay for the company's offerings. Furthermore, because charging different prices for the same product creates arbitrage opportunities, a company must keep different customer segments apart to ensure that the lower priced items sold to one segment are not resold on a secondary market (such as eBay, Alibaba, and Craigslist) to other segments with a higher willingness to pay. Another important consideration involves managing the perception of price fairness to ensure that buyers perceive the differential pricing as fair based on the sociocultural norms of the market in which the company operates.

Psychological Aspects of Pricing

Buyers do not always evaluate prices in an objective fashion; instead, their reaction to an offering's price depends on a variety of psychological effects. The most common psychological pricing effects include *reference-price effects*, *price–quality inferences*, *price–quantity effects*, *unit-pricing effects*, as well as *price-tier* and *price-ending effects*.

Reference-Price Effects

To assess the attractiveness of the price of an offering, people typically evaluate it relative to other prices, which serve as reference points. These reference prices can be either internal, such as a remembered price from a prior purchase occasion, or external, such as the readily available price of a competitive offering. By strategically using the reference price, a company can frame the price of its offering in a way that makes it more attractive to potential buyers—for example, by comparing it to a more expensive competitive offering or to a higher regular price for the same offering.

There are several types of internal reference-price points that buyers can use when evaluating an offering's price. Thus, reference prices might reflect the typical price at which the offering is sold. Alternatively, buyers might set the reference price as the last price they paid for the offering. The reference price might also be the "fair" price—that is, the price at which buyers think the product or service should be sold. The reference price might be based on buyers' reservation prices—that is, the highest or the lowest price they are willing to pay for the offering. Furthermore, the reference price might also include buyers' expectations of future price increases or decreases based on their market observations and prior experiences.

Buyers' reference prices are also influenced by the prices of the other market offerings. For example, when buyers are uncertain about how much they ought to pay for a particular product or service, they often use competitors' prices for similar offerings as a reference point. Furthermore, the relative prices of other offerings in a company's product line can serve as reference points and, thus, influence customer demand. For example, restaurants often price wine they are trying to dispose of as the second cheapest in its menu assortment because many customers who are not willing to spend much on wine are often embarrassed to select the least expensive one.

Because buyers often lack accurate price knowledge and do not have a well-defined idea of how much they should pay for a given item, companies use reference points to "frame" an item's price. For example, a $250 set of car floor mats might seem exorbitantly expensive if considered as a separate item but might seem more sensible if purchased along with an $80,000 car. In the same vein, a $100 price tag for a pair of jeans might seem excessive; however, it might seem reasonable when buyers are informed that the price is a markdown from the original price of $250. As these examples show, reference points are important because they shape the way people evaluate prices and make purchase decisions.

Price-Quality Inferences

When evaluating the available options and making purchase decisions, buyers believe they get what they pay for, often employing the dictum "there's no such thing as a free lunch." This heuristic reflects consumers' fundamental belief that price and quality are related, with higher quality implying higher price and, vice versa, that lower priced items are likely to be of lower quality.

Given the prevalence of consumers' belief in the price–quality correlation, some manufacturers have deliberately set their prices to signal exceptional product quality, a pricing policy referred to as image (or prestige) pricing. For example, Screaming Eagle—one of Napa Valley's most expensive wine brands—has priced its flagship wine upwards of $3,000 per bottle—a price that sends a clear signal about the quality of the wine. In the same vein, luxury brands such as Hermès, Louis Vuitton, and Bottega Veneta set premium prices for their products in order to convey an image of quality, exclusivity, and prestige.

The belief that price reflects quality, although popular, is not held by all consumers and across all purchase occasions. Buyers are more likely to use price as a proxy for quality in cases when information about the actual quality of the product or service is not readily available. Furthermore, to draw price–quality inferences, buyers must perceive markets to be efficient, meaning that they believe the prices observed in the market accurately reflect product quality.

Price-Quantity Effects

People tend to be more sensitive to changes in price than to changes in quantity. To illustrate, the sales volume of a ten-pack of hot dogs priced at $2.49 is likely to decline to a greater extent following a $.50 price increase (a ten-pack for $2.99) than following a two-item reduction in unit volume (an eight-pack for $2.49), even though on a per-item basis, the eight-pack is more expensive than the ten-pack. The same principle applies to reducing the weight and size of a product since customers tend to pay more attention to price than to the actual quantity purchased.

The price–quantity effect does not imply that buyers are indifferent to receiving smaller quantities of the product with no price increase. It simply means that they are less dissatisfied with receiving smaller quantities at the same price than receiving the same quantities at a higher price. Furthermore, the price–quantity effect does not depend on customers failing to perceive changes in quantity. Consumers' preference for receiving a smaller quantity of the offering rather than paying a higher price holds even when these changes are transparent and buyers are fully aware of the reduced quantity.

Increases in commodity, transportation, and energy costs have pressured many manu-facturers to consider raising prices to meet their profit goals. However, concern that an out-right price increase could lead to a decline in consumption and customer defection to com-petitors' products has prompted companies to reduce the package size and product quantity while leaving the price essentially unchanged. As a result, the past two decades have seen multiple examples of this product-reduction strategy. For example, instead of raising the price of its ice cream, Dreyer's Grand Ice Cream reduced the package size to 1.5 quarts from 1.75 quarts. In the same vein, Frito-Lay reduced the quantity of chips in its bags from 12 to 10 ounces and PepsiCo replaced its 96-ounce jug of Tropicana orange juice with an 89-ounce bottle.

Unit-Pricing Effects

Unit-pricing effects refer to customers' reaction to two different ways in which price can be presented to customers: unit-based pricing and usage-based pricing. Unit-based pricing in-volves expressing the price of an offering in terms of its total cost. In contrast, usage-based pricing reflects the cost of the good spread over a particular time frame. Consider, for ex-ample, Hästens Vividus—a custom-made bed built by master artisans in Köping, Sweden. The bed contains layers of flax, horsetail hair, and cotton and wool batting, which, according to the company make it "the world's most comfortable bed." To make its $150,000 price tag more palatable, Hästens informs potential buyers that if they keep the bed for 25 years and get eight hours of sleep every night, the cost is $2 per hour.[24]

Usage-based pricing also was one of the key factors contributing to the success of the Dollar Shave Club. Rather than pricing its cartridges on a per-item basis, as most cartridges sold through traditional retail channels do, the online startup priced its shaving products on a monthly basis, charging its customers $1 (plus shipping and handling), $6, or $9 for a monthly supply depending on the number of blades per cartridge. Within only a few years of its launch, Dollar Shave Club was able to gain more than ten percent of the wet-shaving market in the United States, most of which came from Gillette, even though on a per-shave basis, Gillette's razors were actually cheaper. Men unwilling to pay $5 per Gillette cartridge (that they were likely to shave with for about three weeks) were paying $9 per month for cartridges that were likely to be of inferior quality thinking that they were saving money.

Price-Tier and Price-Ending Effects

Price-tier effects reflect people's tendency to think of individual prices in terms of levels or tiers, rather than as a continuum. While this price categorization helps minimize cognitive effort and simplify the way people evaluate pricing information, it also can lead to biased percep-tions of the actual prices because of the ways people encode prices into distinct tiers. For ex-ample, an item priced at $1.95 is typically encoded in the "$1+" price tier, whereas an item priced at $2.00 is typically classified in the "$2+" price tier. As a result, paying $1.95 for an item is more likely to be associated with spending $1 rather than $2.

Related to price-tier effects are *price-ending effects*, whereby customers' perception of prices is a function of the price endings. Some of the effects of price endings can be readily observed in the case of price-tier effects, whereby people are more sensitive to changes in price endings across different price tiers than within the same price tier. For example, the difference in prices of items that cost $1.45 and $1.48 is perceived to be smaller than the difference in prices of items that cost $1.49 and $1.51, even though the actual price difference is greater in the former case.

In addition to influencing price-tier perceptions, price endings can influence perceived prices by suggesting the presence of a bargain or a discount. For example, prices ending in 9 are often perceived as offering a better deal than prices ending in other digits—a finding commonly attributed to the fact that in many countries consumers have been culturally conditioned to associate prices ending in 9 with discounts and better deals. Apart from influencing price perceptions, price endings can also influence the perceived quality of the company's offering. For example, while prices ending in 9 might create the perception of a discount, prices ending in 0 and 5 might create the perception of quality. This effect is often attributed to the fact that prices ending with 0 and 5 are easier to remember, retrieve from memory, and evaluate. This ease in processing the pricing information can, in turn, translate into perceptions of quality.

Setting the Price to Create Company Value

Because sales volume and profits are a function of price, setting the right price can be an important driver of a company's ability to achieve its goals. Some of the key issues when setting an offering's price involve determining an offering's cost structure, defining the company's pricing goals, and choosing the pricing format. These issues are discussed in more detail in the following sections.

Determining an Offering's Cost Structure

Market demand and a company's cost structure are two key factors that determine the range of prices that allow an offering to profitably exist in a market. Market demand, driven by customer willingness to pay, sets the ceiling for the price that a company can charge for its offering. In contrast, the company costs involved in developing, promoting, and distributing the offering set the floor for profitable pricing.

The key factors that merit consideration in determining an offering's cost structure include the magnitude of the offering's fixed and variable costs, as well as the ways in which costs vary as a function of the scale and scope of the processes involved in designing, communicating, and delivering the offering.

Fixed and Variable Costs

Based on whether they depend on the production quantity, the total costs associated with an offering can be divided into two categories: *fixed costs* and *variable costs*.

Fixed costs are expenses that do not fluctuate with output volume within a relevant period. Typical examples of fixed costs include research-and-development expenses, mass-media advertising expenses, rent, interest on debt, insurance, plant-and-equipment expenses, and salary of permanent full-time employees. Even though their absolute size remains unchanged regardless of output volume, average fixed costs per unit become progressively smaller as volume increases. These savings result from spreading the fixed costs over a larger number of output units.

Unlike fixed costs, which do not depend on the produced quantity, **variable costs** are expenses that fluctuate in direct proportion to the output volume of units produced. For example, the cost of raw materials and expenses incurred by consumer incentives such as coupons, price discounts, rebates, and premiums are commonly viewed as variable costs. Other expenses, such as distribution channel incentives and salesforce compensation, can be classified as either fixed or variable costs depending on their structure (e.g., fixed salary vs. performance-based compensation).

Deciding which costs are fixed and which costs are variable depends on the time horizon. For example, in the short run, the salaries of permanent full-time employees will be considered fixed costs because they do not depend on output volume. In the longer run, however, a company may adjust the number and/or salaries of permanent employees based on the demand for its products or services—a scenario in which these costs would be considered variable rather than fixed. Thus, in the long run, all costs could be considered variable.

An important concept related to that of fixed and variable costs is break-even analysis. Generally speaking, break-even analysis aims to identify the point at which the benefits and costs associated with a particular action are equal and beyond which profit occurs. Common types of break-even analyses include break-even of a fixed-cost investment, which indicates the unit or dollar sales volume at which the company is able to recoup a particular fixed-cost investment; break-even of a price cut, which reflects the increase in sales volume needed for a price cut to have a neutral impact on company profit; and break-even of a variable-cost increase, which identifies the sales volume at which a company neither makes a profit nor incurs a loss after increasing variable costs. The different types of break-even analyses are discussed in more detail in Chapter 6.

An Offering's Cost as a Function of Scale and Scope of Production

The costs of an offering are not set in stone: They often vary as a function of the quantity produced and the synergies among different types of offerings in the company's portfolio. The effects of these two factors are commonly referred to as *economies of scale* and *economies of scope*.

Economies of scale refer to the tendency of greater manufacturing and sales volume to lead to a decrease in per-unit costs. This relationship between production output and unit costs is closely related to the concept of the *experience curve*: The more experience a firm has in producing a particular offering, the lower its costs. A classic example of economies of scale and experience-curve pricing is the Ford Model T, where the goal of creating an affordable car resulted in scaling up production in a way that dramatically reduced the costs of each automobile.

Note that the relationship between costs and production volume is not monotonic: As the output volume increases, marginal costs tend to decrease initially until they reach the point at which they begin to increase, leading to diseconomies of scale. Thus, rather than the company experiencing continued decreasing costs with increasing output, diseconomies of scale can lead to an increase in marginal costs when output is increased. Diseconomies of scale can be caused by a variety of factors that are typically related to managing an increasingly large workforce and complex production logistics.

Economies of scope involve synergies among different offerings in a company's portfolio and are based on the notion that the average total cost of production tends to decrease as the number of different goods produced increases. Economies of scope are conceptually similar to economies of scale in that an increase in size typically leads to lower costs. Unlike economies of scale, however, where cost savings stem from increasing the scale of production for a single offering, economies of scope refer to cost savings resulting from synergies among different offerings in a company's portfolio. For example, Microsoft can develop both a word processing program and a spreadsheet program at a lower average cost than if two different companies were to produce each program separately. This is because both programs (Word and Excel) share a common platform and are promoted and distributed (often as a bundle) using the same channels.

As in the case of economies of scale, economies of scope do not always lead to a cost advantage: In many cases a firm producing a variety of different offerings is less efficient than separate firms that specialize in the production of a single offering. Diseconomies of scope often stem from the relative benefits of specialization, whereby focusing on a single product or service enables a company to achieve scale of production and gain the relevant experience—an advantage that could outweigh the potential benefits associated with synergies among different offerings.

Defining the Company's Pricing Goals

When setting the price for an offering, a company must first decide on the overall monetary and strategic goals it aims to achieve. In this context, one important consideration is whether the offering should focus on gaining market share while sacrificing some of the profit margin or on maximizing the per-unit profit at the expense of sales volume. The corresponding two pricing strategies—penetration pricing and skim pricing—are illustrated in Figure 3 and outlined in more detail below.

Figure 3. Penetration, Skim, and Loss-Leader Pricing

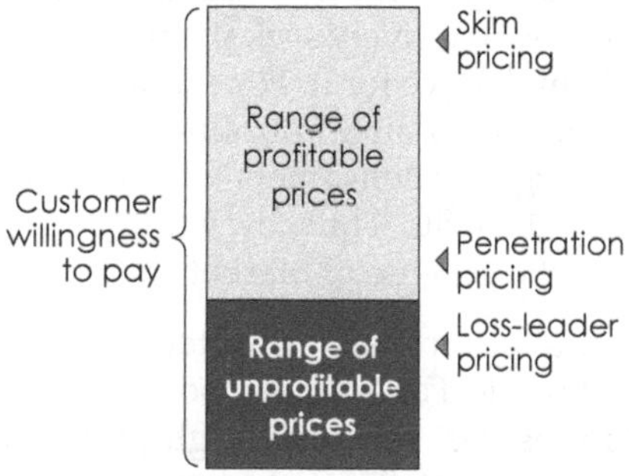

Penetration Pricing

Penetration pricing involves setting relatively low prices in an attempt to gain higher sales volume, albeit at lower profit margins. A classic example of penetration pricing comes from Swedish retailer IKEA, known for its affordable furniture and household items. Although the low prices make each sale less profitable, the high sales volume generated by the low prices more than offsets the low margins. Another example of penetration pricing is Dollar Shave Club, which was able to gain share from the premium-priced market leader Gillette by introducing a low-priced offering featuring a free razor and a monthly supply of cartridges starting at $1.

A particular case of penetration pricing is *loss-leader pricing*, whereby a company sets a low price for an offering (often at or below cost) in an attempt to increase the sales of other offerings. A retailer might set a low price for a popular item in an attempt to build store traffic, thus increasing the sales of other, more profitable items. For example, on Black Friday—one of the busiest shopping days in the United States when many consumers do their

Christmas shopping—many retailers drop the prices on a few high-demand items, such as the most popular children's toy, to attract buyers to their stores in the hope of making up loss-leader deficits with profit from other products that customers purchase during their shopping trip.

An extreme version of penetration pricing is *freemium pricing*, whereby a company gives away a restricted (either in terms of functionality or duration) version of the offering for free in an attempt to introduce potential buyers to its offering, gain market share, and ultimately convert some of the buyers to the paid, fully functional version of the offering. Examples of companies using the freemium model include Dropbox, Box, Evernote, Survey Monkey, Slack, Spotify, and Amazon Web Services. Freemium pricing is most often used for offerings with negligible variable costs that make the marginal cost of giving away a free item close to zero, as in the case of purely digital offerings.

In general, penetration pricing is more appropriate in cases where (1) demand is relatively elastic, such that lowering the price is likely to substantially increase sales volume, (2) the target market is increasingly competitive, (3) cost is a function of volume and, as a result, significant cost savings are expected as cumulative volume increases, (4) being the market pioneer can lead to a sustainable competitive advantage, and (5) the company has the resources to mass produce the offering.

Skim Pricing

Skim pricing involves setting a high price to "skim the cream" off the top of the market. Skim pricing targets customers who actively seek the benefits delivered by the offering and are willing to pay a relatively high price for it. For example, when launching a new generation of mobile phones, manufacturers often introduce a product line that contains a fully featured, high-price offering targeting consumers who seek the most benefits and are willing to pay a premium for these benefits. Thus, by setting high prices, skim pricing maximizes profit margins, usually at the expense of market share.

Skim pricing is also used to attract early adopters willing to pay higher prices at the initial stages of the product life cycle. For example, popular books, videogames, movies, and music albums are initially released at relatively high prices, targeting customers who are willing to pay a premium to be among the first to experience the offering. Skim pricing is also very common, if not universal, in the case of luxury offerings that target the higher end of the market. Indeed, because luxury products and services are by definition expensive and exclusive, skim pricing is the rule rather than the exception.

In general, skim pricing is more appropriate in cases where (1) demand is relatively inelastic and lowering the price is not likely to substantially increase sales volume, (2) there is little or no competition for the target segment, (3) cost is not a direct function of volume, and significant cost savings are not achieved as cumulative volume increases, (4) being the market pioneer is unlikely to result in a sustainable competitive advantage, and (5) the company lacks the capability to mass produce the offering.

Managing Price Dynamics

Company prices are not immutable. Once set, they often evolve over time based on factors such as supply and demand, competitive offerings, and the overall market environment. Moreover, in some cases, rather than setting the prices at which target customers would buy its offerings, a company might let the prices be set dynamically by the market forces. The key methods that companies use to dynamically manage prices involve *price adjustments*, *auction pricing*, and *reverse pricing*.

Price Adjustments

Unlike the traditional approach, in which prices remain relatively stable and demand is stimulated by incentives, an increasing number of companies have adopted *dynamic pricing*, which involves a range of prices that change frequently to adapt to market conditions. Dynamic pricing is a common practice in industries such as hospitality, travel, and energy, where supply is constrained and cannot be varied to accommodate fluctuation in demand.

For example, time-based pricing is commonly used in the hospitality industry, where higher prices are charged during the peak season and other high-demand periods. In the same vein, airlines set prices taking into account factors such as the day of the week, time of day, and the number of seats available. Such dynamic pricing aims to align the available inventory with customer demand in a way that enables the company to maximize revenues by narrowing its focus on customers with the highest willingness to pay.

In addition to being driven by inventory considerations, price dynamics might stem from a company's desire to maximize revenue based on customers' willingness to pay for the company's products and services. For example, a retailer might vary the price of sodas, beer, and ice cream depending on the weather, charging higher prices to skim the market demand or, alternatively, charging lower prices to drive traffic and create a favorable price image.

One common instance of dynamic pricing is *surge pricing*. However, unlike the general case of dynamic pricing, which can involve price fluctuations in both directions (price increases as well as price decreases), surge pricing exclusively involves premium pricing. Surge pricing is often used by electric utilities to raise prices in periods of high demand. Another common example of surge pricing involves Uber, which charges surge rates as a multiplier of the base fare during periods of high demand.

On some occasions companies can also permanently lower their prices to accommodate changes in the market in which they operate. Unlike sales promotions, which typically involve short-term monetary incentives, *price rollbacks* are relatively permanent changes in a company's base prices. For example, Walmart, known for its everyday low pricing, uses lasting price rollbacks rather than temporary price discounts to deliver greater value to its customers.

An important issue in dynamic pricing is managing customers' perceptions of the fairness of the company's prices. Raising prices based solely on customer demand and the availability of alternative options can breed resentment from the public and damage the company's brand image. This is particularly true for products and services that are basic necessities, such as utilities, public transportation, and pharmaceutical products.

Auction Pricing

An auction is a process in which potential buyers place competitive bids on goods or services, which are then sold to the highest bidder. The auction model is commonly used for unique items such as art, antiquities, and rare artifacts; for items that must be sold within a given time frame; and when sellers are willing to let the market set the price of the items being sold. The three most common types of auctions include English auctions, Dutch auctions, and sealed-bid auctions.

English auctions start with a suggested opening bid reserve or a starting price that is set by the seller. As buyers try to outbid one another, the price of the item is raised progressively until either the auction is closed or no higher bids are received. In *Dutch auctions*, the price of an item is lowered until it gets a bid, and the first bid made is the winning bid. Thus, unlike English auctions, where the price rises as bidders compete, in Dutch auctions the price declines as the auction progresses. Finally, in *sealed-bid auctions*, all bidders simultaneously submit sealed bids to the auctioneer, and the highest bidder usually wins the items. Unlike the English auction, where bidders can submit multiple bids based on previous bids by others, in sealed-bid auctions each bidder submits a single bid and cannot adjust the bid based on competing bids.

The above three types of auctions have pros and cons that determine their usage. Thus, an English auction is typically used in real estate, art, antiques, and vehicles. Companies that use English auctions include fine art auction houses Christie's and Sotheby's and online auctioneers eBay and Taobao. Dutch auctions are often used in financial markets (e.g., the Department of the Treasury uses Dutch auctions to raise funds for the U.S. Government) as well as in certain commodity markets (e.g., Aalsmeer Flower Auction in the Netherlands—the world's largest flower auction—is set up as a Dutch auction). Sealed-bid auctions are often used when soliciting requests for proposals (RFP) for longer term service, development, and manufacturing contracts (when used for procurement purposes, the winning RFP bid is often the lowest rather than the highest).

Sellers use auctions in cases when there is considerable uncertainty about the optimal price of an item, both in terms of the item's objective value as well as how much potential buyers are willing to pay for it. Thus, rather than trying to guess the ideal price of its offerings, a company might let market forces set the price based on buyers' willingness to pay. Auction pricing is also very common in the case of unique items such as art, antiques, and real estate where the seller aims to identify the buyer who has the highest willingness to pay for each item. In addition to helping set the price for unique items, auction pricing is used to set spot prices in commodity industries where the supply and demand constantly fluctuate.

Reverse Pricing

Reverse pricing (also referred to as name-your-own pricing) is similar to auction pricing in that buyers have to place a bid for the item they wish to acquire. Unlike auctions, where buyers directly compete with one another, in reverse pricing buyers submit their bids to the company, which then decides how many and which bids to accept. Companies utilizing reverse pricing include Priceline.com, Groupon, and eBay.

A particular form of reverse pricing is *pay-what-you-want pricing*. This pricing format is similar to reverse pricing in that buyers set the purchase price of a given item. The key difference is that in reverse pricing the seller has the ability to reject bids that do not meet certain criteria, such as a minimum purchase price or volume. In contrast, in the pay-what-you-want approach the seller does not control the price set by the buyer. Pay-what-you-want pricing is used primarily when the marginal costs of the offering are low, such as in the case of digital content: information, music, and video. Pay-what-you-want pricing is also used when the average price paid by consumers is likely to be higher than the cost of the offering and thus has the potential to generate additional sales while minimizing the risk of financial loss.

One of the first major cases of customer-determined pricing was the album *In Rainbows* by English rock band Radiohead, self-released in 2007 as a pay-what-you-want download. Another notable example is The Metropolitan Museum of Art, which lets New York residents determine how much they should pay for admission tickets. Letting customers set prices has a number of limitations. The most obvious problem is free riding, whereby customers pay less than what they think the product or service is worth. In addition, many customers might not have realistic perceptions of the costs associated with different items and end up paying significantly less than an item's actual cost to the company. As a result, the practical application of pay-what-you-want pricing is rather limited.

Setting the Price in a Competitive Context

Companies do not set prices in isolation: Their prices reflect the competitive environment in which they operate. Indeed, because a company's ultimate goal is to create greater value for its target customers than the value created by its competitors, the pricing policies of competitors have a direct impact on the customer value created by the company. Therefore, to ensure market success, a company must assess the price-to-benefit ratio of its offerings vis-à-vis those of the competition, clearly understand the antecedents and consequences of price wars, and develop a policy on how to respond to a threat of a price war. These issues are discussed in the following sections.

Competitive Price–Benefit Analysis

The price–benefit analysis examines the price–benefit tradeoff across the company's different market offerings. At the heart of the price–benefit analysis is the notion that a company's focus should not be on price alone but also on the offering's value, defined as a function of the perceived benefits and perceived price. The price–benefit relationship is best illustrated using competitive price–benefit maps, which reflect the perceived price–benefit tradeoffs associated with a particular offering in a competitive context (Figure 4).

Figure 4. Competitive Price– Benefit Map

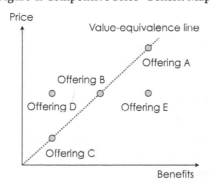

The value-equivalence line in Figure 4 represents offerings for which the ratio of perceived benefits and perceived price is the same: higher benefit, higher priced offerings are positioned toward the upper right (Offering A); lower benefit, lower priced offerings are positioned toward the lower left (Offering C). Offerings A, B, and C deliver equivalent value, with Offering A delivering higher benefits at a premium price and Offering C delivering fewer benefits at a lower price. Offerings below the value-equivalence line (Offering E) deliver superior value relative to the offerings on or above the value-equivalence line, whereas offerings above the value-equivalence line (Offering D) deliver inferior value relative to the offerings on or below the value-equivalence line.

In a truly efficient market, all offerings should lie on the value-equivalence line. In reality, however, offerings might vary in the value they deliver to customers; some offerings (Offering E) deliver superior value (higher benefits at a lower price), whereas others (Offering D) deliver inferior value (lower benefits at a higher price). These value discrepancies are likely to influence the market shares of the offerings, such that value-advantaged options are likely to gain share, whereas value-disadvantaged options are likely to lose share. This implies that, over time, the sales of offerings A and B are likely to shift to Offering E, and the sales of Offering D are likely to shift to offerings B (and ultimately E) and C.

An important aspect of price–benefit analysis is that it reflects perceived rather than actual benefits and prices of the available offerings. This is important because customer perceptions of an offering's price depend on a variety of factors (some of which were discussed earlier in this chapter), such that the perceived price might not adequately reflect an offering's actual price. Moreover, just because an offering has a particular feature does not imply that this feature will translate into a meaningful customer benefit. In other words, customers might not accurately perceive the offering's performance and misconstrue its true benefits. Because customers' behavior reflects their subjective beliefs about the offering's price and benefits, understanding these beliefs and incorporating them in a company's pricing is the key to creating market value.

Understanding Price Wars

Price wars are very common in competitive markets. Price wars can involve price reductions offered directly from manufacturers to end users (price discounts, volume discounts, and coupons). Price wars also might involve price cuts and incentives offered by manufacturers to retailers, which, in turn, might prompt retailers to lower their prices, thus provoking a price war. Price wars can also be initiated by retailers who aggressively compete for the same customers.

Price wars often start when a company is willing to sacrifice margins to gain sales volume. Price cuts, the forerunner of price wars, are popular among managers because they are easy to implement and typically produce fast results, especially when a company's goal is to increase sales volume.

Not every price cut, however, leads to a price war. The likelihood that a price cut will trigger a price war depends on several factors:

- **Offering differentiation.** Price wars are more likely when offerings are undifferentiated and can be easily substituted, such that a price cut is likely to instantly attract competitors' customers.

- **Cost structure.** Companies are more likely to engage in price wars when significant economies of scale can be achieved by increasing volume and both the company and its competitors stand to gain if they increase their output.

- **Market growth.** Price wars are more likely to occur when markets are stagnant, and to grow sales a company has to steal share from its direct competitors.

- **Customer loyalty.** Companies are more likely to engage in price wars in markets in which customers are price sensitive (meaning that they are not brand loyal and are willing to trade off performance for lower price) and their switching costs are low.

Price wars are easy to initiate but costly to win. Winning a price war often comes at the expense of a significant loss of profits, making it more of a Pyrrhic victory than a true success. Price wars are detrimental to a company's profitability for several reasons:

- **Fixed-cost effect.** Price reductions have an exponential impact on profitability. To illustrate, in the absence of an increase in sales volume, reducing the price of an offering with a 10% profit margin by 1% will result in a 10% decrease in operating income.

- **Competitive reaction.** Because in most cases competitors can easily match price cuts, they are rarely sustainable. Firms with similar cost structures can quickly lower their prices in response to a competitor's action.

- **Increased price elasticity.** Price wars often result in a shift in customers' future price expectations, such that the lowered prices become the reference points against which future prices are judged.

- **Brand devaluation.** Emphasis on price tends to erode brand power. This effect is exacerbated by the heavy price-focused communication campaigns that tend to accompany most price wars (because a company needs to promote the low price so that it can generate sufficient incremental volume to offset the lost profits resulting from the decrease in price).

Price wars rarely enable companies to achieve their strategic goals, and in most cases the only beneficiaries of a price war are the company's customers. In general, the best strategy for a company to win a potential price war is to avoid it.

Circumventing Price Wars

Even companies not seeking a price war are often confronted with a scenario in which a competitor initiates a price cut. The gut reaction of most managers in such cases is to respond with a matching price cut. This reaction, however, is often premature and suboptimal. Only after evaluating the antecedents and likely consequences of the price cut can a company identify the optimal response strategy. A relatively simple approach for developing a strategic response to a competitor's price cut is outlined below.

- **Verify the threat of a price war.** Price wars are often caused by miscommunication of pricing information or misinterpretation of a competitor's goals. For example, when competitive prices are not readily available (e.g., in contract bidding), a company might incorrectly believe that a particular competitor has significantly lowered its price. It is also possible that a competitor's price decrease is driven by internal factors, such as clearing inventory (e.g., prior to introducing a new model), rather than by an intention to initiate a price war. Thus, before responding to a competitor's actions, it is imperative to validate whether the threat of a price war is real.

- **Evaluate the likely impact of the competitor's actions.** To determine the best course of action, a company must first identify which of its own current and potential customers are most likely to be affected by competitors' price cuts, assess the likely response of these customers to the price cut, and consider their value to the company. In certain cases, a company might choose to abandon markets that have no strategic importance and in which customer loyalty is low.

- **Develop segment-specific strategies to address the competitive threat.** There are three basic strategies to respond to the threat of a price war: staying the course, repositioning an existing offering by lowering its price and/or increasing its benefits, and adding new offerings. The decision to stay the course and ignore a competitor's price cut reflects a company's belief that the price cut will not have a significant impact on the company's market position, that the price cut is not sustainable and will dissipate by itself, or that serving the customer segment targeted by the price cut is no longer viable for the company. In contrast, repositioning the existing offering reflects a company's view that the market has fundamentally changed and the value of its offering must be realigned with the new market realities. Alternatively, a company might launch a downscale extension (a fighting brand) to attract price-sensitive customers without discounting its premium offering (see Chapter 16 for a discussion of these strategies).

Using a systematic approach to evaluate the threat of a price war and develop an appropriate response is paramount to sustaining the profitability of the market in which a company competes and ensuring the company's long-term success in this market. A visceral reaction to a competitor's price cut can be as detrimental to a company's future as the very action that provoked the company's response.

SUMMARY

Price defines the monetary aspect of the value a company's offering aims to create and capture in the market. When setting the price, managers must consider two types of factors: *strategic factors* that deal with the offering's target market (customers, competitors, collaborators, company, and context), and *tactical factors* that deal with the ways in which price interacts with the other attributes of the offering (product, service, brand, incentives, communication, and distribution).

To set the optimal price, a manager must understand the relationship between the offering's price and customer demand. P*rice elasticity* reflects the degree to which changing the price influences sales volume. High price elasticity means that a small change in price leads to a large change in sales volume, whereas low elasticity means that the decrease in sales volume resulting from the change in price is relatively small.

Because buyers' willingness to pay is one of the key market characteristics, companies use pricing as a targeting tool (a practice referred to as price segmentation). Commonly used price-segmentation criteria include purchase quantity, time of purchase or use, and distribution channel.

Because buyers do not always evaluate prices in an objective fashion, companies often use *psychological pricing* that takes advantage of a variety of effects stemming from behavioral economics, such as reference-price effects, price–quality inferences, price–quantity effects, unit-pricing effects, as well as price-tier and price-ending effects.

When setting an offering's price, a company can employ one of two core strategies: skim pricing and penetration pricing. By setting high prices, *skim pricing* maximizes profit margins, usually at the expense of market share. In contrast, *penetration pricing* involves setting relatively low prices in an attempt to gain higher sales volume, albeit at lower margins.

Company prices are not immutable: Once set, they often evolve over time based on factors such as supply and demand, competitive offerings, and the overall market environment. The key methods that companies use to dynamically manage prices involve price adjustments, auction pricing, and price negotiation.

The *price–benefit analysis* examines the price–benefit tradeoff across the different market offerings. At the heart of the price–benefit analysis is the idea that a company's focus should not be solely on price but also on the offering's value, defined as a function of the perceived benefits and perceived price. The price–benefit relationship is illustrated with price–benefit maps, which reflect the perceived price–benefit tradeoffs associated with a particular offering in a competitive context.

Competing on price often results in a *price war*, which typically starts when companies are willing to sacrifice margins to gain market share. Price wars are likely to occur when offerings are undifferentiated, when capacity utilization is low, when significant economies of scale can be achieved by increasing volume, when markets are mature and a company has to steal share from its direct competitors to grow sales, and when customers' price elasticity is high and switching costs are low.

An effective approach for developing a *strategic response to a price cut* calls for verifying the validity of the threat of a price war, prioritizing customers who are most likely to be affected by a competitor's price cut based on their value to the company and price elasticity, and developing segment-specific strategies to address the competitive threat. Price wars rarely enable companies to achieve their strategic goals, and usually the only beneficiaries of a price war are the company's customers. In most cases, the best strategy for a company to win a potential price war is to avoid it.

MARKETING INSIGHT: KEY PRICING CONCEPTS

Captive Pricing: See *complementary pricing*.

Competitive Pricing: Pricing method that uses competitors' prices as benchmarks for price setting. A popular version of this approach, referred to as *competitive-parity pricing*, involves setting the offering's price in a way that puts it at parity with that of competitors.

Complementary Pricing: Pricing method applicable to uniquely compatible, multipart offerings, whereby a company charges a relatively low introductory price for the first component of the offering and higher prices for the other components. Classic examples include razors and blades, printers and cartridges, and cell phones and cell phone service. The unique compatibility of the offering's components is crucial to the success of complementary pricing—for example, only the printer manufacturer should be able to sell cartridges that fit its printers.

Cost-Plus Pricing: Pricing method in which the final price is determined by adding a fixed premium to the cost of the product. Cost-plus pricing is used in industries where profit margins are relatively stable. See also *markup pricing*.

Cross-Price Elasticity: The percentage change in the quantity of a given offering sold caused by a percentage change in the price of another offering.

Deceptive Pricing: The practice of presenting an offering's price to the buyer in a way that is deliberately misleading. Deceptive pricing is illegal in the United States.

Demand Pricing: Pricing method that involves setting prices based on customers' willingness to pay for the benefits afforded by the company's offering.

Experience-Curve Pricing: Pricing method based on an anticipated lower cost structure, resulting from scale economies and experience-curve effects.

Image Pricing: Pricing method that involves setting a high price for the purpose of signaling the high quality of an item. See also *price signaling.*

Loss-Leader Pricing: Pricing method that involves setting a low price for an offering (often at or below cost) in an attempt to increase the sales of other products and services. For example, a retailer might set a low price for a popular item in an attempt to build store traffic, thus increasing the sales of other, more profitable items.

Markup Pricing: Pricing method that involves adding a standard markup to the cost of the offering. Markup pricing is very similar to cost-plus pricing, with the key difference that rather than being calculated as an item-specific dollar amount (as in the case of *cost-plus pricing*), the added premium is calculated as a percentage of an item's cost. Because of its standardized nature, markup pricing is more common among intermediaries (such as wholesalers, dealers, and retailers) that carry large quantities of different items. For example, a wholesaler might add a standard percentage markup to all of the offerings it distributes based on the cost of the goods sold.

Predatory Pricing: Pricing method that involves selling below cost with the intent of driving competitors out of business. Predatory pricing is illegal in the United States.

Prestige Pricing: Pricing method in which the price is set at a relatively high level for the purpose of creating an exclusive image for the offering.

Price Fixing: Pricing method in which companies conspire to set prices for a given product or service. Price fixing is illegal in the United States.

Price Segmentation: Pricing method that involves charging different buyers different prices for goods of equal grade and quality.

Price Signaling: (1) Pricing method that aims to capitalize on price–quality inferences (higher priced products are also likely to be higher quality), primarily used when the actual product benefits are not readily observable (also known as prestige pricing); (2) Indirect communication (direct price collusion is prohibited by law) between companies aimed at indicating their intentions with respect to their pricing strategy.

Product-Line Pricing: Pricing method in which the price of each individual offering is determined as a function of the offering's place in the company's product line.

Second-Market Discounting: Pricing method in which a company charges lower prices in more competitive markets, such as when exporting goods to developing countries.

Two-Part Pricing: See *complementary pricing.*

Yield-Management Pricing: Pricing method in which the price is set to maximize revenue for a fixed capacity within a given time frame (frequently used by airlines, hotels, and cruise ships).

CHAPTER ELEVEN

MANAGING INCENTIVES

But wait, there's more!
— Ron Popeil, inventor
and infomercial salesman

Incentives are inducements that aim to enhance the value of an offering by increasing its benefits or, more frequently, by reducing its costs. The ultimate goal of incentives is to incite action on the part of the company's customers, collaborators, and employees. Because they typically are used to increase sales, incentives are often referred to as sales promotions. The key aspects of designing and managing incentives are the focus of this chapter.

Managing Incentives as a Value-Creation Process

Incentives enhance the value of an offering by providing additional benefits or reducing costs. Most incentives are temporary in nature and are designed to facilitate sales by enabling the company to respond in a timely manner to changes in the market, such as a decline in customer demand, competitive price discounts, time-defined company goals, pressure from channel partners, or a weak economy.

Incentives are one of the seven attributes defining the company's offering. Working with the other offering attributes—product, service, brand, price, communication, and distribution—incentives aim to enhance the offering's value for target customers, collaborators, and the company (Figure 1). Accordingly, a manager's ultimate goal is to design incentives that create optimal value for target customers, collaborators, and the company.

Figure 1. Managing Incentives as a Value-Creation Process

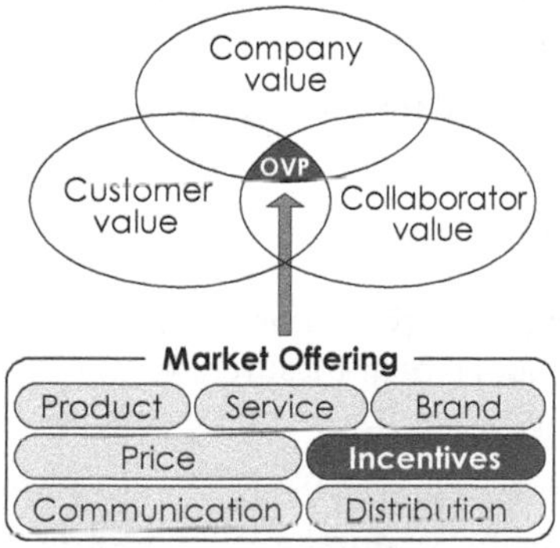

Depending on the entity for which they aim to create value, most incentives fall into one of three categories: incentives given to *customers* (coupons, loyalty programs, sweepstakes, contests, and premiums); incentives given to the company's *collaborators*, most often channel partners (price cuts, volume discounts, allowances, and co-op advertising); and incentives given to the company's *employees* (awards, bonuses, rewards, and contests).

In addition, incentives can be either *monetary* (e.g., volume discounts, price reductions, coupons, and rebates), or *nonmonetary* (e.g., premiums, contests, and rewards). Unlike monetary incentives, which typically aim to reduce an offering's costs, nonmonetary incentives typically aim to enhance the offering's benefits. The most common types of incentives are outlined in Figure 2.

Figure 2. Incentive Types

	Monetary incentives	Nonmonetary incentives
Customer incentives	Coupons, rebates, volume discounts, price reductions	Premiums, rewards, sweepstakes, loyalty programs, prizes, contests
Collaborator (trade) incentives	Slotting, stocking, advertising, display, and market-development allowances; spiffs; volume discounts and rebates; off-invoice incentives; cash discounts; inventory financing	Contests, bonus merchandise, buyback guarantees, sales support and training
Company incentives	Monetary bonuses and rewards	Nonmonetary bonuses and rewards, recognition awards, contests

The key aspects of customer, collaborator, and company incentives are outlined in more detail in the following sections.

Customer Incentives

Customer incentives are inducements that aim to enhance the value of an offering for its target customers. Customer incentives can be offered by the producer as in the case of manufacturer incentives and by channel members as in the case of retailer incentives. Because retailers have direct contact with buyers at the point of purchase, in addition to their own incentives they also implement incentives on behalf of manufacturers (also referred to as pass-through incentives). For example, a manufacturer might engage retailers carrying its products to distribute and redeem coupons, offer a two-for-one promotion, or temporarily lower the price on some of its products.

Based on the nature of the reward involved, customer incentives can be divided into two types: *monetary* and *nonmonetary*.

Monetary Customer Incentives

Monetary incentives aim to increase the value of the offering by reducing its costs, thus providing customers with an inducement to purchase the offering. The most common types of monetary incentives include *coupons, rebates, volume discounts*, and *temporary price reductions*.

- **Coupons** are certificates that entitle the buyer to receive a price reduction for a given product or service at the time of purchase. Coupons are the oldest and arguably most widely used form of customer incentives. They are often used as a means of price segmentation because they are effective with price-sensitive customers, who are willing to trade off time and effort (by locating the coupon and using it at the point of purchase) in order to save money. In addition to entitling customers to a price reduction, coupons also help create and enhance customers' awareness of the company's offering. Coupons are most often distributed as free-standing inserts (FSI) in newspapers and magazines, online, via direct mail, or at the point of purchase. Coupons can also be affixed to the product (as in the case of coupons offering instant discounts), or they can be placed inside the package or generated at the time of purchase at the checkout counter (as in the case of bounce-back coupons redeemable on the next purchase of the same or a related item).

- **Rebates** are cash refunds given to buyers after they make a purchase. Rebates are less popular than coupons and usually require greater effort from buyers (e.g., filling out the rebate form) as well as the disclosure of certain personal information (e.g., buyer's name and the mailing address to which the rebate will be sent). Most rebates require time to be processed and, as a result, the customer might have to wait weeks or sometimes months to receive the monetary compensation offered by the rebate. An exception to the latter aspect of rebates are instant rebates that are redeemed at the time of purchase. Because customers effectively end up paying a discounted price, instant rebates are functionally similar to temporary price reductions.

- **Volume discounts** are price reduction offers that are conditional on the purchase of multiple items. By incentivizing buyers to purchase larger quantities, volume discounts allow retailers to transfer some of their inventory (and, hence, reduce inventory costs) to the buyer, who now will have to store larger quantities of the purchased items. Volume discounts are popular among retailers who are trying to free up inventory space (e.g., for a higher margin item), in the case of perishable products, as well as for products (e.g., food and beverage offerings) where a larger purchase quantity is likely to increase consumption and, therefore, the total size of the market.

- **Temporary price reductions** involve a straightforward lowering of the offering's price without requiring buyers to take any additional action such as bring a coupon, fill in a rebate form, or buy multiple items. Temporary price reductions are akin to changing an offering's price, with the key difference that the changes are not permanent. (In fact, the short-term nature of temporary price reductions is the reason why they are considered an incentive-related decision rather than a pricing decision). In addition, temporary price reductions are typically framed as a discount off the original price. As a result, the original price now serves as a reference point against which customers assess the attractiveness of the promotional offer.

Nonmonetary Customer Incentives

Nonmonetary incentives typically aim to enhance the value of the offering by increasing its benefits rather than lowering its costs. The most common types of nonmonetary customer incentives are *premiums, prizes, contests, sweepstakes, games,* and *loyalty programs.*

- **Premiums** are bonus products or services offered for free or at deeply discounted prices as an incentive to purchase a particular offering. Premiums can be delivered instantly with the purchase (packaged with the product) or can require the customer to send in a proof of purchase to receive the premium. A popular form of premium is the buy-one-get-one (or two-for-one), where the buyer receives a bonus item identical to the item purchased. Another common type of premium are toys included with the purchase of products consumed by kids, such as cereal and fast-food meals. For example, McDonald's' decision to include toys with its Happy Meals made it de facto the largest toy retailer on a unit basis, distributing close to a billion toys per year.

- **Prizes** offer customers the opportunity to win an award as an incentive for purchasing a particular offering. Unlike premiums, where the reward is given with every purchase, in the case of prizes the actual reward is given to a relatively small number of participants. Prizes can be both monetary and nonmonetary. For example, Pepsi's *Twist and Win* promotion involved specially marked Pepsi products with various instant awards that ranged from cash to free gas, drinks, and movie tickets imprinted under the bottle cap.

- **Contests, sweepstakes, and games** involve prizes that typically require customers to submit some form of entry to participate. Contests typically require a proof of purchase, whereas sweepstakes are usually not contingent on customers purchasing the offering. Winners are selected by a panel of judges (in the case of contests), by a drawing (in the case of sweepstakes), or by an objective criterion such as points collected (in the case of games).

- **Loyalty programs** involve rewards related to the frequency, volume, and type of products and services purchased. Loyalty programs can be both monetary, such as cash rewards, and nonmonetary, such as frequent-flyer airline awards, frequent-stay hotel awards, and loyalty points that can be converted into bonus products and services. Unlike most of the other types of incentives, loyalty programs primarily target a company's existing customers and are designed to ensure their long-term loyalty as well as increase the quantity purchased by these customers. In addition to retaining its current customers, loyalty programs can attract new customers who are assessing the pros and cons of competing brands prior to deciding to patronize a particular company. For example, American Airlines—which in 1981 was one of the first major companies to introduce a loyalty program—launched its frequent-flyer program as a tool to move away from competing purely on price to building a loyal customer base.

The Pros and Cons of Customer Incentives

Customer-focused incentives offer multiple benefits to companies. Incentives are most frequently used to increase the sales of an offering. To this end, companies often use incentives to attract new customers as well as to encourage more frequent and larger purchases by existing customers. In addition, companies use incentives to stimulate demand in product categories where consumption depends on the purchase quantity. For example, customers who have purchased a larger amount of food than usual because of a sales promotion are often likely to end up consuming more food just because it is readily available.

Incentives can also encourage customers to purchase a company's offering within a time frame consistent with the company's goals. For example, a sales promotion run during the last quarter of the accounting year can help a company meet the desired annual sales goal. Furthermore, because sales promotions are easy to initiate and generate a positive (albeit often short-term) customer response, companies find them an increasingly effective tool not only to gain new customers but also to rebuff competitors' efforts to steal their customers.

In addition to helping the company increase sales, incentives enable the company to optimize the value of the offering for different customers by selectively offering incentives to particular customer segments. For example, a company might optimize profits by selectively offering discounts to economically disadvantaged customers, frequent buyers, and high-volume buyers while having less price-sensitive segments pay full price.

Despite their advantages, customer incentives have a number of drawbacks. First, most incentives have a short-term effect, which limits their ability to create a sustainable competitive advantage. Indeed, most sales promotions cause an initial peak in sales followed by a return to pre-promotional sales levels. Furthermore, in many cases the promotional peak is followed by a post-promotional dip below the initial baseline because buyers take advantage of the promotion to purchase larger than usual quantities of the goods on sale and stockpile them for future consumption.

Incentives can also cannibalize regular-price sales from customers who would have purchased the offering without incentives. In this context, a portion of the company's promotional activities are likely to end up subsidizing sales that would have occurred anyway. The larger the company's market share and the less targeted its sales promotions, the more likely it is that such cannibalization will take place. Consequently, the company can end up spending money and effort selling discounted goods to customers who would have purchased them at the regular price.

In addition, frequent use of incentives can "train" customers to anticipate promotions and time their purchases accordingly. As a result, buyers become accustomed to purchase primarily on the basis of a discounted price rather than on the basis of the benefits associated with the product, service, and brand aspects of the offering. Moreover, frequent use of incentives leads to communication that involves advertising sales promotions rather than informing buyers about the nonprice benefits of the company's offering.

The complex nature of customer incentives and their multiple advantages and drawbacks call for a careful evaluation of the specific circumstances in which they are used. To this end, a manager must clearly identify the market opportunity that should be addressed (or the problem that should be solved) to ensure that the use of incentives will indeed produce the desired outcome and that incentives are the most effective means (compared to the other marketing tactics) to achieve that outcome.

Collaborator Incentives

Most collaborator incentives are offered to downstream members of a distribution channel, including wholesalers, distributors, dealers, and retailers. These incentives, also referred to as trade incentives, can be used to achieve a variety of goals: to acquire shelf space for new products as in the case of slotting allowances; to encourage distributors to carry higher levels of inventory to avoid stock-outs as in the case of stocking allowances, inventory financing, and volume discounts; and to encourage distributors to promote the company's offerings as in the case of advertising and display allowances. Similar to customer incentives, trade incentives can be either *monetary* or *nonmonetary*.

Monetary Collaborator Incentives

Monetary incentives involve payments or price discounts given by the manufacturer to channel members as encouragement to carry a particular offering or as an inducement to promote an offering to customers. Common monetary incentives include *slotting, stocking, cooperative advertising, display,* and *market-development allowances; spiffs; volume discounts; volume rebates; off-invoice incentives; cash discounts;* and *inventory financing.*

- **Slotting allowances** are incentives paid to a channel member—a wholesaler, dealer, or retailer—to allocate shelf space for a new product. Slotting allowances are designed to offset the costs associated with inventorying the new items, redesigning store shelves, and informing the employees about the new offerings.

- **Stocking allowances** are incentives paid to a distributor to carry extra inventory in anticipation of an increase in demand. Stocking allowances are often used in conjunction with extensive advertising campaigns and consumer incentive programs that are likely to lead to a spike in demand for the promoted offering.

- **Cooperative advertising allowances** are incentives paid by the manufacturer to channel members in return for featuring the manufacturer's offerings in their advertisements. The magnitude of the allowance can be determined as a percentage of the distributor's advertising costs or as a fixed amount per unit.

- **Display allowances** are incentives paid by the manufacturer to channel members in return for prominently displaying the manufacturer's products and services. Display allowances can involve end-of-aisle displays (endcap displays), larger and better shelf space, as well as free-standing displays featuring manufacturers' products.

- **Market-development allowances** are incentives offered to channel members in return for creating demand for the company's products. Market-development allowances are often used by manufacturers to create awareness of their offerings in local markets by leveraging retailers' knowledge and influence in these markets.

- **Spiffs** are incentives such as cash premiums, prizes, or additional commissions given directly to the salesperson (rather than to the retailer) as a reward for selling a particular item. Because they encourage the retailer's sales personnel to "push" the product to customers, spiffs are often referred to as "push money." The term "spiff" stems from the use of the word in the middle of the 19th century in reference to somebody smartly dressed (hence *to spiff up*—to improve the appearance of a place, a product, or a person).

- **Volume discounts** are price reductions offered to channel members based on the volume of a manufacturer's products purchased, with higher volumes typically associated with greater discounts.

- **Volume rebates** are incentives paid by the manufacturer to a distributor as a reward for achieving certain sales-quantity benchmarks. For example, a car manufacturer might offer a volume rebate to dealers only if they have sold a certain number of cars per month.

- **Off-invoice incentives** refer to any temporary price discounts offered by manufacturers to channel members. Off-invoice incentives are offered for a fixed period of time for the purpose of encouraging retailers to purchase larger quantities of the manufacturer's products and/or to pass some of the price reduction through to consumers in order to stimulate demand.

- **Cash discounts** are price reductions for payments made instantly or within a predefined time frame prior to the invoice due date. For example, a company might offer a two percent discount if an invoice due in 90 days is instead paid in 30 days.

- **Inventory financing** involves loans provided to a distributor for acquiring manufacturers' goods. Inventory financing can be structured as an inventory-backed revolving line of credit or a short-term loan made to the retailer by the manufacturer. Inventory financing is particularly relevant for retailers that must pay manufacturers in a shorter period than it takes them to sell the merchandise and receive payments from their customers.

Most monetary allowances are offered to channel members as a reward for conducting promotional activities on behalf of the manufacturer, and these allowances are typically implemented as a discount from the wholesale price rather than as a separate promotional payment. From an accounting standpoint, depending on the way they are structured, trade allowances can be considered as a discount to the channel or as a separate marketing expense.

Nonmonetary Collaborator Incentives

Nonmonetary incentives involve rewards given by the manufacturer to channel members as encouragement to carry a particular offering or as an inducement to promote an offering to customers. Common nonmonetary incentives include *buyback guarantees*, *sales support and training*, *bonus merchandise*, and *contests*.

- **Buyback guarantees** are agreements that the manufacturer will buy back from channel members product quantities not sold within a certain time frame. The purpose of buyback guarantees is to encourage channel members to carry larger inventory (in order to avoid stock-outs) by minimizing their financial risk.

- **Sales support and training** involve various forms of aid offered to familiarize distributors with the offering and facilitate sales. This form of trade promotion is common in industries with more complex offerings that require sales support staff to be versed in the product specifics and be able to explain them to customers.

- **Bonus merchandise** involves free goods offered as a reward for stocking a particular item or in lieu of a monetary allowance. Thus, rather than giving channel members monetary compensation for carrying a particular good, the manufacturer can provide extra units of its merchandise at no extra cost.

- **Contests** involve performance-based rewards such as vacation trips, cars, and monetary compensation given to the best performing individuals or teams among a company's collaborators. Contest winners can be determined based on factors such as the number of units of a particular product sold, the number of new accounts opened, and the number of promotional activities launched.

The Pros and Cons of Collaborator Incentives

Collaborator-focused incentives offer multiple benefits to companies. These incentives can help persuade channel members to carry a company's offerings, making these offerings readily available to target customers. Incentives can further persuade channel members to carry larger inventories of their offerings in order to ensure against stock-outs. Trade allowances can induce channel members to promote the company's offerings by securing prime shelf space, placing point-of-purchase product displays, and otherwise promoting the company's offerings. Collaborators can also facilitate the implementation of pass-through promotions by delivering the company's incentives such as coupons, price discounts, and bonus offerings directly to customers. Finally, trade incentives such as spiffs, contests, bonus merchandise, and volume discounts and rebates can help motivate channel members to push the company's offerings.

Despite their advantages, trade incentives have a number of drawbacks. A key drawback are the high costs associated with the design and implementation of trade incentives. Indeed, as consolidated retailers gain power, they are in a stronger position to demand compensation from manufacturers for all activities designed to support their offerings. Retailers, on the other hand, are faced with rapidly evolving buyer preferences, a growing number of new product introductions, and ever-increasing competition, which, in turn, force them to streamline their operations and demand compensation for all incremental activities in order to achieve their profit goals.

In addition to their high costs, trade incentives can lead to channel conflicts stemming from the different goals of manufacturers on the one hand and channel members on the other. For example, incentives such as spiffs that are paid directly to the salesforce can put the interests of the manufacturer at odds with the interests of the retailer: The salesforce is motivated to push the offerings of a particular company that might not fit with the optimal profit-maximization strategy of the retailer. Furthermore, the offering promoted by the company might not be the best option for the retailer's customers, which, in turn, can damage this retailer's reputation among its customers.

To determine whether to provide incentives to each of the company's collaborators, as well as the type and magnitude of these incentives, a manager must carefully examine the value that its offerings create for collaborators and how these incentives are aligned with the company's strategic goals. Indeed, because incentives are easy to implement and often have immediate impact, managers can be tempted to use them as a universal tool to bolster sales volume. In this context, considering both the pros and cons of incentives is essential for the development of a sound market strategy.

Company Incentives

Although often overlooked, company incentives can play an important role in managing a company's offering. Similar to customer and collaborator incentives, company incentives can be divided into two categories: *monetary* and *nonmonetary*.

Monetary Company Incentives

Monetary incentives are often used to supplement the regular compensation received by employees in the form of a salary or commissions. They are similar to commissions in that they depend on employee performance and are typically conditional on achieving a specific performance benchmark such as units sold, sales revenues, and customer satisfaction. The most common forms of employee monetary incentives are cash bonuses and contests.

- **Monetary bonuses** are monetary rewards for employees—managers, customer service representatives, and salesforce—who meet certain performance benchmarks. Monetary bonuses can involve direct cash payments, or they can be tied to the company's performance as in the case of stock options.

- **Monetary contests** are performance-based rewards given to the best performing employees. Unlike monetary bonuses, which are given to all employees that have achieved certain performance outcomes, contests reward only the top performer(s).

Monetary incentives can be an effective means for companies to manage employees' compensation in a way that reflects their overall performance while at the same time introducing a competitive component. Indeed, the use of incentives given only to top performers (as in the case of contests) enables the company to motivate employees by benchmarking their performance based not only on the goal set by the company but also on the levels attained by top achievers.

Nonmonetary Company Incentives

Nonmonetary incentives are a popular form of employee incentives that are used either in combination with or as a replacement for monetary incentives. Unlike monetary incentives, where benefits are expressed using a common currency, nonmonetary incentives vary widely in the type of benefit received by employees. The most common types of nonmonetary incentives include bonuses, contests, and awards.

- **Nonmonetary bonuses** include a variety of incentives such as vacation incentives (e.g., extra vacation days), travel incentives (e.g., business class travel and a company car), and entertainment incentives (e.g., expense account).

- **Nonmonetary contests** involve performance-based nonmonetary rewards such as vacation trips, cars, free merchandise, and other prizes. Similar to monetary contests, nonmonetary contests reward only the best performers.

- **Recognition awards** acknowledge an employee's professional achievements and are an important component in creating and managing a company's culture by underscoring the company's values and the behaviors it aims to encourage. Common recognition awards include certificates of appreciation, employee of the month/quarter/year awards, and leadership and management awards.

The popularity of nonmonetary incentives can be attributed to several factors. First, nonmonetary awards acknowledging employee achievements can be more meaningful than a relatively small amount of cash to employees who would like to make a difference and appreciate the fact that their work is valued by the company. In addition, compared to cash, nonmonetary incentives can be perceived as being of a more personal nature, which, in turn, helps build an emotional bond between the company and its employees. Finally, in some cases, a company can acquire the benefits awarded to the employee at a significantly lower cost than their market value, thus making the nonmonetary awards more cost effective for the company.

The Pros and Cons of Company Incentives

Company-focused incentives can help motivate employees to increase productivity and achieve higher levels of performance, foster teamwork, and stimulate creativity. Incentives are a particularly common tool for motivating the salesforce in order to achieve greater sales effort, foster lead development and conversion to sales, promote new products and services, and stimulate off-season sales. Incentives are also often used to motivate the company's management by recognizing their leadership skills and rewarding them for the company's overall performance.

An important benefit of incentives is their variety, which enables the company to match the nature of the reward with the benefits sought by individual employees. Thus, the company can reward some of its employees with additional monetary compensation, whereas other employees might derive greater benefit from nonmonetary benefits such as extra vacation time, free merchandise, or recognition of their exemplary work ethic. Apart from their functional and monetary benefits, incentives can also deliver important psychological benefits by demonstrating that the company cares about its employees and appreciates their achievements.

In addition to increasing employee productivity, teamwork, and creativity, incentives can play an important role in attracting new employees and retaining a company's current workforce. To this end, companies use a variety of incentives including signing bonuses, moving expenses, and temporary housing in order to increase the likelihood of hiring and retaining excellent employees by "sweetening" their compensation package. Offering short-term incentives rather than a more permanent compensation package can also help the company address the uncertainty involved in hiring new employees and hedge its bets by minimizing long-term commitments.

Company incentives are not without shortcomings. Similar to the way in which customers and channel members get habituated to incentives, employees might become accustomed to receiving incentives, which, in turn, might make these incentives less effective. In addition, competitive incentives such as contests can end up being detrimental to the company's culture, engendering a competitive rather than collaborative environment. In the same vein, rewarding top performers to boost their motivation might end up demotivating those who were not rewarded. Finally, without a diligent performance-monitoring system in place, productivity-based incentives might encourage some employees to adopt unethical (and sometimes illegal) work practices, such as circumventing legal requirements and regulations, delivering inferior product quality, and misrepresenting the company's offering to buyers.

A classic example of counterproductive behavior induced by pay-for-performance incentives is the snake-catching bounty introduced in India during British rule. In order to free Delhi from a plague of snakes, the city's governor introduced a bounty on cobra skins. Because catching cobras is rather challenging, the reward was quite high. This, in turn, created a profitable business of farming snakes and collecting a reward for their skins. As the number of bounty claims increased exponentially, it became clear that the incentive was ineffective, and the governor decided to abandon the snake-catching initiative. Once farming cobras was no longer profitable, the snakes were released into the city streets, aggravating the original problem.[25]

To ensure that performance-based incentives serve their purpose and will not backfire by promoting unethical or otherwise counterproductive behavior, managers should carefully consider the behavioral implications of the proposed incentives. When used judiciously, and in a way that accounts for employee abuse of the company's reward policies, incentives can have a significant impact on company performance and the value that the company creates and captures in the market. Therefore, designing a meaningful incentives program aimed at attracting, motivating, and rewarding company employees while monitoring their performance can play a key role in enabling the company to achieve market success.

Managing Incentives in a Competitive Context

Compared to the other marketing tactics, incentives are relatively easy to implement and, as a result, many companies rely on incentives to better align the value of their offerings with the current market conditions. The widespread use of incentives as a universal value-management tool underscores the importance of identifying whether and how to use incentives in a way that benefits target customers, the company, and its collaborators. The key aspects of managing incentives to create market value—using incentives as a means of competitive differentiation, managing push and pull promotions, and communicating incentives—are discussed in the following sections.

Using Incentives as a Means of Competitive Differentiation

In the ideal scenario, incentives create market value and generate sales that could not be achieved by the other marketing tactics. While most incentives are able to boost the value of an offering in the short term, this boost in many cases is short-lived, often having adverse consequences on the offering's ability to create market value in a sustainable fashion.

Sales promotions often fail to create long-term value because of the ease with which competitors can match, and thereby negate, the competitive advantage they create. Moreover, by focusing buyers' attention on the monetary aspect of the offering, sales promotions systematically erode the power of the offering's brand by implicitly endorsing the view that the competing offerings are de facto commodities that can only be differentiated by price. Accordingly, sales promotions in general, and price promotions in particular, should be viewed as ancillary means rather than main tools to achieve competitive differentiation.

Not all incentives are detrimental to the company's ability to create a sustainable competitive market position for its offerings. Incentives that are directly related to the benefits of the company's offering and are aligned with the positioning of the company's offering can help strengthen the company's market position and increase the power of its brand. Incentives that can benefit the company's long-term market position include loyalty programs as well as premiums, prizes, contests, and games that are directly related to the benefits delivered by the company's offering. For example, airline, hotel, and credit card loyalty programs enhance the brands of these companies. In the same vein, Coca-Cola's "look under the cap" promotion helps the company maintain top-of-mind awareness by offering consumers the opportunity to win a variety of prizes based on the unique code under the bottle cap.

Managing Push and Pull Promotions

An important aspect of managing a company's promotional activity involves determining the balance between customer-focused and channel-focused promotions. In this context, two core approaches can be identified: push promotions and pull promotions. These two types of promotions differ in the flow of incentives and communications between the company, its channel partners, and target customers (Figure 3). Here the term "promotion" is used in a more general sense to refer both to incentives (sales promotions) and communication.

Figure 3. Push and Pull Promotions

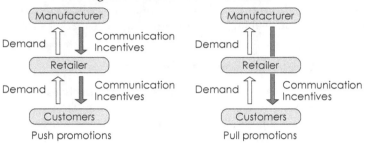

Push promotions   Pull promotions

Push Promotions

Push promotions stimulate demand for a company's offering by incentivizing channel members so that they have a vested interest to push the product downstream to end users. For example, the manufacturer can offer large trade allowances and discounts on its products and services to retailers. These promotions help generate store traffic, giving retailers a vested interest in selling the product. The manufacturer can also educate a retailer's salesforce about the benefits of its offerings and provide the retailer with promotional materials, thus facilitating the sales process.

The advantages of push promotions are that they are easier for the manufacturer to implement, since in this case the promotional activities are outsourced to channel members. In addition, because a large number of consumers make their buying decisions at the point of purchase, store-level promotions can be very effective in influencing their choices. The growing power of retailers demanding competitive trade discounts and allowances makes it even more difficult for manufacturers to ensure that their offerings are readily accessible to their target customers without relying on push promotions.

Despite their multiple benefits, push promotions have several important drawbacks. A key downside of push promotions is that in most cases they do not enable the manufacturer to directly promote its brand and build brand loyalty among its customers. Indeed, because in this case retailers carry out most of the communication and sales promotion, manufacturers do not have direct contact with customers and must rely on channel members to inform customers about the benefits of its offerings. The challenge here is that retailers are not always interested in building strong manufacturer brands because as these brands gain strength their dependence on retailers tends to decline, which in turn erodes retailers' power. This misalignment of the ultimate goals of manufacturers and retailers often leads to retailers not implementing the push promotions as intended by the manufacturer. For example, a retailer might decide not to pass through price discounts as the manufacturer intends and instead leave prices unchanged, keeping the discount for themselves. Another important downside of push promotions is the opportunity cost, whereby excessive spending on trade promotions can drain the company's promotional budget, hindering its ability to build strong brands and create a loyal customer base.

Pull Promotions

Pull promotions create demand for a company's offering by promoting the offering directly to end users, who in turn demand the offering from intermediaries, and ultimately "pull" it through the distribution channel. To illustrate, the manufacturer can extensively advertise its products and services to end users and promote its offerings using means such as coupons, rebates, games, and contests.

The advantage of pull promotions is that they enable the company to interact with its customers without the involvement of an intermediary. Companies can use this direct line of communication to promote the benefits of its offerings and associate these benefits with its brand, thus building a meaningful brand image in the minds of its customers. The ability to build customer loyalty and a strong brand can play a crucial role for manufacturers that are trying to gain power over retailers. Indeed, faced with customer demand for a manufacturer's offerings, retailers are likely to feel pressured to carry these offerings in order to please their customers, which, in turn, gives the manufacturer some leverage over retailers.

One of the main drawbacks of pull promotions is the increasing cost of effectively reaching target customers. Customers are constantly bombarded with a multitude of messages, making it difficult to break through the clutter to communicate the company's message and build a meaningful brand image. And while many companies have managed to create direct lines of communication with their current customers through mobile apps, loyalty programs, and online forums, attracting new customers has become more challenging. Another drawback of pull promotions is the increasing complexity of implementing a successful customer-focused communication and sales promotion program, which requires a certain level of market knowledge and expertise in design and delivery to carry it out in an effective and cost-efficient manner. As a result, companies that lack such expertise often choose to allocate a greater portion of their promotional budget to push promotions and delegate their implementation to channel members.

Summary

Incentives aim to increase the value of an offering by increasing its benefits or reducing costs. Most incentives are temporary in nature and are designed to enable the company to respond in a timely manner to changes in the market such as a decline in customer demand, competitive price discounts, pressure from channel partners, or a weak economy.

Companies use incentives for a variety of reasons: to retain their current customers and attract new ones, to ensure collaborator support, as well as to increase the productivity and ensure the loyalty of their employees. When developing incentives, a manager's ultimate goal is to enhance the value an offering creates for target customers, the company, and its collaborators.

Most incentives fall into one of three categories: customer incentives, collaborator incentives, and company incentives.

Customer incentives can be divided into monetary incentives that typically aim to reduce an offering's costs (coupons, rebates, volume discounts, and temporary price reductions) and nonmonetary incentives that often aim to enhance the offering's benefits (premiums, prizes, contests, sweepstakes, games, and loyalty programs).

Most *collaborator incentives* are offered to members of the distribution channel and involve slotting, stocking, advertising, display, and market-development allowances; spiffs; volume discounts and rebates; off-invoice incentives; cash discounts; and inventory financing. Similar to customer incentives, trade incentives are either monetary (discounts and allowances) or nonmonetary (buyback guarantees, sales support and training, bonus merchandise, and contests). Trade incentives can have multiple objectives such as gaining distribution coverage, encouraging channel members to stock the offering at certain inventory levels (to avoid stock-outs or to transfer inventory from the manufacturer to distributors), and encouraging channel members to promote the company's offering.

Company incentives commonly involve rewards for employees who meet certain performance benchmarks. These incentives include performance-based awards such as monetary and non-monetary bonuses, employee recognition awards, and contests.

Managing promotions calls for finding the right balance between customer-focused and channel-focused promotions. *Push promotions* create demand for a company's offering by incentivizing channel members, who in turn push the product downstream to end users. *Pull promotions*, on the other hand, create demand for a company's offering by promoting the offering directly to end users, who in turn demand the offering from intermediaries and ultimately "pull" it through the channel.

CHAPTER TWELVE

MANAGING COMMUNICATION

A good advertisement is one which sells the
product without drawing attention to itself.
— David Ogilvy, founder of Ogilvy & Mather

Communication informs target customers, collaborators, and company employees and stakeholders about the benefits of the company's offering. Communication is one aspect of marketing that has undergone dramatic changes in the past decade and is continuing to evolve rapidly. Despite these changes, there are a number of enduring marketing principles that are at the heart of successful communication campaigns. The core principles of marketing communication are outlined in this chapter.

Communication as a Value-Creation Process

Market success is rarely possible without an effective communication campaign that creates awareness of the company's offering among its target audience. The role of communication as a tool for creating market value, the key trends in communication management, and the process of developing a viable communication campaign are discussed in the following sections.

Communication as a Tool for Creating Market Value

Communication informs the relevant market entities — target customers, collaborators, and the company — about the specifics of the offering. Companies spend billions of dollars each year to advise buyers about the availability of their offerings, explain the benefits of these offerings, spread the word about price cuts, and promote product and corporate brands. In the words of Leo Burnett, founder of the Leo Burnett advertising agency, *Advertising says to people, "Here's what we've got. Here's what it will do for you. Here's how to get it."*

Communication is one of the seven attributes that define a company's offering. Unlike the first five attributes — product, service, brand, price, and incentives — which largely define the value of the offering, communication informs target customers about various aspects of the offering. As a result, communication creates value by informing different market entities — target customers, collaborators, and the company employees and stakeholders — about the offering's optimal value proposition (OVP). Therefore, when developing a communication campaign, a manager's ultimate goal is to inform target customers, collaborators, and company employees and stakeholders about the offering and the ways in which it will create market value (Figure 1).

Figure 1. Communication as a Value-Creation Process

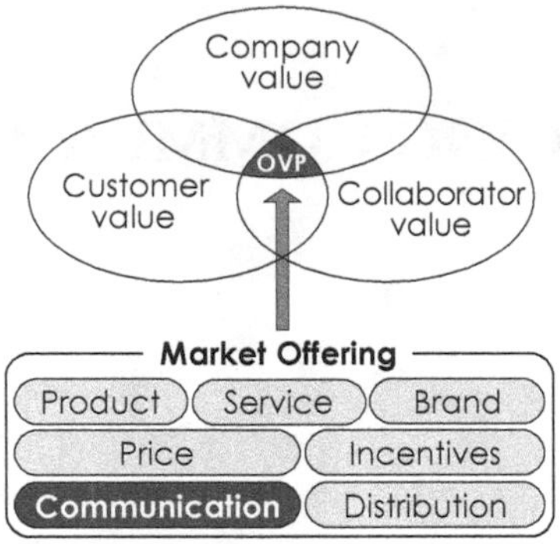

Based on the target audience, there are three types of communication: customer-focused, collaborator-focused, and company-focused (internal). While all three types of communication are important, the one that is the most complex and typically absorbs most of a company's resources is customer-focused communication. Collaborator-focused and internal communication share many commonalities with customer-focused communication but are typically more straightforward to implement. Accordingly, the remainder of this chapter will focus on the communication a company aims at its customers.

Developing an Effective Communication Campaign

The changes in the ways companies interact with their customers add an extra layer of complexity to the task of effectively managing communication campaigns. This complexity highlights the importance of using a systematic approach—such as the G-STIC framework outlined in Chapter 3—to communicate the company's offering. Consistent with this framework, managing communication can be defined by five key actions: setting the communication *goal*, articulating the communication *strategy*, designing the communication *tactics*, *implementing* the communication campaign, and *controlling* (evaluating) the campaign results (Figure 2).

Figure 2. The G-STIC Framework for Managing Communication

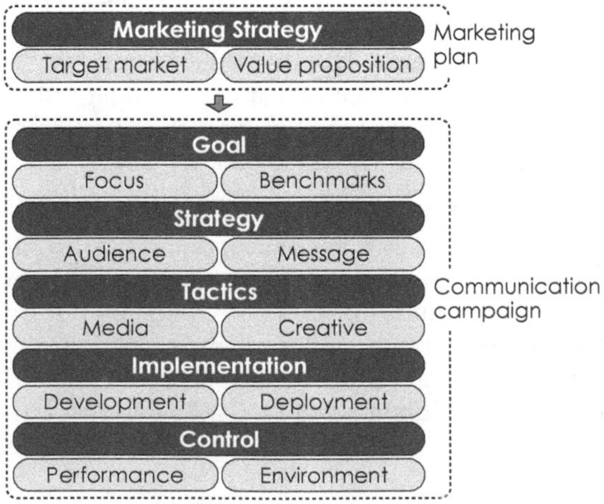

A company's communication campaign is guided by its overarching marketing strategy, defined by the choice of target market and the company's value proposition for this market. Building on this marketing strategy, the communication campaign starts with setting a *goal*, defined by its *focus*, which delineates the key criterion for the success of the communication campaign, and performance *benchmarks*, which outline the quantitative and temporal criteria for reaching the communication goal. Following articulation of the goal is the development of a communication *strategy* and, specifically, the identification of the target *audience* and the *message* that will be communicated to this audience. The communication strategy is then translated into *tactics*, which involve determining the specific *media* used to transmit the message and the *creative* execution that aims to express the message in the chosen media format. Next, is the *implementation*, which involves the practical execution—*development* and *deployment*—of the campaign. Finally, *control* measures the *performance* of the campaign while monitoring for changes in the *context* in which communication takes place.

The key aspects of developing a communication campaign—setting communication goals, identifying the target audience, developing the message, selecting the media, designing the creative execution, and evaluating communication effectiveness—are outlined in the following sections.

Setting Communication Goals

Communication goals articulate the particular outcomes that a company aims to achieve with its communication campaign in a specific period of time. As in the case of the company's overall goal, setting the communication goal involves two main decisions: identifying the *focus* of the company's actions and defining the performance *benchmarks* to be achieved. These two aspects of setting the communication goal and the factors that influence their selection are discussed in more detail below.

Defining the Focus of the Communication Campaign

The focus identifies the key criterion for the success of the communication campaign. It is the metric defining the desired outcome of the company's communication activities. Based on their focus, there are three types of communication goals: *creating awareness, building preferences*, and *inciting action*.

- **Creating awareness.** A communication campaign might aim to make the target audience aware of a company's offering. For example, a toy manufacturer might want to inform its target customers about a new toy, a retailer might want to communicate its new sales promotions, and a movie studio might want to create awareness of an upcoming movie release. In cases when the company launches a new-to-the-world product or service, the communication might also aim to create awareness of the entire product category. For example, when launching its video streaming service, Netflix had to inform its customers about its offering while in the process explaining the benefits of the entire fixed-fee-based streaming business model. Creating top-of-mind awareness of the entire product category is also a common communication goal for many industry associations tasked with promoting the consumption of a particular good such as cotton, milk, and alternative energy.

- **Building preferences.** A communication campaign might also aim to create and strengthen customer preference for the offering by enhancing the offering's desirability. Preference-building goes beyond generating awareness of the company's offering among the target audience to convey the value it creates. This value can be expressed in terms of its superiority to another offering, as in the case of comparative advertising, or by focusing on the offering's ability to fulfill customers' needs without necessarily comparing it to another offering, as in the case of noncomparative advertising.

- **Inciting action.** A communication campaign might aim to motivate customers to engage with the offering and take an action such as obtaining more information about the company's offering, visiting a retailer that carries it, and ultimately purchasing it. For example, a pharmaceutical company might encourage consumers to contact a doctor to obtain more information about a particular drug, a car manufacturer might encourage buyers to visit its dealerships, and an electronics manufacturer might encourage shoppers to buy its newest device.

These three goals are interdependent, such that some can be viewed as prerequisites for others. Thus, enhancing an offering's attractiveness implies that target customers are already informed about the offering's existence. Similarly, a call for action implies that customers are already informed about the offering and find it desirable. Therefore, when determining the focus of its communication campaign, a company must be cognizant of customers' awareness and beliefs about its offering(s), prioritize the outcomes it aims to achieve, and ensure that these outcomes are aligned with its overall marketing goals.

Defining Performance Benchmarks

Performance benchmarks outline the quantitative and temporal criteria for reaching the communication goal. Consequently, there are two types of performance benchmarks that define the company's communication goal:

- **Quantitative benchmarks** define the specific milestones to be achieved by the company with respect to its focal communication goal. For example, a company might aim to create awareness of a new offering among 50% of its target customers, increase by 20% the number of buyers who prefer its brand to its primary competitors, or increase traffic to the company's website by two million visitors. Quantitative benchmarks can be expressed in either relative terms (e.g., increase awareness by 20%) or absolute terms (e.g., generate two million incremental visits).

- **Temporal benchmarks** identify the time frame for achieving a particular milestone. Setting a timeline for achieving a goal is a key strategic decision because the communication campaign adopted to implement these goals is often contingent on the time horizon. An aggressive communication goal that aims to achieve a particular outcome in a short period of time will likely require a different campaign than the goal of achieving the same outcome over a longer period of time.

To be actionable, the communication goal should clearly articulate the focus of the campaign and its quantitative and temporal benchmarks. Some communication campaigns define the desired outcome in relative terms, whereas others define the goal as an absolute number. The key principle when choosing the focus and benchmarks of the communication campaign is that they must be consistent with the company's overall marketing strategy and enable the company to create superior value for its target customers, collaborators, and stakeholders.

Determining the Communication Budget

An important aspect of developing a communication campaign is determining the optimal level of expenditures required to achieve the set communication goals. Generally speaking, communication costs can be divided into two categories: costs of developing the creative content and media costs that involve securing communication channels, such as the cost of air time, magazine space, and outdoor billboards. For many companies, and especially those with significant resources allocated for communication, media costs far exceed the costs associated with creative development.

There is no universal method that works for all companies and in all circumstances. Instead, there are three key factors that a company must consider in order to determine the optimal communication budget: its *communication goals*, the *cost of achieving these goals*, and the *available resources*.

- **Communication goals.** The nature of the company's goals—specifically the degree to which they are ambitious in terms of number of customers to be reached, the time frame for reaching them, and the desired outcome—can have a significant impact on the expenditures needed to achieve these goals.

- **Cost of achieving the communication goals.** The cost of achieving the company's communication goals depends on a variety of factors such as the level of benefits created by the offering, the degree to which the offering is differentiated from the competition, the level of communication expenditures by the competition, the effectiveness of competitive communication, the existing level of awareness and acceptance of the offering among target customers, as well as the company's ability to use resources in an effective and cost-efficient manner.

- **Available resources.** The overall level of communication expenditure depends on the company's resources. A small business with limited access to capital is likely to spend less on communication than an established large enterprise or a well-funded startup.

The above three factors are interrelated, such that communication goals are often set while considering the cost of achieving these goals and the resources that the company can allocate to the communication campaign. Indeed, articulating a communication goal without taking into account whether the company has the resources to achieve this goal can be counterproductive and is likely to cause disruptions when implementing the campaign. Setting the communication budget based solely on the resources allocated to running a communication campaign (e.g., as a percentage of sales revenues) without considering the ultimate goals that the campaign aims to achieve can also lead to either underfunding or overinvesting in the campaign.

Designing the Communication Strategy

The communication strategy comprises two key components: the audience targeted by the company's communication and the message that the company aims to convey to this audience. These two aspects of designing a communication strategy—identifying the target audience and developing the communication message—are discussed in the following sections.

Identifying the Target Audience

Identification of the target audience is a key component of developing a communication strategy that can have a significant impact on the effectiveness and cost efficiency of the communicated message. There are two complementary aspects of identifying the target audience: strategic and tactical. Strategic targeting involves identifying the audience targeted by the company's communication. In contrast, tactical targeting involves identifying the specific ways in which the company can reach strategically important audiences with its message in the most effective and cost-efficient way. The two aspects of the target audience—*strategic* and *tactical*—are outlined in the following sections.

Strategic Target Identification

The target audience is the intended recipient of the company's communication. Because communication is one aspect of an offering's tactics, identification of the target audience follows from the strategic choice of target customers for the company's offering. The target audience for the company's communication might differ from an offering's target customers. Target customers are the users of the offering—the entities for whom the company designs its offering. In contrast, the target audience for the company's communications consists of people that the company aims to inform about its offerings.

Most often, the target audience for a company's communication consists of the same customers targeted by the company's offering. This, however, is not always the case. For example, parents buying food and clothing for their kids are often the target audience for a company's communication campaign although they are not the end users. In the same vein, a company selling business software applications might develop a communication campaign targeting senior executives who will ultimately have to approve the purchase even though these executives might never actually use the software. A company might also develop a communication campaign aimed at the purchasing department of a potential client in order to create awareness of the company's offerings, even though the employees working in the purchasing department typically are not the target customers for the company offerings. Accordingly, the target audience can be broader than the offering's target customers and include initiators, influencers, gatekeepers, decision makers, and purchasers involved in selecting, buying, and using the offering.

Tactical Target Identification

Following identification of the target audience is identification of the ways in which the company can reach these customers. The primary goal of tactical targeting is to ensure effective and cost-efficient delivery of the company's communication. An overly broad targeting that includes audiences unrelated to the company's offering is not cost efficient because it wastes resources on reaching individuals that are unlikely to respond favorably to the company's offering. Targeting that is too narrow, on the other hand, is ineffective because it might overlook audiences that are strategically important for the company. Accordingly, tactical targeting is driven by two key principles: *effectiveness*, which reflects a company's ability to reach *all* desired recipients with its communication, and *cost efficiency*, which reflects the degree to which a company's communication efforts are deployed in a way that reaches *only* its target audience.

To enable the company to reach its target audience in the most effective and cost-efficient manner, tactical targeting must answer three main questions: *whom* to reach and *where* and *when* is the optimal opportunity to reach this audience. To address these questions, a company must identify the observable characteristics (the profile) of the strategically viable audience and identify the ideal touch points to inform this audience about the company's offering.

To determine the optimal opportunity (where and when) to reach the target audience, companies increasingly rely on their ability to track people's behavior, including their physical location and online activity. Examining an individual's online activity can help better understand, and even predict, this individual's current needs. For example, the information that an individual visits a particular website, the day and time of this visit, the pages visited, the amount of time spent on each page, the links clicked on, and the searches made enable companies to gain insight into this individual's specific needs and preferences. Furthermore, combining individuals' past online behavior with their current online activity enables companies to develop and serve content that is most likely to appeal to these individuals at a particular point in time.

Geotargeting enables a company to deliver content to its audience based on customers' current geographic location, determined by their mobile devices. Geotargeting is particularly important because location contains information about a customer's environment at a given time, which, in turn, makes it easier to deliver a relevant message that is aligned with the particular stage in this customer's decision journey. For example, delivering a message featuring a sales promotion to a customer visiting a grocery store can help the company increase the chances that this person will not only pay attention to the advertisement but also be more likely to change his or her behavior in response to the communication content.

Developing the Communication Message

Following identification of the target audience, the second component of a company's communication strategy aims to develop the message to be communicated to this audience. Here, a manager must choose the specific aspect(s) of the offering on which to focus the communication campaign. The essence of the communicated message and the decision of which offering attributes to promote are discussed in the following sections.

Determining the Message Content

The message is the information that the company aims to share with the target audience. The specifics of the company's message depend on which aspects of its offering the company aims to promote. Accordingly, the message can involve one or more of the other attributes defining the company's offering: *product, service, brand, price, incentives,* and *distribution*.

- **Communicating product and service information** informs the target audience about the specifics of the company's products and services, detailing their key benefits such as performance, reliability, durability, and ease of use.
- **Communicating the brand** informs the audience about the identity and meaning of the company's brand to create a unique, evocative image in customers' minds.

- **Communicating the price** informs the target audience about the monetary cost of the company's offering—its actual price as well as the total cost of ownership, including shipping, setup, maintenance, and disposal costs.

- **Communicating incentives** informs the target audience about the different sales promotions associated with the offering, such as temporary price reductions, volume discounts, rebates, coupons, and premiums.

- **Communicating distribution** informs the target audience about the offering's availability and the ways to obtain the offering.

Depending on its communication goals, a company can choose to promote one or more aspects of its offerings. For example, consider Cadillac, a division of General Motors that builds luxury vehicles worldwide. Based on its communication goals, Cadillac can tailor its message in a way that emphasizes different aspects of the company's offering. Thus, it might focus on the benefits of the *product*, emphasizing the design, performance, and comfort of its vehicles. The company might also communicate different aspects of its *service*, such as its OnStar emergency, security, and connectivity service, as well as its certified auto repair service and its automobile financing service.

Rather than focusing on the specific aspects of its cars and related service, Cadillac might focus its communication campaign on building its *brand*, emphasizing its roots as one of the oldest automobile brands in the world, its reputation of being at the forefront of innovation, and its image of luxury, performance, and prestige. Cadillac might also choose to advertise the *prices* at which its vehicles are sold—for example, to highlight the affordability of some models and the exclusivity of others. Another communication goal that Cadillac might pursue is to inform its target customers about *incentives* such as cash-back offers, price discounts, and special financing. Finally, Cadillac might choose to inform target customers about the *availability* of its offerings by informing them of the location of its dealerships.

Deciding Which Benefits to Promote

Another important aspect of developing the communication message is deciding how many and which benefits of the offering to promote. Here, more is not always better. Even though the notion of promoting all relevant benefits of the offering might sound appealing, cramming a plethora of benefits into a single communication campaign might be counterproductive by making it less likely that these benefits will register in buyers' minds. Therefore, a company must carefully consider the pros and cons of promoting different benefits and focus on those that are most likely to produce the desired impact on buyers' behavior.

The key principle guiding the choice of the message to be communicated is that it must be consistent with the overarching communication goals. This principle follows from the general notion that the strategy of any action must be aligned with the ultimate goal this action aims to achieve. For example, if the company's communication goal is to inform customers about the functional benefits of the offering, the message should focus on its product and service aspects. In contrast, if the goal is to inform customers about an ongoing or future sales promotion, the message should focus on the offering's incentives. Similarly, if a company has introduced a new distribution channel, it might benefit from focusing its communication on informing customers about the availability of its offering.

An important consideration when deciding on the message content is the degree to which the information contained in the message can lead to a change in customers' knowledge, beliefs, and behavior toward the company's offering. To this end, managers must take into account the principle of diminishing returns. This principle implies that the marginal impact of improving a company's performance on a given attribute tends to decrease over time as the company invests resources in improving that attribute. In the context of designing the communication message, this principle implies that the market impact of promoting the same benefit will decline over time.

For example, when launching a new offering, a company might benefit from promoting its performance and unique benefits. On the other hand, if target customers are already aware of the benefits of the company's products and services, focusing on other aspects of the offering—such as building the offering's brand and informing customers about the offering's price, incentives, and availability—might prove to be a more effective allocation of the company's resources. Thus, to increase the effectiveness of its communication campaign, a company must identify the areas in which additional information can have the greatest impact on the target audience and design its message accordingly.

Selecting the Media

The media defines the particular means the company uses to convey its message to the target audience. Based on the entity that initiates the communication, media can be divided into two types: *outbound* and *inbound*.

Outbound Media

Outbound media involves channels used for communication that are initiated by the company. Outbound media can be divided into three main types: *paid*, *owned*, and *earned*.

Paid Media

Paid media involves marketing communication in which a company relays its message using media owned by a third party and absorbs most or all of the media costs (e.g., the cost of air time and print space). The key advantages of paid media are its reach and the fact that the company can largely control the content of its message. For example, a company can reach millions of people with a Super Bowl commercial featuring company-developed content promoting its offerings. The main downside of paid media is that the company must pay to gain access to the audience reached by the media and in most cases does not have exclusive use of the media, giving it little or no control over other messages that appear in close proximity to its own message. Popular forms of paid media include media advertising, direct advertising, personal selling, event sponsorship, and product placement.

The choice of the appropriate media and the allocation of resources across different types of media are a function of the effectiveness and cost efficiency with which different media outlets are able to communicate the company message. For example, advertising and personal selling typically present the company's message in a more direct way to an audience that is fully aware of advertisers' efforts to influence their preferences and behavior. In contrast, event sponsorship and product placement tend to influence the target audience in a subtler way, often by leveraging the audience's goodwill toward the organization partnering with the company or the individual using the offering. In addition, compared to event sponsorship and product placement, which tend to be place- and time-specific, advertising is readily scalable across different regions and can be repeated as needed to have the maximum impact.

Owned Media

Owned media involves marketing communications in which a company relays its message using its own media channels. The key advantages of using media owned by the company are that there are no payments to a third party for media rights and the company retains exclusive use and control of the media. The key downside of owned media is its limited reach, which means the company might incur additional expenses to drive traffic to its own media channel. Popular owned media formats include the company's physical and virtual space, product packaging, experiential events, direct mail, personal selling, and samples.

As is the case with paid media, the choice of the particular type of company-owned communication channel depends on this channel's effectiveness and cost efficiency. The use of a company's own physical and virtual real estate, product packaging, direct email, and virtual samples (e.g., free digital products and service trials) tends to be the least costly for the company, whereas personal selling, experiential events, and the distribution of physical samples tend to be associated with higher costs. In most cases, the higher costs associated with some of the company's own channels reflect the greater effectiveness of these channels at relating the company's message to the target audience. Note, however, that the effectiveness of the different channels is not always directly related to their cost, meaning that less expensive channels are not always less effective than costlier channels. In this context, a company's goal when choosing the optimal channel mix is to identify the channels that have the highest likelihood of engaging and informing the target audience at minimal cost to the company.

Earned Media

Earned media involve marketing communications in which a company's message is relayed using media owned by a third party at no cost to the company. The three most popular forms of earned media are press coverage, social media,[26] and word of mouth. These three types of media are similar in that neither the media source nor the content of the message is owned or directly controlled by the company. At the same time, they differ in that press coverage typically relies on professionally managed media outlets, whereas social media and word of mouth primarily involve interpersonal communication.

A key advantage of earned media is that the company does not have to pay for the media as it does for a space in a newspaper, air time on a radio show, or a physical billboard. Another important advantage of earned media is that because the message comes from a third party that typically has no vested interest in the company's offering, it is often viewed as more credible than a message directly sponsored by the company. The key downside of earned media is that because the company does not pay for the media, it does not control the message and, hence, cannot ensure that the conveyed message is consistent with the company's strategic goals.

Inbound Media

Inbound media involves communication initiated by other entities—customers, collaborators, company employees and stakeholders, and the general public—rather than the company. For example, consumers might not just passively view a company's advertisements; they might actively seek out information by conducting an online search, visiting a company's website, or talking to a salesperson. In this case, rather than trying to reach out to target customers to pique their interest and provide them with relevant information, a company's aim is to address inquiries from customers who have already displayed interest in the company and its offerings.

Inbound media formats vary depending on the nature of the communication channel in which they take place. Common types of inbound media include online search, personal interaction, phone, online interactive forums, regular mail, and email.

- **Online search** involves customers actively seeking offering-relevant information across different formats: text, video, and audio. The growth of online search is in part attributable to the effectiveness of popular search platforms such as Google, YouTube, Amazon, Siri, and Alexa, which put relevant product information at customers' fingertips. The popularity of online search has also led to the development of search marketing tools such as search engine optimization (SEO) and search engine marketing (SEM).

- **Personal interaction** is perhaps the oldest form of inbound communication, allowing customers with questions about the company's offerings to interact directly with company representatives. This form of communication is particularly important for establishing and maintaining personal relationships with customers and building and maintaining customer loyalty.

- **Phone communication** enables customers to interact with the company to receive relevant information and address specific issues related to the company and its products. It is similar to personal interaction except that it is not conducted face to face.

- **Online interactive forums**, such as online live chat, enable the company to connect with website visitors, understand their needs and objectives, and provide them with the information they need. The advantage of this type of media is that it gives customers an opportunity to interact instantly with the company without leaving the company website. In addition, from a company's perspective, this type of communication can be very cost efficient because it lends itself to automation (e.g., using artificial intelligence to generate meaningful responses to customer inquiries).

- **Mail** and **email** are alternative forms of inbound media that benefit customers who prefer to communicate by articulating their thoughts more carefully and in a format that preserves the specifics of the interaction for future reference.

During the past decade, the importance of inbound media has increased dramatically, with online search becoming the key inbound media format. Despite the popularity of online search, the other types of inbound media also play an important role in company communication by adding an interactive component to the search process. The key to managing inbound media is understanding the ways customers learn, consider, buy, and use the offering and providing them with a venue to connect with the company to increase the value they derive from the company's offerings.

Designing the Creative Execution

The creative execution defines the specific implementation of the company's message. It translates the company's communication strategy into a message that is tailored to the specific type of media that can best convey information to target customers. The creative aspect of the offering's communication aims to express the offering's value proposition in a way that will resonate with and engage its target customers. Thus, rather than merely enumerate the specific attributes or benefits of the offering, the creative solution must translate the company message into a meaningful and engaging story.

The key to developing an effective creative solution is maintaining the balance between the marketing and the entertainment components of the communication campaign. Because of the ever-growing competition to capture buyers' attention, companies are often tempted to develop overly creative campaigns designed to break through the clutter of competitive messages. While creativity per se is a virtue, in business communication creativity should never be achieved at the expense of the marketing content. *We want consumers to say, 'That's a hell of a product' instead of, 'That's a hell of an ad,'* notes Leo Burnett, whose namesake agency created some of advertising's most well-known characters and campaigns of the 20th century, including Tony the Tiger, the Pillsbury Doughboy, and the Marlboro Man.

The creative solution is media specific. Thus, print advertising involves decisions concerning the copy (wording of the headline and the body text), visual elements (pictures, photos, graphics, and logos), format (size and color scheme), and layout (the arrangement of different parts of the advertisement). Radio advertising involves decisions dealing with the text (wording of the dialogue and narration), audio (music, dialogue, and sound effects), and duration (length). Television advertising involves decisions concerning the visual elements (imagery), text (wording of the dialogue, voice-over narration, and printed text), audio (music, dialogue, and sound effects), and duration (length of the commercial).

Developing the creative solution to convey the communication message involves three basic elements: *message source*, *message appeal*, and *message complexity*.

Message Source

An important aspect of translating the communication strategy into an engaging story is deciding on the source of the company message—that is, who will be telling the story. For example, the source of the message can be the company in general, as in the case of an advertisement merely listing the features and benefits of the company offering. Alternatively, the message can stem from a company employee or stakeholder that represents the company, as in the case of an employee discussing the benefits of the offering or the company's CEO making an announcement in response to an issue concerning a company's offering.

The message does not need to come from the company or its employees. It can come from the public, as when ordinary users share their experiences with the company's offering. It can also stem from independent experts discussing and ultimately endorsing the company's offering, such as medical professionals promoting a particular drug. Finally, the source of the message can be a celebrity—a movie star, supermodel, or socialite with a large social media following—who endorses the company's offering either for monetary compensation (paid endorsers) or because of a real appreciation for the offering (unpaid endorsers).

The influence of the source on the ultimate impact of the message depends on the expertise, likability, and trustworthiness of the source. Thus, the greater the specialized knowledge of the source, the greater the potential impact of the message conveyed by this source. In addition, messages from sources that are likable, physically attractive, engaging, witty, and overall favorably regarded tend to be more influential. Source trustworthiness that reflects the degree to which the source truly believes in the message can further amplify the message and enhance the ultimate impact of company communication.

Message Appeal

Message appeal reflects the approach used to communicate the company's message. Most creative solutions involve one of two types of appeals: information-based and emotion-based.

- **Information-based appeals** typically rely on methods such as factual presentations (straightforward presentations of the relevant information), demonstrations (illustration of the offering's key benefits in a staged environment), problem-solution examples (identifying a problem and showcasing an offering that will eradicate the problem), product comparisons (offering A is better than offering B), slice-of-life stories (illustration of the offering's key benefits in everyday use), and testimonials (endorsements of the offering by ordinary users or celebrities). Information-based appeals assume rational processing on the part of the recipient.

- **Emotion-based appeals** typically play on people's feelings. Broadly speaking, there are two types of emotional appeals: positive appeals that revolve around love, romance, and joy, and negative appeals that evoke fear, guilt, and shame. Positive appeals focus on emotional states that individuals look forward to and try to achieve, whereas negative appeals focus on emotional states that people try to avoid. For example, consumers might be encouraged to buy a particular brand of toothpaste to either make them more attractive to their romantic partners (positive appeal) or to prevent tooth decay (negative appeal). Both types of appeals can be effective depending on the specific market situation, including the type of offering being promoted; consumers' beliefs, needs, and preferences; and the competitive context.

Information-based appeals tend to be more effective when consumers are likely to be paying more attention to and thinking about the message in order to adequately comprehend its content. Emotion-based appeals, on the other hand, can be effective even when consumers are less involved and are not paying very close attention to the message. In this context, the choice of message appeal calls for careful consideration of recipients' level of involvement when processing the company's communication.

Message Complexity

Communication messages vary in complexity: Some have a relatively straightforward message and others involve multifaceted messages that are more complex. For example, some messages present one-sided arguments touting the benefits of the offering, whereas others involve two-sided messages presenting arguments in favor of and against the offering. In addition, messages can be noncomparative, focusing on the offering's ability to fulfill a particular customer need, or comparative, demonstrating the offering's ability to fulfill a given customer need better than the alternative options.

A key factor in determining the optimal message complexity is the level of involvement of the target audience and, specifically, the degree to which the recipients have the cognitive resources to process the message and elaborate on its content. Thus, a more complex message might not be appropriate for an audience that is relatively uninvolved because these customers do not care about the product, perceive the product to be a commodity with few differences between brands, or are distracted and not paying attention to the message content. For example, many consumers might not care much about learning the differences between different brands of paper tissues and, as a result, process the information contained in the message in a haphazard manner. At the same time, in certain circumstances, such as purchasing professional equipment, providing detailed product specifications can be beneficial for articulating the ways in which the company's offering creates superior customer value.

Ensuring a fit between the complexity of the message and the willingness and ability of the audience to process this message is important because a mismatch can be counterproductive. For example, a comparative ad that aims to demonstrate the contrast between the company's offering and its competitors might create the erroneous impression that the products are similar to each other. This is because processing contrast-based messages requires greater effort on the part of the recipients compared to messages that focus on a single offering. Less involved recipients also might fail to grasp the essence of a comparative message and simply aggregate the stated pros and cons of the offering without considering the arguments for why the advantages of the offering outweigh any disadvantages.

The mismatch between the complexity of the message and the target audience's level of involvement is one of the most common problems in creative execution. This mismatch often stems from the difference in the involvement levels of the marketing managers and the creative team designing the message and the recipients of the message. Bombarded with hundreds of ads and promotional offers every day, consumers increasingly pay less attention to each individual message and, as a result, are less likely to allocate the cognitive resources needed to delve into the complex reasoning embedded in a given message. In contrast, the manager and the creative team that generates the communication are deeply involved with the offering and with developing a memorable message that will also enable the marketing team to showcase its creativity. The disparity between overly involved marketers and uninvolved consumers can lead to counterproductive outcomes when the company message is either ignored by consumers or, even worse, is misconstrued to mean the opposite of what was intended.

Evaluating Communication Effectiveness

Depending on the company's goals, communication might aim to achieve different outcomes. Therefore, a meaningful approach to evaluating communication effectiveness is to link the particular performance metrics to the overarching communication goals. Accordingly, communication effectiveness can be assessed based on its ability to *create awareness*, *build preference*, and *incite action*.

Measuring Awareness

Measuring awareness can involve assessing whether the target audience has been exposed to the offering's message, has understood the message, and can recall the message.

Measuring *exposure* aims to establish whether a company's communication has reached its intended audience. To this end, a company can assess the number of people who view a particular television program, read a newspaper, or visit a website, and use this as a basis to determine the number of people who have been exposed to a company's message. In addition to measuring exposure, communication effectiveness can involve assessing *understanding*, which reflects the degree to which the target audience has comprehended the communication message. For example, a company can conduct a focus group to test whether the target audience has comprehended the intended message of its communication campaign.

Another popular measure of communication effectiveness is assessing *recall*, the degree to which the target audience remembers the company's advertisement and, more important, its message. Two types of recall can be measured: aided and unaided.

Aided recall refers to a person's ability to remember whether they have been exposed to a particular communication and/or the content of the communication message when explicitly asked about it. To assess aided recall, respondents are typically given a list of brand names following the presentation of a series of advertisements and asked to recall whether they have seen any of these brands in a given period of time (e.g., during the past week). In contrast, unaided recall refers to a person's ability to spontaneously recall an advertisement without being directly prompted to do so. To assess unaided recall, respondents are typically asked to recall all brands they have seen advertised in a given period of time.

Measuring Preferences

Measuring preferences involves assessing the degree to which the company's communication was able to form, strengthen, or change customer beliefs about its offering(s). A common approach to measuring preferences is assessing customers' brand-specific beliefs before and after they have been exposed to a company's communication.

Because preferences for established brands (which often are among the largest advertisers) are difficult to change with a single communication, companies often measure the attitude toward the advertisement (rather than the beliefs about the offering) on the premise that if the target audience likes the advertisement, then this attitude will translate into liking the company's offering. While this approach is not without merit, the connection between customers liking the advertisement and their attitude toward the advertised brand has not been validated. Thus, the mere fact that the audience likes the company's communication does not necessarily mean that the company has achieved its strategic goals.

An alternative approach to measuring preferences is asking the target audience to make a *choice* among different offerings before and after being exposed to the company communication. The greater the relative choice share of the offering following the company communication, the more effective this communication is. In addition to asking customers to make a choice, companies often measure customers' behavioral intentions — for example, by asking respondents to indicate the likelihood of purchasing the product within a given time frame.

Preferences can also be captured by monitoring social media activity, including blog entries, social media posts, as well as shared photos and videos. Because in this case preferences are usually embedded in the broader context of the conversation and are often not explicitly stated, companies use a variety of data analysis methods for extracting and interpreting the information relevant to the company's offering to infer individuals' preferences.

Measuring Behavior

Measuring behavior involves assessing customer actions resulting from the company's communication, such as buying the offering; contacting the company to inquire about the offering, visiting a company's stores, showrooms, or website; and clicking on a company's online banners.

Intuitively, it might seem that sales are the best measure of communication effectiveness. This, however, is not always the case. The problem with relying on sales as a measure of effectiveness is that most often the impact of communication is not immediate (especially in cases of brand-building communication). As a result, the impact of communication is typically confounded with a variety of unrelated factors such as changes in price, incentives, competitive actions, and purchase cycle, which makes it difficult, if not impossible, to disentangle the unique contribution of communication from the observed changes in sales volume.

Furthermore, evaluating the behavioral impact of a communication campaign depends on the type of message conveyed. Thus, communicating incentives such as price discounts tends to have an immediate impact on sales, whereas brand-building communication takes much longer to produce visible results. This differential impact implies that using sales as a benchmark of effectiveness is likely to underestimate the impact of brand-building communication and overestimate the role of incentive-focused communication.

Measuring the effectiveness of a communication campaign also depends on the type of media used. In cases where the media are directly linked to performance measures (such as in direct marketing, personal selling, and online advertising), actual behavior can be used to evaluate the effectiveness of the communication campaign. Linking media to performance in this way, however, creates an *attribution bias*, whereby the communication formats that produce directly measurable results are exclusively credited for the outcome of the communication campaign.

Crediting media formats that produce an immediate and measurable impact often comes at the expense of other media formats such as public relations, social media, and event sponsorship, which create market value even though their impact cannot be measured directly. Thus, even though click-throughs and online searches lead to directly measurable outcomes, these outcomes often are a consequence of a company's coordinated efforts to create awareness, generate interest, and build preferences for its offerings. To accurately evaluate the effectiveness of a company's communication campaign, a manager must consider the way different components of the campaign interact with one another and use the appropriate measures to assess the unique contribution of each communication activity.

SUMMARY

Communication informs the relevant market entities — target customers, collaborators, and the company employees and stakeholders — about the specifics of the company's offering. Developments during the past decades have dramatically altered the way companies communicate with their current and potential customers. The key changes in communication management involve micro-targeting, inbound communication, peer-to-peer communication, geolocation, predictive analytics, occasion-based targeting, and measurability.

The development of a communication campaign is guided by the G-STIC framework, which involves five key decisions: setting the communication *goal*, articulating the communication *strategy* (identifying the target audience and developing the communication message), designing the communication *tactics* (selecting the media and developing the creative solution), *implementing* the communication campaign, and *controlling* (evaluating) the campaign results.

Setting *communication goals* involves identifying the focus of the company's actions and defining the performance benchmarks to be achieved. The *focus* of the communication campaign can involve creating awareness of the offering, building preference for the offering, and inciting an action such as purchasing the offering. *Performance benchmarks* outline the quantitative and temporal criteria for reaching the communication goal. A company's communication goals can be related to the customer decision journey, with different stages of the customer journey associated with different goals.

An important aspect of developing the communication campaign is determining the *budget* required to achieve the communication goals. The optimal level of communication expenditures is determined by three factors: available resources, communication goals, and the cost of achieving these goals.

The *target audience* encompasses the recipients of the company's communication. Identification of the target audience involves two aspects: strategic and tactical. Strategic targeting involves identifying the target audience based on the value that the company can create and capture from it. In contrast, tactical targeting involves identifying the specific ways in which the company can reach strategically important audiences with its message in the most effective and cost-efficient way.

The communication *message* can involve one or more of the attributes defining the company's offering: product, service, brand, price, incentives, and distribution. Thus, an important aspect of developing the communication message is deciding which and how many attributes to promote. The key principle in designing the communication message is that it should be aligned with the company's overarching communication and marketing goals.

The *media* defines the means used by the company to convey its message to the target audience. Based on the entity initiating the communication, there are two general types of media: outbound media, involving communication initiated by the company, and inbound media, involving communication initiated by the public. Outbound media can be further divided into three main types: paid, owned, and earned.

The *creative solution* involves translating the company's message into the language of the selected media format. Developing the creative solution to convey the communication message involves three key decisions: message source, message appeal, and message complexity.

A meaningful approach to *evaluating* communication effectiveness is to tie it to the communication goals. Accordingly, communication effectiveness must be assessed based on its ability to create awareness, build preference, and incite action.

MARKETING INSIGHT: KEY COMMUNICATION CONCEPTS

Above-the-Fold (ATF) Communication: Based on the specific location of an advertisement in the publication, there are two types of placements: above-the-fold, which refers to the upper half of the front page of a newspaper where the important news stories are often located, and below-the-fold (BTF), which refers to the lower half of the front page of a newspaper. In online communication, ATF refers to the viewable space on a webpage when it first loads, whereas BTF refers to the part of a webpage that cannot be seen without scrolling down.

Above-the-Line (ATL) Communication: Based on the type of media, communication is divided into two categories: Above-the-line (ATL) communication, which encompasses mass-media advertising such as television commercials, radio, and print advertisements; and below-the-line (BTL) communication, which includes public relations, event sponsorship, personal selling, and direct mail. Historically, the term ATL was used in reference to communication for which an advertising agency charged a commission to place in mass media, whereas the term BTL was used in reference to communication that involved a standard charge rather than a commission. Currently, the terms ATL and BTL are used loosely to indicate an emphasis on mass media (ATL) versus one-on-one communication and customer and trade incentives (BTL).

Advertising Awareness: The number of potential customers who are aware of the offering. Awareness is a function of the total volume of advertising delivered to the target audience and the number of exposures necessary for the target audience to become cognizant of the offering. In cases where a single exposure is sufficient to create awareness, the awareness level equals the advertising reach.

$$\text{Awareness} = \frac{\text{Reach} \cdot \text{Frequency}}{\text{Number of exposures needed to create awareness}}$$

Advertising Elasticity: The degree to which a change in advertising leads to a change in awareness, preferences, or behavior of the target audience. The higher the advertising elasticity, the more likely it is that increasing advertising expenditures can produce favorable results—increase awareness, strengthen preferences, and incite action.

Advertising Frequency: The number of times the target audience is exposed to an advertisement in a given period. Also used in reference to the number of times an advertisement is repeated in a specific medium during a specific period.

Advertising Reach: The size of the audience that has been exposed to a particular advertisement at least once in a given period (multiple viewings by the same audience do not increase reach). Reach can be stated either as an absolute number or as a fraction of a population. For example, if 40,000 of 100,000 different households are exposed to a given commercial at least once, the reach is 40%.

Affiliate Marketing: A communication strategy that involves revenue sharing between advertisers and online content providers. An affiliate is rewarded based on specific performance measures such as sales, click-throughs, and online traffic.

AIDA: Communication model outlining the key steps in the process of converting advertising to sales. The AIDA framework posits that the consumer decision process involves four key steps: attention, interest, desire, and action. According to the AIDA framework, before making a purchase decision consumers need to be made *aware* that the offering exists and be stimulated to take some *interest* in the offering. Then, a *desire* must be created among consumers to purchase the offering, which must be translated into *action* that leads to the actual purchase of the offering.[27]

Awareness Rate: The number of potential customers aware of the offering relative to the total number of potential customers.

Below-the-Fold (BTF) Communication: See *above-the-fold communication.*

Below-the-Line (BTL) Communication: See *above-the-line communication.*

Carryover Effect in Advertising: Impact of an advertising campaign that extends beyond the time frame of the campaign. To illustrate, an advertising effort made in a given period might generate sales in subsequent periods.

Comparative Advertising: Advertising that directly contrasts two or more offerings.

Competitive Parity Budgeting: Budget allocation method based on matching competitors' absolute level of spending or the proportion per point of market share.

Cooperative Advertising: Advertising in which a manufacturer and a retailer jointly advertise their offering to consumers. For example, a manufacturer can pay a portion of a retailer's advertising costs in return for the retailer featuring its products, services, and brands.

Cost Per Point (CPP): Measure used to represent the cost of a communication campaign. CPP is the media cost of reaching one percent (one rating point) of a particular demographic. See also *gross rating point (GRP).*

$$CPP = \frac{\text{Advertising cost}}{\text{GRP}}$$

Cost Per Thousand (CPM): Measure used to represent the cost of a communication campaign. CPM is the cost of reaching 1,000 individuals or households with an advertising message in a given medium (M is the Roman numeral for 1,000). For example, a television commercial that costs $200,000 to air and reaches 10M viewers has a CPM of $20. The popularity of CPM derives in part from its functioning as a good comparative measure of advertising efficiency across different media (e.g., television, print, and online).

$$CPM = \frac{\text{Advertising cost}}{\text{Total impressions}} \cdot 1,000$$

Creative Brief: An outline of the key aspects of the communication campaign designed to guide the creative development. The creative brief typically includes the communication goal, the target audience, the message to be communicated, and the choice of media.

Gross Rating Point (GRP): A measure of the total volume of advertising delivery to the target audience. GRP is equal to the percent of the population reached times the frequency of exposure. To illustrate, if a given advertisement reaches 60% of the households with an average frequency of three times, then the GRP of the media is equal to 180. GRP can also be calculated by dividing gross impressions by the size of the total audience. A single GRP represents 1% of the total audience in a given region.

$$GRP = \text{Reach} \cdot \text{Frequency}$$

Impression: A single exposure of an advertisement to one person.

Institutional Advertising: Advertising strategy designed to build goodwill or an image for an organization (rather than to promote specific offerings).

Point-of-Purchase Advertising: Promotional materials displayed at the point of purchase (e.g., in a retail store).

Public Relations: A specific type of communication activity that aims to manage a company's relationship with society at large. There are three defining aspects of public relations as a form of communication. First, it is often directed not only to the company's customers, collaborators, and stakeholders but also to the general public. Second, it is a form of institutional communication that deals with issues concerning the reputation of the entire company rather than merely providing information about a particular offering. Third, it is most prominent at times of company crisis, a significant change in the company's business model, or a major shift in a company's internal and external policies. Public relations can involve the same types of media as other forms of communication, including advertising, event sponsorship, direct mail, press coverage, social media, and word of mouth.

Public Service Announcement (PSA): Nonprofit advertising that uses free space or time donated by the media.

Reminder Advertising: Advertising designed to maintain awareness and stimulate repurchase of an already established offering.

Search Engine Marketing (SEM): A process of promoting the company's offerings by increasing its ranking in the list of (paid) results returned by a search engine. Unlike the search engine optimization (SEO) approach, which aims to increase the website rank organically, SEM aims to attract more visitors using paid search such as pay-per-click listings and advertisements.

Search Engine Optimization (SEO): A process of optimizing a company's website to increase the number of visitors by ensuring that the site appears high on the list of results returned by a search engine. For example, a travel agency can optimize its website (e.g., by embedding the key search terms in the website, streamlining the website content, and linking it to external content) in a way that allows it to show up first when customers enter the word "travel" in their browsers.

Share of Voice: A company's communication expenditures relative to those of the entire product category.

$$\text{Share of voice} = \frac{\text{Advertising spend for an offering}}{\text{Advertising spend for the category}}$$

Target Rating Point (TRP): A measure of the total volume of advertising delivery to the target audience. TRP is similar to GRP, but its calculation uses only the target audience (rather than the total audience watching the program) as the base. Thus, a single TRP represents 1% of the targeted viewers in any particular region.

Top-of-Mind Awareness: The first brand identified by respondents when asked to list brands in a given product category.

Wearout: A decrease in the effectiveness of a communication campaign because of decreased consumer interest in the message, often resulting from repetition.

CHAPTER THIRTEEN

MANAGING DISTRIBUTION CHANNELS

If you make a product good enough, even though you live in the depths of the forest,
the public will make a path to your door . . . But if you want the public
in sufficient numbers, you better construct a highway.

—William Randolph Hearst, American newspaper publisher

Distribution channels deliver the company's offerings to its target customers. Managing distribution channels involves designing and streamlining the process of delivering a company's offering in a way that creates value for target customers, the company, and its collaborators. The key aspects of managing distribution channels are the focus of this chapter.

Distribution as a Value-Creation Process

A company's distribution channel can involve three main types of entities: *merchants* such as retailers, wholesalers, dealers, and distributors that buy and resell the company's offering; *agents* such as brokers and sales representatives that help connect buyers and sellers; and *facilitators* such as transportation companies and banks that facilitate the exchange of goods and money between the company and its customers.

Creating market value by bringing manufacturers and customers together is at the heart of any distribution channel. The role of distribution channels as a tool for creating market value and the key channel functions are outlined in the following sections.

Distribution as a Tool for Creating Market Value

Distribution involves the channel(s) used to deliver an offering to a company's customers and collaborators. Working together with the other marketing tactics defining the offering—product, service, brand, price, incentives, and communication—distribution aims to create an optimal value proposition (OVP) for the relevant market entities: the company, its customers, and its collaborators (Figure 1). In this context, a manager's ultimate goal is to design distribution channels that create superior value for target customers in a way that benefits the company and its collaborators.

To effectively fulfill their value-delivery function, distribution channels must be aligned with the other attributes of the offering. Thus, an offering's distribution depends on its *product* and *service* attributes, such that novel, complex, and undifferentiated products often benefit from channels offering higher levels of sales support. Distribution must also be consistent with the offering's *brand*, such that lifestyle brands like Ralph Lauren, Lacoste, and Gucci benefit from using channels that enable them to exercise greater control to ensure a consistent brand image. Distribution also depends on *price*, with low-price, low-margin offerings typically associated with channels providing lower levels of service, and high-price, high-margin offerings typically associated with higher levels of service. The choice of a distribution channel also depends on the offering's *incentives*, such that incentive-rich offerings typically call for channels that offer frequent sales, whereas offerings that do not rely on incentives are a better fit with channels featuring everyday low pricing. Finally, the choice of a distribution channel depends on the channel's ability to effectively *communicate* the offering's benefits to target customers.

Figure 1. Distribution as a Tool for Creating Market Value

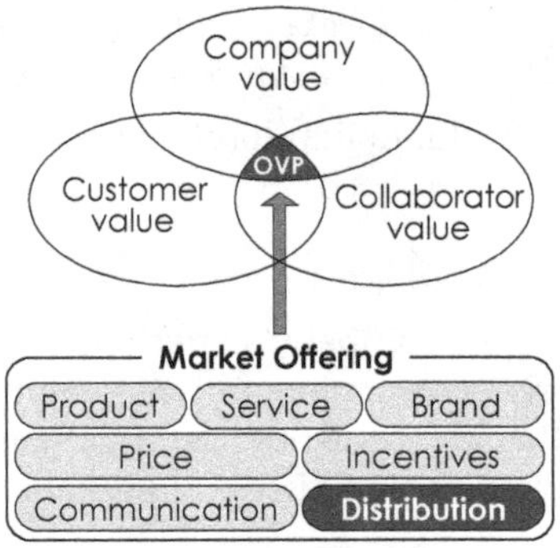

Because distribution is an integral aspect of the value-creation process, the choice of distribution channels depends on the market in which the company operates. Thus, distribution depends on the choice of target *customers*, with mass-market offerings more likely to involve multiple distributors across different geographic markets and niche offerings likely to involve a narrower distribution. The choice of a distribution channel also depends on the goals and resources of the *company*, such that a company seeking market dominance is likely to utilize diverse channels to achieve extensive coverage. An offering's distribution also reflects the balance of power between the company and its *collaborators*, whereby a company might select multiple distributors or open its own retail stores in order to minimize the power of any particular channel. The choice of a distribution channel is also a function of the *competition*, such that a company might seek channels in which its direct competitors are not present or, alternatively, seek channels in which it can compete head-to-head with similar offerings. Finally, distribution depends on the *context*; for example, customers in certain locations might favor smaller, individually operated retail outlets, whereas customers in other locations might favor consolidated superstore chains.

Distribution Channel Functions

The primary function of distribution channels is to deliver the company's offering to its target customers. This function involves delivering the company's product, service, brand, price, and incentives, as well as delivering information about different aspects of the offering. The role of distribution in the value-creation process and the different aspects of delivering the offering's value are outlined below.

- **Product delivery** involves transferring the physical possession and ownership rights of the product from the manufacturer to intermediaries (wholesalers, distributors, dealers, and retailers) and, ultimately, to end users. Functions such as transportation, inventorying, sorting, risk hedging, and handling returns can be allocated across different members of the distribution channel. For example, a manufacturer might choose to outsource most channel functions to a wholesaler and a retailer who can perform these tasks more effectively and cost efficiently. In the same vein, a retailer might choose to outsource some of the sorting and inventory functions to customers by selling in bulk and letting customers self-select the items they want to purchase.

- **Service delivery** involves customer-focused activities such as customization, repair, technical assistance, and warranty support, as well as collaborator-focused activities such as storage, inventory management, sorting, and repackaging. A company might choose to perform the service-related activities such as repairs, customization, and packaging, or, alternatively, it can delegate these functions to different members of the distribution channel.

- **Brand building** provides customers with an opportunity to experience the brand. For example, Apple, Disney, Hermès, and Harley-Davidson retail stores function as channels delivering these brands to their customers. Thus, a company can use its distribution channels as a means of communication to inform buyers about its brands while at the same time letting them experience the essence of these brands. To this end, many accessories, apparel, and cosmetics companies have allocated significant resources to build their brands at the point of purchase by setting up distinct "store-within-a-store" retail locations.

- **Collecting payments** involves collecting and processing payments from customers. Note that unlike other marketing tactics where the flow of items is from the company to its customers, in the case of pricing the flow is reversed: Payments are collected from customers and delivered to the company. In addition to collecting payments, channel members can set the prices at which the company's products and services are sold to customers.

- **Delivering incentives** involves distributing sales promotions such as coupons, rebates, and premiums to customers. A company has two basic options to deliver incentives: It can deliver them directly to target customers or delegate this function to channel members who are in direct contact with target customers. Thus, a manufacturer might adopt a pull strategy by creating and communicating the incentives directly to target customers to drive traffic to retailers that sell its products and services. Alternatively, the manufacturer can adopt a push strategy by offering promotional allowances to retailers who, in turn, develop sales promotions and "push" these promotions to target customers (see Chapter 11 for more detail).

- **Delivering information** involves keeping customers apprised of the different aspects of the company's offering by explaining the product and service benefits, communicating the meaning of its brand, and informing customers about the offering's price and incentives. The information-delivery function of distribution channels is an element of the company's overall communication activities, whereby distribution channels serve as a means of delivering the company's message to target customers.

Even though the primary function of the distribution channel is to deliver the company's offerings to target customers, its functions are not limited to delivering offerings that have already been designed by the company. Channel members also frequently participate in designing and communicating the offerings they deliver. For example, distribution channel members can help define the attributes of the offering, design financing and warranty services, craft the offering's brand, negotiate the sale price, develop point-of-purchase incentives, and shape the company's communication activities.

The flow of goods, services, and information is not always unidirectional. On some occasions the delivery process works in reverse. Thus, in addition to delivering the offering to target customers, distribution channels can process the return of unwanted goods, reusable materials (e.g., printer cartridges), and products and packages for recycling (e.g., beverage containers) and disposal (e.g., batteries). Distribution channels can also handle the reverse flow of payments as in the case of processing refunds, rebates, commissions, and rewards. In addition to managing the reverse flow of products and payments, distribution channels can also manage the information flow from customers to the company by soliciting and collecting customer feedback, suggestions, and complaints.

Distribution Channel Design

The process of designing and managing distribution channels involves several key decisions: *channel structure*, *distribution coverage*, and the *value added by the channel*. The main aspects of these decisions are outlined in the following sections.

Defining the Channel Structure

Channel structure defines the members of the distribution channel and the flow of goods and services from the manufacturer to customers. Based on their structure, channels can be *direct*, *indirect*, or *hybrid* (Figure 2).

Figure 2. Distribution Channel Structure

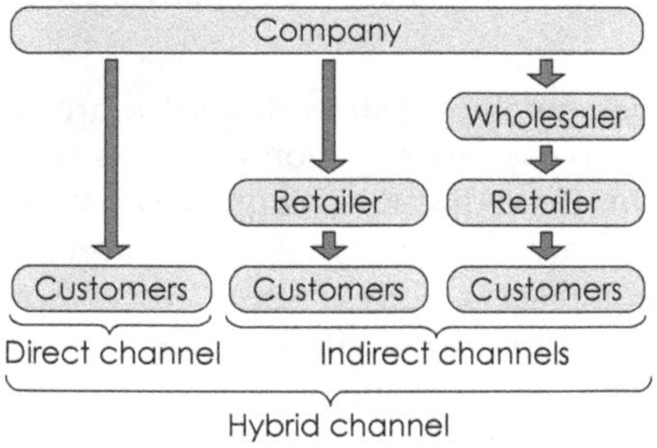

Direct Channels

Direct channels involve a distribution model in which the manufacturer and the end customer interact directly with each other without intermediaries. For example, Apple distributes many of its offerings directly to customers through its own online and brick-and-mortar retail outlets. In the same vein, many luxury brands such as Louis Vuitton, Gucci, Prada, and Hermès have established retail stores that they own and operate. Nestlé distributes its Nespresso coffee pods directly to consumers using its own online and physical retail stores.

When deciding whether to adopt a direct channel structure, a manager must keep in mind the different functions usually performed by the members of the distribution channel that the company would have to perform to create value for its target customers. Some managers erroneously believe that by moving from indirect to direct distribution channels—also referred to as disintermediation—a company can circumvent many of the functions traditionally performed by distribution channels.

Eliminating distribution channels does not eliminate the functions performed by these channels. For example, a manufacturer directly distributing its products has to assume all of the functions that are performed by the intermediaries in an indirect channel, including handling returns, managing service requests, offering financing, managing sales promotions, and informing customers about the specifics of its offerings. Failure to perform these functions can disrupt the company's ability to create market value. For example, eToys—one of the first online toy retailers—launched its operations without an established infrastructure for handling returns and was forced to store thousands of returned items in the hallways of its headquarters.

Thus, the question is not *whether* a particular channel function has to be performed, but *who* will perform this function. In this context, the decision to shift some of the channel functions upstream (to the manufacturer) or downstream (to the retailer and/or customers) is driven by determining who is best able to perform this function in an effective and cost-efficient manner.

Indirect Channels

Most companies do not sell their offerings directly to the public. Instead, they use intermediaries specialized in delivering the company's products and services to target customers. Indirect channels involve a distribution model in which the manufacturer and the end customer interact with each other through intermediaries such as wholesalers, dealers, and retailers. For example, consumer goods companies like Procter & Gamble, Unilever, Coca-Cola, PepsiCo, Mondelēz, and Henkel use a variety of intermediaries ranging from small convenience stores to mega-retailers such as Walmart, Costco, Kroger, Tesco, and Carrefour.

An important decision in developing indirect distribution channels is deciding who should perform the different value-delivery functions. Allocating channel functions involves deciding on the ways in which the other key aspects of the company's offering—product, service, brand, price, incentives, and communication—will be delivered to target customers, and specifically, the roles that different entities—the company, intermediaries, and customers—will play in the value-delivery process.

Indirect channels can involve two types of coordination: contractual and implicit. *Contractual coordination* involves binding agreements among channel members, such as long-term distribution agreements, joint ventures, and franchise agreements. Distribution contracts specify the terms of the business interactions among the members of the distribution channel, including pricing, sales promotions, financing, returns, inventory levels, and delivery schedules. In contrast, *implicit coordination* is more informal and is based on established business practices rather than contractual agreements. The main benefit of implicit coordination is its flexibility. This flexibility, however, comes at the cost of the inability to predict the behavior of the channel members as well as their lower level of commitment, resulting in an unwillingness to invest resources to customize their operations to fit the needs of a particular manufacturer.

Hybrid Channels

Hybrid channels involve a distribution model in which the manufacturer and the end customer interact with each other through multiple channels, both directly and through intermediaries. In this case, a company distributes its offerings directly by taking and fulfilling customer orders while using a variety of indirect channels such as wholesalers, independent retailers, and retail chains. For example, in addition to directly interacting with customers, Apple relies on third-party distributors such as Best Buy, Walmart, and Target to bring its products to market.

Hybrid channels have numerous advantages that stem from combining the benefits of direct and indirect distribution. At the same time, hybrid channels are also subject to many of the disadvantages of both direct and indirect channels. An additional problem with using hybrid channels is the potential for channel conflict in cases when the direct and indirect channels compete for the same customers. Despite their disadvantages, hybrid channels are gaining popularity in markets where manufacturers can readily establish direct online distribution.

Key Considerations in Channel Design

One of the key decisions in defining the channel structure is whether to use intermediaries to reach target customers. The pros and cons of using intermediaries and the ways in which a company should decide on intermediaries are discussed in the following sections.

The Pros and Cons of Using Intermediaries

Collaborating with third parties to deliver a company's offerings to target customers has its advantages and drawbacks. Specifically, using indirect distribution channels offers several important *benefits* to manufacturers: *effectiveness*, *cost efficiency*, *flexibility*, *scale*, and *speed*.

- **Effectiveness.** Indirect distribution typically results in greater effectiveness of the value-delivery process because manufacturers benefit from the assets and competencies of intermediaries. Because channel collaboration enables companies to take advantage of the expertise of others, it can provide channel members with a competitive advantage stemming from greater specialization.

- **Cost efficiency.** In addition to increasing the effectiveness of the value-delivery process, indirect distribution can also increase cost efficiency because each channel member can achieve greater economies of scale and experience by specializing in a given function. Specialization might also encourage channel members to invest in new technologies that they would not invest in if they lacked a larger scale of operations.

- **Flexibility.** Relative to developing the necessary in-house distribution expertise, using intermediaries requires a lesser commitment of resources, thus offering much greater flexibility in terms of adopting new technologies, entering new markets, and exiting existing ones. For example, the development of a new distribution channel requires substantial resources and calls for a long-term commitment, whereas using an already existing distribution channel requires a smaller upfront investment and offers much greater flexibility.

- **Scale.** Compared to direct distribution, the use of intermediaries can ensure broad market coverage that enables a company to reach its target customers. Indeed, most companies lack the scale to develop a proprietary retail network to make its offerings available to all customers. As a result, by using intermediaries, a company can achieve greater market access than it could by using its own channels.

- **Speed.** Indirect distribution enables a company to achieve the desired results much faster than building in-house expertise. For example, a manufacturer can gain access to target markets virtually overnight using an existing distribution chain, whereas launching its own distribution channel, especially a brick-and-mortar one, would take considerably longer.

Despite their numerous benefits, indirect channels have several important *drawbacks* that include *loss of control, limited information, channel conflicts,* and *complex structure.*

- **Loss of control.** Delegating some of a company's activities to an intermediary often leads to loss of control over the selling environment. For example, relying on third parties to deliver its offering to customers greatly diminishes a company's ability to directly communicate with customers and present the offering in a way that draws customers' attention, underscores the offering's benefits, and nudges customers to buy the offering.

- **Limited information.** The use of indirect channels hinders a company's ability to monitor the performance of its offerings and optimize these offerings for the current market conditions. Thus, using intermediaries prevents manufacturers from having direct contact with customers and obtaining firsthand information about their needs and their reactions to the company's offerings.

- **Channel conflicts.** Indirect distribution brings the potential for vertical channel conflicts resulting from different strategic goals and profit-optimization strategies on the part of the company and its intermediaries. For example, a manufacturer might want the retailer to promote its offerings over those of the competition, whereas the retailer might find promoting competitors' offerings more beneficial. Different types of channel conflicts are discussed later in this chapter.

- **Complex structure.** Using multiple intermediaries can result in a complex channel structure that could complicate the management of these channels, leading to inefficiencies in the value-delivery process because of poor channel coordination. Furthermore, because manufacturers have to share the sales revenues with distribution channel partners, inefficiencies in the value-delivery process could lower manufacturers' profit margins.

As with most business decisions, deciding to use indirect distribution and enter into collaborative relationships with different channel members involves weighing the relevant benefits and costs. When the benefits from the collaboration outweigh the corresponding costs for both the producer and channel members, the collaboration is likely to be sustainable. In contrast, when the collaboration fails to create superior value for either party, the collaboration might be dissolved as the partners pursue alternative options such as finding new distribution partners or switching to direct distribution.

Defining the Optimal Channel Structure

Because different channel formats have their own pros and cons, the choice of a particular format ultimately depends on the strategic goals a company aims to achieve with its distribution channel. Thus, a company seeking to rapidly gain presence in diverse markets will be better served by using indirect channels, as these channels are likely to prove more effective and cost efficient. By doing so, however, a company should be willing to give up some of its ability to control the ways in which its offering is presented, sold, and delivered to its customers.

In contrast, a company that prioritizes the image of its offerings and the environment in which it is presented to customers is typically better served by establishing its own distribution channel, allowing the company to exercise greater control over the way in which customers interact with its offerings. As a result, many luxury, fashion, and lifestyle-brand companies end up developing their own retail outlets that they use not only to deliver the company's products to customers but also to build their brands. By choosing to dispense with intermediaries, these companies are willing to accept the higher upfront cost, narrower distribution coverage (in the case of physical stores), and lower levels of customer traffic (in the case of online stores) typically associated with manufacturer-operated retail outlets.

Distribution Coverage

In addition to determining the optimal channel structure, a company needs to decide on the number and type of outlets at which offerings are made available to target customers. In this context, there are three basic types of distribution coverage: *exclusive*, *selective*, and *intensive*.

- **Exclusive distribution** involves a limited number of intermediaries such that a company's offerings are available only in certain markets and only through a particular retailer or distributor. It is often used for specialized and high-end products and services requiring that the distributor have the relevant expertise to offer an experience consistent with customers' expectations and the image of the brand. Exclusive distribution often involves granting territorial rights for selling a company's offerings in exchange for distributors' commitment to these offerings. Exclusive distribution is common for automobiles, fashion, and high-end household appliances. For example, Ford, General Motors, and Chrysler have dedicated dealer networks authorized to sell and service their vehicles.

- **Selective distribution** involves a subset of all the available distribution channels. Selective distribution often uses channels that meet certain criteria such as geographic location, customer profile, level of service, product assortment (including the presence of competitive offerings), price tier, and reputation. For example, fashion companies such as Coach, Burberry, Dolce & Gabbana, and Michael Kors rely on selective distribution by working with high-end shopping malls located in upscale high-traffic areas that are frequented by their target customers.

- **Intensive distribution** involves a wide variety of outlets to ensure that an offering is readily accessible to a large proportion of customers in a given market. It is often used for offerings that target diverse customer segments across different purchase occasions. Intensive distribution is common for snacks, non-alcoholic beverages, and media products such as newspapers and magazines. For example, consumer goods companies such as Procter & Gamble, PepsiCo, Coca-Cola, and Kraft Heinz work with a wide variety of retailers across different geographic regions in order to bring their products to their diverse customer base.

A key advantage of exclusive distribution is the reliance on specialized channels that have the expertise and resources necessary to deliver superior customer value. In addition, exclusive distribution typically involves a relatively close collaboration between the different members of the distribution channel, which often results in a more effective and cost-efficient operation. These advantages, however, come at the cost of having relatively limited coverage and potentially limiting customers' access to the offering. As the distribution coverage increases, the company has to interact with a larger number of outlets that vary in resources and expertise, which, in turn, complicates channel coordination. Greater distribution coverage can also hinder the producer's ability to control channel members and ensure that their actions are aligned with the producer's goals. For example, the larger the coverage, the more difficult it is to ensure that retailers price and promote the offerings as intended by the company.

Value Added by the Channel

In addition to merely distributing a manufacturer's offerings, retailers can create customer value that extends beyond the value created by the products and services they deliver. Based on the incremental value they add, distribution channels comprise a spectrum of options, with value-added distribution channels at one end of the spectrum and streamlined distribution channels at the other.

Value-added distribution channels are defined by the relatively high marginal value they add to the company's offering. Value-added distribution channels can enhance the value of a company's offering by customizing the product to customer needs; offering additional services (e.g., delivery, installation, repair, and disposal); enhancing the offering's brand; informing buyers about the features and benefits of the offering; and providing greater convenience to customers by virtue of factors such as ease of shopping, hours of operation, location, and level of customer service within the store. Common examples of value-added channels are high-end department stores such as Neiman Marcus, Harrods, and Le Bon Marché.

Value-added channels tend to charge manufacturers higher margins for distributing their offerings to offset the cost of the resources required to provide the extra benefits to buyers. Because the value-added model is typically associated with higher retail prices, value-added distributors tend to generate lower sales volume compared to distributors offering fewer benefits at a lower price. As a result, most value-added distributors tend to operate using a high-margin/low-volume profit formula.

Note that the high margins that value-added distributors charge do not always mean that they also sell the company offerings at a higher price point. Indeed, rather than pass the costs of the value-added services to buyers, the company might choose to absorb these costs to keep prices uniform across different distribution channels. For example, Apple stores provide multiple value-added services without charging higher prices because in this case the cost of providing these services is partially built into the price of its products. In addition, Apple's stores serve as a means of informing customers about the company's offerings and creating a positive shopping experience, effectively directing some of the company's communication and brand-building budget into the distribution channel.

Streamlined distribution channels are characterized by the relatively low value they add to the company's offering. Streamlined retailers tend to perform only the most basic channel functions, making the company's products and services available to their target customers without investing extra effort to enhance the offering or to improve the overall shopping experience. Because streamlined channels do not require additional resources in order to provide a basic level of convenience and service to customers, these channels tend to charge manufacturers lower margins for distributing their offerings. Furthermore, because the streamlined model is typically associated with lower retail prices, streamlined retailers also tend to generate higher sales volume compared to value-added distributors. As a result, most streamlined distribution channels, such as Aldi, Carrefour, and Walmart, tend to operate using a low-margin/high-volume profit formula.

An extreme version of streamlined retailers are *fulfillment distributors* that do not perform any function other than distributing the company's offering. Fulfillment distributors act as a logistics arm of the manufacturer, helping the company deliver its offerings to its target customers without expending any effort to promote the offering or provide extensive customer service. Many wholesalers act as fulfillment distributors, providing a minimal level of service and charging a relatively low margin. Fulfillment distributors are somewhat similar in their operations to delivery service companies such as UPS, FedEx, and DHL. The key difference is that unlike shipping companies, which make money by charging delivery fees without being concerned about customer demand, fulfillment distributors are compensated based on sales and, hence, absorb the inventory risk of inaccurately estimating customer demand.

Most *mass-market channels* fall between the value-added and the streamlined distribution models, providing a moderate level of value-added services and collecting standard margins for providing these services. Many of these channels provide additional services—such as premier product placement, sales promotions, and communication campaigns—at an extra cost to the manufacturer reflected in the various promotional allowances charged by the channel members. Because mass-market channels are able to offer both market reach and extended service options, they are commonly used by market leaders and companies that aim to expand their market reach by attracting new customer segments. For example, Procter & Gamble, Unilever, and Nestlé are working closely with Walmart, Costco, Tesco, Carrefour, and Kroger to ensure the availability of their offerings to their broad customer base.

Managing Channel Relationships

Because the company and members of its distribution channel often pursue different goals, their actions are often not perfectly aligned. As a result of this misalignment, channel relationships can spawn tensions arising from the different goals pursued by members of the distribution channel. Such tensions are often facilitated by the power imbalance of the channel members and frequently lead to explicit conflicts.

Channel Power

Channel power refers to the ability of one channel member to exert influence over another member of the same distribution channel. This influence often leads to an imbalance in the value exchange in favor of the more powerful entity. For example, a well-established manufacturer with a strong consumer brand is likely to receive preferential treatment from retailers, including premier shelf space, more favorable margins, discounts, allowances, and more flexible product-delivery schedules. In the same vein, large retailers often receive monetary and nonmonetary benefits from manufacturers, including preferential volume discounts, greater promotional allowances, and customized delivery schedules.

Channel power depends on a number of factors, including the *customer demand* for the offering, the *availability of alternative options*, and the *strategic importance* of the collaboration for each entity.

- **Customer demand.** Companies with differentiated offerings in high demand tend to have more channel power compared to companies with commoditized offerings. For example, manufacturers with strong brands such as Procter & Gamble, PepsiCo, Kraft Heinz, Unilever, and Nestlé have more power when dealing with their channel partners than companies with less powerful brands. In the same vein, high-traffic retailers such as Walmart, Carrefour, Amazon, and Aldi have more power when dealing with suppliers that have undifferentiated offerings.

- **Availability of alternative options.** A company is likely to have more power when there are fewer alternative options providing the same benefits. For example, companies like Walmart, Costco, Carrefour, and Tesco provide manufacturers with access to a broad customer base—a benefit that cannot be readily matched by many of their competitors.

- **Strategic importance.** A company tends to have more power when it accounts for a significant portion of a channel member's profits. As a result, larger entities—both manufacturers and retailers—tend to have more channel power than smaller ones. For example, Walmart is in a position of power when negotiating with small manufacturers because their individual contribution to Walmart's net income is low, whereas Walmart accounts for a substantial part of their profits.

In the past several decades, power has been gradually shifting away from manufacturers that create the goods sold to distributors that control target customers' access to these goods. There are several reasons for this shift in channel power. First, the consolidation of retailers and the proliferation of smaller independent producers have significantly increased the role that channels play in a company's ability to create customer value. Furthermore, the increased availability of customer-generated product information such as product ratings and reviews, product popularity rankings, and the relative ease of identifying alternative options (e.g., similar products searched for or purchased by customers) have heightened the role of retailers as a key source of product-related information.

Heightened retailer power is further facilitated by retailers' increased ability to understand, engage, and maintain relationships with their customers. Because retailers typically are much closer to customers than manufacturers, they are in a much better position to observe, interpret, predict, and influence buyers' behavior. The increased reliance on data analytics has enabled many retailers to link shoppers' profiles reflecting their prior activities to their in-store behavior, and use this information to direct them to offerings that are most likely to fit their current needs and preferences. The access to this information and the ability to influence buyers' behavior gives retailers the upper hand in negotiations with manufacturers, who might not be privy to the wealth of information collected by retailers and are often limited in their ability to influence target customers at the point of purchase.

Channel Conflicts

As with most business relationships, channel collaboration is not without conflicts. Channel conflicts are tensions among entities occupying different levels of the value-delivery chain. Tensions among channel partners are often caused by the differences in their strategic goals and profit-optimization strategies. Depending on the nature of the tension, there are two types of channel conflicts: *vertical* and *horizontal*.

- **Vertical channel conflict** involves tensions between entities within a given distribution channel. The most common type of vertical conflict is that between a manufacturer and a retailer. For example, vertical conflict might involve tensions regarding the size and composition of the manufacturer's product line carried by the retailer. The conflict here stems from the discrepancy between a manufacturer's desire that a retailer carry its entire product line and a retailer's desire to carry only the most profitable offerings from different manufacturers. Vertical conflict can also occur when one entity exercises its power to achieve its strategic goals to the detriment of its channel partner (e.g., the retailer raises product prices to maximize its own profits to the detriment of the manufacturer's profits).

- **Horizontal channel conflict** involves tensions among entities in multiple distribution channels (e.g., a manufacturer and two retailers). Horizontal conflicts occur when a manufacturer targets the same customers utilizing multiple distribution channels that operate with different cost structures and profit margins. For example, a manufacturer selling its products in high-margin, full-service stores and in high-volume, low-margin stores is likely to create channel conflict if the two retailers sell the same product at different prices to the same customers. Horizontal channel conflicts can also involve disagreements concerning the level of service and brand image provided by different outlets carrying offerings from the same producer. For example, a McDonald's franchisee that aims to delight its customers by offering superior service might be unhappy with a franchisee that tarnishes the image of all franchisees by offering inferior service. (This example might also involve a vertical conflict between the franchisee and the franchisor.)

Companies use diverse strategies for managing channel conflicts. A common approach for managing vertical channel conflict involves coordinating the assortment, pricing, and promotion of a company's offerings with the retailer in order to optimize the profitability of both the manufacturer and the retailer. In the same vein, a popular approach for managing horizontal channel conflict involves the development of channel-specific product variants that have minor differences in functionality and, therefore, cannot be directly compared. For example, Procter & Gamble might develop unique packaging for its laundry detergents for large retailers such as Walmart and Costco that is not available in other retail outlets. Mitigating the likelihood of vertical and horizontal channel conflicts is an essential aspect of developing a successful value-delivery strategy that benefits all members of the distribution channel.

Channel Dynamics

Once created, distribution channels do not stay static; they evolve over time. Changes in technology and market structure often lead to reallocation of the functions performed by the different channel members. For example, a manufacturer might decide to create its own direct distribution network, or a retailer might decide to start manufacturing the products it has been selling on behalf of a third party. To this end, a company might decide to insource the activities that were performed by collaborators by creating a new entity or by acquiring (or merging with) an existing entity.

Depending on the relative position of the entities in the value-delivery process, there are two types of channel integration: *vertical* and *horizontal*.

- **Vertical integration** typically involves the acquisition of an entity occupying a different level of the value-delivery chain. Depending on the relative position of the entities, there are two common types of vertical integration: forward and backward. Extending ownership upstream (toward suppliers) is referred to as backward integration, whereas extending ownership of activities downstream (toward buyers) is referred to as forward integration. For example, a retailer acquiring a manufacturer is a form of backward integration, whereas a manufacturer acquiring a retailer to establish its own distribution system is a form of forward integration.

  Vertical integration is favored by companies seeking to control the key aspects of the value-delivery process. For example, ExxonMobil engages in worldwide oil and gas exploration, production, supply, and transportation. Starbucks directly manages all aspects of its business, including sourcing, roasting, distributing, and overseeing how its coffee is served. American Express directly markets to customers, issues its cards, processes the payments through its own network, and directly acquires the merchant relationships. By consolidating the distinct aspects of the value-delivery process, these companies aim to create offerings that consistently deliver superior market value.

- **Horizontal integration** involves acquiring a business entity at the same level of the value-delivery chain. For example, a retailer acquiring another retailer or a manufacturer merging with another manufacturer constitutes horizontal integration. Horizontal integration might occur among entities with similar core competencies—a common scenario for companies seeking economies of scale through consolidation and for those seeking economies of scope through diversification.

  Horizontal integration is favored by companies for a variety of reasons, including gaining access to new markets, acquiring the rights to proprietary technology or research, reducing the competition in strategically important markets, and gaining power over the other entities in the value-delivery chain. For example, Amazon's acquisition of Whole Foods helped the online retailer establish a physical footprint in the grocery market as well as gather information about the food-buying patterns and preferences of many of its own customers.

SUMMARY

Distribution involves collaboration between a company and a set of channel partners—retailers, wholesalers, dealers, and distributors—for the purpose of delivering a company's offerings to target customers. When designing distribution channels, a manager's ultimate goal is to create value for target customers in a way that benefits the company and its collaborators. Channels create market value by delivering the different aspects of the company's offering to target customers: They deliver the company's products and services, enhance the offering's brand, collect payments, distribute and process incentives, and communicate the offerings' benefits to buyers.

Channel structure defines the members of the distribution channel and the flow of goods and services from the manufacturer to customers. Based on their structure, channels can be direct, indirect, or hybrid. *Channel format* defines the distribution coverage and the value added by distribution channels. Channel coverage reflects the number of outlets at which offerings are made available to target customers. Channel value added reflects the marginal benefits created by the members of a company's distribution network. Based on the value they add, channels comprise a spectrum of options, with value-added distribution channels at one end of the spectrum and streamlined distribution channels at the other.

Channel power refers to the ability of one channel member to exert influence over another member of the same distribution channel. This influence often leads to an imbalance in the value exchange in favor of the more powerful entity, which frequently benefits from higher margins, discounts, and allowances; preferential access to scarce resources; premier shelf space; and more favorable product-delivery schedules.

Channel conflict describes tensions among channel members, often caused by differences in their goals. Distribution channels face two common types of channel conflicts: vertical conflicts, which involve different levels of the same channel (e.g., a manufacturer and a retailer), and horizontal conflicts, which involve entities within the same channel level (e.g., two retailers).

Once created, distribution channels evolve. A common form of *channel dynamics* is channel integration, whereby a company insources the activities that were performed by collaborators. Depending on the relative position of the entities in the value-delivery process, there are two types of channel integration: vertical integration, which involves the acquisition of an entity occupying a different level of the value-delivery chain, and horizontal integration, which involves acquiring a business entity at the same level of the value-delivery chain.

MARKETING INSIGHT: RELEVANT DISTRIBUTION CONCEPTS

All-Commodity Volume (ACV): A measure of an offering's availability, typically calculated as the total annual volume of the company's offering in a given geographic area relative to the total sales volume of the retailers in that geographic area across all product categories.

$$ACV = \frac{\text{Total sales of stores carrying the company's offering}}{\text{Total sales of all stores}}$$

Channel Captain: A member of the distribution channel that, by virtue of its power, is able to coordinate the activities of the other channel members. A channel captain can be a manufacturer such as Procter & Gamble and Unilever, a wholesaler such as Alibaba and W. W. Grainger, or a retailer such as Amazon and Walmart.

Detailers: Indirect salesforce promoting pharmaceuticals to doctors and pharmacists so that they recommend the brand to the consumer.

Drop Shipping: Distribution method in which the product ordered in a store is shipped directly from the manufacturer to the customer (instead of the manufacturer shipping it to the retailer who then delivers it to the buyer).

Forward Buying: Increasing the channel inventory, usually to take advantage of a manufacturer's promotion or in anticipation of price increases.

Merchandisers: Indirect salesforce that offers support to retailers for in-store activities such as shelf location, pricing, and compliance with special programs.

Parallel Importing: The practice of importing products from a country in which the price is lower to a country in which the same product is priced higher. A hypothetical example of this practice is importing drugs from Canada to the United States. In most cases, parallel importing is illegal in the United States.

Reverse Logistics: The process of reclaiming recyclable and reusable materials and returns for repair, remanufacturing, or disposal.

PART FOUR

MANAGING GROWTH

INTRODUCTION

You will either step forward into growth
or you will step back into safety.
— Abraham Maslow, American psychologist

Growth is at the heart of every business enterprise. Without a viable growth strategy, a company is in danger of losing its market position and being engulfed by competitors. Therefore, to sustain and enhance its market position, a company must constantly seek novel ways to grow its current markets and capture new ones. To this end, companies seek to foster growth by exploring new opportunities, identifying new markets, and uncovering new customer needs.

Three aspects of managing growth merit attention: how to manage a company's market position, how to design and launch new offerings, and how to manage the company's relationship with its customers. These three aspects of managing growth are discussed in Chapters 14–16. Specifically, these chapters address the following topics: *gaining and defending market position*, *developing new offerings*, and *managing product lines*.

- **Gaining and defending market position** focuses on creating and sustaining growth in a competitive environment. A key driver of an offering's market position is managing sales growth that stems from adoption of the offering by new customers as well as increased usage by the offering's existing customers. The key aspects of gaining and defending market position — pioneering new markets and managing sales growth — are discussed in Chapter 14.

- **Developing new offerings** is the engine driving sustainable growth. The development of new products, services, and brands enables companies to strengthen their market position by capturing new opportunities to create market value. The key issues in developing new offerings — managing risk, the stage-gate approach, and understanding the adoption cycle of new products — are the focus of Chapter 15.

- **Managing product lines** aims to align the individual offerings in the company's product line. The key aspects of product line management — product lines as a means of creating market value, managing product-line extensions, and managing product lines in a competitive context — are discussed in Chapter 16.

The selection of a growth strategy is ultimately determined by the company's goals and strategic resources, as well as by the market in which it creates value. To successfully grow its business, a company must constantly seek new ways to create value for its customers, collaborators, and stakeholders. An integrative approach to managing growth that stems from the fundamental marketing principle of value creation is outlined in the following chapters.

CHAPTER FOURTEEN

GAINING AND DEFENDING MARKET POSITION

Opportunities multiply as they are seized.
—Sun Tzu, Chinese military strategist

In today's competitive business environment, the pressure to grow is unrelenting. To stay relevant, a company must constantly seek new avenues for growth. If a company is not growing, it is inevitably declining by relinquishing its market position to the competition. The key aspects of managing growth—managing a company's market position and managing sales growth—are the focus of this chapter.

Managing Market Position

Managing a company's market position is central to its ability to create and capture market value. The essence of market position as a business concept, common strategies for gaining and defending market position, the pros and cons of pioneering new markets, and the core competencies that substantiate a company's market position are discussed in the following sections.

Market Position as a Business Concept

Depending on the frame of reference, a company's market position can be defined in different ways: as a share of the market in which it competes, as a share of mind among its target customers, and as a share of target customers' hearts.

- **Share of market** reflects a company's share of the market in which it competes. Market share can be defined in terms of the number of units sold within a given period of time (usually annually) or in terms of the monetary value of these units. For offerings sold at similar price points, monetary and unit-based measures of market share are likely to coincide. For offerings sold at different price points, unit-based market share can be more informative because it reflects the sales volume independently of the price at which different offerings are sold. At the same time, focusing exclusively on unit share can be dangerous because without a corresponding increase in revenues, increase in sales volume might lead to profit erosion.

- **Share of mind** reflects the degree to which a company's target customers are aware of its offerings. Share of mind can be thought of as the extent to which a company's products, services, and brands are associated with a particular customer need or category. A high share of mind means that the names of the company's offerings are likely to be the first that comes to customers' minds when they think about a particular need or product category. For example, Kleenex is often the first facial tissue brand that comes to mind, Band-Aid has a leading share of mind in the adhesive bandage category, Rollerblade has top-of-mind awareness in inline skating, and Gillette enjoys the mindshare lead in shaving.

- **Share of heart** reflects the degree to which a company's target customers have a personal connection with the company and its offerings. A high share of heart means that customers have a deep emotional connection with the company's offerings. Brands that have established leadership in gaining a share of customers' hearts have managed to become lovemarks—a term coined by Kevin Roberts, former CEO Worldwide of the advertising company Saatchi & Saatchi. Brands like Harley-Davidson, Porsche, and Apple have developed a loyal following that includes many customers who have become company evangelists voluntarily advocating on behalf of these brands.

The above three measures of market position, although related, do not necessarily overlap. Thus, a company might have a high market share because of low prices and extensive distribution coverage without necessarily having a strong share of mind or heart. In the same vein, a company's high share of mind might not necessarily translate into a high market share if it is high priced and/or has weak distribution. For example, Twinkies snack cakes enjoyed a high share of mind even after the manufacturer Hostess Brands went bankrupt and stopped making them. Likewise, companies like Porsche, Tesla, and Ferrari enjoy a high share of consumers' hearts and minds while having a relatively small market share.

In general, companies that are able to increase their share of customers' hearts and minds are poised to gain share in the market in which they compete and achieve market leadership positions as have Amazon, Apple, Facebook, and McDonald's. Thus, even though market position is typically measured in terms of market share, a company's share of customers' hearts and minds is a precursor of its market share and, hence, is a key driver of this company's market position.

A company's market share depends on the way in which the market is defined. The broader the definition of the market, the more competitors it is likely to include and, hence, the smaller the company market share is likely to be. For example, the market share of Vitaminwater—a vitamin-enhanced mineral water—will vary depending on whether its sales are compared to those of other vitamin-enhanced mineral water brands, to sales of all energy drinks including Red Bull and Powerade, or to sales of all soft drinks including Coca-Cola, Pepsi, and Gatorade.

In competitive markets, companies are constantly jockeying to solidify their market position and gain competitive advantage. The constantly evolving nature of the competitive landscape calls for developing dynamic strategies to manage a company's market position. In this context, companies are presented with two perennial questions: how to gain market position and how to defend their current market position. We discuss these two questions in the following sections.

Gaining Market Position

From a competitive standpoint, a company can gain share by using four core strategies: stealing share from competitors already serving the market, growing the market by attracting new customers to the category, growing the market by increasing sales to current customers, and creating new markets. These four strategies are outlined in more detail below.

Steal-Share Strategy

The *steal-share strategy* refers to a company's activities aimed at attracting customers from its competitors rather than trying to attract customers who are new to the product category. Examples of the steal-share strategy include Apple targeting Windows users rather than targeting customers who have never had a computer, Dollar Shave Club targeting Gillette customers rather than those who are just starting to shave, and T-Mobile targeting Verizon and AT&T customers rather than those who are subscribing to a wireless service for the first time. A company's steal-share strategy can vary in breadth: It can narrowly target customers of a specific competitor (e.g., Pepsi targeting Coke customers), or it can broadly focus on the competitor's market as a whole (e.g., RC Cola trying to steal share from cola market leaders such as Coke and Pepsi).

The steal-share strategy is illustrated in Figure 1, in which the dark-shaded segment represents the company's current market share, and the light-shaded segment represents the share it aims to gain from the competition. Because of its focus on attracting only competitors' customers, the steal-share approach is also referred to as the *selective demand strategy*.

Figure 1. Steal-Share Strategy

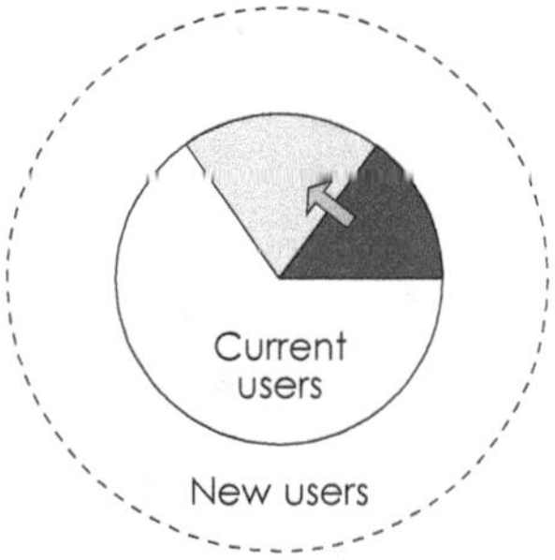

To succeed in attracting competitors' customers, a company needs to present these customers with a compelling value proposition. In this context, there are two main steal-share strategies: a *benefit-differentiation strategy* and a *cost-differentiation strategy*.

- **Benefit differentiation** aims to steal share from the competition by demonstrating the superiority of the company's offering on functional attributes such as performance, reliability, and durability and/or by its ability to create psychological value, such as conveying emotions and enabling customers to express their identity. Based on the offering's price point, there are three benefit-differentiation strategies: premium positioning (greater benefits at a higher price), price-parity positioning (greater benefits at the same price), and dominant positioning (greater benefits at a lower price).

- **Price differentiation** aims to steal share from competitors by virtue of the offering's price advantage. Based on the offering's benefits, there are two price-differentiation strategies: a "same-for-less" positioning (lower price for the same benefits) and a "less-for-less" positioning (lower price for lower benefits). A particular form of the "same-for-less" strategy is cloning, which involves emulating a competitor's offering, usually with slight variations to avoid patent, trademark, and copyright infringement liability.

In cases when a company is trying to gain share from established competitors, the steal-share strategy usually involves comparative positioning, whereby the company's offering is directly compared to those of its competitors. Comparative positioning is less likely to be utilized by the market leader because by comparing itself to a lesser known competitor the company ends up creating awareness of and sometimes even implicitly promoting the competitor's offering. For example, an underdog in the personal computer market, Apple directly compared its offerings to Microsoft-based personal computers, which comprised the vast majority of the market. By the same token, Samsung directly compared its Galaxy mobile phones to the market leader iPhone.

Market-Growth Strategy

Unlike the steal-share strategy, which targets competitors' customers, the market-growth strategy aims to attract customers who are new to the category (Figure 2). For example, an advertising campaign promoting the benefits of smart watches builds the entire category by encouraging first-time buyers to purchase a smart watch rather than to switch from another brand of smart watches. Because of its focus on increasing the overall category demand, the market-growth strategy is also referred to as *primary demand strategy*.

Figure 2. Market-Growth Strategy

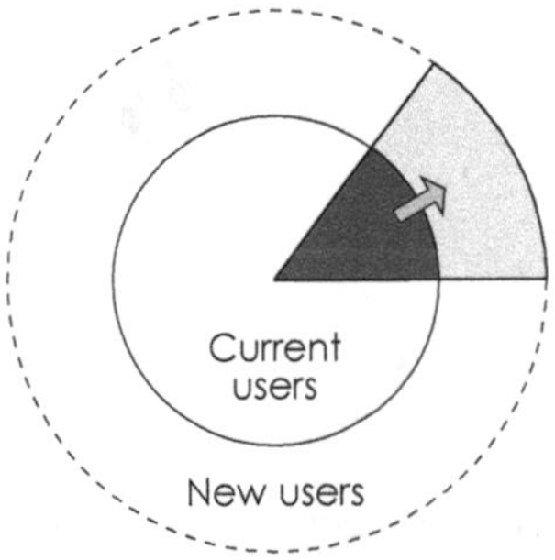

Since the market-growth strategy is aimed at growing the entire market, it typically benefits *all* companies competing in that market. Therefore, this strategy is usually adopted in the early stages of an offering's life cycle when the overall market growth is high and competition is not yet a primary issue. In addition, because offerings tend to gain share proportionately to their current market position, in the case of mature products the market-growth strategy is likely to benefit the market leader.

A notable exception to the scenario illustrated in Figure 2 is a company whose offering has a superior value proposition relative to the competition (because of a technological breakthrough, the addition of unique product benefits, or a price advantage), making it likely to gain a disproportionately large share (relative to its current market share) of new customers. In this case, both a small-share company and the market leader can benefit by using a market-growth strategy (Figure 3). For example, a pharmaceutical company that has developed a proprietary drug that is more effective than the competition might focus on generating primary demand in the belief that the majority of new customers will prefer its offering.

Figure 3. Market-Growth Strategy for a Superior Offering

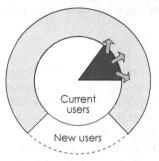

Because it aims to increase the size of the entire market, the market-growth strategy rarely involves comparative positioning. Instead, to grow the market, a company is likely to relate the benefits of its offering to customers' needs and underscore the ways in which the offering will fulfill these needs.

Market-Penetration Strategy

The market-penetration strategy aims to grow sales by increasing the quantity purchased by the company's own customers rather than explicitly trying to "steal" competitors' customers or attract new buyers to the product category (Figure 4). For example, Listerine encourages its customers to use its mouthwash twice a day rather than once, Starbucks' loyalty programs entice customers to visit its coffee shops more frequently, and Campbell urges its customers to eat soup in the summer.

Figure 4. Market-Penetration Strategy

The competitive impact of market penetration varies based on buyers' behavior and, specifically, whether the sales volume stems from substituting competitive offerings for the company's products and services or results from incremental demand that expands the overall category usage. When the market-penetration strategy leads to switching behavior, with customers buying larger quantities of the company's offerings instead of buying competitors' offerings, the net effect of this strategy is very similar to that of the steal-share strategy. The only difference is that instead of directly stealing competitors' customers, the company is stealing a share of purchases that its customers would have made from the competition. In contrast, a market-penetration strategy that leads to an increase in sales without necessarily stealing share from the competition—a common scenario in categories such as food, beverage, and apparel where the quantity purchased and consumed by customers can be influenced by marketers—is akin to growing primary demand that expands the overall category usage.

Market-Creation Strategy

The market-creation strategy is similar to the market-growth strategy in that a company gains market position by attracting customers who are not using any of the products and services offered in a given category (Figure 5). The key difference is that instead of attracting new customers to an existing market in which the company faces numerous rivals, the company defines an entirely new category in which direct competitors are absent. Companies that have created new markets include eBay (online peer-to-peer marketplace), Netflix (digital streaming), Facebook (social networking), Groupon (group-based discounts), Uber (ride-sharing), and Airbnb (short-term lodging).

Figure 5. Market-Creation Strategy

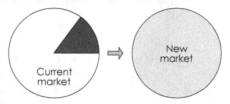

Because of its focus on uncontested markets, the market-creation strategy often leads to high profit margins and rapid growth—a scenario that inevitably attracts new market entrants. Therefore, to sustain its position in the newly created market, a company must begin to fashion a sustainable competitive advantage as soon as it starts creating the new market.

Defending Market Position

Because business success inevitably attracts competition, in addition to thinking about how to expand its offerings, a company must develop strategies to defend its market position. There are four basic ways in which a company can react to a competitor's actions aiming to erode its market position: *stay the course*, *enhance its offering* (increase its benefits or lower the price), *reposition its offering* (move upscale or downscale), and *launch new offerings*. These strategies are illustrated in Figure 6 and discussed in more detail in the following sections.

Figure 6. Defensive Market Strategies[28]

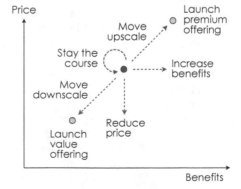

Stay the Course

Staying the course can be a viable response to changes in the market conditions. The decision to ignore a competitor's action(s) reflects a manager's belief that this action either will have no impact on the company's market position or that the competitive threat is not sustainable and will dissipate by itself. For example, a manager might decide that its upscale offering will not be affected by the entry of a low-price, low-quality competitor and, therefore, not consider this action a direct threat. In the same vein, a manager might not react to a competitor's price reduction in the belief that this low price is not sustainable in the longer term.

Staying the course can also reflect a manager's belief that there is simply not enough information to decide whether and how to act, and that additional data must be gathered to identify the best course of action. Indeed, without having a clear understanding of the challenges facing the company and their root cause, any action can end up being counterproductive, complicating rather than improving the situation.

Enhance the Existing Offering

A popular strategy to defend a company's market position is to enhance the attractiveness of its current offerings. This can be achieved by one of two routes: *increasing the offering's benefits* or *lowering its price*.

- **Increasing an offering's benefits.** One approach to increase the attractiveness of an offering is to increase the customer benefits it creates. To this end, a company might enhance the functional benefits of the offering (by improving the offering's performance), increase the monetary benefits (by enhancing the financial value of the offering), and increase the psychological benefits (by strengthening the offering's image). For each of these strategies, the increase in the offering's benefits must be meaningful to lead to a change in customer behavior; adding attributes that are irrelevant to target customers is not likely to enhance the offering's customer value.

- **Lowering an offering's price.** Rather than increase an offering's benefits, a company might increase the offering's value by lowering its monetary costs. To this end, a company might outright reduce the price of its offering and offer monetary incentives such as price discounts, coupons, and rebates. Lowering an offering's costs using price incentives (rather than lowering the offering's price) is the prevalent strategy because it is easier to modify at a later point when market conditions have changed.

The choice of a particular strategy—increasing benefits or lowering costs—depends on the company's overarching strategy. Thus, targeting customers who prioritize performance over price calls for enhancing an offering's performance, whereas targeting price-sensitive customers is better aligned with lowering the offering's price. In the same vein, the choice of a particular strategy to enhance an offering's value is a function of the company's competencies and assets. A company with a strong research and development background might focus on augmenting the offering's benefits with innovative new features. In contrast, a company focused on operational logistics and mass production might choose to compete on price rather than offer a higher level of benefits.

Reposition the Existing Offering

Unlike enhancing the company's offering, which is usually associated with a relatively minor increase in its benefits or a decrease in price, repositioning involves a more dramatic change in the benefits and the price of the offering. There are two ways in which a company can reposition its offering: *move upscale* or *move downscale*.

- **Upscale repositioning** involves modifying the value proposition of an offering by moving it into a higher price tier. In this case, the company not only increases the benefits of an offering but also increases the offering's price. For example, in the late 1990s the German manufacturer of upscale writing instruments Montblanc repositioned its offerings in the United States by withdrawing from office supplies stores such as Office Depot and Staples; upgrading its product line to include luxury watches, jewelry, and leather goods; and investing in its own stores and luxury boutiques.

- **Downscale repositioning** involves modifying the value proposition of an offering by moving it into a lower price tier. Unlike enhancing an offering by lowering its price, in this case the company lowers the price of an offering while also decreasing its benefits. Because it typically leads to lower profit margins, downscale repositioning is rarely used as a strategy to defend a company's market position.

The decision to move upscale or downscale is usually determined by the company's strategic vision and, specifically, whether it is focused on margins, willing to sacrifice sales volume, or aims to compete on volume, albeit at lower profit margins. To be effective, repositioning must be aligned with the needs of the target customers, the competitive offerings, and the company's goals and resources.

Launch a New Offering

In addition to repositioning its existing offerings, a company can respond to competitive actions by adding new offerings to its product line. A product-line extension is similar to repositioning, with the key distinction that instead of modifying the value proposition of an existing offering, the company launches a new offering with a different value proposition. There are two common product-line extension strategies: *vertical* and *horizontal*.

- **Vertical extensions** are new offerings differentiated by both benefits and price, with higher priced offerings delivering a higher level of benefits. A popular strategy to fight low-priced rivals involves launching a *fighting brand*—a downscale offering introduced to shield the core offering from low-priced competitors. A slightly more complex approach to dealing with low-priced competitors is the *sandwich strategy*, which involves both the introduction of a downscale offering and upscale repositioning of the core brand. An alternative approach to deal with low-priced rivals is the *good–better–best strategy*, which involves introducing both an upscale and a downscale offering, resulting in a three-tier product line. These three strategies are discussed in more detail later in this chapter.

- **Horizontal extensions** are new offerings that are differentiated primarily by functionality and not necessarily by price (e.g., a sedan vs. a minivan). As product categories mature, their user base becomes more diverse, calling for specialized offerings tailored to the needs of different customer segments. Consequently, the pioneer might preempt the competition by extending its product line with offerings tailored to each strategically important customer segment.

A detailed discussion on managing product lines and the pros and cons of vertical and horizontal line extensions is offered later in this chapter.

Pioneering New Markets

Based on the domain in which the company becomes the first mover, there are several types of pioneers: *technology pioneer*—the company that first introduces a new technology, *product pioneer*—the company that is first to commercially introduce a new product, and *market pioneer*—the company that first introduces an offering to a particular market. Recognizing the importance of being a technology and product pioneer, the rest of the discussion focuses on market pioneering. In this context, the term *pioneer* or *first mover* refers to the first company to establish its presence in the market.

To be a market pioneer, a company does not need to be a technology pioneer or a product pioneer. In fact, it is often the case that the company first to develop a new technology or first to launch a new type of product is not the company that becomes the market pioneer. To pioneer a market, a company must be the first to gain a leading share of customers' hearts, minds, and wallets.

The Benefits of Pioneering

Pioneering a market offers the incumbent a number of advantages that are not available to later entrants. These advantages include *shaping consumer preferences, creating switching costs, gaining access to scarce resources, creating technological barriers to entry,* and *taking advantage of the learning curve.*

- **Preference formation.** A pioneering company has a unique opportunity to shape customer preferences, creating a close association between its brand and the underlying customer need. For example, Jeep, Google, Amazon, eBay, Twitter, Uber, and Xerox not only helped shape customer preferences but also became synonymous with the entire category.

- **Switching costs.** As a pioneer, a company has the opportunity to build loyalty by creating switching costs for its customers. These switching costs can be functional (loss of the unique benefits created by the pioneer's offering), monetary (the cost of replacing current equipment or a penalty for breaking a contract), or psychological (the cost of learning the functionality of a competitor's offering). For example, iPhone users might find it difficult to switch because of the iPhone's compatibility with other Apple devices (functional cost), the cost involved in purchasing a replacement device and accessories (monetary cost), and the effort involved in learning how to operate a competitive device (psychological cost).

- **Resource advantage.** The pioneer can benefit from securing scarce resources such as raw materials, human resources, geographic locations, and collaborator networks. For example, the pioneer might be able to lock out the competition by securing exclusive access to strategically important mineral resources. Similarly, the pioneer might preempt competitors' access to particular human resources in short supply, such as engineers, designers, and managers. The pioneer may also preempt strategically important geographic locations in both real space (Starbucks, McDonald's, and Walmart) and online (flowers.com, drugstore.com, stamps.com, and cars.com). The pioneer can also preempt the competition by forging alliances with strategically important partners such as distributors or advertisers. For example, Nike offered exclusive long-term contracts to promising athletes early in their careers, thus precluding competitors from collaborating with these athletes when their careers took off.

- **Technological barriers.** The pioneer can create technological barriers to prevent competitors from entering the market. For example, the pioneer can establish a proprietary technological standard (e.g., operating system, communication protocol, or video compression algorithm) that can give it a leg up by forcing later entrants to make their offerings compatible with this standard. Apple's iOS and Google's Android operating systems created technological standards that gained wide adoption, thus erecting entry barriers for new competitors.

- **Learning curve.** The pioneer can also benefit from learning curve advantages, allowing it to heighten its technological know-how, productivity, and efficiency as it gains experience over time. The rate at which these advantages can be acquired by the competition is defined by the nature of the learning curve, such that a steeper slope means a quick increment of skill over time, making it easier for competitors to catch up with the pioneer. (Although in conversational language steep learning curve means a difficult learning process, a learning curve with a steep start actually represents rapid progress.)

Given the multiple benefits for the company that pioneers a given market, one might conclude that the company that is first to invent a new business model, debut a new technology, or launch a new offering will inevitably become the dominant market player. This, however, is not the case. While being a pioneer creates certain advantages, pioneers also face a number of disadvantages.

The Drawbacks of Being a Pioneer

It is far from a sure thing that the pioneer will succeed in becoming the market leader. This is because pioneers face a distinct set of challenges that might impede rather than facilitate their market success. The three most common challenges include *free riding, incumbent inertia*, and *market uncertainty*.

- **Free riding.** A later entrant might be able to benefit from the pioneer's resources, including its investments in technology, product design, customer education, regulatory approval, and infrastructure development at a fraction of the pioneer's cost and effort. To illustrate, after spending millions of dollars to develop the technology and educate the American audience about the advantages of a personal digital recorder, TiVo found itself in competition with cable and satellite operators selling similar services to its already educated customers. A later entrant might also reverse-engineer the pioneer's product and improve on it, while investing only a fraction of the resources required to develop the original product. For example, FedEx built on DHL's idea to start overnight deliveries in the United States, IBM launched its personal computer by building on the earlier product introductions from Apple and Atari, and Best Buy launched a rapid expansion of superstores based on the success of the business model introduced by Circuit City.

- **Incumbent inertia.** Being a market leader often leads to complacency, thus leaving technological and market opportunities open to competitors. To illustrate, IBM's reliance on mainframes, even when mainframes were being replaced by desktops and networked computers, enabled competitors such as Dell and Hewlett-Packard to gain a foothold in IBM's markets and steal some of its most valuable clients. Incumbent inertia might also be driven by a reluctance to cannibalize existing product lines by adopting a new technology or a new business model. For example, brick-and-mortar booksellers such as Barnes & Noble and Borders failed to recognize the importance of e-commerce, allowing Amazon to establish a dominant presence in online book retailing. Incumbent inertia might also result from a "sunk-cost mentality," whereby managers feel compelled to utilize their large investments in extant technology or markets even when technological advancements and market forces make these investments unfeasible. For example, one of the reasons Ford lost its leading market position to General Motors in the 1930s was its reluctance to make the necessary investments to modify existing manufacturing facilities to diversify its product line.

- **Market uncertainty.** Another potential disadvantage in being a pioneer is the uncertainty associated with the offering. Thus, the uncertainty associated with designing the offering and anticipating customers' reaction to this offering is one of the main factors responsible for the high degree of failure involved in pioneering a market. Whereas the pioneer has to deal with the uncertainty surrounding the technology and market demand, a follower can learn from the pioneer's successes and failures and design a superior offering. Because of the uncertainty associated with the introduction of a new offering, companies with strong brands and distribution capabilities might choose to be late-market entrants in order to learn from the pioneer's experience and develop a superior market-entry strategy. These companies use their brand and channel power to gain market share and successfully compete with market pioneers. For example, the first sugar-free soft drink was introduced in the United States by Cott in 1947, and the first sugar-free cola was introduced by Royal Crown in 1962, only to be overtaken by Coca-Cola and PepsiCo, which used their branding and distribution muscle to dominate the consumer soft drink market.

The numerous drawbacks of being a market pioneer suggest that when entering new markets, a company should strive not only to gain share but also to create a business model that cannot be easily copied by its current and future competitors. Because market success inevitably attracts competition, creating a *sustainable* competitive advantage is the key to a successful pioneering strategy.

Building Core Competencies

To gain and defend market position, a firm needs to develop core competencies that will give it a sustainable competitive advantage. A core competency involves expertise in an area essential to the company's business model, allowing the company to create superior market value. From a marketing standpoint, there are six key areas in which a company can develop a core competency: *business process management, operations management, technology development, product development, service management,* and *brand building.*

- **Business process management.** Competency in business management refers to a company's ability to build and manage a viable and sustainable business model that creates market value for the company, its customers, and its collaborators. This competency typically leads to the strategic benefit of *business model leadership.* Examples of companies with demonstrated competency in business innovation include Amazon, Uber, Netflix, Facebook, Google, and Airbnb.

- **Operations management.** Competency in managing operations refers to expertise in manufacturing and supply-chain management. Companies with this competency are proficient at optimizing the effectiveness and cost efficiency of their processes, which typically leads to two strategic benefits: *logistics leadership* and *cost leadership*. Logistics leadership involves proficiency in supply-chain management that enables a company to excel in sourcing, manufacturing, and distribution. For example, Foxconn—arguably the world's largest electronics contract manufacturer and a supplier for companies like Amazon, Apple, Dell, Google, Huawei, Intel, Microsoft, Nintendo, Toshiba, and Xiaomi—stands out for its dynamic, high-volume production of complex electronics products. Examples of companies with demonstrated competency in logistics include UPS, FedEx, and DHL. Cost leadership reflects the company's position as the lowest cost (although not necessarily the lowest price) producer in the market. For example, Walmart's competency in operations management is reflected in its dominant position as a low-cost retailer. Other examples of companies with demonstrated cost leadership include Costco, Carrefour, H&M, and Zara.

- **Technology development.** Competency in technology development refers to a company's ability to devise new technological solutions. This competency typically leads to the strategic benefit of *technological leadership*. Technological leadership involves proficiency in developing new technologies that enable the company to excel in establishing technological standards in markets in which it operates. Examples of companies that have demonstrated this competency include Motorola, BASF, Google, and Intel. Competency in developing new technologies does not necessarily imply competency in developing commercially successful products. To illustrate, Xerox and its Palo Alto Research Center (PARC) have invented numerous new technologies including photocopying, laser printing, graphical user interface, client-server architecture, and the Ethernet but have been slow in commercializing these technologies.

- **Product development.** Competency in product development describes a company's ability to develop products that deliver superior customer value. This competency typically leads to the strategic benefit of *product leadership*. Product leadership involves proficiency in creating new products that enable the company to excel in gaining and sustaining its market position. Examples of companies with demonstrated competency in this area include Apple, Microsoft, Tesla, Johnson & Johnson, and Merck. Note that competency in product development does not necessarily imply competency in technology development. Technologically inferior products delivering superior customer benefits are often more successful than technologically advanced products that fail to meet customer needs.

- **Service management.** Competency in service management reflects a company's ability to develop services that deliver superior customer value and typically leads to the strategic benefit of *service leadership*. Service leadership involves proficiency in initiating and growing customer relationships that enable the company to excel in gaining and sustaining a strong market position. Examples of companies with demonstrated competency in this area include The Ritz-Carlton, American Express, Amazon, Zappos, and Nordstrom.

- **Brand building.** Competency in brand building describes a company's ability to build strong brands that deliver superior customer value. This competency typically leads to the strategic benefit of *brand leadership*, which reflects a company's ability to build and sustain strong brands that capture customers' hearts and minds and engender customer loyalty. Examples of companies with demonstrated competency in this area include Harley-Davidson, Lacoste, Hermès, McDonald's, and Coca-Cola.

The above core competencies are not mutually exclusive; achieving excellence in one area does not prevent the company from excelling in another. To stay competitive, a company must develop competencies in multiple areas. For example, the success of Amazon, Google, and Facebook stems from building core competencies in all of the above domains — from business model development to brand building.

Managing Sales Growth

Sales growth is a key component of a company's efforts to gain and defend its market position and ensure long-term profit growth. Sales growth can be achieved organically by using existing resources, or it can be achieved by acquiring or merging with another company. Here, we focus on organic growth, which is the most common sales growth strategy. Organic sales growth can stem from two sources: an increase in the offering's sales volume and a change in the offering's price. In this section, our focus is on strategies for growing sales by increasing sales volume (the impact of pricing on sales is discussed in Chapters 6 and 10).

Increasing sales volume can be achieved with two core strategies: increasing the rate of adoption of a company's offering by new customers and increasing the offering's sales to existing customers. These two strategies for increasing the sales volume of a company's offerings — *managing adoption* and *managing usage* — are discussed in more detail below.

Managing Offering Adoption

To identify the optimal strategy for increasing sales volume when introducing new market offerings, a company first needs to understand the process by which its target customers adopt new offerings, then identify the impediments to new product adoption in different stages of the process, and, finally, develop an action plan to remove these impediments. These aspects of managing the adoption of new offerings are discussed in more detail below.

Understanding the Adoption Process

From a customer's perspective, the adoption of a new offering can be viewed as a process comprising four main stages: awareness, attractiveness, affordability, and availability. Thus, for customers to adopt an offering, they must be *aware* of the offering, find its benefits *attractive*, perceive the offering to be *affordable*, and have access to the offering, meaning that the offering should be *available* for purchase and use.[29] Because the number of potential customers who ultimately purchase the offering tends to decrease with each progressive step, the adoption process is also referred to as an *adoption funnel* (Figure 7).

Figure 7. The Adoption Funnel

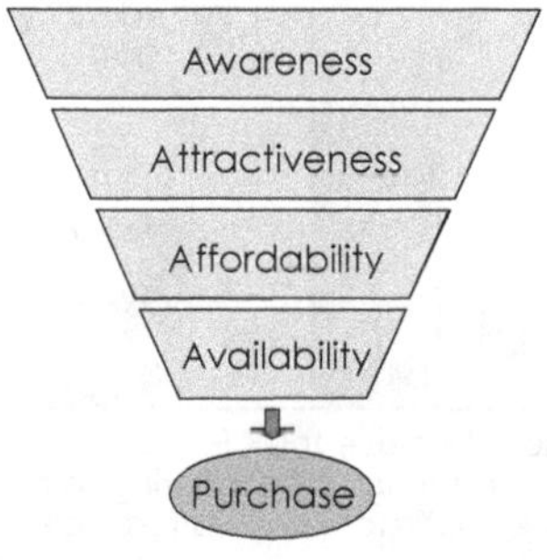

- **Awareness** reflects customers' knowledge of the offering. Awareness can be generated by the company's direct communications with its target customers; by communication initiated by its collaborators; or by third-party communication such as press coverage, social media, and personal communication.

- **Attractiveness** reflects the benefits associated with a given offering, typically considered in a competitive context. Thus, an offering's attractiveness reflects its ability to satisfy a particular customer need better than the competition.[30]

- **Affordability** reflects customers' perceptions of the monetary costs associated with the offering and their ability to cover these costs. Considered together, attractiveness (benefits) and affordability (costs) determine the overall value (utility) of the offering for target customers.

- **Availability** reflects customers' ability to acquire the offering. An offering's availability is a function of the proximity of the distribution channels to target customers and the in-stock availability of the offering in these channels on a day-to-day basis.

Note that the order in which potential buyers experience the different stages of the adoption process might vary. For example, an offering might be available to all potential buyers, but only a few buyers might be aware of it before encountering it on the store shelves. Thus, the sequence of the stages in the adoption funnel can vary across individual customers.

Identifying and Closing Adoption Gaps

Managing product adoption calls for identifying and eliminating impediments at different stages of the adoption process. These impediments, referred to as *adoption gaps*, can be illustrated by mapping the dispersion of customers across different stages of the adoption funnel. The goal of this analysis is to provide a better understanding of the dynamics of the adoption process and identify problematic areas that must be addressed.

The dispersion of customers across different stages of the adoption process can be represented by a series of bars, as shown in Figure 8. Here, the light-shaded part of each bar corresponds to the share of potential customers who have not transitioned to the next stage of the adoption process. The ratio of the light-shaded portion to the dark-shaded portion of the bar reflects the effectiveness of the company's actions at each step in acquiring new customers.

Figure 8. Identifying Adoption Gaps

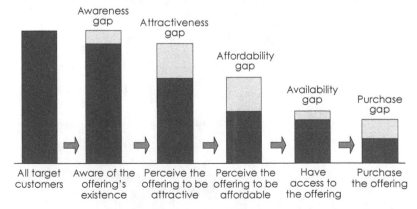

Evaluating the loss of potential customers at each step of the process offers a simple way to identify impediments to adoption. In this context, gap analysis can be used both to pinpoint the problem spots in product adoption and to identify specific solutions to close adoption gaps. The key performance gaps and the common solutions for closing these gaps at the different stages of the adoption process are outlined below.

- **Awareness gaps** call for increasing awareness of the offering among target customers. This type of gap requires improving company communication, which can involve increasing communication spending, streamlining the message, developing a better creative solution, or improving the effectiveness of reaching target customers. In addition to directly communicating the offering to target customers, the company can also partner with collaborators — for example, by engaging in joint (co-op) advertising with its channel partners and by fostering third-party communication such as facilitating publicity about the offering and encouraging media coverage.

- **Attractiveness gaps** call for improving the benefits of the offering. Typically, this is achieved by redesigning the benefit-related aspects of the offering — specifically, its product, service, and brand components. Attractiveness gaps do not always imply that the offering lacks the benefits desired by buyers; they can also stem from buyers' failure to comprehend the offering's benefits. Such gaps in customers' understanding of the offering's benefits can be closed by improving communication and providing target customers with an option to experience the offering via product samples and demonstrations.

- **Affordability gaps** call for lowering the costs of the offering. Lowering the monetary cost might involve lowering the offering's price and adding monetary incentives to decrease the offering's cost to customers. As is the case with attractiveness gaps, affordability gaps do not always imply that the actual cost of the offering is high; they might also result from customers' misperception of the offering's actual costs. Such misperceptions of the offering's cost can be surmounted by communication aimed at correcting customers' erroneous beliefs.

- **Availability gaps** indicate that target customers do not have access to the offering. For example, an offering might be in short supply because a company underestimated its appeal to target customers or because of inadequate distribution coverage. Depending on the cause of the availability gap, improving an offering's availability can involve ramping up production to meet demand, improving the geographic coverage of distribution channels to give target customers better access to the offering, and improving channel operations to reduce stock-outs.

- **Purchase gaps** indicate that even though customers are aware of the offering and find it attractive, affordable, and available, they have not yet purchased the offering — for example, because of time or budgetary constraints. Closing purchase gaps typically involves introducing time-sensitive incentives such as short-term price discounts, coupons, and financing options.

Following identification of the adoption gaps and the means of closing these gaps, a company must evaluate the magnitude of each gap and its impact on sales revenues and profits against the feasibility and the costs associated with closing each gap. This analysis can enable the company to prioritize the adoption gaps and develop an effective and cost-efficient approach to managing sales growth by attracting new customers.

Managing Offering Usage

The discussion so far has focused on growing sales volume by increasing product adoption by new customers. An alternative approach to growing an offering's sales volume involves increasing its usage by current customers and identifying and closing usage gaps.

Understanding Offering Usage

Many purchases are recurring in nature, whether they are products for daily usage such as food, apparel, and cosmetics, or durable goods such as cars, household appliances, and electronics. In this context, managing recurring consumption can have a significant impact on sales volume, especially in cases of frequently purchased high-ticket items.

The total quantity of offerings purchased over time by a given customer depends on several factors, including overall satisfaction with the offering, the frequency with which this customer uses the offering, the quantity used on each usage occasion, and the ease of repurchase. As in the case of customer adoption, these factors can be presented in the form of a funnel illustrating factors influencing repurchase frequency (Figure 9).

Figure 9. The Usage Funnel

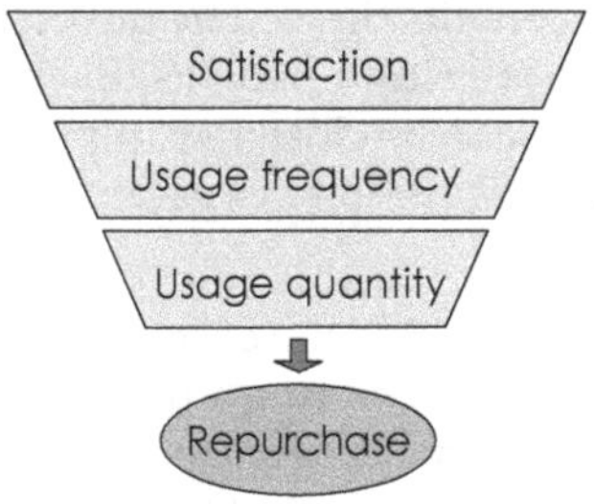

- **Satisfaction** reflects customers' experience with the offering. Unlike the attractiveness stage in product adoption, which is based on expectations of an offering's value, satisfaction reflects the post-consumption evaluation that takes into account customers' actual use of the offering.

- **Usage frequency** reflects the number of occasions on which the offering is used. For example, for cars, usage frequency refers to how often customers drive; for toothpaste, it refers to the number of times people brush their teeth; and for shaving, it indicates how frequently customers shave.

- **Usage quantity** reflects the amount customers use on each occasion. For example, usage quantity for toothpaste depends on the amount of toothpaste people use to brush their teeth. In the case of unit-based products such as printer cartridges, water filters, and razor blades, which customers determine when to replace, usage quantity is defined by the replacement frequency.

- **Ease of repurchase** reflects the ease with which customers can obtain a replacement for the company's offering once it has been consumed.

Identifying and Closing Usage Gaps

A practical approach to closing usage gaps calls for identifying and eliminating impediments at the different stages of product usage. The potential impediments to product usage can be visualized by a series of bars, as shown in Figure 10. Here, the light-shaded portion of each bar corresponds to the share of customers whose consumption behavior is off target, and the ratio of the light-shaded portion to the dark-shaded portion reflects the effectiveness of the company's actions at each step of the consumption process.

Figure 10. Identifying Usage Gaps

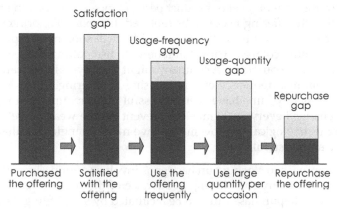

Evaluating the effectiveness of each stage of consumption offers a relatively simple way to identify usage gaps and develop solutions for closing such gaps.

- **Satisfaction gaps** call for improving customers' experience with the offering. Depending on the cause of the satisfaction gap, closing this gap might involve enhancing the benefits and reducing the costs of the offering to make it more competitive and to better align the offering's value proposition with customer preferences.

- **Usage-frequency gaps** call for increasing the rate at which customers use the offering. For example, sales of a laundry detergent can be increased if customers wash their clothes more often, sales of toothpaste can be increased if customers brush their teeth more frequently, and sales of razors can be increased if customers shave more frequently. Sales volume can also be increased by identifying new ways to use the offering. To illustrate, Campbell promotes the use of its soup (usually consumed in winter time) during the summer, and Arm & Hammer promotes baking soda not only for baking but also as a household cleaner and deodorizer.

- **Usage-quantity gaps** call for increasing the amount of product used on each occasion. Usage quantity can be increased by educating customers about the optimal usage quantity. A classic example of this approach is the "rinse and repeat" shampoo advertising campaign. Another approach involves increasing the size of the packaging in categories where bigger package size typically leads to consuming a larger quantity. Usage volume also can be increased by designing the product in a way that ensures dispensing of the optimal quantity per usage occasion. For example, Heinz introduced a plastic squeeze bottle, increased the size of the opening in the bottle neck, and designed the "upside-down bottle" so ketchup can be poured without having to wait for the contents to slide down to the opening of the bottle.

  In cases of unit-based products such as printer cartridges, razor blades, and water filters, usage-quantity gaps call for increasing the frequency with which customers replace the product. Replacement frequency can be managed by informing customers about the optimal usage duration and replacement frequency. For example, to encourage customers to replace their toothbrush, the Oral-B toothbrush features blue bristles that fade to alert users that they need a new brush.

- **Repurchase gaps** call for streamlining the ways in which the offering is replenished after it has been consumed. Closing repurchase gaps can involve enabling customers to monitor the current level of product performance and informing them in a timely manner that the offering needs to be replaced. For example, printers include toner-level indicators to alert users that the cartridge will soon need replacement. Gillette cartridges feature colored strips that fade with use, letting the user know that it is time to replace the cartridge. A company might also invest in educating its customers about the optimal frequency of repurchasing its offering. For example, oil change chains such as Jiffy Lube have been successful in promoting the idea that a car's oil must be changed every 3,000 miles to prevent engine wear—a belief that persisted long after technological improvements have made changing oil that frequently unnecessary and wasteful.[31]

  Another approach to closing purchase gaps involves offering incentives that encourage customers to buy the offering in advance of the need to replace it so that they never run out. Repurchase can also be facilitated by simplifying the process of reordering the offering, such as introducing subscription programs (e.g., Amazon Subscribe and Save) and one-step reordering devices (e.g., Amazon Dash).

Because they deal with recurring purchases, usage gaps often hold greater potential to increase sales volume than do adoption gaps. This is especially true for companies with a dominant position in the market because of the relatively large installed base of users. Optimizing the consumption experience in this case can have a significant impact on the company's ability to grow sales volume.

SUMMARY

A company's *market position* can be defined as a share of the market in which it competes, as a share of mind among its target customers, and as a share of target customers' hearts.

A company can *gain market position* by using four core strategies: stealing share from competitors serving this market (steal-share strategy), growing the market by attracting new customers to the category (market-growth strategy), growing the market by expanding sales to current customers (market-penetration strategy), and creating new markets (market-creation strategy). Because business success inevitably attracts competition, a company needs to develop strategies to *defend its market position*. Common approaches for reacting to a competitor's actions involves staying the course, enhancing or repositioning existing offerings, and adding new offerings.

A company can gain market position by *pioneering new markets*. The key benefits of market pioneering include the opportunity to shape customer preferences, create switching costs for collaborators and customers, preempt scarce resources, create technological barriers to entry, and reap learning curve benefits. The key drawbacks of being a pioneer include free riding by competitors, pioneer inertia, and uncertainty associated with the offering's technology and with customer demand.

To gain and defend market position, a company needs to develop *core competencies* that will give it an advantage over the competition. Core competencies involve expertise in one or more of six key areas: business innovation, operations management, technology development, product development, service management, and brand building.

Sales growth is a key component of a company's efforts to gain and defend its market position. The two core sales growth strategies are managing adoption and managing usage.

Managing adoption deals with acquiring new customers. It focuses on four key factors: awareness, attractiveness, affordability, and availability. A practical approach to managing adoption involves identifying and eliminating impediments (adoption gaps) throughout the adoption process.

Managing usage deals with the ways in which a company's customers use its offerings. It focuses on three key factors: satisfaction, usage frequency, and usage quantity. A practical approach to managing usage involves identifying and eliminating impediments (usage gaps) to repurchasing the offering.

MARKETING INSIGHT: KEY ADOPTION AND USAGE METRICS

A key aspect of managing sales growth involves managing offering adoption and usage. To this end, there are several metrics commonly used to monitor adoption and usage: awareness rate, conversion rate, penetration rate, retention rate, and attrition rate. These metrics are depicted in Figure 11 and described in more detail below.

Figure 11. Key Customer Adoption Metrics

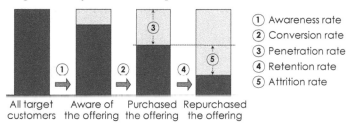

① Awareness rate
② Conversion rate
③ Penetration rate
④ Retention rate
⑤ Attrition rate

All target customers   Aware of the offering   Purchased the offering   Repurchased the offering

Awareness Rate: The number of potential customers who are aware of the company's offering.

Conversion Rate: The number of potential customers who have tried the offering relative to the total number of customers aware of the offering.

$$\text{Conversion rate} = \frac{\text{Current and former customers}}{\text{Potential customers aware of the offering}}$$

Penetration Rate: The number of customers who have tried the offering at least once relative to the total number of potential customers.

$$\text{Penetration rate} = \frac{\text{Current and former customers}}{\text{Potential customers}}$$

Retention Rate: The number of customers who have purchased the offering during the current buying cycle (month, quarter, or year) relative to the number of customers who purchased the offering during the last cycle. Also used in reference to the number of customers who have re-purchased the offering relative to the total number of customers who have tried the product at least once.

$$\text{Retention rate} = \frac{\text{Active customers during the current period}}{\text{Active customers during the last period}}$$

Attrition Rate (Churn Rate): The number of customers who discontinue using a company's offering during a specified period relative to the average total number of customers during that same period.

$$\text{Attrition rate} = \frac{\text{Number of customers who disadopt an offering}}{\text{Total number of customers}}$$

CHAPTER FIFTEEN

DEVELOPING NEW MARKET OFFERINGS

In the middle of difficulty lies opportunity.
— Albert Einstein, theoretical physicist

The development of new offerings is the engine that fuels the growth of a business enterprise. New product success is often attributed to intuition. Indeed, some offerings that stem from intuition do make it big. Yet many others crash and burn. These failures occur because intuition is only one aspect of new product development. The other key ingredient of success is having a systematic approach to developing new market offerings. Such a systematic approach for developing new offerings that create market value is outlined in this chapter.

New Offering Development as a Value Creation Process

New offerings are the key to sustainable growth. The development of new products and services enables companies to gain and sustain their market position by taking advantage of the changes in the market to create superior customer value. Some of the key issues in developing new offerings — managing risk, using the stage-gate approach, and understanding the iterative nature of new product development — are discussed in the following sections.

Managing Risk in Developing New Offerings

Depending on the degree of novelty involved, there are two main types of new offerings: revolutionary offerings that deliver new-to-the-world benefits and evolutionary offerings that involve relatively minor modifications of existing offerings, such as different colors, flavors, tastes, sizes, designs, or packaging variations. Revolutionary offerings such as Netflix, Uber, and Airbnb can disrupt entire industries by providing a set of benefits that cannot be readily matched by their current competitors. In contrast, evolutionary offerings such as different generations of mobile phones, computers, and razors provide higher levels of performance on existing attributes without dramatically changing the competitive playing field. While the concepts discussed in this chapter apply to both revolutionary and evolutionary offerings, the issue of managing risk is particularly relevant in the case of new-to-the-world offerings.

One of the key challenges in developing new offerings is managing the uncertainty associated with launching new products and services. Because uncertainty increases the risk of failure, managing risk is one of the key aspects of developing new offerings. Managing risk involves minimizing the chance that the new offerings will fail, thus wasting the resources expended on their development. There are two types of risk in developing new offerings: market risk and technological risk.

- **Market risk** reflects the uncertainty associated with the five factors (the Five Cs) defining the market in which the company aims to create value. Thus, the customer need that the new offering aims to fulfill might be transient or might exist only for a *customer* segment that is not large enough to justify the development, production, promotion, and distribution costs of the offering. The company's *collaborators* might not allocate the necessary support to ensure the success of the offering. The *company* might not be able to gather sufficient resources to develop and launch the offering. *Competitors* might emulate the company's technology to design a cheaper product or build on the company's technology to develop a functionally superior offering. Finally, the *context* in which the company operates might evolve due to the development of superior technologies; fluctuating sociocultural trends; the state of the economy; new regulatory restrictions; as well as new tariffs, taxes, and fees.

- **Technological risk** reflects the uncertainty associated with the technological viability of the new offering. For example, the desired product features might not be achievable with currently available technologies, product design might not be compatible with the functional requirements, and product reliability might be compromised by the use of new, unproven technologies. Technological risk might also extend the time frame for developing the new offering, which in turn can increase the market risk associated with interim changes in the market.

The high levels of uncertainty and risk associated with the development of new offerings mean that for every offering that succeeds in the market there are many more that fail to gain market traction. The high failure rate calls for using a systematic approach to channel the company's resources to projects that have a higher likelihood of gaining market success while screening out projects that are less likely to succeed.

The Stage-Gate Framework for Developing New Offerings

A popular approach to managing risk calls for breaking down the offering development process into separate components (stages) and introducing benchmarks (gates) that must be met in order for an idea, concept, or product to proceed to the next stage of development. Considered together, the individual steps in the development of a new offering and the corresponding benchmarks form the *stage-gate framework* for developing new offerings.

By outlining a process for designing and validating the business model, the stage-gate framework helps minimize risk and optimize allocation of the company's resources. In this context, the stage-gate framework enables a company to apply a systematic approach to the development of new offerings and ensure that the product development process results in an offering that will create value for target customers while enabling the company and its collaborators to reach their goals.

The stage-gate approach breaks down the process of developing new offerings into individual components and introduces checkpoints (gates) that aim to ensure that the offering is likely to create and capture market value. A streamlined version of the stage-gate framework for developing new offerings involves five key stages—*idea discovery, concept development, business model design, offering development,* and *commercial deployment*—separated by hurdles that aim to validate the actions taken in the previous step (Figure 1).

Figure 1. The Stage-Gate Framework for Developing New Offerings

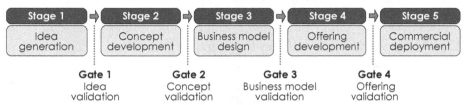

The key components of the stage-gate approach can be summarized as follows:

- **Idea generation.** The development of a new offering starts with the discovery of an unmet market need and the generation of an idea that addresses this need in a novel way. Ideas can be derived from different sources: They can stem from the company (e.g., by virtue of marketing research and employee suggestions), from customers (e.g., via customer feedback and crowdsourcing), and from collaborators (e.g., suppliers, distributors, and co-developers). The idea discovery is followed by a validation of the soundness and the key assumptions of the underlying idea.

- **Concept development.** The validated idea is further refined and fleshed out to create a detailed sketch of the initial concept that delineates the key technological and market aspects of the proposed offering. This step is followed by concept validation, which evaluates the technological feasibility and the desirability of the concept by target customers.

- **Business model design.** The validated concept evolves into a business model that articulates the company's target market, defines the value created and captured by the company in this market, and outlines the key aspects of the company's offering. This stage is followed by business model validation, which evaluates the offering's ability to fulfill the identified customer need in a way that creates value for the company and its collaborators.

- **Offering development.** The design of a viable business model is followed by the development of the resources needed to create the company's offering as well as the design and production of the actual offering. This stage is followed by the offering's validation in which its business viability is tested. Typically, validation involves testing the product by releasing it on a smaller scale. In cases when manufacturing the actual product is complex and/or costly, the company might develop and launch a scaled-down version of the offering in a test market. In addition to assessing customers' response to the offering, market testing can also be conducted to improve the design and functionality of the offering before commercializing it.

- **Commercial deployment** involves deploying the new product in the target market. To minimize risk and go-to-market expenditures, a company might initially deploy its offering in selected markets that are the least costly to reach and where customers are most likely to adopt it. Once the offering gains traction in these markets, a company can expand its reach and make the offering available to all target customers.

The ultimate goal of the stage-gate approach is to develop an offering that is *desirable* (target customers find it attractive), *feasible* (it is technologically possible), and *viable* (it can create value for the company). Thus, idea generation is usually focused on the desirability and viability of the offering, concept development combines desirability with feasibility, and business model design aims to ensure that all three criteria are met prior to developing and commercializing the offering.

The Development of New Offerings as an Iterative Process

The stage-gate framework presents a stylized version of the process of developing a new offering. In reality, the development of a new offering is not always a linear process in which the initial idea evolves into a successful market offering. Rather, it is an *iterative process* of discovering a novel idea and translating this idea into a viable market offering. In this context, the development of new offerings involves a series of iterations — *realignments* and *pivots* — aimed to create a desirable, feasible, and viable market offering.

- **Realignments** are relatively minor changes to an idea, concept, or offering that do not substantially alter its core attributes. Realignment typically involves making tactical changes and modifying certain aspects of the offering without changing its core value proposition.

- **Pivots** are major changes that involve going back to the drawing board and modifying some (or all) of the key aspects of the initial idea, concept, or core functionality. Pivots are *strategic inflection points* that change the fundamentals of the new offering's value proposition.

Because of the high uncertainty typically associated with the development of new offerings, realignments and pivots are the rule rather than the exception. It is not unusual for a project to pass the idea-generation stage and subsequently fail to convert into a desirable and feasible concept. In the same vein, a project might reach the implementation stage and be unable to secure the resources (e.g., intellectual property, raw materials, or capital) necessary to develop the offering. When this happens, the company must go back to the previous stage(s), reevaluate their validity, and, if necessary, restart the project until the offering can overcome the hurdles set to help ensure its market success.

A prominent example of pivoting involves *The Point*, a social media company designed to facilitate fundraising. The problem The Point was trying to solve was that people were reluctant to donate because of concerns about the social relevance of the cause involved and the reputation of the fundraising organization. To address these concerns, the company enabled the fundraising entity to set a tipping point—a certain amount of money or number of participants required for the program to be activated. The actual donations were not collected until the set goal was met, thus assuring potential donors that they were contributing to a socially relevant cause supported by many other donors.

Despite being a promising idea that addressed what appeared to be a valid customer concern, The Point did not gain much traction with its target audience. There was one bright spot though: A growing number of consumers used the website to find lower prices and sales, and the most successful campaigns were those that enabled consumers to combine their buying power to save money. Following this trend, The Point redefined its business model to focus on business owners rather than fundraisers and created an entirely new value proposition: enabling vendors to set a tipping point that would activate a promotional offer. Participating vendors could benefit from the new business generated by the promotional offer without having to pay anything if their offer did not generate sufficient customer demand. Pivoting to redefine its business model turned the struggling social media fundraising company The Point into *Groupon*, the multibillion-dollar deal-of-the-day company.

Idea Generation

The development of a new offering begins with the generation of an idea that identifies an unmet market need and a novel way to address this need. The idea can involve a new technology, a new approach to brand building, a new pricing mechanism, a new way of managing incentives, new channels of communication, or a novel distribution method. The different approaches to generating new ideas, the essence of problem-solving and experience-enhancing ideas, and the process of idea validation are discussed in the following sections.

Generating New Ideas

Companies use different strategies to come up with new ideas. Based on the specific way in which ideas are born, there are two basic ways in which business ideas are generated: *top down* and *bottom up*.

Top-Down Idea Generation

Top-down idea generation starts with identifying a market opportunity and is followed by an invention that addresses this opportunity (Figure 2). When exploring a market opportunity, the company seeks to identify an important customer problem that it can solve better than the available alternatives. Accordingly, top-down idea generation starts with a market analysis to identify an unmet need that the company can fulfill better than the competition.

Figure 2. Top-Down (Market-Driven) Idea Generation

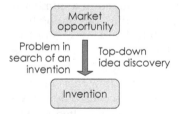

Top-down idea generation has resulted in a number of successful products designed to seize an identified market opportunity. Apple's iPod addressed the need for a user-friendly device that enables people to carry their favorite music with them. Apple's iPhone addressed the need for a user-friendly device that combines the functionality of a mobile phone, a personal digital assistant, a music player, and a camera. Apple's iPad addressed the need for a portable, user-friendly mobile device that offers enhanced iPhone functionality with a larger display.

In the same vein, Procter & Gamble designed Swiffer to address the need for a cleaning tool that is more effective than a mop and cuts down on cleaning time. Herman Miller designed the Aeron chair to address the need for an office chair that is both comfortable and stylish. Tesla designed its Model S sedan to address the need for an environmentally friendly, fuel-efficient, premium car that is fast, spacious, and stylish. Dyson formulated its iconic vacuum cleaner to fulfill the need for a vacuum that retains its suction with usage. Uber offered a solution to customers who needed fast, convenient, and reliable transportation. Airbnb offered housing to travelers seeking less expensive and more personalized alternatives to traditional hotels.

The top-down approach is arguably the most common way of generating business ideas. Because it starts with identifying a market opportunity, it is more likely to result in an offering that fulfills a real market need and, thus, more likely to create market value. At the same time, the top-down approach does not guarantee that a meaningful solution to the unmet need can ultimately be identified: A company might end up spinning its wheels trying to address a problem that cannot be solved using current technologies.

Bottom-Up Idea Generation

Bottom-up idea generation starts with an invention, followed by identification of a market need that can be fulfilled by this invention (Figure 3). Unlike top-down idea generation, the invention here is not driven by an identified market need but by technological innovation. In this context, the bottom-up approach to idea generation is more often the province of scientists in research labs than managers in marketing research departments.

Figure 3. Bottom-Up (Invention-Driven) Idea Generation

Bottom-up idea generation has resulted in a number of successful products that stem from technological innovation. Penicillin—an antibiotic used to combat bacterial infections—was discovered by Scottish biologist Alexander Fleming, who noticed that the fungus growing on contaminated Petri dishes had killed the staphylococci bacteria he was researching. Post-it Notes were invented by a 3M chemist who created a very weak pressure-sensitive adhesive while trying to come up with a super strong adhesive for use in the aerospace industry. The microwave was discovered by a Raytheon Corporation engineer who noticed that the chocolate bar in his pocket melted when he walked in front of a vacuum tube generating microwaves.

Likewise, velcro was discovered by a Swiss engineer who found during a hiking trip that the hooks in burrs clung to anything loop-shaped—in this particular case, his pants and his dog's fur. Rogaine (minoxidil)—the popular over-the-counter drug for treating hair loss—was originally used to treat high blood pressure; however, patients taking drugs containing minoxidil began to notice increased hair growth on their balding scalps, as well as on other parts of their bodies. Viagra, the multi-billion-dollar erectile dysfunction drug, resulted from a Pfizer Company drug that was not particularly effective in treating angina, a condition constricting the vessels that supply blood to the heart. Teflon, the widely used nonstick coating for cookware and other products, was the discovery of a DuPont engineer searching for a better refrigerant.

Even though bottom-up idea generation starts with an invention, to evolve into a successful market offering the invention must address a viable market opportunity. Novel technology per se is not a reason for a company to develop a new offering. While new technologies are often an important factor, the key driver of market success is the company's ability to apply this technology to address an unmet market need. Idea generation, whether top down or bottom up, should always be linked to the market value it creates.

To transform a technological invention into a viable business idea, the company must identify a problem that this invention can solve and the market value it can create. Therefore, even though successful products can be born serendipitously from a technological invention, the top-down approach is the preferred idea generation method in new product development. Because the success of an offering ultimately depends on its ability to deliver market value, by starting with identifying market opportunities a company can increase its chances of developing an invention that will enjoy market success.

Problem-Solving and Experience-Enhancing Ideas

To create value, an offering must increase customers' well-being by fulfilling an unmet need. Based on the degree to which a particular need has been activated, there are two types of ideas: *problem-solving ideas* designed to address a problem faced by customers and *experience-enhancing ideas* designed to improve on an existing solution to a given problem.

- **Problem-solving (must-have) ideas** provide a solution to an important unmet need that customers actively seek to fulfill. Because problem-solving ideas address an essential need that customers deem unresolved, offerings stemming from these ideas are typically easy to communicate and tend to be rapidly adopted by customers.

- **Experience-enhancing (nice-to-have) ideas** improve on an offering that fulfills a given need reasonably well in order to provide customers with an even greater level of satisfaction. Because experience-enhancing ideas address a need that is not considered a problem, the resulting offerings are adopted at a much slower rate than problem-solving offerings.

Problem-solving and experience-enhancing ideas can also be defined in terms of customer pain and gain. Problem-solving ideas can *alleviate customer pain* by eliminating an important source of dissatisfaction. Experience-enhancing ideas, on the other hand, can be perceived as a means of providing *customer gain* because they improve on an already satisfactory offering. Thus, problem-solving ideas typically lead to the development of *must-have* offerings — products and services that customers immediately see the value of. In contrast, experience-enhancing ideas result in *nice-to-have* offerings that customers view as discretionary.

The distinction between problem-solving and experience-enhancing offerings is important because customers more eagerly embrace offerings that provide a solution to a problem than offerings that aim to enhance an already satisfactory experience; as a result, problem-solving offerings enjoy faster adoption than experience-enhancing ideas. Because it takes much longer for customers to understand the benefits of experience-enhancing offerings and recognize their value, a company must expend greater resources to inform customers about the advantages of such offerings.

Identifying the likely speed of adoption of the innovation is important at the later stages of new product development when the company must build a business model around the idea. Indeed, many companies have failed to achieve their growth projections because of the erroneous belief that they could easily educate their customers and change their behavior to appreciate the benefits of offerings that did not address a pressing problem (pain point) faced by these customers. For example, many software companies, including Microsoft, Adobe, and Intuit, have had a difficult time inducing their customers to upgrade to the most recent versions of their offerings because the earlier versions are perfectly capable of fulfilling the needs of these customers. Facing the same predicament, the product-upgrade cycle of many consumer electronics manufacturers—including Apple, Samsung, and LG—is slowing down because consumers are satisfied with the performance of their current offerings.

Idea Validation

Idea validation assesses the soundness of the idea for the proposed offering and the validity of its assumptions. Typically, idea validation involves a preliminary assessment of the *desirability* and *viability* of the offering—namely, whether an offering based on this idea is likely to fulfill an unmet customer need and do so in a way that benefits the company. To validate an idea, a manager should ask the following questions:

Does the idea present a solution that will fulfill an unmet customer need?

Would an offering based on this idea create value for the company?

When evaluating ideas, a company can make two types of errors. The first error is failing to reject an idea that has no merit and is unlikely to result in a successful market offering. The second type of error involves making the opposite mistake—rejecting a good idea. Given the high rate of new product failures, one might conclude that failing to reject bad ideas is more common than rejecting good ones. This, however, is not necessarily correct. In addition to stemming from poor ideas, new product failures can be caused by a high rejection rate of good ideas, as well as by the inherent technological and market risk associated with new product development.

In order to proceed to the next stage of concept development, the company must be able to answer the above questions. If these questions cannot be satisfactorily addressed, the idea must be redefined.

Concept Development

Concept development is a process that aims to minimize the risk inherent in product development by creating a simplified version of the offering that can be used to determine the offering's level of desirability and feasibility. Because bringing new offerings to market typically requires a large expenditure of time, money, and effort, a company can streamline the product development process by first creating and validating a concept that captures the essential features of the offering prior to developing the actual offering.

Prototyping

Concept development typically involves creating a scaled-down version, commonly referred to as a *prototype* (from the Greek πρωτότυπον, meaning *primitive form*). Prototyping aims to refine and flesh out a potentially viable idea and create an initial version of the company's offering with a minimum investment of time, money, and effort. Prototypes need not be functional products; they might merely be rough models of the offering created for the purpose of eliciting the reaction of potential customers. The ultimate goal of prototyping is to evaluate target customers' response to the core benefit of the offering and mold the offering in a way that maximizes its market potential. Illustrating the importance of prototyping is the MIT Media Lab credo, "Demo or Die," which stresses that ideas have little value to customers or the company unless they are expressed in tangible, practicable form.

Prototypes can vary in complexity. Some prototypes involve relatively simple representations of the underlying concept, such as a diagram illustrating the functionality of the offering, a drawing delineating the overall look and feel of the offering, or a rudimentary model that is limited to the key functionality of the offering and addresses the most important aspect of the proposed product or service. Other prototypes might involve more advanced versions of the offering both in terms of their design and functionality. Based on their level of complexity, different prototypes are employed at different stages of the new product development process. Simpler prototypes are more likely to be employed at the idea-generation and concept-development stages of the offering. In contrast, more complex prototypes tend to be employed at the more advanced stages of new product development, such as during the offering-development stage.

Prototyping is not a linear process in which the initial idea naturally evolves into a viable prototype. Rather, prototyping typically involves testing the key assumptions of the initial concept in order to improve it — a process referred to as *validated learning*. Validated learning begins even before the prototype is conceived. It starts with observing the market, identifying an unmet need, and generating an idea for an offering that addresses this need. This idea is then turned into a prototype that captures the core concept of the offering and is tested to ensure its desirability and feasibility. This process is repeated until a satisfactory outcome is achieved, and the company can proceed to design a business model before building and launching the actual offering (Figure 4).

Figure 4. The Validated-Learning Approach

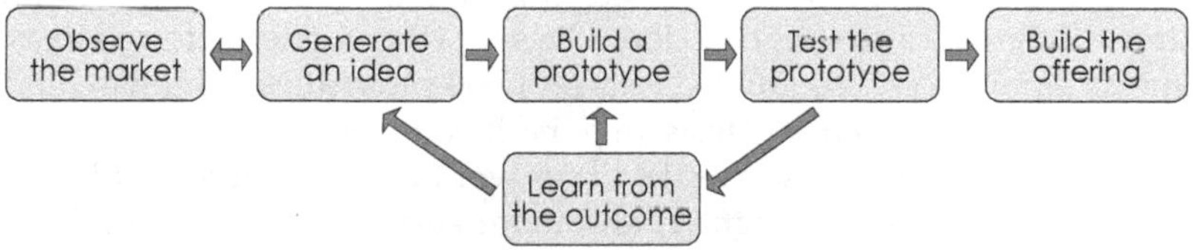

Validated learning is based on data, not gut feeling. It typically involves empirical tests aimed at optimizing the initial concept by varying different attributes of the offering and evaluating their impact on its feasibility and desirability. Stepwise product development, combined with experimentation aimed at verifying the key assumptions guiding the development process, is the hallmark of the validated-learning approach. Rather than conducting *all* market research prior to developing the offering — a legacy approach favored by many corporations — the validated-learning approach is an iterative process of designing, testing, and modifying different aspects of the offering.

To ensure that the new offering is well received in the market, companies rigorously test prototypes at different stages of their development. There are two types of prototype tests:

alpha testing, which involves an evaluation of the product within the company, and *beta testing*, which tests the product with end users. The more novel and complex the offering, the greater amount of alpha and beta testing it is likely to undergo. Beta testing is particularly important for products and services that have multiple applications and are used by different customers in different contexts. For example, new software products and services typically go through extensive user testing to ensure their functionality across different platforms and applications.

Concept Validation

Concept validation assesses the soundness of the core concept underlying the proposed offering. Concept validation typically addresses two factors: the feasibility of the offering to determine if creating the offering is technologically possible, and its desirability to assess whether target customers find the offering attractive. Accordingly, to validate the concept behind the offering, a manager should ask the following questions:

> *Is the offering feasible? Can a functional prototype of the offering be built? Can a fully functional version of the offering be built?*

> *Does the core concept of the offering appeal to its target customers? Does it address the identified customer need better than the alternative options? Are different attributes of the offering optimized to create customer value?*

In order to proceed to the next stage of business model design, a company must validate the core concept underlying the company's offering. If the concept cannot be validated, the company must pivot and redefine the concept. If after multiple iterations the concept cannot be validated, the company must step back and reevaluate the underlying idea.

To illustrate, inventor Sir James Dyson—whose prior inventions include the eponymous transparent vacuum cleaner, the energy-efficient Airblade hand dryer for public restrooms, and the bladeless Air Multiplier fan—spent over four years developing his Supersonic hair dryer. The development of the hair dryer involved a rigorous validation process that included making in excess of 600 prototypes before reaching the final design. Over 100 engineers were involved and more than 250 patents were filed during the development of the new hair dryer. To create a perfect hair dryer, Dyson, who is often referred to as the "Steve Jobs of domestic appliances," conducted tests on 1,000-plus miles of human hair both in his labs and through more than 200 user tests. In pursuit of perfection, engineers also conducted over 7,000 acoustic tests to ensure that the dryer would be sufficiently quiet. The result: a hair dryer that is faster, quieter, lighter, and more aesthetically pleasing than any other product in its category.

Business Model Design

Development of a viable concept is followed by designing a business model that delineates the ways in which an offering will create and capture market value. Unlike concept development, which focuses on the feasibility and the desirability of the offering, business model design also focuses on the offering's viability—the ability of the offering to create value for the company.

Designing the Business Model

Designing the business model involves three key components (discussed in detail in Chapter 2): identifying the *target market*, articulating the offering's *value proposition* in that market, and delineating the key attributes of the *market offering* (Figure 5).

Figure 5. The Key Components of a Business Model of a New Offering

- The **target market** delineates the market in which a company's offering strives to create value. The target market comprises target customers, competitors, collaborators, the company, and the market context.

- The **value proposition** describes the value that the company plans to create for target customers and collaborators as well as the value that the company aims to capture for its stakeholders.

- The **market offering** defines the ways in which the company will create, communicate, and deliver value to its target customers, collaborators, and stakeholders. Specifically, this involves delineating the product, service, brand, price, incentives, communication, and distribution aspects of the offering.

The creation of market value is the ultimate goal of the business model. Accordingly, the success of an offering is determined by the degree to which it can create value for its target customers, collaborators, and the company. Thus, the design of a business model for a new offering is guided by three key questions:

How does the offering create value for target customers? How does it fulfill customer needs better than the alternative options?

How does the offering create value for the company's collaborators? How does it enable the company's collaborators to achieve their goals better than the alternative options?

How does the offering create value for the company? How does it enable the company to achieve its goals better than the alternative options?

The key principles involved in developing the value proposition and the process of creating customer, company, and collaborator value maps were discussed in detail in Chapter 2.

Business Model Validation

The ultimate goal of the business model is to create market value. To this end, the initial idea undergoes a number of pivots and realignments, resulting in a sustainable business model. Pivots and realignments in designing the company's offering are guided by three key principles: *desirability*, *feasibility*, and *viability*.

- **Desirability** reflects the degree to which target customers find the offering attractive. Because customer value is a function of benefits and costs, an offering's desirability might be hindered by its inability to deliver the benefits sought by customers and by the high costs—money, time, and effort—associated with the offering. For example, Crystal Pepsi, a clear, caffeine-free alternative to regular colas, failed despite a massive promotional campaign because consumers did not find the concept of a clear cola appealing. Lisa, a personal computer designed by Apple in the early 1980s, failed largely due to its $10,000 price tag that far exceeded customers' willingness to pay for the device.

- **Feasibility** reflects the degree to which the company has the ability to build an offering that has the functionality desired by customers. Feasibility is a function of current technologies and the company's ability to utilize these technologies. For example, until recently long-range electric cars were not feasible because of limited battery capacity. Ultimate examples of projects that are not considered feasible are a perpetual motion machine and a time machine.

- **Viability** reflects the degree to which an offering is capable of creating value for the company. The viability of an offering from a for-profit perspective is reflected in its ability to generate profits. Viability is typically a function of the expected revenue streams from an offering and its cost structure. The inability to align revenues and costs is often a precursor of market failure. For example, despite its high-profile promotional campaign and a widely recognized brand, online pet supply retailer Pets.com lost money on most of its sales and ultimately went out of business due to its weak fundamentals.

Because a company's success is driven by the desirability, feasibility, and viability of its offerings, the sustainability of the business model is determined by the answers to the following three questions:

Do target customers find the offering attractive?

Does the company have the resources to build the offering?

Can the offering create value for the company?

The desirability, feasibility, and viability aspects of the offering are typically related, such that failure to meet acceptable levels on one dimension is also likely to lead to failure on other dimensions. Thus, an offering that is undesirable to customers would likely not prove to be viable because it would not generate sufficient customer demand to create value for the company. In the same vein, an offering that is not technologically feasible would also fail the desirability test because the offering that can actually be built would not fulfill customer needs.

Offering Development

Offering development is the process of creating the actual offering that the company will introduce in the market. This process involves two main steps: *developing the resources* necessary for the business model to be put into action and *producing the market offering*.

Developing the Core Resources

To succeed, a company must have the necessary resources to implement its business model. It is common for a company not to have all of the resources necessary to create and launch the offering. Thus, after the business model has been designed, the logical next step is to develop the necessary resources by building, outsourcing, or acquiring them.

Resource development involves several activities that can be tied to the resources needed to ensure a company's ability to create market value (discussed in Chapter 4). These activities include: (1) establishing the *business infrastructure*, which includes activities such as procuring manufacturing equipment, developing sales and service call centers, and building the necessary information technology links; (2) developing *supply channels* to obtain the materials needed to create the offering; (3) recruiting, training, and retaining *skilled employees* who can contribute the required technological, operational, and business expertise; (4) gathering the relevant *knowledge* to enable the company to implement different aspects of the offering's business model; (5) developing ancillary *products and services* that act as an ecosystem for the new offering; (6) developing *communication channels* to educate target customers about the offering; (7) developing *distribution channels* through which the offering will be delivered to target customers; and (8) providing *access to capital* to secure the financial resources needed to implement the business model.

To gain the resources needed to successfully launch the new offering, a company might adopt one of two different strategies. First, the company might create its own resources by internally developing its assets and capabilities or by acquiring the necessary resources from a third party. Alternatively, rather than building its own resources, a company might choose to collaborate with other entities that have the resources required to develop, manufacture, distribute, and promote the offering, and leverage these resources without assuming ownership of them.

As with most business decisions, entering into a collaborative relationship with other entities to gain the resources needed for offering development involves weighing the relevant benefits and costs. On the *benefit* side, collaboration enables each party to take advantage of the other's expertise, providing both entities with a competitive advantage stemming from greater specialization. Furthermore, collaboration can also increase cost efficiency because each collaborator can achieve greater economies of scale and experience by specializing in a given function. In addition, collaboration requires a lesser commitment of resources in comparison to developing the necessary in-house expertise, thus offering much greater flexibility in terms of switching technologies, entering new markets, and exiting existing ones. Finally, collaboration enables a company to achieve the desired results much faster than building in-house expertise.

Despite its numerous benefits, collaboration has several important *drawbacks*. First, delegating certain aspects of a company's activities to an external entity often leads to loss of control over the process of developing and managing the offering. Furthermore, outsourcing key activities tends to weaken a company's core competencies and its ability to drive innovation. Outsourcing also might enable collaborating entities to develop a set of strategic competencies, thus becoming a company's potential competitor. For a collaboration to be sustainable, its benefits must outweigh the potential drawbacks, such that the collaboration creates value for both the company and its collaborators.

Developing the Market Offering

Developing the market offering involves turning the offering concept (prototype) into the actual product and service that the company will introduce in the market. To this end, producing the offering involves deployment of the company's resources—its own as well as those of its collaborators—needed to implement the business model.

Developing the offering often involves advanced prototyping and market testing to ensure that the offering will succeed in creating market value. The amount of prototyping and testing done is influenced by a variety of factors such as product novelty, product complexity, and the investment required to modify the offering after it has been launched. New-to-the-world products warrant more market testing than products that involve slight modifications from what is already available in the market. More complex products are more likely to benefit from market testing compared to simpler products. Products that require high levels of investment to be modified after launch (e.g., retooling the manufacturing plant to modify the design of a car) are in greater need of advanced prototyping and market testing compared to products that can be modified relatively easily post launch.

An important decision in producing the new offering is whether to start by developing the ultimate, fully functional version of the offering or to initially develop a simplified version that features only the key functionality of the offering. In this context, a company may consider developing a *minimum viable offering*—the simplest version of the offering that is able to deliver the primary benefit(s) sought by target customers. The alternative to developing a minimum viable offering—developing a fully functional, full-scale offering without previously testing a simplified version—requires substantial investment at a time when market and technological uncertainty are relatively high. As a result, a company risks losing significant resources should some of its assumptions about the market and the technological feasibility of the offering prove to be incorrect. Rather than taking the risk of building a full-scale product or service, starting with a relatively simple version of the offering and validating this version prior to developing the final version reduces the uncertainty associated with bringing new products to market.

Commercial Deployment

Commercial deployment involves informing target customers about the company's offering and making the offering available to these customers. Because large-scale rollouts are associated with greater uncertainty and higher costs, companies often test the offering by initially launching it in a few selected markets prior to introducing it to all target customers. Thus, commercial deployment often includes two steps: *selective market entry*, which involves deploying the offering in selected markets, and *market expansion*, which involves making the offering available to the entire target market.

Selective Market Entry

Market entry via selective deployment aims to test the offering in a natural environment and observe how target customers, competitors, and company collaborators react to the offering. Because of its smaller scale, selective market deployment enables the company to be more agile in adjusting different aspects of the offering in order to maximize its market impact.

The subset of target customers that is the focus of the offering's initial deployment is also referred to as the *primary target*. The primary target is typically the low-hanging fruit that the company initially targets to prove the viability of its business model, fine-tune the offering, and generate a stream of revenue. The choice of the primary target is driven by three key factors: *target attractiveness*, *resource efficiency*, and *scale sufficiency*.

- **Target attractiveness** reflects the degree to which customers in a given market are likely to adopt the company's offering. Prioritizing customers based on the likelihood that they will adopt the offering typically follows *the path of least resistance*. Thus, the likelihood that customers will be among the first to adopt a company's offering depends on whether they (1) have the need that the offering aims to solve, (2) view this need as a problem that needs solving, and (3) actively seek a way to address this problem. Customers for whom all three conditions hold are the most likely to adopt the company's offering and, hence, also the most likely to be chosen as the primary target. Customers for whom only the first condition holds—those who can benefit from the company's offering but are reasonably satisfied with the status quo—are the least likely to be selected as primary targets (Figure 6).

Figure 6. The Path of Least Resistance

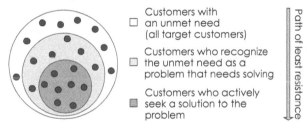

- **Resource efficiency** reflects the company resources needed to communicate and deliver the offering to target customers. In choosing its primary target, companies often follow *the path of least resources*, determined by the company's ability to effectively and cost efficiently communicate and deliver the offering to these customers. For example, a company might choose its primary target because these customers are already aware of the company's brand and the company has the distribution channels in place to reach these customers (Figure 7). Note that the identification of customers based on the costs of informing them about the offering and delivering the offering often takes place simultaneously, as the company seeks to identify segments that are characterized by relatively low communication *and* distribution costs.

Figure 7. The Path of Least Resources

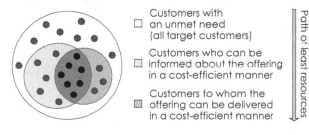

- **Scale sufficiency** reflects the minimum size of the primary market needed to ensure that this market is viable from the company's standpoint. The choice of the primary market can be facilitated by the assessment of the *minimum viable target*—the smallest subset of target customers that is of adequate size to generate the revenue needed to sufficiently offset the company's costs of producing, promoting, and distributing the offering.

The primary target is defined by the convergence of the path of least resistance, the path of least resources, and the minimum viable scale. Therefore, when choosing a primary target for a new offering, a company should focus on markets (1) in which customers have a burning unresolved problem that they are actively seeking to address, (2) that can be easily reached by the company, and (3) that are large enough to enable the company to achieve its goals.

Market Expansion

Market expansion involves going beyond the primary target to include all customers for whom the company's offering aims to create value. Market expansion is the next logical step following successful deployment of the company's offering in its primary target market.

To expand beyond the primary target market, a company needs to (1) scale up the operations involved in the production of the offering, (2) promote the offering to all target customers, and (3) ensure that the offering is available across the entire target market. During market expansion, a company is typically moving into more challenging markets in which customers are less likely to immediately recognize the value of its offering and are more difficult to reach. As a result, the time, effort, and resources involved in market expansion are likely to exceed those involved in initial market deployment.

Because broader markets tend to involve customers with more diverse needs and preferences, market expansion often involves a shift from a single offering to a product line comprising offerings tailored to the different needs and preferences of its customers. Thus, a company might start with a single offering targeting its most likely adopters, and, as it expands to the broader market over time, introduce variations of this offering that are likely to appeal to different customers within the target market. The increased assortment of company offerings associated with market expansion, in turn, calls for additional resources to ensure the success of these offerings in the broader market. The issue of managing product lines is discussed in more detail in Chapter 16.

SUMMARY

New product development is an iterative process of discovering a novel idea and translating this idea into a viable, successful market offering through a series of realignments and pivots. New product development is commonly represented as a sequence of actions (stages) separated by hurdles (gates) that the new offering must overcome. This stage-gate approach divides the innovation process into five key stages—idea generation, concept development, business model design, offering development, and commercial deployment—separated by gates that aim to validate the actions taken in the previous step.

Innovation begins with *generating an idea* that pinpoints an unmet market need and suggests a novel way to address this need. Ideas can be generated top down, by starting with identifying a market opportunity, or bottom up, by starting with an invention and then seeking a market need it can fulfill. The top-down approach is the preferred idea generation method.

Concept development embodies a potentially viable idea by creating an initial version of the offering. It aims to reduce market and implementation risk by designing the offering in an effective and resource-efficient way and typically evolves from a description of the product's core benefits to a prototype that features the offering's core functionality. Prototype testing can involve an evaluation of the product within the company (alpha testing) and testing the product with customers (beta testing).

Business model design involves identifying the target market, articulating the offering's value proposition in that market, and delineating the key attributes of the market offering. Business model validation assesses the ability of an offering to create market value on three key dimensions: desirability (does the offering create value for target customers), feasibility (can the offering actually be built as conceived), and viability (does the offering create value for the company and its collaborators).

Offering development turns the conceptualized offering into an actual offering that is ready for market launch. Offering development involves two components: gathering the necessary resources to put the business model into action and producing the actual offering.

Commercial deployment informs target customers about the company's offering and makes the offering available to these customers. To minimize risk and resources, companies often deploy the offering in selected (primary) markets to test its viability before making the offering available to the entire target market. Identifying the primary market is guided by three key factors: target attractiveness, resource efficiency, and scale sufficiency. Market expansion involves ramping up the facilities involved in the offering's production, promoting the offering to all target customers, and ensuring that the offering is available to the entire target market.

MARKETING INSIGHT: PRODUCT–MARKET GROWTH FRAMEWORK

The Product–Market Growth framework (also referred to as the Ansoff matrix) outlines four key sales-growth strategies by linking the customer segments served by the company to the company's product-development opportunities.[32] This framework is typically presented as a 2×2 matrix in which one of the factors represents the type of product (current or new) and the other factor represents the type of customers (current or new). The resulting four product–market strategies—*market penetration, market development, product development*, and *diversification*—are illustrated in Figure 8 and described in more detail below.

Figure 8. The Product–Market Growth Framework

	Current customers	New customers
Current products	Market penetration	Market development
New products	Product development	Diversification

- *Market penetration* aims to increase sales of an existing offering to a company's current customers. A common market-penetration strategy involves increasing the offering's usage rate. To illustrate, airlines stimulate demand from current customers by adopting frequent-flyer programs, cereal manufacturers enclose repurchase coupons in their offerings, and orange juice producers promote drinking orange juice throughout the day rather than only for breakfast. Companies following a market-penetration strategy employ a variety of tactics directed at current customers, such as increasing the value of the offering (e.g., by lowering the price and running sales promotions), increasing awareness of the offerings (e.g., by increasing advertising and personal selling), and improving the availability of the offering (e.g., by increasing the density of the distribution channels and making the process of acquiring the offering more convenient).

- *Market development* aims to grow sales by promoting existing offerings to new customers. To illustrate, a company that has its products and services available in a particular geographic area (e.g., a city, state, or a country) might choose to expand its operations by entering a new market. The market expansion need not be defined in geographic terms: It can be defined in terms of demographic characteristics such as age, gender, and ethnicity, among others. In business markets, a company can expand its operations by looking to acquire a different type of company based on factors such as size, industry, and growth potential. Tactics employed by companies following a market-development strategy are similar to those used by companies following a market-penetration strategy, with the key difference that instead of focusing on their current customers they focus their efforts on customers they do not currently serve.

- *Product development* aims to grow sales by developing new (to the company) offerings for existing customers. This strategy is similar to the market penetration strategy in that it aims to fulfill the needs of the company's current customers. Where these two strategies part ways is in how they fulfill customer needs: Rather than trying to sell more of its current offerings to current customers, companies following the product-development strategy focus their efforts on developing new offerings. Unlike companies following market-penetration and market-development strategies that focus their efforts on tactics such as pricing, incentives, communication, and distribution, companies following a product-development strategy typically focus their efforts on creating new products, services, and brands. The other tactics, although relevant, play a relatively less important role, aiming to support the introduction of the company's new offerings.

- *Diversification* aims to grow sales by introducing new offerings to new customers. This approach is similar to the market-development strategy in that it goes beyond a company's current market. It is also similar to the product-development strategy in that it extends a company's current product line. What differentiates this approach from the other three market-expansion strategies is that the company does not rely on two of its key resources—its customer base and its portfolio of offerings. Because both the offering and the customers are new to the company, this approach tends to be riskier than the other product–market growth strategies.

The four strategies defined by the product–market growth framework are not mutually exclusive: A company can pursue multiple market-expansion strategies to grow sales revenues and enhance its market position. However, a company using multiple growth strategies needs to prioritize these strategies and allocate resources based on the extent to which these strategies enable the company to achieve its strategic goals.

CHAPTER SIXTEEN

MANAGING PRODUCT LINES

The essence of the beautiful is unity in variety.
— William Somerset Maugham, British novelist

A n important aspect of gaining and defending a company's market position involves organizing and managing the individual offerings as part of a company's product line. In this context, product-line management aims to optimize the value delivered by the individual offerings that are contained in a company's portfolio. The key aspects of managing a company's product line — managing vertical and horizontal extensions, managing product-line cannibalization, and using product lines to gain and defend market position — are the focus of this chapter.

Product Lines as a Means of Creating Value

The core principle in designing and managing product lines is that the company's offerings — considered individually and as a whole — should create superior value for target customers, the company, and its collaborators. The ways in which product lines create value for these three market entities are outlined in more detail below.

Product Lines as a Means of Creating Customer Value

Product lines create value for customers by providing them with offerings that more closely match their needs. Indeed, the more extensive a company's product line, the greater the chance that individual customers will find their "ideal" option. Product lines can also create customer value by appealing to a customer's desire for variety with offerings that are differentiated on relatively minor attributes (e.g., flavor, scent, and color). Finally, an extensive product line can appeal to a customer's desire for freedom of choice and to the feeling that they are not forced to choose from a limited roster of options.

Despite the multiple benefits that product lines can create for target customers, increasing the number of available options is not without drawbacks. One such drawback is that a greater number of options can lead to customer confusion stemming from the inability to choose among the available alternatives. Indeed, although the premise for offering a greater variety of options is that it allows consumers to identify their "ideal" option, providing consumers who do not have well-defined preferences more options can backfire by complicating their decision. As a result, buyers might defer making a purchase decision or select a competitor's offering with a smaller variety of options that are easier to choose from.

Product Lines as a Means of Creating Collaborator Value

Product lines can benefit collaborators by enabling the company to customize its offering to match the specific needs of its collaborators. For example, product lines can help minimize conflicts that might occur among distribution channels with different cost structures, such as mass-market retailers and specialty stores that offer the same product at different price points to the same customers. Companies can address such conflicts by developing product lines comprising different versions of the same product that vary on minor attributes such as color, packaging, and optional features. For example, a toy manufacturer might develop two different versions of the same toy: a higher priced one for high-end toy stores and a lower priced one for mass-market stores. To ensure that shoppers do not feel overcharged by the high-end store, the toys sold in these two outlets feature different packaging and functionality, thus making it difficult for shoppers to compare offerings across retailers.

A downside of a large product line from a retailer's standpoint is that having to carry a greater number of options tends to increase costs while also taking valuable shelf space. Thus, while a manufacturer's preference is that retailers carry its entire product line (and none of the competitors' options), a retailer's profit-optimization strategy often involves carrying only the most profitable offerings from competing manufacturers rather than a single company's entire product line.

Product Lines as a Means of Creating Company Value

Product lines can benefit the company by creating additional sources of revenue and profits. Thus, the more comprehensive a company's product line, the greater the company's ability to create superior value for different customer segments. Product lines can also create value for the company by helping it deal with the competition. Having a product line that targets multiple customer segments can help a company deter market entry by new competitors, which are less likely to target customers whose needs are already fulfilled by an existing offering. In addition, product lines can "crowd out" existing competitors by taking up premier shelf space in distribution channels.

Despite their multiple benefits, product lines have several important drawbacks for companies. The most obvious drawback is the increase in product development, manufacturing, distribution, and management costs associated with developing multiple offerings. In addition, designing and managing a product line can pull resources from the offerings that drive a large part of the company's profits. There is also the potential danger that instead of attracting new customers, the new offerings might end up cannibalizing the sales of the company's existing offerings.

Designing Product Lines and Product Platforms

Most companies manage portfolios that include multiple products. Even companies that start with a single product over time develop additional products targeting customers that seek different benefits and vary in their willingness to pay. In this context, an important aspect of product management involves aligning the individual products with the needs of target customers in a way that maximizes customer value while enabling the company and its collaborators to achieve their goals. The two key aspects of managing product portfolios — *designing product lines* and *designing product platforms* — are outlined in more detail below.

Designing Product Lines

Product lines comprise products that aim to address similar customer needs, typically in the context of the same category. A company can have a single product line or multiple product lines, each containing a group of related products. For example, the Volvo product line targeting the consumer market consists of four types of automobiles — sedan, cross-country, hatchback, and SUV/crossover — each of which includes different product variants.

Product lines that target different customer needs using distinct technologies are grouped into *product portfolios*, which include all products and product lines within the company. For example, in addition to its line of consumer vehicles, Volvo's product portfolio includes a line of commercial trucks utilizing both gasoline and natural gas. The relationship between individual products, product lines, and product portfolios is illustrated in Figure 1.

Figure 1. Product Portfolio and Product Lines

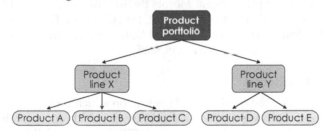

When designing their product lines, companies often designate one of their products as the flagship offering. The flagship product typically is the most widely known, best-selling, and/or highly admired offering that represents the quality of the company's product line. For example, Tide is the flagship product for Procter & Gamble's line of laundry detergents, Coke is the flagship product for Coca-Cola, and Mercedes S-Class is the flagship car for Daimler. Because of the strategic importance of flagship products, companies tend to invest heavily in their development and are very diligent when it comes to modifying these products. For example, while introducing a variety of new vehicles — including an SUV (Cayenne and Macan), an affordable sports car (Boxster), and a sedan (Panamera) — Porsche strived to preserve the distinct design and performance of its flagship high-end sports car, the 911 Carrera.

Product-line design aims to ensure that each individual product within the product line targets a particular customer segment and has a unique value proposition that aims to fulfill the needs of this segment. Thus, in addition to designing each product to create superior customer value relative to the competition, product-line design aims to ensure that the different offerings in the company's product line are distinct from one another and do not target the same needs of the same customers.

A key challenge in designing product lines is maintaining the balance between introducing sufficient product variety to address the needs of different customer segments without the potential side effect of confusing customers or encouraging cannibalization. Indeed, if customers are confused when presented with multiple options and cannot determine which product best matches their needs, they might decide to postpone making the purchase or,

alternatively, choose a competitors' offering. In the same vein, product lines comprising offerings that are similar in functionality but vary in price are likely to lead to sales of the low-
priced offerings cannibalizing the sales of the high-priced ones.

The key principle in designing product lines is that each product should be developed
to address the needs of a particular customer segment and that different products should
not compete for the same customer segments.[33] Designing (as well as extending and trim-
ming) product lines without a clear understanding of the underlying customer needs each
individual product aims to fulfill and without considering the consequences of product cannibalization and customer confusion can be detrimental to the company's market position
and bottom line.

To better differentiate their product lines and avoid confusion, companies often associate
different product lines with unique brands, each having a different identity and meaning in
customers' minds. For example, General Motors distinguishes its product lines by associating them with distinct brands such as Chevrolet, Buick, and Cadillac; Microsoft brands its
product lines as Windows, Office, and Xbox; and Unilever's product lines are delineated by
brands such as Dove, Axe, Lipton, Knorr, and Surf.

Designing Product Platforms

Product platforms provide the common architecture on which products are built. Platforms
encompass the shared components, designs, technologies, and processes that enable a company to create a set of distinct products that can fulfill the needs of different target customers. A product platform can lead to a range of products based on the same core architecture
but with varying features. Unlike product lines, which are typically organized around the
different customer benefits created by the company's offerings, product platforms reflect
the internal processes involved in developing, manufacturing, promoting, and distributing
the products defining a company's product line (Figure 2).

Figure 2. Product Platforms and Product Lines

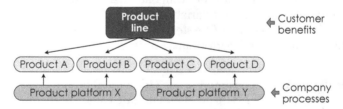

The schematic representation of the relationship between product platforms and product lines shown in Figure 2 is somewhat oversimplified. In reality, most products encompass
different components or modules, each sharing a platform with a similar component of another product. As a result, each product in a company's product line can stem from multiple
platforms. For example, an automobile can share multiple modules—the power system,
chassis, wheels, suspension, and electronic control units—with other automobiles in the
company's product line. To illustrate, Volkswagen uses a common platform across a variety
of individual car models promoted under four brands: Audi, Škoda, Seat, and Volkswagen.
Likewise, General Motors uses common automotive architectures—labeled using the English names of letters of the Greek alphabet such as alpha, epsilon, and gamma—across many
of its cars manufactured under the Chevrolet, Buick, Cadillac, and Holden brands. Procter

& Gamble uses the same set of ingredients in Tide, Ariel, and Cheer for the U.S., European, and Japanese markets, respectively. Black & Decker uses the same universal motor in more than 100 different consumer power tools.

Product platforms have a different strategic focus than individual products. In platform development, the focus is on streamlining the processes to achieve scale and scope and optimize the use of company resources. In this context, the use of platforms enables companies to achieve a higher degree of standardization across the individual offerings in their product lines, which, in turn, leads to less complex production processes, more efficient use of resources, higher levels of productivity, and lower production costs. In contrast, in developing individual products, the focus is on customization and differentiation in order to create a distinct offering that can create superior value for target customers. By developing a set of common elements that are shared among different products, platform-based design addresses the fundamental tradeoff between customers' desire for distinct products that fulfill their idiosyncratic needs and companies' desire to manufacture standardized products in the most cost-efficient manner.

The ubiquity of product platforms stems from the multiple advantages they offer to manufacturers. One of these advantages is the reduced development and production costs associated with the use of product platforms. Indeed, because they are composed of modules shared across multiple types of products, product platforms can lead to significant economies of scale and scope in designing and producing these modules. Furthermore, reliance on already developed modules, processes, and technologies can dramatically speed up the process of developing new products and bringing them to market. In addition, by enabling the company to pool resources across different products and develop a set of common modules, product platforms can lead to technological breakthroughs that are less likely to occur when resources are dedicated to a single product.

The benefits of using product platforms come with several potential drawbacks. One such drawback is that product platforms, almost by definition, impose constraints on the ways in which products are designed, produced, and managed, which, in turn, can curb radical innovation and lead to less innovative products. Furthermore, because they involve shared components, technologies, and designs, product platforms can encourage the development of products that are very similar in their functionality and appearance, which can lead to customer confusion as well as dilution of the brands associated with these products. Finally, because product platforms become the backbone of the development and manufacture of multiple product lines, they can be very difficult and costly to update or switch out of once they become obsolete.

The discussion so far has focused on internal product platforms that are developed to streamline the design, manufacture, promotion, and distribution of the company's own products. In addition to traditional product platforms, *network platforms* designed to be shared across different companies (Figure 3), have seen rapid growth in the past two decades. For example, Amazon has developed Amazon Marketplace as a platform that can be used by external vendors, Apple developed iTunes as a platform for distributing digital content, and Google developed Google Ads (formerly AdWords) and AdSense as digital advertising platforms. As the complexity of designing, manufacturing, promoting, and distributing individual products increases, companies tend to shift to external platforms that specialize in a particular process and allow them to benefit from economies of scale and scope.

Figure 3. Network Product Platforms

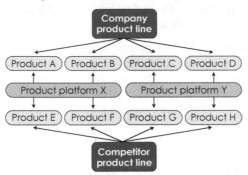

By providing access to resources that might otherwise be out of reach for smaller companies, network platforms effectively lower the barriers to market entry while simultaneously spurring new product development. As a result, platform-based innovators can develop new products and enter new markets much faster, more effectively, and at a lower cost. By providing access to resources needed to develop and launch new products, platforms effectively reduce the scale that individual manufacturers must achieve to be viable, which, in turn, can increase the assortment of custom-tailored products available in the market.

The advancement of networked platforms presents a competitive challenge to companies with their own proprietary platforms. Indeed, outsourcing some of the company's core activities to an external platform might lead to a fundamental change in the design, production, promotion, and distribution processes, as well as the company's entire business model. Switching to a network-platform-based model also implies that a company might have to abandon its current production facilities and equipment, reduce its workforce, as well as share proprietary information with third parties and relinquish control over product development, promotion, and distribution. As a result, despite the multiple benefits of networked product platforms, some companies choose to develop and manage their products using internal product platforms rather than rely on a third-party platform.

Managing Product-Line Extensions

A common approach to building product lines involves starting with a single offering and then adding related offerings, commonly referred to as product-line extensions. Depending on the relationship between the incumbent offering and the added offering(s), product-line extensions can be divided into two types: *vertical* and *horizontal*. These two types of extensions are discussed in more detail in the following sections.

Managing Vertical Product-Line Extensions

Vertical product-line extensions involve adding new offerings in different price tiers. Specifically, a company might add an offering that delivers a higher level of benefits at a higher price in the case of an *upscale vertical extension*, or an offering that delivers a lower level of benefits at a lower price in the case of a *downscale vertical extension*. The two types of vertical extensions—upscale and downscale—are illustrated in Figure 4 and discussed in more detail below.

Figure 4. Vertical Product-Line Extensions

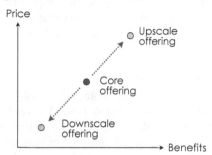

Managing Upscale Product-Line Extensions

Upscale extensions involve extending the company's product line by adding an offering that delivers a higher level of benefits at a higher price compared with the core offering. One of the main reasons for introducing an upscale extension is to capture a more lucrative, higher margin market. For example, to gain a foothold in the growing market for professional tools, leading home improvement company Black & Decker introduced DeWalt—a line of professional, high-end power tools (discussed in detail in Appendices A and B in the last part of this book). Upscale extensions are often used to follow customers through different stages of their life cycle by creating offerings that fit their evolving needs and changing buying power. For example, building on the success of its low-priced cars, Volkswagen introduced the more upscale Jetta and Passat aimed at customers who seek larger, better performing vehicles.

In addition to providing access to higher end markets, upscale extensions can provide synergies with existing offerings. For example, adding an upscale offering can lift the image of the low-end offerings in the company's product line. Introducing a line of premium, award-winning Gallo-branded wines helped E. & J. Gallo Winery strengthen the image of its core offerings. Companies also introduce upscale extensions to gain a competitive advantage in developing advanced technologies. For example, car manufacturers often develop high-performance versions of their vehicles to strengthen their core competencies and further the advancement of technologies that can be used in their mass-produced lower end models.

Despite their multiple advantages, upscale extensions present numerous challenges. Developing upscale offerings usually requires specific resources that a company specializing in lower tier products and services might not readily possess. The lack of such resources might prevent a company from developing an offering that can successfully compete in the upscale market. For example, launching an upscale apparel brand requires a variety of specific resources such as knowledge of fashion trends, product development know-how, high-end manufacturing capabilities, a reputable brand, and access to specialized suppliers and upscale distribution channels that a lower end manufacturer might not have.

Because most companies do not readily have the resources necessary to introduce higher quality offerings, successful organic (internally developed by the company) upscale extensions usually take time to implement and are not very common. Instead, companies often gain access to upscale markets by acquiring existing high-end offerings. This acquisition strategy is illustrated by Fiat's entry into the racing car market with the acquisition of Ferrari; Volkswagen's acquisition of Bentley, Bugatti, and Lamborghini; and Marriott's acquisition of Ritz-Carlton.

Managing Downscale Product-Line Extensions

Downscale extensions involve extending the company's product line by adding an offering that delivers a lower level of benefits at a lower price. Downscale extensions are driven by a company's desire to increase its customer base by attracting less affluent customers who are currently not served by its offerings. Examples of downscale extensions include Armani's launch of Armani Exchange, Mercedes' introduction of the A-Class, and Gap's introduction of Old Navy stores.

The main appeal of downscale extensions is the high volume of sales resulting from serving customers in lower socioeconomic tiers. Downscale extensions also enable companies to gain access to customers early in their life cycle by providing a lower entry point for a company's offerings. For example, Audi and BMW's "1" series cars provide access to younger customers, who despite current constrained resources are likely to evolve into a lucrative customer segment in the future.

Downscale extensions are especially beneficial to companies operating in industries requiring high fixed-cost investments—such as the airline, hotel, and automotive industries—in which economies of scale might be achieved. For example, many upscale car manufacturers—including Mercedes, BMW, and Porsche—have opted to use their design and manufacturing resources to develop downscale product offerings. Downscale extensions are quite popular among managers seeking to achieve quick results because they build on the company's existing resources and are often easier to implement than upscale extensions.

Despite their numerous advantages, downscale extensions have a number of significant drawbacks. A key concern is the threat of cannibalization of higher end offerings by the downscale extension (discussed in more detail later in this chapter). In cases when the extension carries the same brand as the upscale offering, the downscale offering can also weaken the brand by creating undesirable associations with a low-quality/low-priced offering. Another area of concern is that downscale extensions yield lower margins compared to higher end offerings and, as a result, they need to generate substantial sales volume to be profitable. Furthermore, serving price-conscious customers can be challenging because these customers tend to be less loyal and are more likely to switch to lower priced competitive offerings.

Managing Horizontal Product-Line Extensions

Offerings in a horizontally differentiated product line typically belong to the same price tier and differ primarily in the type of benefits they offer (Figure 5). Unlike vertical extensions, in which the different levels of offering benefits can be clearly ordered in terms of their attractiveness (for example, Ritz-Carlton is likely to be regarded as more attractive than Marriott, and a luxury car is likely to be viewed as more appealing than an economy car), horizontal extensions do not imply such universal preference ordering. Instead, horizontal extensions are differentiated on benefits that are idiosyncratic and are likely to vary in their attractiveness across customers. For example, different designs, styles, colors, and flavors are likely to appeal to different tastes without necessarily implying differential pricing. Thus, even though prices might vary across horizontally differentiated offerings, they are not the key differentiating factor.

Figure 5. Horizontal Product-Line Extensions

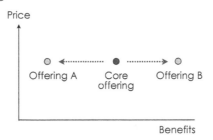

Horizontal extensions create value by providing customers with offerings that better match their preferences. Unlike vertical extensions, which provide a better preference match in a different price–quality tier, horizontal extensions aim to accommodate customers' tastes within the same price–quality tier. By providing an assortment of diverse options, horizontal extensions help companies fulfill the needs of customers with different tastes while satisfying the variety-seeking behavior of these customers. For example, Colgate-Palmolive, Procter & Gamble, and Unilever have introduced more than a hundred varieties of toothpaste to appeal to consumers' diverse tastes in order to provide individual customers with a greater variety of options to choose from.

Because they draw on a company's existing resources, horizontal extensions are often easier to implement than vertical extensions. Moreover, because they are sold at similar price points and have a similar cost structure, horizontal extensions have profit margins comparable to those of the existing offerings, thus attenuating cannibalization concerns—a key advantage over downscale extensions.

Despite their multiple benefits, horizontal extensions have several important drawbacks. Because customers vary in their tastes, horizontal extensions often call for expansive product lines, which in turn increase the complexity and the costs associated with developing and managing the offerings in these product lines. In addition to greater complexity and costs, extensive assortments of similar options can lead to customer confusion and choice deferral, especially in cases when customers are unable to readily ascertain which of the available options best matches their preferences.

Managing Product-Line Cannibalization

When extending its product line, a company's goal is to generate additional sales and profits by stealing share from the competition and/or bringing new users into the category. Ideally, all the sales generated by the new offering will come from competitors' offerings or from growing the overall category. In reality, however, this is rarely the case. A common consequence of launching a new offering is that in addition to stealing share from competitors it can cannibalize some of the company's current offerings.

Product-line cannibalization is illustrated in Figure 6. Figure 6A depicts the market prior to the introduction of the new offering; Figure 6B depicts the "ideal" scenario, in which the new offering steals share exclusively from competitive offerings; and Figure 6C depicts the more typical scenario, in which the new offering steals share from both the competitive offerings and the company's own offering.

Figure 6. Product-Line Cannibalization

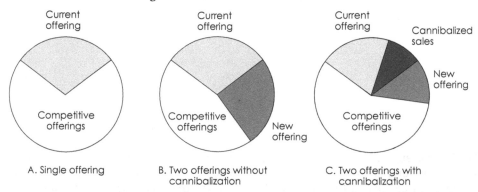

A. Single offering   B. Two offerings without   C. Two offerings with
                             cannibalization   cannibalization

Cannibalization describes a scenario in which the sales of one offering come at the expense of the sales of another offering from the same company. Cannibalization is not always problematic, and on certain occasions a company might actively seek to cannibalize the sales of some of its offerings. For example, by launching a newer version of its flagship offering, a market leader might aim to cannibalize its current flagship offering in order to provide customers with a better experience and gain higher profit margins.

Cannibalization is a primary concern in the case of downscale product-line extensions because they typically have lower profit margins than the offerings they end up cannibalizing. To minimize the possibility of cannibalization, a company needs to ensure that its downscale extension is substantially differentiated from its current offerings. This means that differentiation on price must also involve differentiation on benefits, such that lower price is associated with a lower level of benefits. Indeed, when the new offering provides the same benefits as the incumbent offering at a lower price, customers have no reason to prefer the higher priced offering and will ultimately gravitate toward the lower priced extension. Therefore, meaningful differentiation is key to sidestepping cannibalization.

When differentiating its downscale extension, a company walks a fine line between curbing potential cannibalization by ensuring that the downscale extension is not more attractive than the incumbent offering and building the market for the downscale extension by bolstering its appeal. In its desire to minimize cannibalization, a company can stretch its downscale extension so far that it becomes inferior to those of its direct competitors. For example, in an effort to avoid cannibalization, Intel overstretched its downscale extension, Celeron, making its performance subpar to its low-priced competitors. Over-differentiation can also involve overpricing the lower end offering. Gap Warehouse, the forerunner of Old Navy, failed because in an effort to avoid cannibalizing sales in Gap's core stores it set relatively high prices, which put it at a disadvantage relative to its direct competitors.

Poorly differentiated downscale (lower priced) vertical extensions are not the only cause of cannibalization; poorly differentiated horizontal extensions can result in cannibalization as well. Even when offerings in horizontal product-line extensions are priced at parity and have similar margins, a company's overall profitability might decrease when a larger number of company offerings ends up chasing the same number of customers. Thus, when the newly added offerings in a company's product line address the same need of the same target customer as the existing offerings, extending a product line can ultimately lead to substitution between offerings rather than stimulating new demand. In this case cannibalization is likely to hurt a company's bottom line because the increased costs of developing new offerings are not offset by a corresponding increase in sales volume.

Cannibalization is of primary concern when the margins of the new offering are lower than those of the offering being cannibalized, which means that every time a customer buys the new, lower margin offering instead of the higher margin one, the company generates lower profits. A key issue, therefore, is how much cannibalization a company can afford before the new offering produces a net loss. The maximum amount of cannibalization of an existing offering by a new one is given by the *break-even rate of cannibalization*. Assessing the break-even rate of cannibalization is discussed in more detail at the end of this chapter.

Managing Product Lines in a Competitive Context

In addition to creating value for customers, product-line extensions can help companies gain and sustain market position by optimizing a company's value proposition relative to its competitors. Three of the most popular competitive product line strategies—the *fighting-brand strategy*, the *sandwich strategy*, and the *good–better–best strategy*—are outlined in more detail below.

The Fighting-Brand Strategy

A common strategy to compete with low-priced rivals involves launching a fighting brand—an offering that matches or undercuts the competitor's price (Figure 7). For example, to compete with low-price rivals while preserving the market position of its flagship Marlboro brand, Philip Morris aggressively priced its Basic cigarette label, making it a fighting brand. Similarly, Procter & Gamble launched Oxydol laundry detergent as a low-price alternative to its flagship brand, Tide.

Figure 7. The Fighting-Brand Strategy

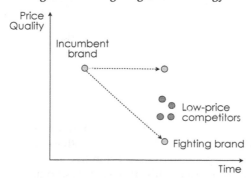

Fighting brands are created specifically to combat low-priced rivals that are encroaching on the company's incumbent offering. Rather than tackle the threat head-on and lower the price of its core offerings, the fighting-brand strategy involves introducing a lower priced, lower quality offering to address the needs of price-conscious consumers while leaving intact the value proposition of the original offering. In addition to protecting the company's premium offerings, fighting brands enable the company to reach a new market segment of price-conscious customers willing to accept a lower level of performance in order to receive a lower price.

Despite its popularity, the fighting-brand strategy has certain limitations. Thus, in some cases the introduction of a lower priced offering might lead to cannibalization, whereby customers who normally would have purchased the company's premium offering now purchase the lower priced, lower margin offering. Such cannibalization is particularly likely in cases when the premium and the low-priced offering carry the same brand name—an approach that, in addition to facilitating cannibalization, has the potential to dilute the image of the offering's brand. Moreover, the fighting-brand strategy assumes a two-tiered market in which some buyers care about quality more than price and others are willing to sacrifice quality for price. In reality, however, the market structure might be more complex and a different strategy, such as good–better–best (discussed later in this section), might be more appropriate.

The Sandwich Strategy

The sandwich strategy involves introducing a two-tiered product line comprising a high-quality offering and a low-priced offering, effectively sandwiching low-priced competitors. This strategy is typically achieved by launching a downscale extension while simultaneously moving the existing offering upscale (Figure 8). For example, in anticipation of an inflow of cut-price competitors following the patent expiration of its blockbuster prescription drug Prilosec, AstraZeneca introduced a low-priced, over-the-counter version (Prilosec OTC) and at the same time replaced Prilosec with Nexium—a premium-priced and slightly more effective version of the drug.

Figure 8. The Sandwich Strategy

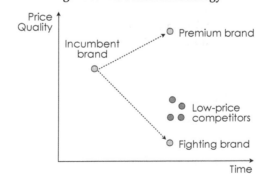

The sandwich strategy resembles the fighting-brand strategy because in both cases the incumbent brand introduces a low-priced offering. Where the sandwich strategy differs from the fighting-brand strategy is that in addition to introducing a downscale offering it also moves the core offering upscale. This upscale repositioning of the incumbent offering reflects the change in the target market following the introduction of low-price offerings by competitors. Indeed, after the incumbent offering loses some of its price-sensitive customers to lower priced rivals, the remaining customers are, on average, less price sensitive and more quality oriented. As a result, the incumbent offering is no longer optimally positioned for these customers (it is underpriced) and can benefit from moving upscale.

The sandwich strategy is an effective approach for dealing with lower priced competitors in cases when buyers have clearly articulated preferences for either quality or price. At the same time, this strategy might backfire in markets where buyers have uncertain preferences. In such markets, buyers often prefer options that offer a compromise among the extreme alternatives rather than either the high-quality or the low-price option. To illustrate, when choosing from a set composed of a high-priced/high-quality offering, a low-priced/low-quality offering, and an average-priced/average-quality offering, buyers often select the middle option because it allows them to avoid trading off price and quality. In this case, trying to "sandwich" the low-priced brand by simply launching a fighting brand and moving the core brand upscale without offering a mid-price/mid-quality option might be counterproductive because the "sandwiched" competitor might benefit from becoming the compromise option.

The Good–Better–Best Strategy

The good–better–best strategy involves introducing a downscale offering (fighting brand) as well as an upscale offering (premium brand) while preserving the core brand. The good–better–best strategy is similar to the sandwich strategy in that it involves the introduction of a low-priced offering. However, instead of a two-tiered product line that involves an upscale repositioning of the core brand, the good–better–best strategy calls for launching a new premium offering that yields a three-tiered product line (Figure 9).

Figure 9. The Good–Better–Best Strategy

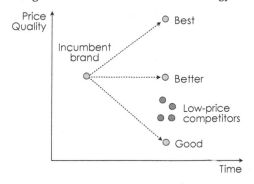

The good–better–best strategy can be illustrated by Apple's response to low-priced competitors of its iPod music player. Instead of directly competing with lower priced offerings, Apple extended its product line downscale by first introducing the iPod Shuffle and then the iPod Nano. The iPod's good–better–best product line reflects Apple's view of the market as comprising three key segments: a segment seeking a fully functional player (iPod), a segment seeking basic functionality (iPod Nano), and a segment seeking a low-priced offering with limited functionality (iPod Shuffle). The good–better–best strategy is also exemplified by Gap's three-tiered structuring of its retail stores: Old Navy, Gap, and Banana Republic.

The good–better–best strategy works well in tiered markets comprising three key segments: a quality-focused segment, a price-focused segment, and a segment seeking a compromise between high quality and low price. In such three-tiered markets, the two-pronged sandwich strategy would not work because moving the core offering upscale without having a mid-tier option leaves the company vulnerable to competitive offerings of mid-point quality and price. In addition to being an effective tool to fend off cut-price competitors in three-tiered markets, the good–better–best strategy could also be effective in markets in which buyers have uncertain preferences and are likely to select the middle option in order to avoid making a tradeoff between price and quality.

Despite its advantages, the good–better–best strategy also has important limitations. One such limitation is that this strategy requires that the company have the necessary resources to develop three different market offerings that vary in the level of benefits they provide to customers while ensuring that each offering delivers value to its target segment. The introduction of multiple offerings is also likely to result in additional product development and management costs that put additional pressure on the company to increase sales revenues. Finally, in the absence of clearly delineated differences in performance between the good, better, and best offerings, the lowest priced offering is likely to cannibalize the sales of the higher priced offerings, eroding the company's sales revenues and profits.

SUMMARY

Product-line management aims to optimize the market value created by a company's offerings. A key principle of managing product lines is that each offering should have its own unique value proposition that fits the needs of a particular customer segment without cannibalizing sales of other offerings.

Product lines comprise products that aim to address similar customer needs, typically in the context of the same category. Product lines that target different customer needs using distinct technologies are grouped into product portfolios.

Product platforms provide the common architecture on which a group of products is built; they comprise a set of shared components, designs, technologies, and processes that can lead to a range of products based on the same core architecture but with varying features.

A common approach to building product lines involves starting with a single offering and then adding related offerings, commonly referred to as *product-line extensions*. There are two types of product-line extensions: vertical and horizontal.

Vertical extensions involve adding new offerings that are in different price tiers. Depending on the price tier of the newly added offering, vertical extensions can be upscale (in a higher price tier) or downscale (in a lower price tier). One of the main reasons for introducing an upscale extension is to capture a more lucrative, higher margin market. Downscale extensions are typically driven by a company's desire to increase its customer base by attracting less affluent customers who are currently not served by its offerings.

Horizontal extensions aim to accommodate customers' tastes within a given price–quality tier. An important concern with downscale extensions is cannibalization, which describes a scenario in which the sales of the company's new downscale offering come at the expense of the sales of the incumbent offering.

In addition to optimizing the value for target customers, product-line management can help a company defend its market position against the competition. Popular competitive product-line management strategies include the *fighting-brand strategy*, the *sandwich strategy*, and the *good–better–best strategy*.

MARKETING INSIGHT: ASSESSING THE BREAK-EVEN RATE OF CANNIBALIZATION

The break-even rate (BER) of cannibalization indicates the maximum proportion of the new offering's sales volume that can come from the existing offering(s) without the company incurring a loss. The greater the break-even rate of cannibalization, the larger the percentage of an incumbent offering's sales a new offering can cannibalize while still having a positive impact on the company's bottom line (Figure 10).

Figure 10. Break-Even Rate of Cannibalization

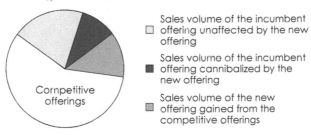

☐ Sales volume of the incumbent offering unaffected by the new offering

■ Sales volume of the incumbent offering cannibalized by the new offering

▨ Sales volume of the new offering gained from the competitive offerings

The break-even rate of cannibalization is derived as follows: To avoid loss of profit across all offerings, profit from the new product must be equal to or greater than the lost profits from cannibalization:

$$\text{Profit}_{\text{New offering}} \geq \text{Lost profit}_{\text{Old offering}}$$

Because profit is a function of unit volume and unit margin, the above equation can be modified as follows:

$$\text{Volume}_{\text{New offering}} \cdot \text{Margin}_{\text{New offering}} \geq \text{Lost volume}_{\text{Old offering}} \cdot \text{Margin}_{\text{Old offering}}$$

When the two sides of the equation are equal, the new offering is breaking even with respect to cannibalization of the old offering. In this case, the above equation can be represented as follows:

$$\frac{\text{Lost volume}_{\text{Old offering}}}{\text{Volume}_{\text{New offering}}} = \frac{\text{Margin}_{\text{New offering}}}{\text{Margin}_{\text{Old offering}}}$$

The left part of the equation is the ratio of sales volume of the old offering that was lost because of cannibalization by the new offering, which is the definition of the break-even rate of cannibalization (BER$_C$).[34] Hence:

$$\text{BER}_C = \frac{\text{Margin}_{\text{New offering}}}{\text{Margin}_{\text{Old offering}}}$$

For example, consider a company launching a new product priced at $70 with variable costs of $60, which cannibalizes the sales of an existing product priced at $100 that also has variable costs of $60. In this case, Margin$_{\text{New Offering}}$ = $70 – $60 = $10 and Margin$_{\text{Old Offering}}$ = $100 – $60 = $40. Therefore, the break-even rate of cannibalization can be calculated as follows:

$$\text{BER}_C = \frac{\$10}{\$40} = 0.25$$

The break-even rate of cannibalization in this case is 0.25 or 25%, which means that to be profitable for the company, no more than 25% of the sales volume of the new offering should come from the current offering, which in turn implies that at least 75% of the sales volume should come at the expense of competitors' offerings and/or from increasing the overall size of the market.

PART FIVE

MARKETING TOOLBOX

INTRODUCTION

When the only tool you own is a hammer,
every problem begins to resemble a nail.
— Abraham Maslow, American psychologist

The first four parts of this book presented a theory of marketing and outlined a framework for marketing management. The practical application of this theory and framework is facilitated by a set of tools that help managers accomplish common business tasks, which include identifying target markets and designing a business model. These two tasks are briefly outlined below, and the application of the marketing theory and framework to these tasks is discussed in more detail in the following chapters.

- **Identifying target markets** focuses on deciding which customers the company should tailor its offering to and which customers it should ignore. A systematic approach to identifying target customers, which builds on the theory presented in Chapter 4, is outlined in Appendix A. The process of identifying target customers is illustrated with a concrete example delineating the process of segmentation and targeting.

- **Generating a business model** involves developing the key aspects of an offering's strategy and tactics. The key aspects of a company's business model are captured in a market value map that outlines the specific ways in which an offering creates value for its target customers, collaborators, and the company. A systematic approach to generating a business model and market value maps, which build on the theory presented in Chapter 2, is outlined in Appendix B.

The generalized knowledge reflected in the key marketing concepts, principles, and frameworks can help managers circumvent common errors stemming from over-dependence on intuition and gut feel. By bridging marketing theory with managerial practice, the tools outlined here aim to facilitate the use of a systematic approach to identifying market opportunities, solving business problems, and creating market value.

SEGMENTATION AND TARGETING WORKBOOK

> *There is nothing so useless as doing efficiently*
> *something that should not be done at all.*
> — Peter Drucker, founder of
> modern management theory

Deciding which customers to serve is a defining aspect of a company's strategy. It influences all other aspects of the target market — competitors, collaborators, the company's resources necessary to serve these customers, and the context in which the company operates. The fundamental role that identifying target customers plays in defining a company's business model highlights the importance of applying a systematic approach to targeting. Accordingly, this chapter presents an application of the targeting framework outlined in Chapter 4. Specifically, it outlines the key steps of the process of identifying target customers and illustrates the process of segmentation and targeting with a concrete example.

The Process of Identifying Target Customers

Identifying target customers can be represented as a sequence of steps a company should take to decide which customers to target. Specifically, a company's targeting decision is represented by three key processes: *strategic targeting analysis*, *tactical targeting analysis*, and *target selection*. These processes and the corresponding decisions are summarized in Figure 1 and outlined in more detail below.

Figure 1. Identifying Target Customers

Strategic targeting
- Define the key value drivers
- Segment the market
- Assess segment attractiveness
- Assess segment compatibility
- Select strategically viable segment(s)

Tactical targeting
- Define the segment profile
- Assess tactical viability of segment(s)

- Select target segment(s)

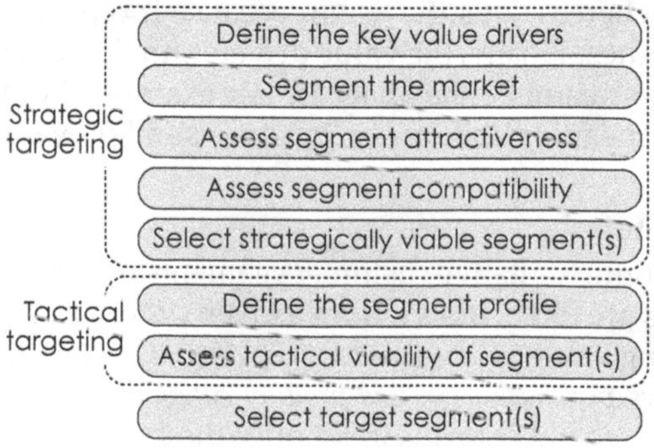

- **Strategic targeting** aims to identify which customers the company will target and which it will ignore — a decision based on the needs of these customers and the company's ability to fulfill these needs. Accordingly, the first step of analysis involves defining the key attributes (value drivers) that create customer value. This step is followed by segmenting the market into groups of customers with similar preferences based on the value they expect to receive from and can create for the company. The purpose of this segmentation is to select strategically viable segments that are compatible with the company's resources and at the same time can create value for the company.

- **Tactical targeting** aims to find effective and cost-efficient ways to reach the strategically viable segments. To this end, the company must identify the readily observable characteristics (profile) of the strategically viable target customers and evaluate the tactical viability of pursuing this segment.

- **Target selection** follows analysis of the strategic and tactical viability of targeting different segments and involves the ultimate decision of which segment(s) the company will pursue. Depending on its strategic goals and resources, a company might choose to target a single segment or multiple segments. In cases when a company decides to pursue multiple segments, it must develop a separate business model for each target segment.

The different steps in identifying target customers are outlined in more detail in the following sections and are supplemented with a practical example that illustrates the process of identifying target customers in the context of a particular company.

Step 1: Define the Value Drivers for the Category

A common approach to segmentation is to start by identifying the *value drivers* — the relevant attributes that buyers consider when making a choice. The identified customer value drivers become the criteria that will guide the process of defining market segments and identifying target customers.

When identifying the value drivers, it is important to ensure that they are indeed *relevant*, meaning that buyers consider them when making a choice, as well as *comprehensive*, meaning that all relevant attributes are identified and included in the analysis. In addition, the attributes identified as value drivers should be *specific*. For example, "reliability" is a relatively specific attribute, whereas "quality" is not because it typically refers to the combination of all nonprice attributes. Finally, the value drivers should be relatively *independent* from one another in order to streamline the analysis. For example, "precision" and "accuracy" are likely to overlap in meaning and, hence, produce similar evaluations.

Step 2: Segment the Market

The next step involves identifying tentative customer segments based on the value that customers within these segments are likely to seek from a given product category. A good starting point is to ask the following value-related questions: *What motivates customers' purchases? On what occasions do customers purchase from this product category? What needs are customers trying to fulfill?* The goal of these questions is to identify the key customer segments—that is, groups of customers who are very similar in their buying behavior within each segment and at the same time are very different across segments.

Once the tentative segments have been identified, the next step is to define the value sought by each segment. A practical approach to defining the needs of a segment is to rate the importance of each attribute of an offering for all of the tentatively identified segments. For example, one might use a three-point rating scale with levels "high," "moderate," and "low," where "high" indicates that a particular attribute is very important to a given segment and "low" indicates that it is relatively unimportant. Note that the three-point scale described here is for illustration purposes only; any scale that rank-orders the importance of different attributes can work. In general, the more nuanced the scale, the greater its ability to detect relatively minor differences among segments.

Not all of the identified value drivers necessarily differentiate the segments: Some attributes might be equally important to all segments. For example, durability might be considered an important factor by all segments, whereas color might be viewed as relatively unimportant by all. This is not a problem; it merely indicates that these attributes are non-diagnostic with respect to the ability to differentiate among the tentatively identified segments.

Defining potential target segments is often a trial-and-error process that stems from a manager's intuition about the different types of buyers in a given market. Accordingly, it is important to ensure that the intuitively defined segments represent different groups of customers. It is quite possible that the first attempt at identifying viable market segments does not produce a viable segmentation. In such cases, one must go back to the "drawing board" and revise the initial segmentation. The number of iterations to achieve a valid segmentation depends largely on a manager's experience and knowledge of the particular market. Some managers might derive the "right" segmentation from the beginning, whereas others might go through several iterations to arrive at a valid customer segmentation.

Step 3: Assess Segment Attractiveness

Segment attractiveness reflects the ability of the customers in this segment to create value for the company. Evaluating segment attractiveness aims to answer the question of whether the members of a particular segment have the resources to create value for the company and whether they can create greater value than those in non-chosen segments. The evaluation of segment attractiveness is based on the assessment of two types of value: monetary value, which reflects a segment's ability to generate profits for the company, and strategic value, which reflects a segment's ability to create nonmonetary benefits that are of strategic importance for the company.

A practical approach to assessing segment attractiveness involves evaluating each segment with respect to its ability to create monetary and strategic value for the company. For example, one might use a three-point rating scale with levels "high," "moderate," and "low," where "high" indicates that a particular segment is extremely attractive and "low" indicates that it is relatively unattractive to the company (a more nuanced scale can offer greater accuracy).

Step 4: Assess Segment Compatibility

Following the analysis of segment attractiveness is the analysis of segment compatibility—that is, the degree to which the company can create superior value for this segment. In order to provide this assessment, the manager needs to know the competitive context in which customers will evaluate the company's offering. Therefore, evaluating segment compatibility begins with identifying the competitors for each of the identified customer segments.

Once relevant competitors have been identified, the next step is to evaluate the company's ability to fulfill the needs of each target segment better than the competition. Segment compatibility can be assessed by evaluating the benefits of the company's offering relative to the competition on each of the relevant attributes (identified in Step 1). For example, one might use a three-point rating scale with levels "high," "moderate," and "low," where "high" indicates that a particular offering performs very well on a given attribute and "low" indicates that it performs rather poorly on that attribute (a more nuanced scale can offer greater accuracy).

Step 5: Select the Strategically Viable Segment(s)

Following analysis of the attractiveness and compatibility of the identified segments is the selection of the strategically viable segment(s). This involves selecting the target segment that best meets the attractiveness and compatibility criteria.

Deciding on the viability of each segment typically involves a binary (yes/no) decision indicating whether pursuing a particular set of customers is a strategically viable option for the company. Note that in some cases a company might decide to pursue a strategically important segment even though it does not readily have the resources necessary to create superior value for these customers. In such cases, the company's decision to target this segment is predicated on its ability to build the deficient resources—a strategy that typically involves the investment of significant resources and/or a longer time horizon.

Step 6: Define the Profile(s) of the Strategically Viable Target Segment(s)

The goal of this step is to identify the readily observable characteristics (profile) of the strategically chosen segment(s) that can be used to communicate and deliver the offering in an effective and cost-efficient manner. This is important because without knowing the profile of its target segment(s) a company faces the risk of not reaching all target customers and/or not reaching them in a cost-efficient manner.

To identify the profile of the strategically viable segment(s), a company can rely on four types of factors: demographic factors (e.g., age, gender, and income), geographic factors (e.g., state, city, and current location), psychographic factors (e.g., values, interests, and hobbies), and behavioral factors (e.g., type of media viewed and distribution channels used). These factors are then used to identify the touch points at which the company can communicate and deliver the offering to its customers.

Step 7: Assess the Tactical Viability of the Strategically Viable Segment(s)

Assessing the tactical viability of serving the identified segment(s) involves an assessment of the company's ability to reach this segment in a cost-efficient manner. This step takes into account the company's access to communication and distribution channels to reach this segment as well as the cost of gaining access to such channels. Note that for tactical purposes each segment can be divided into sub-segments reflecting different channels through which the company can reach these customers to communicate and deliver the offering. The rationale for creating sub-segments is that although customers in the strategically identified segment(s) are similar with respect to their needs, they still could vary with respect to ways the company can best communicate with them and deliver its offering.

Step 8: Select Target Customer Segment(s)

Selecting the optimal target segment yields the ultimate *go* or *no-go* decision with respect to the identified customer segments. Because the strategic segments are defined by the varying needs of customers across segments, in most cases a company can target only one segment with a particular offering. Should a company find multiple customer segments viable, it should develop a unique value proposition and market offering for each target segment.

The Targeting Workbook

The process of identifying target customers can be presented as a matrix that encompasses the key aspects of the targeting decision (Figure 2). By imposing logical structure on the process of market segmentation and targeting, this matrix can also serve as a worksheet guiding the identification of a company's target customers.

Figure 2. The Targeting Workbook

		Step 2 ⟹ **Customer value analysis**				Step 4 ⟹ **Compatibility analysis**		
Step 1 ⟱ **Value drivers**		Customer segments			Company offering	Competitive offerings		
		Segment A	Segment B	Segment C		Offering X	Offering Y	Offering Z
Strategic targeting	Attribute 1							
	Attribute 2							
	Attribute 3							
	Attribute 4							
	Attribute 5							
	Segment attractiveness				⟸ Step 3			
	Segment compatibility				⟸ Step 4 ⟵			
	Strategic viability				⟸ Step 5			
Tactical targeting	Segment profile				⟸ Step 6			
	Tactical viability				⟸ Step 7			
	Target selection				⟸ Step 8			

Because articulating the key drivers of customer value is an integral aspect of targeting, the analysis underlying the selection of target customers is also the basis for defining the offering's value proposition. Thus, the development of a value proposition directly follows from the targeting analysis and is an integral aspect of the development of a sound market strategy. The ultimate success of an offering is determined by the degree to which its value proposition is aligned with the needs and resources of its target customers. In this context, identifying target customers and designing a value proposition for these customers are the two aspects of an iterative process that culminates in the development of an internally consistent and viable marketing strategy. The process of developing a value proposition and a business model for the identified target markets is discussed in detail in Appendix B.

Segmentation and Targeting Workbook Example: Black & Decker

The process of identifying target customers can be better understood when illustrated with a specific example that highlights the decisions involved at each step of the targeting analysis. Accordingly, the following example focuses on Black & Decker, a large U.S. manufacturer of power tools and accessories, and the process by which it identified an underserved customer segment.[35]

Step 1: Defining the Value Drivers for the Category

Black & Decker's market analysis reveals five key attributes—power, reliability, service, brand image, and price—as the main factors that buyers of power tools consider when making a choice. These are the attributes on which Black & Decker needs to create superior value (relative to the other power tool manufacturers) for its target customers.

Step 2: Segmenting the Market

Based on the occasions on which power tools are used, initial market analysis suggests two segments: a *consumer segment*—buyers who use power tools around the house, and a *commercial segment*—buyers who purchase power tools for business use. Next, these segments need to be validated to ensure that (1) buyers in these two segments are different from one another in the value they derive from power tools and (2) that buyers within each of these two segments are very similar in their needs and preferences.

In Black & Decker's case, power and reliability are very important for commercial buyers but are of much lower importance to consumers, who care most about price and are moderately concerned with the brand of power tools they buy (Figure 3). The importance of service, brand, and price for commercial users, however, is much more difficult to pinpoint. There are reasons to argue that these three attributes are relatively unimportant to some of these buyers and reasons to argue that they are extremely important to others.

Figure 3. Customer Value Analysis Workbook (Two Segments)

	Customer segments	
Attributes	Consumer	Commercial
Power	Low	High
Reliability	Low	High
Service	Low	Medium – High
Brand	Medium	Low – High
Price	High	Low – Medium

The consumer–commercial segmentation is not effective because customers in the commercial segment exhibit significant variation in the importance they assign to service, brand image, and price. This variation means that this segment is heterogeneous and has to be segmented further to produce homogeneous (uniform) segments that have minimal within-segment variance in customer needs.

Subsequent analysis reveals that the commercial segment comprises two sub-segments: *tradesmen*—small businesses and independent contractors such as carpenters, plumbers, and electricians working in residential construction—that use power tools on the job; and *industrial buyers*, such as companies that purchase power tools for employee use. Once these sub-segments are taken into account, the resulting segments are fairly uniform with respect to customer preferences within each segment and yet reflect significant differences in customer preferences across segments (Figure 4).

Figure 4. Customer Value Analysis Workbook (Three Segments)

Attributes	Customer segments		
	Consumer	Tradesman	Industrial
Power	Low	High	High
Reliability	Low	High	High
Service	Low	High	Medium
Brand	Medium	High	Low
Price	High	Low	Medium

The customer value analysis shows that whereas customers in the two commercial segments — tradesmen and industrial buyers — share the belief that power and reliability are paramount, tradesmen place much greater importance on brand image and service. In other words, having fast repair service is more important for tradesmen than for industrial buyers, many of whom have their own service support. Furthermore, having tools that carry a professional brand can help enhance the professional image of tradesmen and is more important to them than to industrial buyers, who are purchasing the power tools for use by employees on commercial projects. Finally, the larger volume purchased by industrial buyers makes many of them more price sensitive than the tradesmen, who often buy a single tool.

Step 3: Assessing Segment Attractiveness

Analysis of the attractiveness of the identified customer segments reveals that all three segments — consumer, tradesman, and industrial — are attractive with respect to their ability to create value for Black & Decker. At the same time, even though the tradesman segment is the fastest growing of the three segments, Black & Decker's share of that segment is much lower compared to that of the other two segments. Accordingly, the tradesman segment presents the greatest market opportunity and is rated as a priority for Black & Decker.

Step 4: Assessing Segment Compatibility

Black & Decker's top competitors for the tradesman segment include Makita (the market leader, with nearly a 50% share), Milwaukee Tools, and Ryobi. In this context, analysis of the compatibility of the tradesman segment involves evaluating the performance of Black & Decker's offerings vis-à-vis its key competitors — Makita, Milwaukee Tools, and Ryobi — on each of the attributes identified in Step 1. The resulting attribute performance matrix is shown in Figure 5. The customer analysis ratings depicted in Figure 5 reflect the importance of each attribute for the tradesman segment, and competitive analysis ratings reflect the performance of each competitor on these attributes.

Figure 5. Compatibility Analysis Workbook (Tradesman Segment)

Attributes	Attribute importance	Market offerings			
		B&D	Makita	Milwaukee	Ryobi
Power	High	Medium	High	High	Medium
Reliability	High	High	High	High	High
Service	High	Medium	Medium	Medium	Low
Brand	High	Low	High	High	Low
Price	Low	Medium	High	High	Medium

The analysis depicted in Figure 5 indicates that Black & Decker is at parity with its key competitors in terms of reliability and service, and lags behind Makita and Milwaukee Tools in terms of power and brand image. With respect to price—an attribute that is of relatively low importance for tradesmen—Black & Decker is superior to Makita and Milwaukee Tools and on a par with Ryobi. This analysis suggests that to be at parity with the competition in the tradesman segment, Black & Decker must increase the power of its offerings and dramatically improve its brand image. Furthermore, Black & Decker could create a competitive advantage in terms of service, which would put it ahead of the competition. Finally, given the relatively low importance of price to the tradesman segment and Black & Decker's price advantage over Makita and Milwaukee Tools, there is room for Black & Decker to raise prices, provided that it can create superior value on the other attributes.

Step 5: Selecting the Strategically Viable Segment

Based on the value they can create for the company, tradesmen present the most attractive segment for Black & Decker. However, to successfully target the tradesman segment, Black & Decker must improve its offerings on two key dimensions—power and brand image. Improving the brand image is crucial because it is one of the attributes that target customers care most about and an attribute on which Black & Decker's brand is viewed to be vastly inferior to its top two competitors. Improving the power of its tools is also imperative for Black & Decker given its primary importance to target customers and competitors' advantage on that dimension. Furthermore, because tradesmen view service as a top priority, Black & Decker might also consider improving its service even though it is at parity with the competition. In this context, although its current offering is not optimal for the tradesman segment, Black & Decker can pursue this segment provided that it allocates resources to improve the power, service, and brand image of its offerings.

Step 6: Defining the Profile of the Strategically Viable Segment

Black & Decker's goal now is to identify effective and cost-efficient ways to reach tradesmen to communicate and deliver its offerings. The behavioral profile of tradesmen indicates that they read industry magazines such as *Builder* and *Electrical Contractor*, visit builder trade shows, and frequent home improvement stores.

Step 7: Assessing the Tactical Viability of the Strategically Viable Segment

To reach tradesmen, Black & Decker might advertise in industry magazines, such as *Builder* and *Electrical Contractor*, that are favored by the tradesman, promote the product at trade shows, as well as use point-of-purchase displays at home improvement retailers. To make its products readily available to tradesmen, Black & Decker might further focus its distribution efforts on retail outlets catering to these customers, including large home improvement centers such as Home Depot and Lowe's, smaller hardware chains such as Ace Hardware, and independently owned hardware stores. The above analysis suggests that the tradesman segment can be readily accessed via established communication and distribution channels and, hence, is viable from a tactical perspective.

Step 8: Selecting a Customer Target

Given the market opportunity associated with the tradesman segment, Black & Decker's ability to develop a value proposition compatible with the needs of this segment, and its ability to reach this segment in an effective and cost-efficient manner, Black & Decker can decide to go ahead with developing an offering for this segment.

To create value for the tradesman, Black & Decker must offer powerful and reliable tools from a trusted brand backed by dependable service (see Figure 4). To this end, Black & Decker must allocate resources to develop an offering that is superior to (or at least at parity with) the competition in terms of power, brand image, and service. Given the relatively low importance of price and the relatively high prices of its key competitors, Black & Decker might consider raising its prices—a strategy that not only can contribute to its bottom line but also can help build its brand reputation as a high-quality power tool. The specifics of Black & Decker's business model for creating value for the tradesman segment are outlined in Appendix B.

The Targeting Workbook

Black & Decker's segmentation and targeting analysis can be summarized in a targeting matrix, which outlines the key aspects of the process of identifying target customers (Figure 6).

Figure 6. The Targeting Workbook: Black & Decker

	Value drivers	Customer value analysis — Customer segments			Black & Decker	Compatibility analysis — Competitive offerings		
		Consumer	Tradesman	Industrial		Makita	Milwaukee	Ryobi
Strategic analysis	Power	Low	High	High	Medium	High	High	Medium
	Reliability	Low	High	High	High	High	High	High
	Service	Low	High	Medium	Medium	Medium	Medium	Low
	Brand image	Medium	High	Low	Low	High	High	Low
	Price	High	Low	Medium	Medium	High	High	Medium
	Segment attractiveness	Medium	High	Medium				
	Segment compatibility	Low	High	Low	← Improve on power, brand, and service			
	Strategic viability	Low	High	Low				
Tactical analysis	Segment profile	–	Behavioral profile	–				
	Tactical viability	–	High	–				
	Target selection	–	Yes	–				

Note that Black & Decker's focus on the tradesman segment does not mean that other segments are not viable for the company. Rather, the segmentation and targeting analysis aims to identify market opportunities — segments in which Black & Decker is underperforming and has viable potential for growth.

For brevity, segment compatibility and the subsequent analyses shown in Figure 6 focus only on the most attractive segment (the tradesman). Assessments of the attractiveness and the strategic viability of the tradesman segment are based on the assumption that Black & Decker can develop the resources necessary to target this segment (power, brand, and service). The behavioral profile of the tradesman segment is defined by a set of characteristics, including reading industry magazines such as *Builder* and *Electrical Contractor*, attending homebuilder trade shows, and frequenting home improvement and hardware stores.

THE BUSINESS MODEL WORKBOOK

Innovation is not the product of logical thought,
although the result is tied to logical structure.

— Albert Einstein, theoretical physicist

An offering's business model delineates the ways in which a company creates value in a particular market. The ultimate goal of the business model is to design an offering that will create superior value for target customers in a way that benefits the company and its collaborators. Building on the theory presented in Chapter 2, here we illustrate the key aspects of the process of generating a business model.

Developing a Market Value Map

The business model is the master plan that charts the way in which a company can reach its goals. It streamlines the process by which a company identifies its target market, defines its value proposition in this market, and develops an offering that creates value for its target customers, its collaborators, and stakeholders. Having a clearly articulated, logical, and sustainable business model is a prerequisite for any business enterprise.

The business model comprises two key components: strategy and tactics. The strategy identifies the market in which the company operates and outlines the ways in which an offering will create market value. Tactics, on the other hand, describe the actual offering that will create value in the target market. The strategy and tactics are intricately related: The strategy defines an offering's tactics, and tactics embody the offering's strategy.

The key aspects of a company's business model are captured in a market value map that outlines the specific ways in which an offering creates value for its target customers, collaborators, and the company. The primary purpose of a value map is to outline the key aspects of the business model and serve as a workbook that lays out the company's strategy and tactics. The market value map presents the business model in a schematic way, enabling managers to clearly articulate the key aspects of the company's business model.

The market value map follows the structure of the business model and delineates the three key components — *the target market, the value proposition,* and *the market offering* — that define the offering's strategy and tactics. Accordingly, the market value map is represented as a matrix: The left side outlines the key elements of the business model strategy — the target market (customers, collaborators, company, competitors, and context) and the value proposition (customer value, collaborator value, and company value). The right side outlines the market offering defined by its seven key attributes (product, service, brand, price, incentives, communication, and distribution). The key components of a market value map are shown in Figure 1.

Figure 1. The Market Value Map

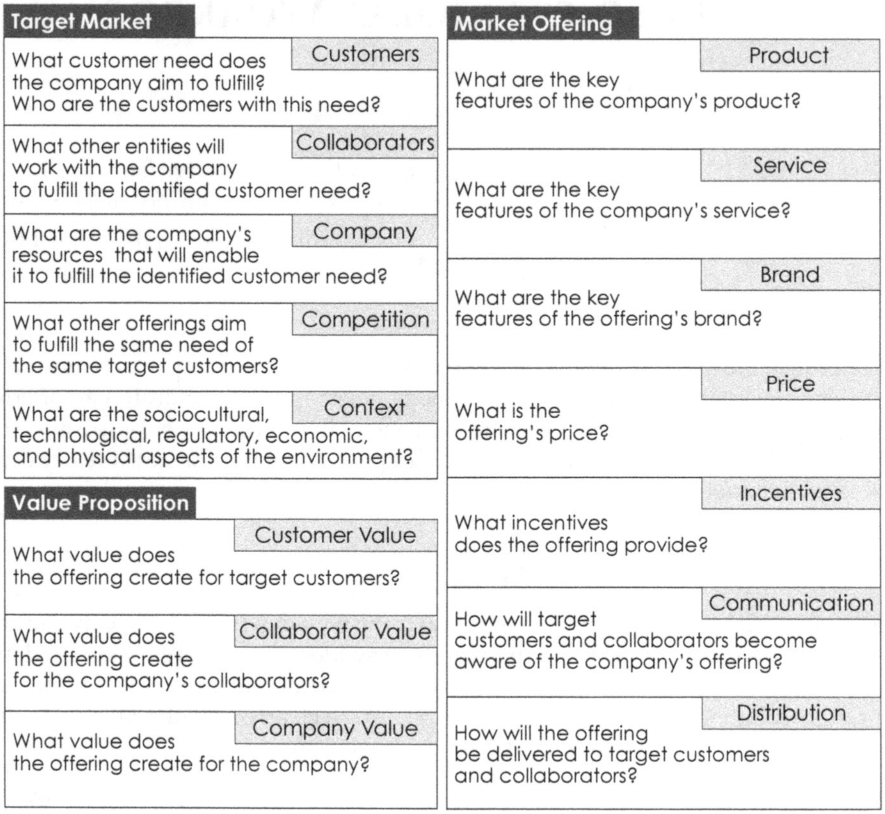

Target Market	Market Offering
Customers What customer need does the company aim to fulfill? Who are the customers with this need?	**Product** What are the key features of the company's product?
Collaborators What other entities will work with the company to fulfill the identified customer need?	**Service** What are the key features of the company's service?
Company What are the company's resources that will enable it to fulfill the identified customer need?	**Brand** What are the key features of the offering's brand?
Competition What other offerings aim to fulfill the same need of the same target customers?	**Price** What is the offering's price?
Context What are the sociocultural, technological, regulatory, economic, and physical aspects of the environment?	**Incentives** What incentives does the offering provide?
Value Proposition	**Communication** How will target customers and collaborators become aware of the company's offering?
Customer Value What value does the offering create for target customers?	**Distribution** How will the offering be delivered to target customers and collaborators?
Collaborator Value What value does the offering create for the company's collaborators?	
Company Value What value does the offering create for the company?	

The market value map offers an overview of the ways in which an offering creates value for the three relevant market entities—customers, collaborators, and the company. Because each of these entities requires its own value proposition and employs different tools to create value, the market value map can be represented as three separate maps: the *customer value map*, the *collaborator value map*, and the *company value map*.

- The **customer value map** outlines the key aspects of the company's offering for target customers and the way in which this offering will create value for these customers.

- The **collaborator value map** outlines the key aspects of the company's offering for its collaborators and the way in which it will create value for these collaborators.

- The **company value map** outlines the key aspects of the company's offering and the way in which this offering will create value for the company.

These three value maps define a company's business model from the viewpoint of each of the three market entities involved in the value-creation process. Because the market success of the company's offering depends on the degree to which it can create value for its customers, collaborators, and the company, the three value maps must clearly identify the ways in which the company offering will create superior value for each of these entities. The key aspects of developing customer, collaborator, and company value maps are outlined in the following sections.

Developing a Customer Value Map

The customer value map outlines the way in which a company's offering can fulfill the needs of its target customers better than the competition. The customer value map consists of four building blocks: target customers, the competition, the customer value proposition, and the customer offering. The core components of the customer value map are shown in Figure 2 and are outlined in more detail in the following sections.

Figure 2. The Customer Value Map

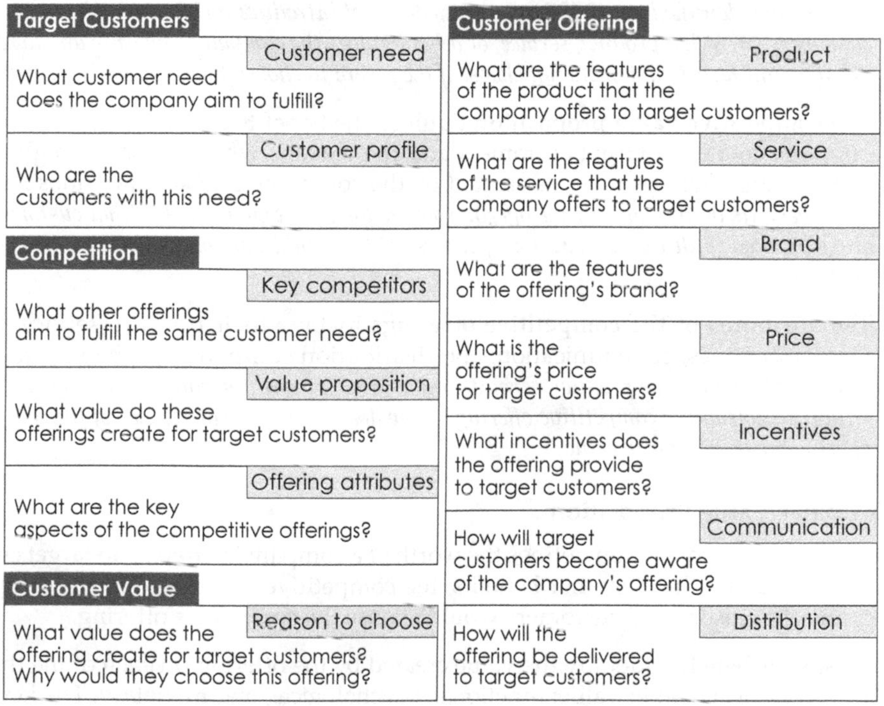

Target Customers

Target customers are the buyers for whom the company is developing its offering. Identifying target customers involves identifying an unmet customer need that the company intends to fulfill and defining the profile of customers with this need.

- The **customer need** identifies a problem faced by customers that the company aims to address with its offering. The key questions that a manager should ask are: *What customer need does the offering aim to fulfill? How common is this need? Do customers view this need as a problem that has to be solved and actively seek alternative means to fulfill this need?*

- The **customer profile** identifies the observable characteristics of target customers that the company can use to communicate and deliver its offering to these customers. The key questions are: *Who are the customers that have the need the company aims to fulfill? What demographic characteristics of these customers can the company use to reach them? What behaviors of these customers can the company use to reach them?*

Competition

The competition consists of the alternative offerings that fulfill the same need of the same customers as the company's offering. Competitors are identified by their value proposition for target customers and the attributes defining the competitive offerings.

- **Key competitors** are the alternative offerings that target customers can use to achieve their goals. The key questions here are: *What means are target customers currently using to fulfill the identified need? If the company does not introduce its offering, what would these customers do? What product, service, or behavior does the company's offering aim to replace? What would target customers <u>not</u> choose if they were to choose the company's offering?*

- The **competitive value proposition** outlines the benefits and costs that competitive offerings create for target customers and the reasons why customers might prefer competitive offerings to those created by the company. The key questions here are: *What benefits do the competitive offerings create for target customers? What customer costs are associated with the competitive offerings? Why would customers choose a competitor's offerings?*

- The **attributes of the competitive offerings** involve their product, service, brand, price, incentives, communication, and distribution components. The key questions here are: *What are the product, service, brand, price, incentives, communication, and distribution aspects of the competitive offering? How does each of the attributes of the competitive offering create customer value?*

The Customer Value Proposition

The customer value proposition defines the worth of a company's offering to target customers. It is identified by the customer benefits, the competitive advantage of the company's offering, and the reason why customers would choose the company's offering.

- **Customer benefits** identify the value created by the offering on each of the three dimensions of customer value: functional, psychological, and monetary. The key question here is: *What functional, psychological, and monetary benefits does the offering create for its target customers?*

- The **competitive advantage** is the ability of an offering to fulfill a particular customer need better than the alternative options. The key questions here are: *Why should target customers choose the company's offering instead of using alternative means of fulfilling the identified need? What are the points of dominance, points of parity, and points of compromise of the company's offering relative to the competitive offerings?*

- The **reason to choose** is the key factor that will motivate customers to buy and use the company's offering. The key questions here are: *What is the primary reason for customers to choose the company offering? How would customers justify choosing the company's offering?*

Customer Offering

The customer offering is defined by the seven attributes—product, service, brand, price, incentives, communication, and distribution—that delineate the company's offering and the value that these attributes create for target customers. The key questions here are: *What are the key features of the product, service, brand, price, and incentives the company offers to its customers? How will target customers become aware of the offering? How will the offering be delivered to target customers? How will different attributes of the offering create customer value?*

Developing a Collaborator Value Map

The collaborator value map outlines the ways in which an offering can help the company's collaborators achieve their goals better than the competitive offerings. Similar to the customer value map, the collaborator value map consists of four building blocks: collaborators, the competition, the collaborator value proposition, and the collaborator offering. The core components of the collaborator value map are shown in Figure 3 and are outlined in more detail in the following sections.

Figure 3. The Collaborator Value Map

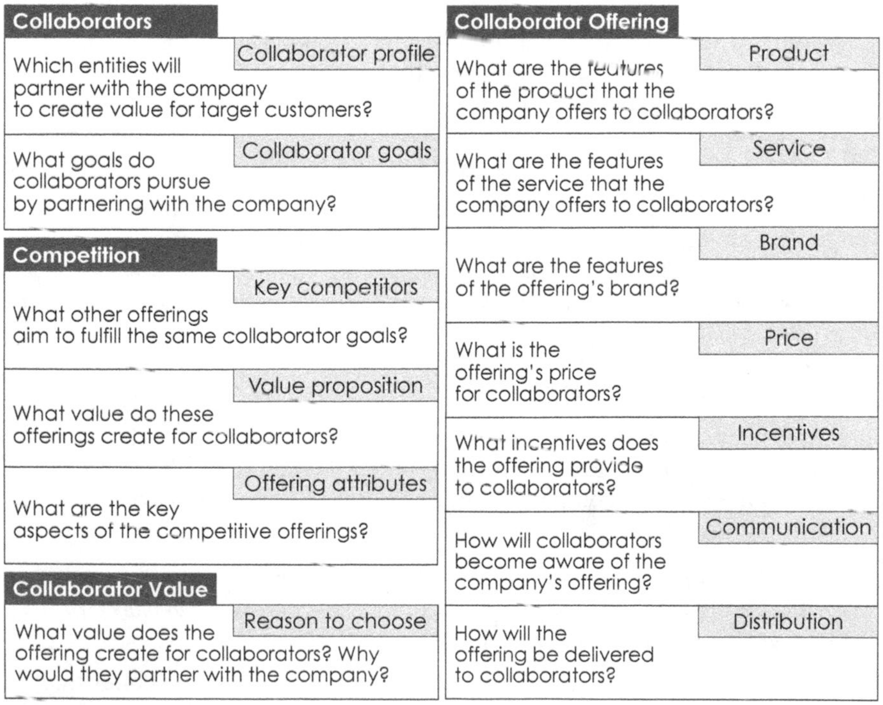

Key Collaborators

Collaborators are entities working with the company to create value for target customers. Identifying collaborators has two aspects: defining the profile of the partnering entities and their resources, and identifying the goals that these entities aim to achieve by partnering with the company.

- The **collaborator profile** reflects the key aspects of the partnering entity, such as resources, location, size, and industry. The key questions here are: *What resources needed to create superior value for target customers is the company looking to outsource? Which entities have the resources the company lacks and is looking to outsource? What are the key characteristics of these entities?*

- **Collaborator goals** are the outcomes that collaborators want to achieve through collaboration. The key question here is: *What monetary and strategic goals do collaborators aim to achieve by partnering with the company?*

Competition

The competition consists of the alternative offerings that target the same goals of the same collaborators that the company does. The competition is defined by the key competitors, their value proposition for collaborators, and the attributes of the competitive offerings.

- **Key competitors** are the alternative means that company collaborators can use to achieve their goals. The key questions here are: *What are potential collaborators currently doing to achieve their goals? If they do not partner with the company, what will these collaborators do? What offering does the company aim to replace with its offering?*

- The **competitive value proposition** reflects the benefits and costs created by the competitive offerings for collaborators and the reasons why collaborators might prefer competitive offerings to those created by the company. The key questions here are: *What benefits and costs do the competitive offerings create for collaborators? What is the primary reason why collaborators might prefer a competitive offering to the company offering?*

- The **attributes of the competitive offerings** involve their product, service, brand, price, incentives, communication, and distribution components. The key questions here are: *What are the product, service, brand, price, incentives, communication, and distribution aspects of the competitive offerings? How does each attribute of the competitive offerings create collaborator value?*

The Collaborator Value Proposition

The collaborator value proposition defines the worth of an offering to the company's collaborators. The collaborator value proposition is identified by the collaborator benefits, the competitive advantage of the company's offering, and the reason why collaborators would choose the company's offering.

- The **collaborator benefits** identify the value created by the offering on two value dimensions: monetary and strategic. The key question here is: *What monetary and strategic benefits does the offering create for collaborators?*

- The **competitive advantage** reflects the ability of the company's offering to address collaborators' goals better than the alternative options. The key questions here are: *Why should collaborators choose to partner with the company instead of using alternative means to achieve their goals? What are the points of dominance, points of parity, and points of compromise of the company's offering relative to the competitive offerings?*

- The **reason to choose** identifies the key factor(s) that would motivate collaborators to partner with the company. The key questions here are: *What is the primary reason* *for collaborators to partner with the company? How would collaborators justify choosing the company's offering?*

Collaborator Offering

The collaborator offering represents the collaborator aspect of the market offering. It is defined by the seven attributes—product, service, brand, price, incentives, communication, and distribution—that delineate the company's offering and the value that each of these attributes creates for collaborators. The key questions here are: *What are the key features of the product, service, brand, price, and incentives the company offers to its collaborators? How will the offering be communicated to collaborators? How will the offering be delivered to collaborators? How will different attributes of the offering create collaborator value?*

Developing a Company Value Map

The company value map outlines the ways in which the offering can enable the company to achieve its goals better than it can with alternative options. The company value map has a structure similar to the customer and collaborator value maps and consists of four building blocks: the company, the alternative options, the company value proposition, and the company offering. The core components of the company value map are shown in Figure 4 and are outlined in more detail in the following sections.

Figure 4. The Company Value Map

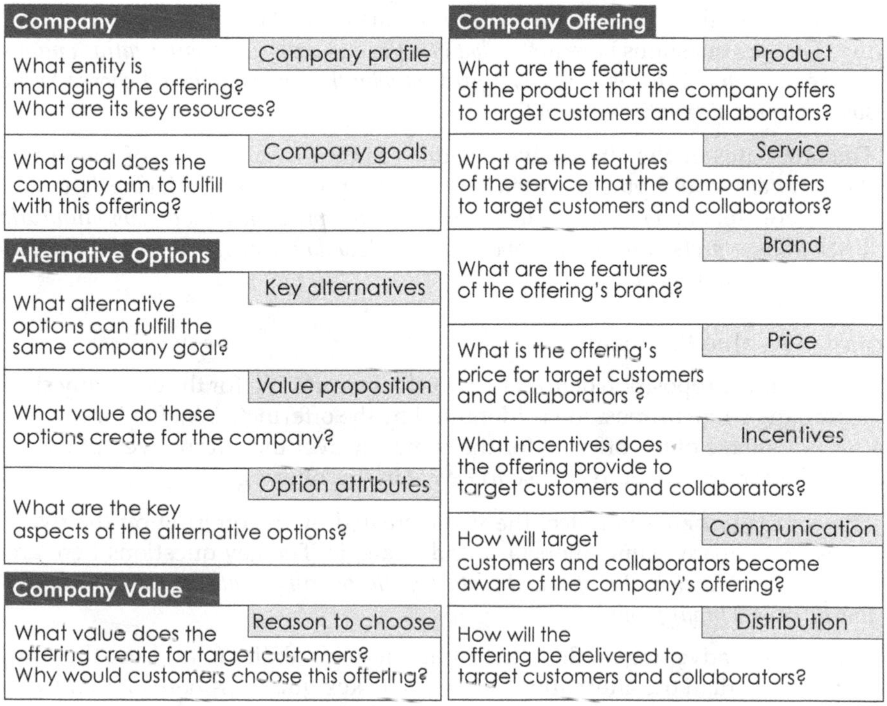

Company	
Company profile What entity is managing the offering? What are its key resources?	
Company goals What goal does the company aim to fulfill with this offering?	

Alternative Options	
Key alternatives What alternative options can fulfill the same company goal?	
Value proposition What value do these options create for the company?	
Option attributes What are the key aspects of the alternative options?	

Company Value	
Reason to choose What value does the offering create for target customers? Why would customers choose this offering?	

Company Offering	
Product What are the features of the product that the company offers to target customers and collaborators?	
Service What are the features of the service that the company offers to target customers and collaborators?	
Brand What are the features of the offering's brand?	
Price What is the offering's price for target customers and collaborators?	
Incentives What incentives does the offering provide to target customers and collaborators?	
Communication How will target customers and collaborators become aware of the company's offering?	
Distribution How will the offering be delivered to target customers and collaborators?	

The Company

The company is the entity in charge of the offering. The company is defined by two factors: the company profile and the goals that the company aims to achieve with the offering.

- The **company profile** outlines the key aspects of the entity (e.g., a specific business unit of the company) in charge of the offering. The key questions here are: *What entity is in charge of the offering? What resources does the company have to fulfill the identified need of the target customers?*

- **Company goals** are the strategic and monetary outcomes that the company aims to achieve with the offering. The key question here is: *What monetary and strategic goals is the company pursuing by creating the offering?*

Alternative Options

From a company's perspective, alternative options are the different means that could enable the company to achieve its goals. The alternative options are identified by their value proposition for the company and by the specific attributes defining these options.

- **Key alternatives** are the other options that compete with the focal offering for the company's resources. The key questions here are: *What is the company currently doing to achieve its goals? What alternative offerings could enable the company to achieve its goals? What would the company give up if it chooses to invest in this offering?*

- The **value proposition of the alternative options** reflects the benefits and costs created by the options the company could pursue instead of investing in the focal offering. The key questions here are: *What benefits and costs do the alternative options create for the company? What is the primary reason why the company would choose to invest resources in the alternative options?*

- The **attributes of the alternative options** are the characteristics of the options that the company could pursue instead of investing in the focal offering. The key questions here are: *What are the product, service, brand, price, incentives, communication, and distribution aspects of the alternative options? How do the attributes of the alternative options create company value?*

The Company Value Proposition

The company value proposition defines the worth of an offering for the company stakeholders. The company value proposition is identified by the offering's benefits for the company, the relative advantage of the offering for the company over the alternative options, and the reason why the company would choose to invest in this offering.

- The **company benefits** reflect the value created by the offering on the two dimensions of company value: monetary and strategic. The key questions here are: *What monetary and strategic benefits and costs does the offering create for the company? What is this offering's profit formula?*

- The **relative advantage** reflects the focal offering's ability to address the company's goals better than the alternative options. The key questions here are: *Why should the company choose to invest resources in the focal offering instead of using alternative means to* *achieve its goals? What are the points of dominance, points of parity, and points of compromise of the focal offering relative to the alternative options?*

- The **reason to choose** is the key factor(s) that would motivate the company to invest in this offering. The key questions here are: *What is the primary reason for the company to pursue this offering? How would the company management justify choosing this offering?*

The Company Offering

The company offering represents the company aspect of the market offering. It is defined by the seven attributes—product, service, brand, price, incentives, communication, and distribution—that delineate the offering and the value that each of these attributes creates for the company. The key questions here are: *What are the key features of the product, service, brand, price, and incentives the company offers to its customers and collaborators? How will the offering be communicated to target customers and collaborators? How will the offering be delivered to target customers and collaborators? How will different attributes of the offering create company value?*

Business Model Workbook Example: Black & Decker (DeWalt)

The key components of a company's business model and the corresponding value maps can be illustrated with a company-specific example, which builds on the Black & Decker example introduced in Appendix A. In this context, the business model of the newly formed division of Black & Decker—DeWalt Industrial Tool Company—is outlined in the DeWalt market value map and detailed in the customer, collaborator, and company value maps.[36]

The Market Value Map (DeWalt)

DeWalt's business model and market value map are defined by three key components: the *target market* (the Five Cs), the *value proposition* for the relevant market entities—customers, the company, and its collaborators—and the key attributes of the *market offering*—product, service, brand, price, incentives, communication, and distribution. The specifics of DeWalt's business model are outlined in the market value map presented in Figure 5.

Figure 5. The Market Value Map (DeWalt)

TARGET MARKET	DESCRIPTION
Customers	Tradesmen—small businesses and independent contractors working in residential construction and using power tools on the job
Collaborators	Distribution channel partners: Wholesale distributors (serving smaller retailers), large home improvement centers (Home Depot, Lowe's), smaller hardware chains (Ace Hardware, ServiStar), and independently owned hardware stores
Company	DeWalt Industrial Tool Company (a business unit of Black & Decker, launched in 1992 to serve the tradesman segment)
Competition	Makita Electric (50% market share), Milwaukee Tools (10% market share), Ryobi (9% market share)

Context	*Economic context:* Recession, resulting in high unemployment, limited money supply (credit), and increased inflation
	Business context: Rapid growth of new home construction and remodeling prior to the recession, consolidation of home improvement retailers, and rise of big-box home improvement centers Home Depot and Lowe's
	Regulatory context: Price dumping allegations against some of the Japanese manufacturers, including Makita, raising the possibility of imposing import duties on certain tools imported from Japan

VALUE PROPOSITION	DESCRIPTION
Customer value	High-performance, reliable tools backed by a national service and quality commitment unparalleled in the power tool industry
Collaborator value	High-performance, reliable tools backed by a national service and quality commitment; large promotional budget to generate traffic; superior trade profits
Company value	Potential to increase market share from 8% to 50%, increase margins from 5% to 10%, increase the valuation of the company by creating a new brand, ensure a leadership position in the growing tradesman segment, and solidify Black & Decker's relationship with retailers by becoming a single-source supplier for both consumer and professional segments

OFFERING	DESCRIPTION	CUSTOMER VALUE
Product	Thirty-three high-performing power tools (drills, saws, sanders, and plate joiners) and 323 accessories designed to maximize power, precision, ergonomics, durability, and reliability	*Benefits:* Performance (power, precision, and ergonomics), durability, and reliability
Service	*Loaner Tool Policy:* DeWalt will lend a tool during the repair period	*Benefits:* Minimized downtime (fast service and loaner availability), professional training, technical support, accurate diagnostics
	48-Hour Service Policy: If a repair is not completed in 48 hours, DeWalt will provide a new tool for free	
	Technical Support: Experts are available by phone at 1-800-4DEWALT to assist with DeWalt products, service, repair, or replacement	
	Free Service: DeWalt will maintain the tool and replace parts free during the first year of ownership	
	Warranty: DeWalt will warranty materials and workmanship for one year	
	Diagnostics: DeWalt Certified Service Centers will diagnose problems quickly and accurately	
Brand	*Brand name:* DeWalt® (replaces the Black & Decker Professional brand)	*Benefits:* Brand designed for professional (not consumer) use
	Brand logo: **DeWALT**	*Costs:* New brand with unknown reliability
	Brand color: Yellow	
	Brand associations: High-performance industrial tools; "no downtime" company	
	Related brands: Black & Decker (service centers)	

Price	*List price:* Premium price tier (10% higher than Makita)	*Costs:* Price paid
Incentives	*Loyalty programs:* Preferred Contractor Program	*Benefits:* Price discounts
Communication	*Message:* Create awareness of the new offering; build the DeWalt brand to create customer brand loyalty. Taglines: *DeWalt. Guaranteed Tough* and *High Performance Industrial Tools** *Media:* Industry magazines (*Builder* and *Electrical Contractor*; $1M budget); trade shows; direct-mail catalogs ($300K budget); point-of-sale displays at home improvement retailers ($200K budget); ten vans visiting job sites promoting DeWalt products ($1M budget)	*Benefits:* Awareness of the offering and its specifics
Distribution	*Product:* Home improvement centers (Home Depot, Lowe's), hardware chains (Ace Hardware, ServiStar), and independent hardware stores *Service:* 117 Black & Decker authorized service centers with a dedicated DeWalt counter *Returns:* DeWalt will accept returns for any reason within 30 days from the date of purchase	*Benefits:* Product accessibility (wide distribution network), service accessibility (wide service network), peace of mind (30-day return policy)

The market value map shown in Figure 5 outlines DeWalt's business model. The ways in which DeWalt offerings create value for its target customers, collaborators, and the company are further detailed in its customer, collaborator, and company value maps, which are presented in the following sections.

The Customer Value Map (DeWalt)

The ways in which DeWalt creates value for its target customers is centered around four main components: *target customers*, the *competition*, the *customer value proposition,* and *customer offering* (Figure 6).

Figure 6. The Customer Value Map (DeWalt)[37]

STRATEGY	DESCRIPTION
Customers	*Overview:* Tradesmen—small businesses and independent contractors working in residential construction and using power tools on the job *Customer needs:* Performance (power, precision, and ergonomics), reliability, service, and professional image *Customer demographics:* Small businesses and independent contractors (carpenters, plumbers, and electricians) working in residential construction. Tradesmen represent 28% ($420M) of the US power tools market and are the fastest growing segment (9%) of this market *Customer behavior:* Use power tools on the job; read trade press (*Builder* and *Electrical Contractor*); visit trade shows and home improvement stores including large home improvement centers such as Home Depot and Lowe's, smaller hardware chains such as Ace Hardware and ServiStar, and independently owned hardware stores

Competition	*Key competitors:* Makita Electric (50% market share), Milwaukee Tools (10% market share), Ryobi (9% market share) *Competitive value proposition:* Reliable power tools; used by most contractors (Makita) *Offering attributes:* Wide variety of competitively priced power tools	
Value proposition	*Benefits:* High-performance, reliable tools backed by a national service and quality commitment unparalleled in the power tool industry *Competitive advantage:* More reliable than the competition *Positioning:* "No downtime" performance (reliability/service commitment)	

TACTICS	DESCRIPTION	VALUE
Product	Thirty-three high-performing power tools (drills, saws, sanders, and plate joiners) and 323 accessories designed to maximize power, precision, ergonomics, and reliability	*Benefits:* Performance (power, precision, and ergonomics) and reliability
Service	*Loaner Tool Policy:* DeWalt will lend a tool during the repair period *48-Hour Service policy:* If a repair is not completed within 48 hours, DeWalt will provide a new tool free of charge *Technical Support:* Experts are available by phone at 1-800-4DEWALT to offer assistance regarding DeWalt products, service, repair, or replacement *Free One-Year Service Contract:* DeWalt will maintain the tool and replace worn parts free any time during the first year of ownership *One-Year Warranty:* DeWalt will warranty materials and workmanship for one year *Superior Diagnostics:* DeWalt Certified Service Centers use state-of-the-art testing equipment to diagnose problems quickly and accurately	*Benefits:* Minimized downtime (fast service and loaner availability), professional training, technical support, accurate diagnostics
Brand	*Brand name:* DeWalt® (replaces the Black & Decker Professional brand) *Brand logo:* **DEWALT.** *Brand color:* Yellow *Brand referents:* High-performance industrial tools; "no downtime" company; guaranteed tough	*Benefits:* Brand designed for professional (not consumer) use *Costs:* New brand with unknown reliability
Price	*List Price:* Premium price tier (10% higher than Makita)	*Costs:* Price paid
Incentives	*Loyalty programs:* Preferred Contractor Program	*Benefits:* Price discounts

Communication	*Message:* Create awareness of the new product line and service program; build the DeWalt brand to create customer brand loyalty. Taglines: *DeWalt. Guaranteed Tough* and *High Performance Industrial Tools** *Media:* Industry magazines (*Builder* and *Electrical Contractor*; $1M budget); trade shows; direct-mail catalogs ($300K budget), point-of-sale displays at home improvement retailers ($200K budget); ten vans visiting job sites promoting DeWalt products ($1M budget)	*Benefits:* Awareness of the offering and its specifics
Distribution	*Product:* Large home improvement centers (Home Depot /Lowe's), smaller hardware chains (Ace Hardware /ServiStar), and independently owned hardware stores *Service:* 117 Black & Decker authorized service centers with a dedicated DeWalt counter *Returns:* DeWalt will accept returns for any reason within 30 days from the date of purchase	*Benefits:* Product accessibility (wide distribution network), service accessibility (wide service network), peace of mind (30-day return policy)

* A specific example of customer communication in the print media features a plate joiner (a woodworking tool used to join two pieces of wood together) following the headline: "The Joint Chief." The advertising copy reads: "The key to a plate joiner's performance is its fence. And that's what makes the DeWalt plate joiner a real stand-out in its field. Because the DeWalt fence lets you make a great variety of joints and move with speed and precision from one kind to another. And the angles are covered with an integral fence which tilts 0-90 degrees. The fence is calibrated from 0-90 degrees so you can make the cut at exactly the proper angle. The fence can also be located on the inside or outside of a mitered joint, according to your preference. In addition, flush cuts can be made at 0 degrees without having to remove the fence. Rack and pinion control provides easy, accurate height adjustment and keeps the fence parallel to the blade. With this feature, the risk of making an inaccurate cut is virtually eliminated. And this rack and pinion control is a feature unique to DeWalt. So, if you haven't decided which plate joiner to get, you don't have to guess anymore. All you have to do is try DeWalt. You'll add it to your staff immediately."[38]

The Collaborator Value Map (DeWalt)

The ways in which DeWalt creates value for its collaborators is defined by four main components: *collaborators*, the *competition*, the *collaborator value proposition*, and the *collaborator offering* (Figure 7).

Figure 7. The Collaborator Value Map (DeWalt)

STRATEGY	DESCRIPTION
Collaborators	*Overview:* Distribution channel partners *Collaborator profile:* Wholesale distributors (serving smaller retailers), large home improvement centers (Home Depot, Lowe's), smaller hardware chains (Ace Hardware, ServiStar), independently owned hardware stores *Collaborator goals:* Increase profits; generate traffic; enhance brand image
Competition	*Key competitors:* Makita Electric (50% market share), Milwaukee Tools (10% market share), Ryobi (9% market share) *Competitor value proposition:* Established brand with 50% market share (Makita) that brings traffic, revenues, and profits *Offering attributes:* Variety of power tools with standard trade margins

Value proposition	*Value proposition:* High-performance, reliable tools backed by a national service and quality commitment unparalleled in the power tool industry; supported by a large promotional budget to generate customer traffic; backed by Black & Decker; offering superior trade profits *Positioning:* More profitable for the retailer than the competition	
TACTICS	**DESCRIPTION**	**VALUE**
Product	Thirty-three high-performing power tools (drills, saws, sanders, and plate joiners) and 323 accessories designed to maximize power, precision, ergonomics, and reliability; aimed to replace the Black & Decker Professional product line	*Benefits:* Superior product line better fitting the needs of tradesmen than the Black & Decker Professional line it replaces *Costs:* Discontinuing Black & Decker Professional products; introducing DeWalt products
Service	Trade support provided by Black & Decker (ordering, inventory management, returns)	*Benefits:* Superior trade support compared to that for the Black & Decker Professional line
Brand	*Brand name:* DeWalt® (replaces the Black & Decker Professional brand) *Brand logo:* **DEWALT** *Brand color:* Yellow *Brand referents:* Profitable	*Benefits:* Adding the DeWalt brand to a retailer's brand portfolio helps solidify Black & Decker's image as a go-to shop for tradesmen
Price	*Price:* Trade margins 5% higher than Makita *Price protection:* Price protection from discounters (e.g., halting supplies to price-cutting retailers) to prevent horizontal channel conflict	*Benefits:* Superior margins relative to Black & Decker Professional; price protection from discounters *Cost:* Price paid
Incentives	*Point-of-sale promotions:* Trade incentives to ensure retailer "push"	*Benefits:* Trade incentives provide additional source of revenue
Communication	*Message:* Create awareness of the new product line and service program; build the DeWalt brand to create retailer loyalty. Tagline: *There's only one thing about DeWalt that's not tough: Making a profit** *Media:* Trade shows (National Association of Home Builders); Black & Decker salesforce	*Benefits:* Increased store traffic from DeWalt customer communication
Distribution	*Product:* Distributed through the existing Black & Decker channels; direct distribution to home improvement stores, and indirect (wholesaler) distribution to hardware stores. $20M inventory buildup at launch to ensure product availability and avoid stock-outs *Returns:* DeWalt will accept returns for any reason within 30 days from the date of purchase	*Benefits:* Distributed by the same company (Black & Decker); sufficient inventory available at the time of launch; peace of mind (return policy) *Costs:* Ordering and inventorying DeWalt products; reverse logistics for the remaining Black & Decker Professional products

* A specific example of collaborator communication for print media features a plate joiner (a woodworking tool used to join two pieces of wood together) following the headline: "There's only one thing about DeWalt that's not tough: Making a profit." The advertising copy reads: "In developing the complete line of DeWalt high-performance industrial tools and accessories, we've kept you in mind. By doing everything possible to make them profitable for you to sell. And this is what we've done. We've put together easy-to-understand pricing programs tailored to your specific needs. We've got a salesforce dedicated to helping the tools sell through. They'll be out on job sites putting tools in your customers' hands, creating demand and sales for you. All tools come with a 30-Day No Risk Satisfaction Guarantee plus a full 1-year warranty. And with our quick-return repair service, which includes a free loaner program, your customers will never have a problem with down time. Why are we doing all this? Because at DeWalt, we believe selling tools that work hard shouldn't have to be hard work. And, above all, it should make you a solid profit."[39]

The Company Value Map (DeWalt)

The ways in which DeWalt offerings create value for the company is defined by four main components: the *company*, the *alternative options*, the *company value proposition*, and the *company offering* (Figure 8).

Figure 8. The Company Value Map (DeWalt)

STRATEGY	DESCRIPTION
Company	*Company profile:* DeWalt Industrial Tool Company (a business unit of Black & Decker, launched in 1992 to serve the tradesman segment) *Company goals:* Increase revenues and profits; gain leadership in the growing and profitable tradesman market
Alternative options	*Key alternatives:* Promote the existing Black & Decker tools to tradesmen instead of launching the DeWalt line of tools *Value proposition:* Lower cost (compared to developing new products and building a new brand) *Offering attributes:* Existing product line branded as Black & Decker, promoted in trade magazines, and offered through current channels
Value proposition	*Monetary value:* Potential to increase market share from 8% to 50%, increase margins from 5% to 10%, and increase the valuation of the company by creating a new brand *Strategic value:* Ensures leadership positioning in the growing tradesman segment. Solidifies Black & Decker's relationship with retailers by enabling retailers to have a single-source supplier for consumer and professional segments *Positioning:* "No downtime" performance (reliability and service commitment)

TACTICS	DESCRIPTION	VALUE
Product	Thirty-three high-performing power tools (drills, saws, sanders, and plate joiners) and 323 accessories designed to maximize power, precision, ergonomics, and reliability ("the banner of quality")	*Benefits (strategic):* R&D innovation can benefit other product lines; the new product line establishes a quality benchmark for Black & Decker *Costs (monetary):* Product development and production costs

Service	*Customer service:* Loaner tool policy, 48-hour service policy, technical support, free one-year service contract, one-year warranty, superior diagnostics *Trade service:* Retailer support (ordering, inventory management, returns)	*Benefits (strategic):* Builds customer loyalty; offers sustainable competitive advantage over Makita *Costs (monetary):* Service implementation costs
Brand	*Brand name:* DeWalt® (replaces the Black & Decker Professional brand) *Brand logo:* **DeWALT.** *Brand color:* Yellow *Brand referents:* High-performance industrial tools; "no downtime" company; guaranteed tough; profitable for retailers and Black & Decker	*Benefits (strategic):* Identifies the offering to create customer loyalty; builds brand (DeWalt) equity *Costs (monetary):* Brand-building expense
Price	*Price:* Premium price tier (10% higher than Makita and Black & Decker Professional)	*Benefits (monetary):* Captures customer value in the form of revenues *Benefits (strategic):* Premium price enables Black & Decker to invest in product development, service, brand building, and promotion
Incentives	*Loyalty programs:* Preferred Contractor Program *Point-of-sale promotions:* Trade incentives to ensure retailer "push"	*Benefits (strategic):* Stimulates customer demand *Costs (monetary):* Incentives expenses *Costs (strategic):* Monetary customer incentives could have detrimental impact on the DeWalt brand
Communication	*Customer communication:* $1M advertising in industry magazines (*Builder* and *Electrical Contractor*); $300K direct mail; $1M van promotion program; $200K point-of-sale displays; trade shows *Trade communication:* Black & Decker salesforce; trade shows	*Benefits (strategic):* Creates awareness of the offering; builds the DeWalt brand *Costs (monetary):* Communication expenses
Distribution	*Product:* Distributed through the existing Black & Decker channels offering direct distribution to large home improvement centers (Home Depot, Lowe's) and indirect (wholesaler) distribution to smaller hardware chains (Ace Hardware, ServiStar) and independent hardware stores. $20M inventory buildup at launch to ensure product availability and avoid stock-outs *Service:* 117 Black & Decker authorized service centers with a dedicated DeWalt counter *Returns:* 30-day return policy	*Benefits (strategic):* Solidifies Black & Decker's relationship with retailers by offering a comprehensive product portfolio *Costs (monetary):* Cost of making DeWalt available to the trade, cost of discontinuing Black & Decker Professional, cost of processing returns

References

Chapter 1

Peter Drucker, *The Practice of Management* (New York, NY: Routledge, 2017).

Philip Kotler and Kevin Lane Keller, *Marketing Management,* 15th ed. (Upper Saddle River, NJ: Prentice Hall, 2016).

Nirmalya Kumar, *Marketing as Strategy: Understanding the CEO's Agenda for Driving Growth and Innovation* (Boston, MA: Harvard Business School Press, 2004).

Alice Tybout and Bobby Calder, *Kellogg on Marketing* (New York, NY: John Wiley & Sons, 2010).

Chapter 2

David Aaker, *Strategic Market Management,* 10th ed. (New York, NY: John Wiley & Sons, 2013).

Alexander Chernev, *The Business Model: How to Develop New Products, Create Market Value and Make the Competition Irrelevant* (Chicago, IL: Cerebellum Press, 2017).

Mark Johnson, Clayton Christensen, and Henning Kagermann, "Reinventing Your Business Model," *Harvard Business Review* 86 (December 2008).

Jagdish Sheth and Rajendra Sisodia, *The 4 A's of Marketing: Creating Value for Customer, Company and Society* (New York, NY: Routledge, 2012).

Chapter 3

Tim Calkins, *Breakthrough Marketing Plans: How to Stop Wasting Time and Start Driving Growth,* 2nd ed. (New York, NY: Palgrave Macmillan, 2012).

Alexander Chernev, *The Marketing Plan Handbook,* 5th ed. (Chicago, IL: Cerebellum Press, 2018).

James Collins and Jerry Porras, "Building Your Company's Vision." *Harvard Business Review* 74, (September–October 1996), pp. 65–77.

Simon Sinek, *Start With Why: How Great Leaders Inspire Everyone to Take Action* (New York, NY: Penguin Group, 2011).

Chapter 6

David Aaker, *Strategic Market Management,* 10th ed. (New York, NY: John Wiley & Sons, 2013).

Clayton Christensen, Taddy Hall, Karen Dillon, and David Duncan, "Know Your Customers' 'Jobs to Be Done,'" *Harvard Business Review* 94 (September 2016), pp. 54–60.

Malcolm McDonald, *Market Segmentation: How to Do It and How to Profit from It,* 4th ed. (New York, NY: John Wiley & Sons, 2012).

Alice Tybout and Bobby Calder, *Kellogg on Marketing,* 2nd ed. (New York, NY: John Wiley & Sons, 2010).

Chapter 7

Patrick Barwise and Sean Meehan, *Simply Better: Winning and Keeping Customers by Delivering What Matters Most* (Boston, MA: Harvard Business School Press, 2004).

Roger Best, *Market-Based Management: Strategies for Growing Customer Value and Profitability,* 6th ed. (Upper Saddle River, NJ: Prentice Hall, 2012).

W. Chan Kim and Renée Mauborgne, *Blue Ocean Strategy: How to Create Uncontested Market Space and Make the Competition Irrelevant* (Boston, MA: Harvard Business School Press, 2005).

Al Ries and Jack Trout, *Positioning: The Battle for Your Mind,* 20th Anniversary Edition (New York, NY: McGraw-Hill, 2000).

Chapter 8

Tim Ambler, *Marketing and the Bottom Line: The New Methods of Corporate Wealth,* 2nd ed. (London: Pearson Education, 2003).

Jim Collins, *Good to Great: Why Some Companies Make the Leap and Others Don't* (New York, NY: HarperCollins Publishers, 2001).

Paul Farris, Neil Bendle, Phillip Pfeifer, and David Reibstein, *Key Marketing Metrics: The 50+ metrics every manager needs to know* (Harlow, UK: FT Publishing International, 2017).

Thomas Peters and Robert Waterman, *In Search of Excellence: Lessons from America's Best-Run Companies* (New York, NY: HarperCollins Publishers, 2006).

Chapter 9

Tim Brown, *Change by Design: How Design Thinking Transforms Organizations and Inspires Innovation* (New York, NY: HarperCollins Publishers, 2009).

Clayton Christensen, *The Innovator's Dilemma: When New Technologies Cause Great Firms to Fail* (Boston, MA: Harvard Business School Press, 1997).

Donald Lehmann and Russell Winer, *Product Management*, 4th ed. (Boston, MA: McGraw-Hill/Irwin, 2006).

Youngme Moon, "Break Free from the Product Life Cycle," *Harvard Business Review* 83 (May 2005), pp. 87–94.

Chapter 10

Leonard Berry and A. Parasuraman, *Marketing Services: Competing Through Quality* (New York, NY: Free Press, 2004).

Dwayne Gremler, Mary Jo Bitner, and Valarie Zeithaml, *Services Marketing: Integrating Customer Focus Across the Firm*, 6th ed. (Boston, MA: McGraw-Hill/Irwin, 2012).

Bernd Schmitt, *Customer Experience Management* (New York, NY: John Wiley & Sons, 2003).

Venkatesh Shankar, Leonard Berry, and Thomas Dotzel, "A Practical Guide to Combining Products and Services," *Harvard Business Review* 87 (November 2009), pp. 94–99.

Chapter 11

David Aaker and Erich Joachimsthaler, *Brand Leadership* (New York, NY: Simon and Schuster, 2012).

Alexander Chernev, *Strategic Brand Management*, 2nd ed. (Chicago, IL: Cerebellum Press, 2017).

Jean-Noël Kapferer, *The New Strategic Brand Management: Advanced Insights and Strategic Thinking*, 5th ed. (London, UK: Kogan Page Publishers, 2012).

Kevin Lane Keller, *Strategic Brand Management: Building, Measuring, and Managing Brand Equity*, 4th ed. (Upper Saddle River, NJ: Prentice Hall, 2012).

Alice Tybout and Tim Calkins, *Kellogg on Branding* (Hoboken, NJ: John Wiley & Sons, 2005).

Chapter 12

Ronald Baker, *Implementing Value Pricing: A Radical Business Model for Professional Firms* (Hoboken, NJ: John Wiley & Sons, 2010).

Walter Baker, Michael Marn, and Craig Zawada, *The Price Advantage,* 2nd ed. (Hoboken, NJ: John Wiley & Sons, 2010).

Hermann Simon, *Confessions of the Pricing Man: How Price Affects Everything,* (New York, NY: Springer, 2015).

Thomas Nagle, John Hogan, and Joseph Zale, *The Strategy and Tactics of Pricing: A Guide to Growing More Profitably*, 5th ed. (Upper Saddle River, NJ: Pearson/Prentice Hall, 2010).

Chapter 13

George Belch and Michael Belch, *Advertising and Promotion: An Integrated Marketing Communications Perspective*, 10th ed. (Boston, MA: McGraw-Hill/Irwin, 2014).

Roddy Mullin, *Sales Promotions: How to Create, Implement, and Integrate Campaigns that Really Work*, 5th ed. (Philadelphia, PA: Kogan Page Publishers, 2010).

Scott Neslin, *Sales Promotion* (Cambridge, MA: Marketing Science Institute, 2002).

Thomas O'Guinn, Chris Allen, Angeline Scheinbaum, and Richard Semenik, *Advertising and Integrated Brand Promotion*, 7th ed. (Boston, MA: Cengage, 2018).

Chapter 14

George Belch and Michael Belch, *Advertising and Promotion: An Integrated Marketing Communications Perspective*, 10th ed. (Boston, MA: McGraw-Hill/Irwin, 2014).

Jonah Berger, *Contagious: Why Things Catch On* (New York, NY: Simon & Schuster, 2016).

Tom Duncan, *Principles of Advertising and IMC*, 2nd ed. (New York, NY: McGraw-Hill/Irwin, 2005).

Yoram Wind and Catharine Findiesen Hays, *Beyond Advertising: Creating Value Through All Customer Touchpoints* (New York, NY: Wiley, 2016).

Chapter 16

Anne Coughlan, Dr. Sandy Jap, *A Field Guide to Channel Strategy: Building Routes to Market* (Scotts Valley, CA: CreateSpace 2016).

Julian Dent, *Distribution Channels: Understanding and Managing Channels to Market* (London, UK: Kogan Page Publishers, 2011).

Robert Palmatier, Louis Stern, and Adel El-Ansary, *Marketing Channel Strategy*, 8th ed. (New York, NY: Routledge, 2017).

V. Kasturi Rangan and Marie Bell. *Transforming Your Go-to-Market Strategy: The Three Disciplines of Channel Management.* (Boston, MA: Harvard Business Press, 2006).

Chapter 18

Clayton Christensen, *The Innovator's Dilemma: The Revolutionary Book That Will Change the Way You Do Business* (New York, NY: HarperCollins Publishers, 2011).

Clayton Christensen and Michael Raynor, *The Innovator's Solution: Creating and Sustaining Successful Growth*, (Boston, MA: Harvard Business Review Press, 2013).

George Day, David Reibstein, and Robert Gunther, *Wharton on Dynamic Competitive Strategy* (New York, NY: John Wiley & Sons, 2004).

A. G. Lafley and Roger Martin, *Playing to Win: How Strategy Really Works* (Boston, MA: Harvard Business School Press, 2016).

Chapter 19

Jonah Berger, *Contagious: Why Things Catch On* (New York, NY: Simon and Schuster, 2016).

Alexander Chernev, *The Business Model: How to Develop New Products, Create Market Value and Make the Competition Irrelevant* (Chicago, IL: Cerebellum Press, 2017).

Merle Crawford and Anthony Di Benedetto, *New Products Management*, 10th ed. (New York, NY: McGraw-Hill, 2011).

Nir Eyal, *Hooked: How to Build Habit-Forming Products* (London, UK: Penguin, 2014).

Chapter 20

Robert Buzzell and Frederick Wiersema, "Successful Share-Building Strategies," *Harvard Business Review* 59 (January–February 1981), pp. 135–44.

Nirmalya Kumar, "Strategies to Fight Low-Cost Rivals," *Harvard Business Review* 84 (December 2006), pp. 104–112.

Youngme Moon, *Different: Escaping the Competitive Herd* (New York, NY: Crown Business, 2016).

Mark Ritson, "Should You Launch a Fighter Brand?," *Harvard Business Review* 87 (October 2009), pp. 87–94.

INDEX

NOTES

[1] Peter Drucker, *The Practice of Management* (New York, NY: HarperCollins, 1954).

[2] Ibid.

[3] The view of customer value creation as a process of managing attractiveness, awareness, and availability is a streamlined version of the 4-A framework that delineates *acceptability, affordability, accessibility,* and *awareness* as the key sources of customer value. Because acceptability and affordability can be related to the benefit and cost aspects of the value created by the company's offering, here we use a single term—attractiveness—that captures both the benefit and cost aspects of the offering. See Jagdish Sheth and Rajendra Sisodia, *The 4 A's of Marketing: Creating Value for Customer, Company and Society* (New York, NY: Routledge, 2012).

[4] E. Jerome McCarthy and William Perreault, *Basic Marketing: A Managerial Approach*, 12th ed. (Homewood, IL: Irwin, 1996).

[5] Michael Porter, "How Competitive Forces Shape Strategy," *Harvard Business Review* 57 (March–April 1979), pp. 137–145.

[6] Note that there are cases when a company can increase its market share while lowering its promotional costs. Such instances, however, are not very common as they require a dramatic improvement in the efficiency of the company's marketing activities.

[7] 27 CFR 5.22—The Standards of Identity, Alcohol and Tobacco Tax and Trade Bureau; U.S. Department of Treasury.

[8] Al Ries and Jack Trout, *Positioning: The Battle for Your Mind*, 20th Anniversary Edition (New York, NY: McGraw-Hill, 2000).

[9] Alexander Chernev, "Jack of All Trades or Master of One? Product Differentiation and Compensatory Reasoning in Consumer Choice," *Journal of Consumer Research* 33, no. 4 (2007), pp. 430–44.

[10] www.inc.com/laura-montini/a-lesson-from-harley-davidson-on-perfecting-product-positioning.html

[11] The examples used in this chapter are for illustration purposes only and might not adequately reflect the companies' actual positioning strategies.

[12] Note that the salesforce might serve a dual function—communicating and distributing the offering.

[13] Sigma refers to the Greek letter σ, commonly used in statistics as a measure of the degree of variance in a given population.

[14] Stock Keeping Unit (SKU) is a unique identifier assigned to each distinct product.

[15] Theodore Levitt, "Exploit the Product Life Cycle," *Harvard Business Review* 43 (November–December 1965), pp. 81–94.

[16] Adapted from Theodore Levitt, "Exploit the Product Life Cycle," *Harvard Business Review* 43 (November–December 1965), pp. 81–94.

[17] Adapted from Clayton Christensen, *The Innovator's Dilemma: When New Technologies Cause Great Firms to Fail* (Boston, MA: Harvard Business School Press, 1997).

[18] www.thebalance.com/zappos-company-culture-1918813 and www.entrepreneur.com/article/249174

[19] Nader Tavassoli, Alina Sorescu, and Rajesh Chandy, "Employee-Based Brand Equity: Why Firms with Strong Brands Pay Their Executives Less," *Journal of Marketing Research* 51, no. 6 (2014), pp. 676–690; C. B. Bhattacharya, Sankar Sen, and Daniel Korschun, "Using Corporate Social Responsibility to Win the War for Talent," *MIT Sloan Management Review* 49 (January 2008), pp. 37–44.

[20] Note that, even though associating the brand with new products and services might also change (typically broaden) the brand's meaning, this change is not the goal but rather a consequence of extending the brand.

[21] The accounting rules regarding the inclusion of brand equity on the balance sheets of a company vary across countries. Thus, in the United States, companies do not list brand equity on their balance sheets, whereas in the United Kingdom and Australia balance sheets include the value of the company's brands.

[22] IFRS (2012) *IAS 38. Intangible Assets*, London, UK: International Financial Reporting Standards.

[23] Interbrand, *Interbrand Best Global Brands* (2015), www.bestglobalbrands.com

[24] www.bloomberg.com/news/articles/2016-12-02/hastens-vividus-mattress-review-price

[25] www.theguardian.com/sustainable-business/financial-incentives-bonus-schemes-lloyds-fine

[26] Note that while social media is considered earned media, advertisements embedded in social media (e.g., Facebook, Instagram, and YouTube ads) are a form of paid media.

[27] Walter Scott, *The Psychology of Advertising* (Boston, MA: Small Maynard, 1913).

[28] Adapted from Stephen Hoch, "How Should National Brands Think about Private Labels?" *Sloan Management Review*, 37 no. 2 (1996), pp. 89–102.

[29] Jagdish Sheth and Rajendra Sisodia, *The 4 A's of Marketing: Creating Value for Customer, Company, and Society* (New York, NY: Routledge, 2012).

[30] Attractiveness can also be defined as the combination of both benefits and costs. For the purposes of understanding the adoption process, this chapter uses a narrower view of attractiveness that focuses only on the benefits of a company's offering.

[31] www.scientificamerican.com/article/oil-change-truths/

[32] Igor Ansoff, *Strategic Management* (New York, NY: John Wiley & Sons, 1979).

[33] A notable exception are product lines designed to address customers' variety-seeking needs. For example, a company might create different flavors of yogurt, snacks, and sodas to ensure that customers can fulfill their need for variety without switching to products from another company.

[34] Note that the above equation assumes that the launch of the new offering is not associated with an increase in the fixed costs and that such costs—if they do exist—are included in the margins of the old and the new offerings.

[35] This example illustrates the main steps and the key considerations in the process of selecting target customers; it should not be used as a source of primary data about the company, customer segments, and/or market conditions. The reported data are based on "The Black & Decker Corporation (A): Power Tools Division" (595-057), "The Black & Decker Corporation (B): 'Operation Sudden Impact'" (595-060), "The Black & Decker Corporation (B): 'Operation Sudden Impact'" (596-510), and "The Black & Decker Corporation (C): 'Operation Sudden Impact' Results, 1992–1994" (595-061), Harvard Business School Publishing, Boston, MA.

[36] This example illustrates the main steps and the key considerations in articulating a company's business model; it should not be used as a source of primary data about the company, customer segments, and/or market conditions. The reported data are based on "The Black & Decker Corporation (A): Power Tools Division" (595-057), "The Black & Decker Corporation (B): 'Operation Sudden Impact'" (595-060), "The Black & Decker Corporation (B): 'Operation Sudden Impact'" (596-510), and "The Black & Decker Corporation (C): 'Operation Sudden Impact' Results, 1992-1994" (595-061), Harvard Business School Publishing, Boston, MA.

[37] "The Black & Decker Corporation (B): 'Operation Sudden Impact,'" (595-060), Harvard Business School Publishing, Boston, MA.

[38] Ibid.

[39] Ibid.

CPSIA information can be obtained
at www.ICGtesting.com
Printed in the USA
BVHW060420080321
601082BV00003B/3